Janáček's Operas

Janáček's Operas

A DOCUMENTARY ACCOUNT

John Tyrrell

PRINCETON UNIVERSITY PRESS
PRINCETON, NEW JERSEY

First published in the United States of America in 1992 by
Princeton University Press
41 William Street, Princeton, New Jersey 08540

First published in Great Britain in 1992 by
Faber and Faber Limited
3 Queen Square, London WC1N 3AU

Printed in Great Britain

Library of Congress Cataloging-in-Publication Data

Janacek, Leos, 1854–1928
    Janacek's operas: a documentary account / (edited by) John Tyrrell
        p. cm.
    Letters and other writings, chiefly by Janacek.
    Translated from Czech or German.
    Includes bibliographical references and index.
    ISBN 0–691–09148–X
    1. Janacek, Leos, 1854–1928. Operas. 2. Opera. I. Tyrrell.
John. II. Title.
ML410.J18A4   1992
782.1'092—dc20

                                                         92–16091
                                                              CIP
                                                              MN

TO DR THEODORA STRAKOVÁ
AND IN MEMORY OF
DR OTAKAR FIALA

Contents

List of Illustrations

The illustrations appear by kind permission of the following: Music Division of the Moravian Provincial Museum, Brno (1, 3–5, 7, 8, 10, 11); Prague National Museum, Theatre Division (9 and front jacket).

Preface

There is a charming story of how Janáček used to answer the telephone: 'Janáček – with a long "a"' – an attempt to reconcile his short-vowel dialect with correct Czech orthography. But he did not have much opportunity for this, at least at home: the Janáčeks were not on the phone.[1] To this fact, and that Janáček lived in Brno while many of his friends lived elsewhere, this book owes its existence.

Much of Janáček's life happened in letters. He wrote thousands of them and carefully hoarded all those that he received, often with their original envelopes and stamps. As he grew more famous most of what he sent out was also kept. After his death his *Nachlaß* was faithfully guarded by his widow, and given to Brno University to make up the nucleus of the magnificently comprehensive Janáček archive in Brno.

A systematic attempt to publish Janáček's correspondence was made in the late 1940s, in the eight volumes of the *Janáčkův archiv*. Collections of his correspondence have appeared in isolated journal articles; more recently, Janáček's letters to Mrs Newmarch, to his publishers Universal Edition, and the great collection of letters to Kamila Stösslová have also been published. But with a few exceptions, such as Dr Němcová's concentration of material on the Brno première of *Jenůfa*, or Dr Straková's painstaking trawl through the *Fate* documents, publications of Janáček's letters have focused on particular recipients rather than works.

The object of this book is to present in English the most important documents relating to the genesis and early performances of Janáček's nine operas. A vast quantity of material of unusual richness and fascination has survived, providing a unique insight into Janáček's working methods and attitudes towards his operas. This material helps chart the complicated genesis of problematic works, such as *Fate* and *The Excursions of Mr Brouček*, and depicts the long-drawn-out campaigns to get them produced, notably *Jenůfa* at the Prague National Theatre. Not much seems to be missing. Janáček's letters to

---

1 Not many others in Czechoslovakia were either. The manual exchange which served Brno until 1931, three years after the composer's death, had only 2,000 subscribers.

Gabriela Preissová and Julius Zeyer are obvious gaps; virtually nothing of the Vinohrady Theatre archives survives except for posters – a fact that deprives us of a rich store of indignant letters from the composer. But in such cases the replies to Janáček allow at least a partial reconstruction of events. Where there is little material, such as on *The Beginning of a Romance* or *From the House of the Dead*, I have included most of what there is. Everywhere else I have had to make a rigorous selection, sometimes to fewer than half the surviving letters and documents. In general I have favoured letters which provide an insight into how Janáček set about and composed his operas, and how he regarded them. Letters dealing with publishers' terms, publication and production rights, though most useful to the social historian, have been mostly omitted, or merely referred to. Thus I have given Janáček's correspondence with Fedora Bartošová, his librettist in *Fate*, almost in its entirety, leaving the lawsuit with the Vinohrady Theatre to be represented by one or two important letters. It is not surprising that the later operas yield fewer letters that the middle ones. The later operas, all quickly written, were comparatively trouble-free in their genesis and production. Janáček did not need to discuss them. This is not the case with *Jenůfa*, *Fate* and *The Excursions of Mr Brouček*, all of which occupied Janáček for many years: the material they generated makes up half the book.

I am grateful to Nicholas John of English National Opera for his original suggestion for this book, and for generously allowing me to take it elsewhere when his planned series ran into difficulties. I am similarly grateful to Patrick Carnegy of Faber and Faber for taking it over, and to his successor Helen Sprott for her encouragement and her commitment to the work when it grew far beyond the original estimate. To Michael Hall I owe the idea for the final format and character of the book. Jim Friedman, Ruth Thackeray and Audrey Twine all contributed quite beyond the call of friendship in reading through the manuscript and making innumerable helpful suggestions. The manuscript was also read by Dr Jana Kuchtová, Dr Michaela Freemanová-Kopecká, Dr Milan Poštolka and Dr Bela Poštolková to check my translations from the Czech. Their comments and corrections are most warmly acknowledged; any remaining deficiences are naturally mine. Brad Robinson kindly allowed me to use his German translations of Brod's letters from my earlier book *Leoš Janáček: Káťa Kabanová* and, with Robert Pascall, checked the new translations from the German. I have been especially fortunate in the interest

that Czech scholars have taken in this project and wish to acknowledge the help of Dr Jarmil Burghauser, Dr Eva Drlíková, Dr Zdenka
E. Fischmann, Dr Zora Oppeltová, Dr Bořivoj Srba and Mr Václav
Štěpán, CSc. I owe a special debt to three scholars in particular who
dealt with regular queries from me with heroic fortitude: Dr Jitka
Ludvová, Dr Alena Němcová and Dr Svatava Přibáňová. The last, as
chief Janáček scholar at the Moravian Museum, also looked after my
needs for many years in the Janáček archive and gave generously of
her time and unique knowledge of the material. The personal knowledge of all three scholars has been shamelessly and anonymously
exploited in many of my footnotes and commentaries.

I gratefully record my thanks to the following who have given me
permission to reproduce copyright material: ing. Ladislav Bakala (for
Břetislav Bakala); Mrs Vera J. Bala (for Jan Löwenbach); Dr Jarmil
Burghauser (for Otakar Šourek); Cambridge University Press (for
extracts from John Tyrrell: *Leoš Janáček: Káťa Kabanová*, Cam-
bridge, 1982); Mrs Eva Ducháčková (for Jan Kunc); Mrs Alena
Dunovská (for Ota Zítek); Dr Zdenka Fischmann (for extracts from
Janáček-Newmarch Correspondence, Kabel Publishers, Rockville
Maryland, 1986); Mrs Ilse Ester Hoffe (for Max Brod); Penguin
Books Ltd (for an extract from Sir Charles Johnston's translation of
Pushkin's *Eugene Onegin*); Artuš Rektorys (for his grandfather Artuš
Rektorys); Dr Jiřć Sehnal (for the Music Department of the Movavian
Provincial Museum); Mr Otto Stössel (for Kamila Stösslová); Univer-
sal Edition AG Wien (for Emil Hertzka). I am most grateful to Dr
Richard Klos for his advice on Czech copyright law and his help in
contacting copyright holders.

Any scholar owes a debt to those who came before. I owe much to
Czech Janáček experts who have sought out letters in private
collections, and published and annotated the new documents. With-
out the exemplary work of Dr Theodora Straková and the late
Professor Bohumír Štědroň in particular, the present volume would
be infinitely poorer. But most of all I owe a great debt to the Janáček
archive housed in the Music History department of the Moravian
Provincial Museum. This collection, established by Professor
Vladimír Helfert and added to by Helfert's distinguished successors,
Professor Jan Racek, Dr Theodora Straková, and the present curator
Dr Jiří Sehnal, now forms one of the most impressive collections
devoted to a single major composer anywhere in the world. The book
is my attempt to repay the help, guidance and kindness offered to me
by members of this institution over twenty-five years; I do so by

Notes for the Reader

All documents have been given a code based on letters from the Czech title of the opera followed by a number. The letter codes for each opera are as follows:

SR   *Šárka*
PR   *Počátek románu* (*The Beginning of a Romance*)
JP   *Její pastorkyňa* (*Jenůfa*)
OS   *Osud* (*Fate*)
BR   *Výlety páně Broučkovy* (*The Excursions of Mr Brouček*)
KK   *Káťa Kabanová*
LB   *Příhody Lišky Bystroušky* (*The Cunning Little Vixen*)
VM   *Věc Makropulos* (*The Makropulos Affair*)
ZD   *Z mrtvého domu* (*From the House of the Dead*)

The relevant code is given to each document, whether it is rendered complete or abridged, paraphrased, or a single point extracted from it; the numbers generally (but not invariably) follow a chronological order. At the main (usually first) appearance of a document its code number is always in bold type (e.g. **PR7**); cross references to it are given in normal type (e.g. PR7). Thus to follow the sequence of the alphanumerical codes the reader needs to look not only at the numbers in the margins (for substantial documents) but also for the codes in bold type in the commentaries, where documents may be referred to or briefly quoted.

Occasionally the same document has been split into two or more parts (bearing individual codes). In such cases cross references occur in square brackets at the end of the extract. Such cross references are not given for documents used frequently throughout the book, such as Janáček's autobiography and Stejskalová's reminiscences.

All documents are originally in Czech except for a number written in German: these comprise letters and other writings by Max Brod and Universal Edition, all Janáček's letters to Universal Edition (but not Janáček's letters to Brod), and JP42–4. Brad Robinson translated the letters from Brod in Chapter 6; all the other translations are my own.

Typographical emphases, however made originally, are always shown by italics.

Letters from well-known individuals attached to an institution (and sometimes writing on behalf of the institution) are generally credited to the individual rather than the institution, e.g. letters are shown to come from Šubert, Kovařovic or Ostrčil rather than the Prague National Theatre. Both individual and institution are included in cases where it is helpful or particularly significant. However Janáček's letters to and from Universal Edition are shown as such, whether or not they were addressed to/signed by Dr Emil Hertzka, director of Universal Edition. Janáček usually wrote to the director, but his letters were not necessarily handled by Hertzka, or replies signed by him.

Salutations and sign-offs have been omitted without indication. Any other omissions from letters are indicated thus [. . .]; any ellipses without square brackets come from the writers themselves.

In extracts from books and articles internal omissions are similarly indicated but not omissions before or after the extract quoted.

Abbreviations of first names and surnames are generally filled out (e.g. František Šubert for Fr. Šubert; Mr Kovařovic for Mr Kov., etc). Janáček's occasional misspellings of names are corrected without comment (e.g. Šubert instead of Janáček's 'Šubrt', Schmoranz instead of 'Šmoranc', Noltsch instead of 'Nolč'). Similarly his dialect 'Ukvaldy' has been standardized to 'Hukvaldy.'

Persons who make several appearances in the book are included in the Glossary. Others are identified in square brackets within the text or in the footnotes.

Cross references to commentaries are shown by a plus or minus sign, e.g.:

$$\text{PR25} + = \text{commentary after PR25}$$
$$\text{PR25} - = \text{commentary before PR25}$$

Names of works (operas, novels, etc.) in Czech and other Slavonic languages are given exclusively in English throughout the book. Their original-language titles can be found after the English title in the index (listed under composer, author, etc.). Names of journals, periodicals and other bibliographical sources, however, are left untranslated.

Names of Czech buildings and institutions are given in English if a standard, accepted translation exists (e.g. the Prague National Theatre, Brno Organ School); others (e.g. Hudební matice, Besední dům) are left in Czech, usually with a translation or explanation supplied at the first occurrence. On the other hand, quotations from Janáček's operas are usually given in Czech to aid finding the passages in the scores. Translations are not automatically given for such quotations.

References to individual vocal scores are made thus: vs28 (= vocal score, page 28). They are made when a single published edition exists (by Universal Edition, Vienna), with no possibility of ambiguity, except for *The Cunning Little Vixen*, where references are to the generally available 'second' edition. Readers who find that vs references in this work do not tally with their score may be consoled by the realization that they have a rare and valuable possession.

BmJA   Janáček Archive of the Moravian Regional Museum, Brno

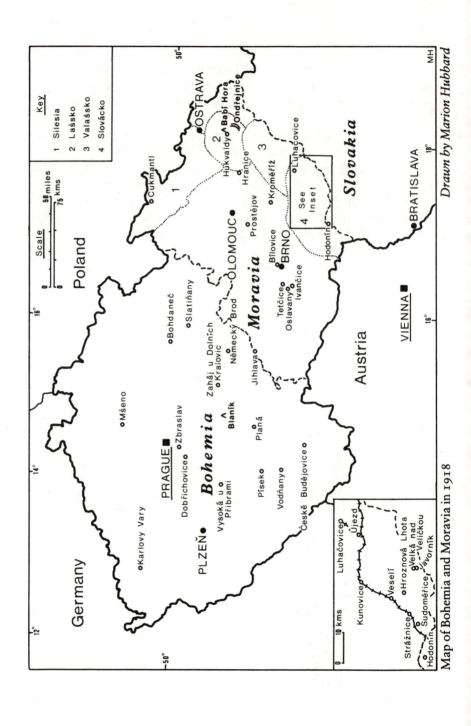

Map of Bohemia and Moravia in 1918

Drawn by Marion Hubbard

Key

1 Silesia
2 Lašsko
3 Valašsko
4 Slovácko

Germany

Poland

Bohemia

Moravia

Slovakia

Austria

PRAGUE

PLZEŇ

OLOMOUC

OSTRAVA

BRNO

BRATISLAVA

VIENNA

Karlovy Vary

Mšeno

Dobřichovice

Zbraslav

Vysoká u Příbrami

Píseko

Vodňany

České Budějovice

Blaník

Planá

Zaháj u Dolních

Kralovic

Německý Brod

Jihlava

Slatiňany

Bohdaneč

Cukmantl

Hukvaldy

Babí Hora

Ondřejnice

Hranice

Kroměříž

Luhačovice

Prostějov

Tetčice

Oslavany

Ivančice

Bílovice

Hodonín

See Inset

Scale

50 miles
75 kms

Strážnice

Veselí

Kunovice

Luhačovice

Újezd

Hroznová Lhota

Velká nad Veličkou

Sudoměřice

Vornik

Hodonín

10 kms

Chronology of Janáček's Life and Works

Premières are all in Brno unless otherwise stated.

	Janáček's life	operas	other works
1854	Born in Hukvaldy, Moravia (3 July).		
1865	Goes to Brno as choirboy at Augustinian Monastery.		
1866	Attends German *Realschule* in Brno.		
1869	Attends Teachers' Training Institute in Brno.		
1870			First sacred chorus.
1872	Qualifies as assistant teacher.		
1873	Choirmaster of men's choral society Svatopluk (to 1878).		First secular male-voice choruses.
1874	Attends Organ School in Prague.		First instrumental pieces (for organ).
1875	Graduates from Prague Organ School; takes state examinations in choral singing, piano and organ.		Instrumental pieces (strings etc).
1876	Choirmaster of Philharmonic Society of the Brno Beseda.		
1877	Conducts Mozart's Requiem; gives piano lessons to Zdenka Schulzová (his future wife).		Suite for Strings.

	Janáček's life	*operas*	*other works*
1878	Takes state examination in violin.		Idyll for Strings.
1879	Conducts Beethoven's *Missa Solemnis*; studies at Leipzig Conservatory (Oct–Feb 1880).		Romance for Violin and Piano.
1880	Studies at Vienna Conservatory (April–June).		'Zdenka Variations' for piano ('op.1').
1881	Marries Zdenka Schulzová (13 July); appointed director of the Brno Organ School (to 1919).		
1882	Begins teaching at the Brno Beseda music school; opening of Brno Organ School; birth of daughter Olga (15 Aug).		
1883	Walking tour with Dvořák.		
1884	Opening of Czech Theatre in Brno; founds and edits *Hudební listy* (to 1888).		Publishes Pieces for Organ.
1885			(Four) male-voice choruses.
1887	Reviews Kovařovic's *The Dogheads*; cure in Cukmantl (Aug).	*Šárka* (1st version).	
1888	Begins to collect folksongs; birth of son Vladimír (16 May); first contacts with Gabriela Preissová.	*Šárka* (2nd version).	
1889			*Valachian* (later *Lachian*) *Dances* for orchestra.

	Janáček's life	*operas*	*other works*
1890	Stops working with Brno Beseda; death of Vladimír (9 Nov).		First folksong collection with Bartoš.
1891		The Beginning of a Romance.	Works based on folksong: *National Moravian Dances* for piano; Suite op.3 for orchestra; ballet *Rákós Rákóczy*, 1st perf., Prague, 24 July.
1892		Prague rejects *Romance.*	
1893	Publishes first feuilleton in *Lidové noviny.*	Contacts with Preissová over *Jenůfa.*	
1894		*Romance* (1st perf. 10 Feb); plans *Jenůfa*; Overture 'Jealousy' (original overture for *Jenůfa*).	
1895	Chairman of the Moravian working committee for the Czechoslavonic Ethnographic Exhibition in Prague.	Begins *Jenůfa.*	
1896	Visits Russia.		
1897	Helps found Russian circle in Brno; publishes first major theoretical writing.	?Completes *Jenůfa* Act 1.	*Amarus*, cantata for soloists, chorus and orchestra.
1899	Publishes singing teaching manual.		(With Bartoš) *Moravian Folksongs, newly collected* (to 1901).
1901		Begins *Jenůfa* Act 2.	*Our Father*, chamber cantata; 5 pieces of *On the Overgrown Path* for piano (pubd).
1902	Takes Olga to Russia.	Completes *Jenůfa* Act 2.	

	Janáček's life	*operas*	*other works*
1903	Death of Olga (26 Feb); founds music section of the Club of the Friends of Art; holiday in Luhačovice; meets Kamila Urválková.	Completes *Jenůfa*; National Theatre (Prague) refuses *Jenůfa*; Brno Theatre accepts *Jenůfa*; begins *Fate*.	*Elegy on the Death of my Daughter Olga*, chamber cantata.
1904	Trip to Warsaw to discuss possible appointment as director of the Conservatory; granted early retirement from Teachers' Training Institute.	*Jenůfa* 1st perf., 21 Jan; *The Farm Mistress* (sketches only).	Four Moravian male-voice choruses.
1905	Chairman of the working committee for Czech folksong in Moravia and Silesia.	*Fate* (1st version) copied.	Piano Sonata 'From the Street – 1. x. 1905'.
1906		*Fate* (2nd version) copied; revises *Jenůfa* (to 1907); *The Mintmaster's Wife* (sketches only); Brno accepts *Fate*.	*Maryčka Magdónova* and *Kantor Halfar* for male-voice chorus.
1907		*Anna Karenina* (sketches only); submits *Fate* to Vinohrady Theatre; revises *Fate* (3rd version).	
1908	Organ School moves to independent building.	Begins *BME**; *Jenůfa* vs pubd; Brno Theatre asks again to perform *Fate*.	Piano Trio 'The Kreutzer Sonata' (lost).
1909			*The Seventy Thousand* for male-voice chorus.

*BME = *The Excursion of Mr Brouček to the Moon.*

	Janáček's life	*operas*	*other works*
1910	Moves to new house in grounds of Organ School; cure in Teplice.	Begins *BME* Act 1 Scene 2	*Fairy Tale* for cello and piano.
1911	*Complete Treatise on Harmony* pubd.	Begins *BME* Act 2; Vinohrady Theatre undertakes to perform *Fate* 1912–13.	*Čárták on Soláň*, cantata for tenor, male chorus and orchestra.
1912	Holiday on the coast of Croatia.		*In the Mists* for piano; *The Fiddler's Child* for orchestra.
1913	Cure in Karlovy Vary.	*Jenůfa* (last perf. in pre-Kovařovic version); completes *BME* Acts 1–2, 1st version; takes Vinohrady Theatre to court over *Fate*.	
1914		Withdraws *Fate* from Vinohrady Theatre.	*The Eternal Gospel* for soloists, chorus and orchestra; Violin Sonata (to 1921); *The Fiddler's Child* for orchestra pubd.
1915	Cure in Bohdaneč.	Kovařovic accepts *Jenůfa*; Janáček returns to *BME*.	*Taras Bulba* for orchestra (1st version).
1916		*Jenůfa*, 1st Prague perf. 26 May; revisions and final version of *BME* Acts 1–2; Act 1 of *BME* engraved; begins *BME* Act 3; *The Living Corpse* (sketches only).	Women's choruses.

	Janáček's life	operas	other works
1917	Meets Kamila Stösslová in Luhačovice.	*Jenůfa* pubd: Czech VS (2nd edition), German VS; *BME* Act 3 completed, Act 2 engraved; composes *BFCE*;* considers revising *Fate*.	*The Diary of One who Disappeared*, song cycle (to 1919).
1918		*Jenůfa*, 1st Vienna perf., 18 Feb; abandons *BME* Act 3; Chlubna orchestrates *Šárka* Act 3; Kovařovic accepts *Brouček*.	*Taras Bulba* (2nd version).
1919	Brno Organ School becomes Conservatory and Janáček its director (to 1920); professor of the master-classes at the Prague Conservatory.	Revises *Šárka* (3rd version); *Brouček* pubd; considers *Káťa Kabanová*.	
1920		Begins *Káťa*; *Brouček*, 1st perf., 23 April.	*The Ballad of Blaník* for orchestra.
1921		Completes *Káťa*, 1st perf., 23 Nov; plans *Vixen*.	
1922		Begins *Vixen*; *Káťa* pubd, 1st Prague perf. 30 Nov.	*The Wandering Madman* for male-voice chorus.
1923		Completes *Vixen*; begins *Makropulos*.	String Quartet 'The Kreutzer Sonata'; ?first sketches for *The Danube*, symphony (unfinished).
1924	70th birthday celebrations.	*Vixen* pubd, 1st perf., 6 Nov.	*Mládí* for wind sextet.

*BFCE = *The Excursion of Mr Brouček to the Fifteenth Century*.

	Janáček's life	operas	other works
1925	Honorary doctorate from Brno university; attends ISCM Festival in Venice.	*Vixen*, 1st Prague perf., 18 May; *Šárka*, 1st perf., 11 Nov; completes *Makropulos*.	Concertino for piano and chamber ensemble; *Nursery Rhymes* for voices and instrumental ensemble.
1926	Visits England.	*Brouček*, 1st Brno perf., 15 June; (1st excursion only) *Makropulos* pubd, 1st perf., 18 Dec.	Sinfonietta for orchestra; *Glagolitic Mass*; Capriccio for piano left hand and chamber ensemble.
1927	Attends ISCM festival in Frankfurt am Main.	Begins *From the House of the Dead*; extends interludes in *Káťa*.	Violin Concerto (first version of overture to *From the House of the Dead*).
1928	Dies in Ostrava (12 Aug).	*Makropulos*, 1st Prague perf. (1 March); completes *House of the Dead*.	Second String Quartet 'Intimate Letters'; *Schluk und Jau*, incidental music (unfinished).
1930		From the *House of the Dead*, pubd, 1st perf., 12 April.	
1934		*Fate*, 1st radio perf., 13 March.	
1935	Kamila Stösslová dies.		
1938	Zdenka Janáčková dies.		
1958		*Fate*, 1st perf., 25 Oct.	

1 Šárka

In the revolt of the women against men's rule recorded in Czech mythic history, Šárka was the boldest and most zealous of the women warriors. Her chief opponent was the young hero Ctirad, whom she tricked into an ambush. She let him find her tied to a tree in the forest, seemingly defenceless and rejected by the women. As he untied her he fell in love with her. She disarmed him and then summoned her warriors hiding nearby to finish him off. However, she had fallen in love with him and in remorse ended her own life.

The name of Šárka first appears in the oldest Czech verse chronicle, the so-called 'Chronicle of Dalimil' dating from the beginning of the fourteenth century. The story of Šárka's erotic and tragic confrontation with Ctirad became a popular subject in early nineteenth-century German and Czech literature and later in the century attracted all the major Czech composers. The third tone poem of Smetana's orchestral cycle *My Fatherland* is called 'Šárka', as is Fibich's penultimate opera. Dvořák, Smetana and Janáček all had contacts with a *Šárka* libretto written by Julius Zeyer (1841–1901), one of the leading Czech symbolist poets.

Zeyer's attraction to this mythical world is evident in his five-part epic poem *Vyšehrad*, published in 1880 and dedicated to his friend, the poet J. V. Sládek. According to Zeyer (SR11), he was invited by Dvořák through the good offices of Sládek to write an opera libretto for him, and seems to have done so by adapting the fourth part of *Vyšehrad*, entitled 'Ctirad' (written in January 1879). Many lines are common to both poem and libretto: it is more likely that they went from the poem to the libretto rather than the other way round. Much of the Indo-European mythology with which Zeyer fleshed out the original Czech legend is incomprehensible in the libretto without a knowledge of the poem.[1]

Reports soon began to circulate that Dvořák was working on a new opera, *Šárka*. The first, in the periodical *Hudební a divadelní věstník* of 20 February 1878 (**SR1**) mistakenly indicated that the libretto would be by 'J.O.V.'(Josef Otakar Veselý, the librettist of Dvořák's opera *The Cunning Peasant*). Another, in *Dalibor* over two years later, was rather nearer the mark:

---

1 The date of the libretto is unknown. The arguments given for its coming after the poem are those of Ladislav Dlouhý (1936, 93–5). The contrary view is less logical and rests only on press reports which mention a plan for an opera, not a finished work.

SR2   'Short reports'

Antonín Dvořák will compose a new opera for which our excellent poets, Messrs Zeyer and Sládek, are writing the libretto. We look forward to Dvořák's latest work being an effective enrichment of the operatic repertory worthy of our national theatre!

Dalibor (10 August 1880)

These reports of Dvořák's composition were premature. From a brief remark in a letter from Sládek to Zeyer a month later (**SR3**, 27 September 1880), it is clear that Dvořák had not yet begun: 'I was at Dvořák's place. He likes *Šárka* a lot, and is full of fire for the work'. Sládek's report may have been wishful thinking. There is little reason to believe that Dvořák would have accepted a libretto with so few opportunities for the sort of set-piece opera that he was still writing at the time. In Zeyer's words (SR11), 'He did not agree with my views on opera.' In his libretto to *Šárka* Zeyer included choruses, but specified the combination of solo voices only in the Act 2 duet between Šárka and Ctirad, and as part of the ritual of the last act. In contrast, Dvořák's next opera, *Dimitrij* (composed 1881–2), has ensembles and concertato finales, among other set pieces. It was not until his extensive revisions of *Dimitrij* in 1894 that a more 'Wagnerian' direction to Dvořák's work can be discerned. Zeyer came from a cultured, cosmopolitan family and during his extensive travels would have had more opportunity than most Czechs of his generation to get to know a wide variety of foreign operas. It is clear from his *Šárka* libretto that he took a Wagnerian view of opera. He described it as a 'music drama' and filled it with many Wagnerian allusions: a chorus of Valkyrie-like women warriors, magic weapons held in waiting for the hero, a love-union in the immolation of hero and heroine.

Perhaps because of Dvořák's lack of interest, the libretto also found its way to Smetana, as is documented by the two following letters from authors both refusing to supply Smetana with librettos on the grounds that he already had two at his disposal:

SR4   Eliška Krásnohorská to Bedřich Smetana   *Prague, 23 February 1882*

[...] I know for certain that you had in your hands two librettos with which you would have been able to carry out your ideal, i.e. of continuing in the style and musical character of *Libuše*; you dream of Czech pagan subjects. I cannot therefore explain why you did not see fit to choose one of these librettos, and I think that you made a mistake if you have completely turned them down. I know one of them [Pippich's *Death of Vlasta*.[1] ... The other [*Šárka*] I don't know

---

1 Karel Pippich's libretto *The Death of Vlasta* was later offered to Fibich and to Dvořák and was set ultimately by Ostrčil, reaching the stage in 1904.

but it comes from someone with a knowledge of music and one could presume therefore that it would be musical and operatic. Possibly it may have been more Wagnerian than Wagner, possibly it had its faults – but surely both these librettos are better than Wenzig's,[1] for instance his *Libuše*, or are at least as good as it? [. . .]

Jaroslav Vrchlický to Josef Srb-Debrnov   *Prague, 11 July 1882*   SR5

In reply to your esteemed letter of 30 June I am honoured to inform you that as far as I know a libretto *Vlasta* exists, by Dr Pippich, and then a libretto *Šárka* by Julius Zeyer. On this point I allow myself the humble observation that if Smetana is not satisfied with the libretto of Mr Pippich, who is a music specialist, or even with the libretto by Mr Zeyer, who is a distinguished poet, my libretto would hardly find favour in his eyes and I would not care to be overtaken by the fate of Mr Zeyer, whose libretto wandered from Ananias to Caiaphas for a whole two years without his receiving from the famous composer any lines of acknowledgement or thanks for such unrewarding work. Do not take it ill if I have no trust in similar enterprises and if I tell you my opinion frankly.

After a decade Zeyer must have realized that it was futile waiting for Dvořák and he published his *Šárka* as a 'music drama' in three instalments, one for each act, in the new theatrical fortnightly, *Česká Thalie* (1 January, 15 January, 1 February 1887). It was here that the young Leoš Janáček saw it. Three years earlier, in 1884, a Czech theatre had opened in Brno, and its productions were regularly reviewed by Janáček himself in *Hudební listy*, the journal that he had founded that year. Janáček had already contemplated a couple of operatic projects, including a somewhat unlikely setting of Chateaubriand's *Les aventures du dernier des Abencérages*.

    Šárka seems to have awakened Janáček's imagination and he set to work quickly. Within a few months, by August 1887, he had completed his setting of Zeyer's text in vocal score and, like several other works of this period, sent it off to his friend and mentor Antonín Dvořák for an opinion. If Dvořák was surprised to see the text he was meant to be setting surfacing in this way, his letters to Janáček do not show it.

Janáček's autobiography (1924)   SR6

Cukmantl [Zuckmantel, now Zlaté Hory] in Silesia. Dr Anděl, the owner of the spa, maintained a Czech society. In the district there was

---

1 Josef Wenzig (1807–76), the author of the (German) texts of Smetana's operas *Dalibor* and *Libuše*.

said to be just one Czech – a chemist. I sent off the vocal score of
Šárka from here to Antonín Dvořák in Prague.

SR7   **Antonín Dvořák to Janáček**   *Vysoká u Přibrami, 6 August 1887*

I've received your opera. Looking through it will need much time. I'll
give you a report later.

SR8   **Antonín Dvořák to Janáček**   *[undated, postmarked Prague, 25*
                                                          October 1887]

Forgive me for not replying for so long, but I imagine that you are in
no great hurry over the matter, and then I also hope that you may
perhaps come to Prague so that we could have a talk about a weighty
matter like this. It's not so easy to write about it. So do come, but no
sooner than the 29th, for I go off tomorrow for about three or four
days to Berlin.

Though Janáček reported (SR10) that Dvořák's assessment went 'quite
well',[1] Dvořák cannot have been wholly enthusiastic, since Janáček then
wrote the piece again, leaving little of the first version intact. Before he did so
he wrote to Zeyer for permission to set his text.

SR9   **Julius Zeyer to Janáček**   *Vodňany, 10 November 1887*

I much regret if this will be unpleasant for you but I cannot consent to
your composing music to my *Šárka*. Believe me, I have very strong
reasons.
    Besides, you yourself can take some of the blame in this matter.
Allow me to say to you that you should surely have asked me first
before sending into the world your outline for an opera to *my* text.
Your music will certainly not be lost because of this; you can use it in
some other way. In any event, my name would only harm you with
the management of the National Theatre since I have only opponents
there.
    Forgive me if I have possibly caused you a nasty moment, remem-
ber that you have also caused me one.

---

1 In suggesting that 'Dvořák only wanted, as usual, "more melody"' (Vogel 1963, 86;
Vogel 1981, 88), Vogel may have been confusing Dvořák's reaction to Janáček's earlier set
of choruses, sent to Dvořák for his comments. The date of the meeting that Vogel gives (29
October) is presumably taken from the first date Dvořák suggested in his letter (SR8).

Janáček's comment (1924) SR10

It was a misunderstanding! I did not know whether I would make a success of my first opera, so I kept quiet – and worked at it for myself. I then sent the finished vocal score to Dr Dvořák for his verdict. It turned out quite well. Only then did I ask Mr J. Z. for his permission. My work was thus not 'in the world' – as J. Z. thought.

Julius Zeyer to Janáček *Vodňany, 17 November 1887* SR11

It seems that you did not receive my first letter and so it becomes my very unpleasant duty to tell you once again that *I do not give my consent* for you to use my *Šárka* as a text for your opera. I have very serious reasons for this, which have absolutely nothing to do with you personally and therefore there is nothing in my conduct to cause you offence. As to your talent I have certainly not the least doubt.

But I must tell you frankly that your conduct is not proper. You take a mistaken attitude when you think that every wretched poet is gratified when some composer or other takes pity on a poem of his. Rather, he can be glad when it is announced to him '*subsequently*' (as you write). All 'changes' and all 'arranging' are then graciously put to him 'for approval'.[1]

Thank you, sir. You probably do not know how offensive you are.

I must add that either Mr Dvořák or you are mistaken. I did not offer either him or anyone else my *Šárka*. He invited me, through the good offices of Prof. Sládek, to write a text for an opera for him. I was glad to comply with his wishes. He did not agree with my views on opera, he did not like my text and so did not compose *Šárka*. I could not really hold this against him and we remained good friends.

So much by way of explanation.

By the date of this letter Zeyer had had three plays produced at the National Theatre but all of them were taken off after two or three performances. In refusing permission to Janáček, Zeyer may have had this in mind, though as Artuš Rektorys suggests,[2] a hostile review of his most recent play, *Libuše's Anger*, published earlier that year in Janáček's journal *Hudební listy*,[3] may

---

1 Zeyer is presumably quoting words from Janáček's letter to him. No letters from Janáček to Zeyer survive.
2 JA ii, 91.
3 The review, signed 'Dr. Hn.' (Jan Herben) and published on 15 February 1887 (*Hudební listy*, iii (1886–7), 69), dismisses the play on both dramatic and poetic grounds and mentions that after the first-night 'success' the theatre was half full on the second night and empty on the third and last night.

also have played its part in his decision. The fact that Dvořák appeared to be recommending Janáček's setting rather than getting on with his own could not have helped. Later, Dvořák became more enthusiastic about Zeyer's libretto, if Sládek's letter to Zeyer can be believed.

SR12   **J. V. Sládek to Julius Zeyer**   *Prague, 15 April 1889*

[...] Yesterday Dvořák met me and launched into a long conversation with me.

He asks you, he says, to allow him to compose *Šárka* and not to offer it to anyone else. He spoke sincerely. He says that when you gave him the piece years ago, 'he was not ready for it yet!' Now he feels that he is at full strength, that he has the courage to take on something so big and also that he understands it. He is completely taken by it and once he begins work on it, he says, he will soon be finished, because the text itself dictates the music to him. He has already described individual scenes to me and generally spoke in a way I have never heard him speak before. He asked me to write to you at once, which is what I am doing. [...]

Dvořák, however, never did compose *Šárka*, though in the mid-1890s, on his return from America, he seems to have sketched a 'Ctirad motif', later used in a changed form for Jirka in *The Devil and Kate*.[1]

It is puzzling that in what must have appeared hopeless circumstances Janáček nevertheless continued to complete his second version (the fair copy of the vocal score is dated 18 June 1888 in Josef Štross's hand), and then to orchestrate the work. He completed two acts in full score and then gave up. Buoyancy over the birth of his son Vladimír (on 16 May 1888) may have sustained Janáček at a time when the project now seemed so hopeless, but why, having got so far, did he not finish it? Possibly the third act, with its lack of vital dramatic features, held little to engage the composer's interest in these changed circumstances. Another factor may have been Janáček's growing enthusiasm for Moravian folksong. His collaboration on a new collection with František Bartoš at about this time, and the fresh possibilities it opened up, seem to have put everything else out of his mind. It was almost thirty years before *Šárka* surfaced again.

SR13   **Janáček to Gabriela Horvátová**   *Brno, 14 January 1918*

[...] I was looking for something in the chest and I found the full score of Acts 1 and 2 of *Šárka*. I didn't even know that it was finished in full score![2] [...]

1 Šourek 1916–33, ii, 27.
2 Act 3 of course remained only in vocal score.

The 'chest' was the famous painted peasant chest, mentioned in the reminiscences of Janáček's servant Marie Stejskalová, who described[1] how Janáček saw it in an antique shop, acquired it and had it repaired and painted. Janáček kept his manuscripts in it and, according to Stejskalová, Mrs Janáčková carefully collected up music which the composer had discarded, and also put it into the chest. This saved many early compositions, including *Šárka*. Janáček himself thought that the work had been lost and, according to Rektorys,[2] that he had burnt it. Indeed he seems not to have responded to the request for information about it by the Dvořák scholar Otakar Šourek in 1917, a year before its discovery.[3]

Otakar Šourek to Janáček   *Prague, [25] January[4] 1917*   SR14

I learnt from my friend Roman Veselý and also from Dr Löwenbach that you have completed an opera on Zeyer's libretto *Šárka*. This was a very surprising, important and joyful piece of news for me, since in the next volume of my work on the life and works of Antonín Dvořák[5] I am currently concerned with Dvořák's intention to set this libretto (in the years 1878–81). Besides, in a forthcoming volume of Dvořák's correspondence, I also have letters addressed to you in which there is mention of your opera.[6]

I would thus, highly honoured Maestro, be enormously grateful to you if you could kindly let me know a few facts about your work, partly in regard to its composition, and, above all, also something about the features and character of the work and what Dvořák, to whom you sent the work for his scrutiny, thought of it at the time. I almost fear to express the request that I might take a look at the score although I think that during one of your visits to Prague even that would not be impossible.

Meanwhile I would accept even the tiniest piece of news from you with sincere thanks.

---

1 Trkanová 1959, 69.

2 JA iii, 88.

3 Nothing in Šourek's description of Janáček's *Šárka* in his Dvořák biography suggests that he had any private information on the work. Nor was Dr Jarmil Burghauser able to find any response to this request in Šourek's archive. I am most grateful to Dr Burghauser for his help in this matter.

4 The letter is dated only 'January 1917' but a draft Šourek made for it, now in the possession of his son-in-law, Dr Jarmil Burghauser, is dated '25 January 1917'.

5 *Otakar Šourek: Život a dílo Antonína Dvořáka* [The Life and Works of Antonín Dvořák], *ii (Prague, 1917).*

6 *Otakar Šourek: Antonín Dvořák přátelům doma* [Dvořák to his friends at home] (Prague, 1941). Letters 197 and 200 concern *Šárka* (= SR7 and SR8).

Whether Janáček had thought of *Šárka* much since he composed it is hard to say. There are no references to it in his correspondence. The successful première in 1897 of Fibich's opera to the same name (see SR32), though to a different libretto, must have seemed like yet another nail in its coffin. Janáček's review of the score two years later[1] was that of an interested rival: detailed, and just a little grudging.

With the sudden success in Prague of *Jenůfa* in 1916 Janáček's position was completely altered. Even before then he had begun to pick up the threads of *The Excursion of Mr Brouček to the Moon*, abandoned in 1913. By October 1916 it was complete in full score and copied out, and over the next few months Roman Veselý made the vocal score (dating his copy of the first scene '5 October 1916'). It appears from Šourek's letter that during this time Janáček must have let slip something about his very first opera to Veselý and to Dr Jan Löwenbach, who was negotiating the publication of Janáček's operas. And once the long-lost score of *Šárka* turned up in the chest early in 1918, Janáček clearly thought it worth his while to salvage it.

His first step, a few months later, was to arrange with his pupil Osvald Chlubna to orchestrate the third act, which Janáček had left in vocal score. Chlubna undertook this task during the summer of 1918.

SR15 Osvald Chlubna: 'A few words on Janáček's *Šárka*'

In front of me on the table lie three slim volumes of the yellowing pages of the vocal score of Leoš Janáček's opera *Šárka*.[2] The last of these volumes, with the heading 'Act 3', Janáček placed before me in 1918 and expressed the wish that I should orchestrate this act. He did not have the time for it and had by then left far behind his former orchestration technique and style.

Today I leaf through it as then, looking at the pages and at my indications for orchestration written into them. In the corner of the first page [of vol. 3] the date 25 May 1918 is written in my hand. So that was the day when I reported to Janáček at his invitation and he asked me to finish the whole opera. By then he had complete faith in me for he knew my work from that time and my artistic capabilities. I could not refuse, but I was anxious and had my doubts. For I knew neither the first nor the second act, I knew nothing of Janáček's orchestration technique in 1887, and so I was unable to resume and continue his style of orchestration. I had been brought up on Straussian orchestration and had mastered it sufficiently to complete

1 Janáček 1899a.
2 BmJA, A 23.522a-c. Chlubna is writing of the second version (1888), in soft bindings, which, after Janáček's revision, became the third version (1918–19). Apart from a few corrections in 1925 this is the final state of the opera. The first version (1887) in one, hard-bound volume, also survives in BmJA (A 30.388).

Janáček's *Šárka*, but I feared that I might perhaps complete it in a different style and thus harm the work. Janáček did not show me the full score and said only that I should finish the third act in any way I knew. And so I continued Janáček's work after thirty years. I began the orchestration on 2 August 1918 and completed the score on 25 August 1918. It is noted on the last page of the vocal score.

Within three weeks I had finished. In the vocal score you will still find today my notes on the orchestration for the distribution of instruments, for the addition of brass, and the whole harmonic structures of the filling-out in sound.[1] And when I handed over the finished score to Janáček, he was pleased.

[SR19]
Opery Leoše Janáčka na brněnské scéně, ed. Václav Nosek (1958)

Janáček's next step, on 20 October 1918 (**SR16**), was to apply to Zeyer's trustees, the Czech Academy of Sciences, for permission to use the text. The poet had died in 1901 and Janáček's request was as easily granted now (**SR17**, 28 December 1918) as it had been once brusquely refused. It was probably only after then that Janáček began to look at the opera more critically.[2] He subjected it to a thorough revision, chiefly of the voice parts, and this necessitated Chlubna's help once again in tying up the loose ends of orchestration, frayed by Janáček's changes.

Janáček to Osvald Chlubna   *Brno, 10 January 1919*   SR18

Call on me this afternoon at 4 o'clock. You have orchestrated the third act of *Šárka* well.

Osvald Chlubna: 'A few words on Janáček's *Šárka*'   SR19

However, on 10 January 1919 Janáček invited me again and asked me to finish off and complete the orchestration of both the earlier acts of *Šárka* according to the revisions he had just made. He had cut many bars and in their place had newly composed other ones which he had stuck into the vocal score without regard to the full score. And finally he said to me 'Do with it what you want.' And so I got the whole of *Šárka*, but also a task which I could not refuse and which I had to fulfil in a most responsible manner.

---

1 This rather obscure phrase refers to the occasional chords sketched in by Chlubna on empty staves at the foot of the manuscript.
2 His letter to Kamila Stösslová of 12 January 1919 (KK1) suggests that work on *Šárka* was recent.

When later I looked at the full score[1] at home, I was horrified. The cuts and the slips of paper stuck into the score followed the harmony and the movement of the parts fairly closely, but only in the vocal score. In the full score it upset the groupings and deployment of individual instruments to such an extent that it was necessary to reorchestrate whole sections to avoid breaks so as not to disturb the flow of the sound, the unity and the thought. Furthermore, some of Janáček's notations were not easy to read on the scratched-out paper, so that some notes had to be deciphered with a magnifying glass. Because of this it even happened that I rewrote the end of the second act into a key different from Janáček's C sharp minor. Janáček and I discovered this only when we looked through the whole opera.

[SR15]
Opery Leoše Janáčka na brněnské scéně, ed. Václav Nosek (1958)

There were also problems with the text, where occasionally Janáček's musical imagination had run ahead of the words and left vocal lines untexted, and for which F. S. Procházka, the librettist of *The Excursion of Mr Brouček to the Fifteenth Century*, was pressed into service:

SR20   **Janáček to F. S. Procházka**   *Brno, 16 April 1919*

I have *Šárka* in fair copy both in full score and vocal score. The Academy has given me the rights to the text.
     I need just a few lines in it.
     Would you do them for me?
     They are underlined in red, the dots indicate the number of syllables.
     I need in particular some sort of song for the noble warriors' exit [Act 1].

SR21   **F. S. Procházka to Janáček**   *Prague, 6 May 1919*

I have done what you asked and do not know if it fits your music, the dynamics of which I don't know for these sentences. I have served you to demonstrate my goodwill, although otherwise this sort of repair is not to my taste. [. . .]

On 12 May, the same day that he thanked Procházka (**SR22**), Janáček wrote to his publishers, Universal Edition, hoping to interest them in the work.

1 Now in the possession of Universal Edition, Vienna.

Janáček to Universal Edition   *Brno, 12 May 1919*   **SR23**

[. . .] I have put in order one of my earlier operatic works,
                                 Šárka.

The representative of the Czech Theatre in Brno will be visiting you
and will bring you the vocal score of *Šárka* for you to look at and
inspect.

If you would like it, I should be delighted to hear it.

The libretto is taken from the world of Czech myths.

The cautious interest that Universal Edition expressed at the time was
however dependent on the piece's acceptance by a theatre (**SR24**, 26 June
1920); although Janáček asked for his score back to show to František
Neumann in Brno (**SR25**, 2 January 1921), Brno presumably was much more
interested in the première of *Káťa Kabanová* later that year to pay attention
to this early work. *Šárka* remained virtually forgotten until 1924, the year of
Janáček's seventieth birthday, which saw a number of commemorative publications. One was Janáček's autobiography, in which he remembered *Šárka*
approvingly:

Janáček's autobiography (1924)   **SR26**

My *Šárka*?

Everything in it is so near to my recent work! A passionate introduction.

The gloom of unhewn forests, reeking of moss.

The figure of *Přemysl* is bound up with this motif:[1]

Šárka's cause was further championed by the professor of musicology at
Brno University, Vladimír Helfert:

1 Janáček quotes here the opening bars of Act 1. Přemysl is the first character to sing, six
bars later.

SR27   **Vladimír Helfert: 'Janáček's unknown operas, 1: *Šárka*'**

Anyone who has formed a picture of Janáček the dramatist exclusively on the basis of *Jenůfa* and the later operas will certainly be surprised if we say that Janáček's *Šárka* is closest in its dramatic style to *Smetana's tragic style* and has evidently grown from it already in this work while searching for its own path. This circumstance is uncommonly interesting for Janáček's artistic development and for the history of our modern music. [...] *At the time it was written Janáček's 'Šárka' was the most perfect and stylistically the purest Czech tragic opera of its time besides 'The Bride of Messina'.*[1]

Hudební rozhledy, i (1924–5) [15 November 1924]

The next year Brno Theatre decided to stage *Šárka* as a belated seventieth-birthday tribute. The request on 2 June 1925 from the Brno Theatre for the vocal score so that it could be copied (**SR28**) crossed with one from Janáček, promising *Šárka* 'in about a fortnight' and at the same time requesting specific help on the libretto. 'Ctirad talks about love like some fifth-form student; perhaps some tougher verbal expression [to fit] the melody will occur to Mr Zítek [the producer]?' (**SR29**: Janáček to František Neumann, 2 June 1925).[2] After a short but intensive final revision during the first four days of his summer break at Luhačovice, Janáček was able to report to his wife on 7 June 1925 (**SR30**) that having worked on *Šárka* for four days, he had sent it off to Brno. Unfortunately he overlooked another gap in the text for which the words had to be supplied later by Ota Zítek.

SR31   **Janáček to Ota Zítek**   *Hukvaldy, 6 November [October] 1925*

Please may I have those few words of Přemysl's in *Šárka*. The music carried me away and there weren't any more words.[3]

---

1 Fibich's *The Bride of Messina* was first given in 1884; his next operas, including the tragic *Hedy* (1896) and *Šárka* (1897), came more than a decade later. Dvořák's next tragic opera after *Dimitrij* (1882) was *Rusalka* (1901). There were not many other Czech tragic operas that Helfert could have had in mind. The most prominent would have been Bendl's *The Child of Tábor* (1892), Foerster's first opera, *Debora* (1893), and Kovařovic's *The Dogheads* (1897).

2 Ctirad talks of love when alone in Act 1: 'Ó, sne o sladké lásce, přelude kouzelný' ['O dream of sweet love, magic illusion']. Janáček was right to draw attention to this (Ctirad continues by inviting the nightingale to sing and the white moon to shine), but presumably nothing more virile occurred to Mr Zítek since the words in this scene remain those of Zeyer.

3 This refers to the expansion of Přemysl's Act 1 solo 'Buď chrabrým' ['Be valorous!']. The words added by Zítek are: 'Poctivě vládni zbrojí svou, síly své užívej moudře a zůstaň věren odkazu slavných předků' ['Wield your weapon honourably, use your strength wisely, and remain faithful to the heritage of your famous forebears'].

Another problem was the title of the work, shared with Fibich's most famous opera, and which seems to have been queried by the theatre. Janáček wrote about this to the conductor and head of opera in Brno, František Neumann:

Janáček to František Neumann   *Brno, 31 October 1925*   SR32

[. . .] It's about the name of *Šárka*.
I will stick to it for these reasons:
1. Zeyer wrote the libretto and called it *Šárka*.
2. It's given in all literary works which deal with Zeyer.
3. I wrote the work with a strong image of Šárka in mind.
4. When people have written about me, and write about me, they always mention *Šárka* among my works.
5. A short name for a tiny work; that's fitting.
6. So let's print it and say it like this:
     Fibich's – *Šárka*
     Janáček's – *Šárka*.
In doing so I will not undermine in any way the value of Fibich's work and promoting myself is the last thing I want to do!
7. That I was first in the world with my *Šárka* carries some weight, though it's only a matter of form.
     Let's not beat our brains any more over this.

The belated première of *Šárka* was given by Neumann in Brno on 11 November 1925, in general to the composer's satisfaction:

Janáček to Ota Zítek   *Brno, 13 November 1925*   SR33

Thank you for the excellent production of my *Šárka*.
     I particularly commend your conception
                 of the humiliated women
in Act 3.[1] That's the only way it can be!
     But that tomb of the dead Libuše![2] I ask – do please comply with my wishes –
     1. that it should be gloomy inside

1 Apart from Šárka's surprise entry, the only women to appear in Act 3 are clearly on the men's side and take part in the funeral laments for Ctirad. Zítek's 'humiliated women' – presumably Šárka's followers, now leaderless after her change of heart – were an addition.
2 Towards the end of Act 1, the young hero Ctirad goes to the funeral vault of the recently dead Czech Princess, Libuše, to collect the magic hammer and shield bequeathed to him.

2. that Libuše should be in a white robe – that's still today the colour of mourning in Slovakia[1] (Javorník) –

3. that the crown on her head should shine

4. that Ctirad should not go *immediately* into the vault, but only when he hides.

On Sunday [15 November], the representative of Universal Edition is coming to the performance to negotiate the printing. I should be pleased if he liked it.

Naturally, thanks to your valuable idea for the humiliated women in Act 3, I will ask for your production – if another theatre should be interested in my *Šárka*.[2]

The fact that Janáček could report that a representative from Universal Edition was coming to see *Šárka* was a minor triumph of persistence on his part. Only a few days earlier the matter sounded far less hopeful:

SR34   **Janáček to Universal Edition**   *Brno, 9 November 1925*

On 11 November is the première of *Šárka*.
   On 12 November I would have to go to Breslau.[3]
   On 14 November in Breslau.
   On 15 November in Brno. It's the second performance of *Šárka*.
   Guests are coming from Prague.
   And all that after eight weeks of illness.[4]
   That would be too much!
   I wrote to Breslau to excuse myself. Another time I will go willingly!
   And you have no interest in *Šárka*?
   Should someone else get it to print?
   And the thing is pretty.

Universal Edition responded immediately (SR35, 11 November 1925) with apologies from the director, Dr Hertzka, that because of his illness he would

1 Or rather in Slovácko; Janáček often wrote 'Slovensko' (Slovakia) for 'Slovácko' (Moravian Slovakia). The village of Javorník is near Velká nad Veličkou, where Janáček conducted important ethnographic research from 1892. According to the ethnographer Dušan Holý (personal communication), the concept of white for mourning is still to be found in this region. Janáček's insistence on it was not to introduce an inappropriate Moravian ethnographic element into the work, but instead to make use of what he regarded as an archaic pre-Christian survival.
2 The only other production of *Šárka* before the 1958 cycle in Brno was in Olomouc in 1938. Zítek was not involved.
3 (now Wrocław) for the première there of *Jenůfa* on 14 November 1925.
4 In a letter to Max Brod dated 25 September 1925 Janáček mentions a 'painful illness' (shingles) that he had been suffering from for three weeks by then.

not be at the première himself, but would send a deputy to the next perform-ance. He also asked Janáček to reserve the vocal score for Universal Edition. Two months later, Janáček sent back a signed contract for *Šárka* (SR36, 14 January 1926 = VM26).

The fate of *Šárka* became one of the obsessions of Janáček's final years. He took it badly that Prague showed no intention of staging it, and exchanged bitter letters over this with Otakar Ostrčil, the head of opera at the National Theatre in Prague, with whom he had had an excellent working relationship (see for instance BR226ff):

Janáček to Otakar Ostrčil   *Prague, 9 January 1926*   SR37

I wanted to stay here for the new production of *Jenůfa*[1] – for which I respectfully thank you – but the refusal of *Šárka* hurts more than you suspect.

Prager Tagblatt (15 January 1926)[2]   SR38

Janáček's *Šárka*, which recently won a decisive success at its première in Brno, having lain unperformed for about forty years, was – as we have heard – turned down by the Prague National Theatre. This is the second time that Prague has not drawn the obvious conclusion from a Janáček success in Brno. *Jenůfa* also remained unperformed by Prague for many years when in Brno it had already become a reper-tory piece.[3] It is astonishing, in the light of *Jenůfa*'s international success, that the Prague theatre management remains unable to learn its lessons.

B[oleslav] V[omáčka]: 'Janáček's *Šárka* in Prague . . .'   SR39

News in the *Prager Tagblatt* that Janáček's *Šárka* was turned down by the Prague National Theatre is, according to information received directly from the head of opera, Otakar Ostrčil, untrue. The opera was not ever submitted to the National Theatre and there have not yet been any negotiations over its inclusion in the repertory. [. . .]

Lidové noviny (20 January 1926)

---

1 Prague National Theatre, 12 January 1926, conducted by Otakar Ostrčil.
2 It is clear from Max Brod's letter to Janáček of 16 January 1926 (JA ix, 196) that the author of this unsigned report was Max Brod.
3 A journalistic exaggeration; from its première in 1904 to its last performance (in 1913) before the Prague première it was performed nineteen times.

SR40 Janáček to Otakar Ostrčil *Brno, 21 January 1926*

Now I'm not going to deal with the affair of my *Šárka* through the newspapers, am I? So I'm writing to you.

You know that I longed to hear *Jenůfa* conducted by you, that I begged you to take it on.

Then I was informed that you refused to perform my *Šárka*.

I was deeply hurt, and I left Prague without delay.

Why has your refusal of my *Šárka* so upset me?

My work lay around for forty-three years[1] since the conceited Zeyer withheld his permission for me to go to the public with the work.

Recently Dr Helfert, having heard about the piece, borrowed it, and published an analysis [SR27] in which he placed it beside *The Bride of Messina* and even one of Smetana's operas; some German writer in *Anbruch* writes of it in a way that I can be proud of.[2]

Now that the work is going to be published, it will be clear what there is in it.

Believe me, the reviews leave me untouched.

But I am not concerned about this now. Mr Vomáčka writes in today's *Lidové noviny*, after speaking to you, that apparently the matter of *Šárka*'s acceptance was not settled since I allegedly never submitted it.

You know only too well that I did not submit *Káťa Kabanová* or *The Cunning Little Vixen* – and these works have been given at the Prague National Theatre.

I was definitely informed, however, that you refused to put on my *Šárka* at the Prague National Theatre.

I ask you therefore for an explanation, for I don't want this matter to be tramped over in the papers.

That I have had not the slightest part in the attacks on you in the *Lidové noviny*, *Prager Tagblatt*, *Locopresse*, etc. I don't need to show.

You were the only one whom I respected, and continue to respect.

---

1 Thirty-eight years at the most, counting from when Janáček began work.

2 'A.K.', in his review of the Brno première of *Šárka*, 'Eine Jugendoper von Janáček', *Musikblätter des Anbruch*, vii (1925), pp.555–6, praised the 'masterly handling of the choruses', and the love duet in Act 2, 'full of true, blossoming melody'. He concluded with the observation that 'had Janáček's *Šárka* been known earlier, Czech opera would have taken another path'. These comments should be seen in the light that 'A.K.' was Alfred Kalmus from Universal Edition, representing the firm's director, and writing for the firm's house magazine.

Otakar Ostrčil to Janáček   *Prague, 31 January 1926*   **SR41**

Forgive me for answering your letter only today. For one thing I had little time, and for another I did not want to respond over-hastily, especially because your departure from Prague before the première of the new production of *Jenůfa* was not at all pleasant for me.

You know my attitude towards you. During my time at the National Theatre I have performed your *Excursions of Mr Brouček* which had not yet been played in Brno, *Káťa Kabanová*, *The Cunning Little Vixen* and now I have prepared a new production of *Jenůfa*. I have directed all premières myself and I have put all that I know into the preparation. The facts speak for themselves and I do not need to defend myself against the attacks of journalists.

As for *Šárka* I had not anticipated that you were interested in its being performed at the Prague National Theatre. On the contrary I observed that your interest in this work was not lively enough for you to complete the full score of it yourself. I assumed that you yourself regarded the performance of this work on the one hand as an interesting retrospective, shedding light on the beginnings of your work, and on the other as an act of piety on the part of the Brno National Theatre towards the first stage work of Moravia's greatest composer. The attitude of the Prague National Theatre towards *Šárka* was essentially different from that towards your later operas, which the theatre naturally applied for of its own accord, although you did not submit them. For the above reasons I did not apply to produce *Šárka* but it is also intolerable for news to be spread about that I turned it down when it was not even submitted.

I look forward however to your new opera *The Makropulos Affair*, and would regard it an honour if you were to entrust it to the National Theatre in Prague for its first performance.

I express my thanks to you for the concluding words of your letter and am yours devotedly,

O. Ostrčil.

At first Janáček tried to link the Prague première of his next opera, *The Makropulos Affair*, with that of *Šárka* (**SR42**: Janáček to Universal Edition, 14 August 1926). This was not an unusual demand. Richard Strauss allowed the National Theatre (rather than the German Theatre in Prague, which had a first option on all new German works) to stage *Der Rosenkavalier* a few weeks after its Dresden première on condition it also staged his early *Feuersnot* (Tyrrell 1988, 49). In its letter to Janáček of 17 August 1926 (**SR43**) Universal Edition applauded Janáček's plan. Later, however Universal became alarmed when Janáček suggested that the timing of the putative Prague *Šárka* might be linked to the appearance in print of the vocal score:

SR44 Janáček to Universal Edition   *Hukvaldy, 20 February 1927*

Concerning Prague:
1. I wanted to make it a condition that *Šárka* would be staged by the National Theatre when the vocal score appears in print.
    But one can't compel love. [. . .]

SR45 Universal Edition to Janáček   *Vienna, 23 February 1927*

From your esteemed letter we gather that you wanted to link the performance of *Šárka* in Prague with the publication of the vocal score. We knew nothing about this before. As a matter of fact, it is intended, in the spirit of our previous communications, to bring out *Šárka* now that *The Makropulos Affair* has been taken care of. The engraving is now under way so that very soon there will be absolutely no reason why the work should not be produced in Prague. Admittedly, of course, there is the question of whether the National Theatre would not prefer to do *The Makropulos Affair* first and then perhaps *Šárka* later. [. . .]

Promising the engraving 'soon' was, however, a familiar story, as an earlier letter (SR46) demonstrates:

SR46 Universal Edition to Janáček   *Vienna, 4 June 1926*

[. . .] When we received the score, we handed it over immediately to our most experienced employee (Dr Pisk, whom I believe you also know), and for several weeks now he has been working on it, comparing the vocal score with the full score bar for bar. There are so many copying errors and wrong notes in the vocal score and also numerous discrepancies between full score and vocal score (cuts, missing parts, etc) that the work goes forward only very slowly. In the next few weeks you will be getting a questionnaire over certain points which cannot be resolved here without your explanation. We would have done you and the composition an ill service had we immediately engraved and printed the vocal score in the state we received it from you. [. . .] I think now that, as soon as your answers to the questionnaire have come in, thus in about a fortnight, we will be able to begin with the engraving and that the vocal score will appear in print during the course of the summer.

But the summer passed, as did that of 1927, so that by the end of the year Janáček had become impatient with what had begun to seem like delaying tactics, though the grounds had now shifted to the matter of a German translation.

Universal Edition to Janáček   *Vienna, 28 December 1927*   **SR47**

[. . .] You have every reason, most esteemed Meister Janáček, to be dissatisfied on account of *Šárka* and *Říkadla*. But we assure you, that the delay over both works is not our fault.
[. . .]
     As far as *Šárka* is concerned, the postponement is entirely due to the question of the translation. You know that the matter of *Šárka* came up virtually simultaneously with that of *The Makropulos Affair*. We were both, however, in agreement that *The Makropulos Affair* should go first, and so *Šárka* had to wait. After *The Makropulos Affair* Dr Brod, to whom I would have much preferred to entrust the translation, had no time and so we still remain today without a translation. I will make one further last attempt over the translation and if the question cannot be solved suitably, I will have the vocal score engraved with the Czech text alone and the engraving begun immediately after the completion of the [Glagolitic] Mass. We would then still be able to finish the Mass, *Říkadla* and *Šárka* before the summer and thereby get all arrears all out of the way.
[. . .]

Universal Edition had approached Max Brod on 25 October 1927 (**SR48**), saying that it was an 'old wish' of Janáček's to see *Šárka* in print, a wish that Dr Hertzka had not yet fulfilled. He wanted to avoid issuing a purely Czech edition since in view of Janáček's growing reputation in Germany he had no doubt that German theatres could be found to take on the work. Brod, however, had declined (**SR49**: to Universal Edition, 5 November 1927). Janáček accepted the Universal Edition proposal outlined in SR47 (**SR50**, undated, ?3 January 1928),[1] and energetically began to try and change Brod's mind:

Janáček to Max Brod   *Prague, 10 January 1928*   **SR51**

I was today, 10 January, at your house at 4 o'clock. I knocked in vain.
     I wanted to speak to you about the translations of
     1. *Šárka* and

---

1 As noted on the letter, Universal Edition received it on 4 January 1928.

2. The Glagolitic Mass.
Yes, and other things as well. The Glagolitic Mass and *Šárka* will
both be easy. But it's urgent. The Glagolitic Mass is meant to come
out by the end of March, and *Šárka* straight afterwards. [. . .]

SR52   **Max Brod to Janáček**   *Prague, 13 January 1928*

[. . .] But I say to you at once that I am so tired out from work that I
cannot take on *anything*. – It will be possible again later, but not
now. – The best thing would be for someone else to translate the
Mass and *Šárka*, while I would take on *From the House of the Dead*,
since this is not so urgent. At the moment I am very, very tired.

Somehow Janáček seemed to have persuaded Brod that he was not quite so
tired, since on 4 February (**SR53**) he reported to Universal Edition that Brod
was prepared to translate *Šárka*, and awaited the vocal score, which, three
days later, Universal Edition announced had been sent (**SR54**, 7 February
1928). But Brod's tiredness was partly diplomatic.

SR55   **Max Brod to Universal Edition**   *Prague, 13 February 1928*

By the same post [. . .] I am sending Janáček's *Šárka* back to you. I
will not translate this opera. Firstly because I have not found in it
anything to attract me. Do not mention this reason to Meister Janáček. In general however – and this is the second reason for my
refusal – I intend from now on to devote myself to my own works
and to withdraw more and more from translation work. Only in
exceptional cases will I take on translations. [. . .]

Janáček's seemingly successful intervention (sr53) with Max Brod thus
merely delayed matters further. Despite the promise by Universal Edition of
publication by the summer of 1928, *Šárka* was unpublished at Janáček's
death, and remains so.

2 *The Beginning of a Romance*

The landscape is a fir plantation (see Plate 1). In the foreground there are tree stumps and piles of split logs. In the middle of the picture there is a coach and four horses. The driver is a rather raffish figure with a monocle, a high, narrow-brimmed hat and a pointed moustache. He is standing, holding the reins and a long whip. There are two other men in the carriage. An older gentleman is sitting in the back, a rather comfortable figure with whiskers, top hat and full coat. A youngish man with glasses, wearing an overcoat and a round military pillbox hat, is lounging with both feet on the driver's seat. With a gloved hand he is gesticulating towards the fourth figure in the picture, in whose direction all three men are looking.

The fourth figure is a peasant girl, standing in the foreground right, looking down modestly, but also observing the other figures. She is wearing an elaborately embroidered folk blouse, rather a plain brown skirt and brown scarf. Barefoot, she is standing by the pile of split logs and seems to have been gathering the firewood which is now tied down on to her wheelbarrow.

What is striking is the contrast between the two parties, a meeting between two worlds. The downcast, slightly sullen (though interested) look of the peasant girl is set against the overtly ribald expressions of the aristocratic party (which includes a large, well-fed dog). The driver and the old gentlemen appraise the girl with rather cruel, knowing smiles. The gesticulating character seems a little different, though it is hard to read his expression since his hand partly obscures his face. The picture is entitled 'The Beginning of a Romance'.[1]

The artist was the young painter Jaroslav Věšín (1861–1915), recently back from his studies in Munich. His painting formed part of the first Czech exhibition in Brno, which was held during July and August 1885 in the rooms of the Readers' Club at the Besední dům [Meeting House].[2] Věšín's painting aroused considerable interest in the press, and wide popularity through the publication of a coloured reproduction of it. Janáček acquired a framed copy, which hung in the sitting room of his flat in Old Brno. Later he took it to Hukvaldy, where he kept it in his study as a memento of his second

---

1 'Počátek románu'; see p.131, fn.1, for an explanation of 'román.' Here 'romance' seems the more appropriate translation. As Fiala has pointed out (1964, 202), the title is more apt for Věšín's picture than for Janáček's opera, which starts *in media res*.

2 The Besední dům was built in 1874 as a cultural centre for Brno Czechs, with a concert hall, meeting rooms such as the Readers' Club [Čtenářský spolek] and restaurant. See also 'Beseda' in Glossary.

opera. It was not, however, the opera's direct inspiration. In between, Věšín's picture provided the title and situation for a short story by Gabriela Preissová:[1]

PR1   Gabriela Preissová: 'My encounters with Thalia'

As the oldest daughter of six children I shared my mother's worries and while only eighteen I married a good and gentle man, Jan Preiss, the accountant of a sugar refinery in Hodonín.

Hodonín had fascinated me when I had been at school there before [for a year, staying with her uncle]. [...] I began to write about the things which surrounded me – my *Tales from Slovácko*. One of the first pieces was called *The Beginning of a Romance* [1886]. The young Leoš Janáček liked this novella so much that he wrote a one-act opera based on it, set to verse by Professor Tichý. It was performed only about three times in Brno. Why this work by Janáček did not establish itself more firmly on the stage I cannot say. Much later I used the material as the main part of my lyrical comedy *Spring in the Manor Village*. As promised, I submitted it to Švanda's Theatre at Smíchov [a suburb of Prague], where it had over fifty performances and country theatres still do well with it.

[JP3]
Divadlo a hudba, i (1941–2)

Gabriela Preissová had arrived in Moravia at a time when the province was beginning to experience a new awareness of its distinctive folk heritage. Early Czech folklorists, in the first half of the nineteenth century, had concentrated on collecting folksongs. But during the 1880s and 1890s the new wave of interest in folk culture in the Czech lands embraced many new aspects such as language, customs, clothing and domestic architecture. It was only just in time. Folk culture was visibly retreating in the face of the railways and heavy industrialization, and by 1880, when Preissová arrived in Hodonín, it was confined largely to the villages and outlying areas.

Like most towns in Moravia at the time, Hodonín had a predominantly German population (Jan Preiss himself never mastered Czech), but Preissová accompanied her husband on his business trips through the surrounding Czech-speaking villages. Hodonín was in fact at the centre of the ethnographic region of Slovácko (Moravian Slovakia – a border area tending towards Slovak language and culture) which, for a Bohemian such as Preissová, would have possessed all the charm and exoticism of a virtually foreign country. She was an observant and impressionable visitor. She collected the

---

1 See Fiala 1964, 199–200 for more details of the exhibition of Věšín's painting, its cultural context and its influence on Preissová.

rich folk embroidery, and got to know the local people and their way of life. Soon, in 1884, she began publishing short stories based on what she had experienced; *The Beginning of a Romance* formed the basis for Janáček's second opera. Its charm lies not in the trivial story (the budding romance between Poluška and the aristocrat is abruptly terminated by the sober realization of class barriers, and Poluška returns contentedly to her humble swain) but in the evocation of folk life through detailed descriptions of costumes and customs. By the time of his first recorded contacts with Preissová, Janáček had begun his musical reorientation, turning his back on his conventional 'German' training, and striking out on new paths offered by his Moravian roots. As someone with allied interests Janáček turned to Preissová for a Moravian opera libretto. His letters to Preissová do not survive but the nature of his request can be inferred from her reply.

Gabriela Preissová to Janáček   *Hodonín, 6 February 1888*   PR2

I heartily regret that I cannot repay your trust and your request as I should wish to. I cannot write when and what I would like to, but must wait for my rare poetic moments – and so for this reason can never promise anyone a contribution. By giving promises and forcing myself I would lapse easily into mere mechanical work into which, as it happens, my promises led me last year – with the result that I published two works that I would have preferred to have seen in the fire. Well, I won't do that again. Should I write something in a musical genre of my own accord I certainly won't forget you.

By the time of their next documented exchange, three years later, Preissová had become a national figure because two of her plays, both set in Slovácko, had been performed at the Prague National Theatre, *The Farm Mistress* (1889) and *Her Stepdaughter* (1890). The first was warmly received, the second created a furore and was taken off after five performances (see Chapter 3). It was *Her Stepdaughter* that Janáček chose to adapt as his third opera, *Jenůfa*. In this light, it is somewhat surprising to see that he turned first to *The Beginning of a Romance*, which, in Preissová's words (PR6) had '*no* deeper dramatic conflict' and which, furthermore, needed to be recast as an opera libretto. Preissová, who had volunteered to find a librettist, first thought of Eliška Krásnohorská. Her most recent libretto, *The Child of Tábor* (composed 1888, performed 1892), was the last of several she wrote for Karel Bendl. By then, however, she had become embittered by the increasingly patronizing attitude taken by the Czech literary establishment towards her librettos for Smetana's last operas.

PR3   Eliška Krásnohorská to Gabriela Preissová   *[undated, sent to Janáček with* PR4*]*

I thank you warmly for the unexpected surprise and for your trust in me and for kindly sending me the interesting draft, which – as you see – I am returning. Remember, dear soul, that after your own bitter experiences you wrote to me that you are weak and that I am strong, and I answered you perhaps in the following vein: 'You are wrong, I'm not so strong that I would wish to suffer those terrible unpleasantnesses which I know from the theatre; I have given up every thought of the theatre, I have said farewell to it and don't want even to hear about it.' – Don't you remember? And yet you must have forgotten about it, otherwise you would not have sent me your draft. Forgive me – I am very fond of you, but I won't wet my pen for the theatre.

Of Mr Janáček I have already heard that he is a solid musician; I have absolutely nothing against him. But spare me, I beg you, from the theatre! It grieves me that I will be forced once again to experience its existence in person when Bendl's opera *The Child of Tábor*, with my libretto, is produced. If I could prevent it, I would do so immediately. But to poke my nose into the theatre of my own free will is something I won't do. You must therefore please forgive my total unwillingness. No argument will move me, I won't do it at any price.

I was surprised, my dear Preissová, that you wanted to entrust your work to me, not simply because you know my aversion to the theatre, but rather more because among your quartet of women bound by love (mere friendship doesn't count with you) is a librettist *par excellence* – Mrs Červinková. If you found the actual versifying troublesome, she certainly would not. [. . .]

PR4   Gabriela Preissová to Janáček   *Oslavany, 2 April 1891*

As you will see from the enclosed letter, Krásnohorská has declined to do the versification for us. I remember that she wrote to me three months ago saying that she would never again in her life write anything for the theatre.

Look through the action yourself, the way I have drafted it for versification. We must wait a while in view of the mourning in Dr Rieger's household; then we'll turn to Mrs Červinková – I really did forget about her, poor thing.

Don't give the enclosed draft to anybody to read, unless Professor Bartoš should wish to see it; I respect him so much that it was only on his account that I embarked on this. But certainly it would have to be an operatic idyll and never a comedy – it has too little action – that is to say, too little *dramatic* action.

Please keep this draft to yourself for the time being until I write to you again; you should then send it directly to Mrs Červinková, who will take it on for our sake. You would have to accompany it with a few words of entreaty.

It seems impossible, given only a couple of days to do it and report back to Preissová, that Janáček set off for Prague to make a personal appeal to Marie Červinková-Riegrová (1854–95), who had provided two excellent librettos for Janáček's friend Dvořák. However, such an impulsive action was quite in character, and is, moreover, suggested by Janáček's remark in his auto-biography: 'And, somewhere in a drawing room of a house in Prague near the Jungmann statue, I begged for the libretto' (PR42). Whether or not the journey was made, the outcome was that he did not get a libretto from Prague and instead looked around for someone local to do it, in this case František Rypáček (1853–1917), a schoolteacher and former colleague of the folklorist František Bartoš. Rypáček's literary efforts – little known outside his connections with Janáček – went under the pseudonym of Jaroslav Tichý.

Gabriela Preissová to Janáček   *Oslavany, 5 April 1891*   PR5

Providing a text for your work is entirely your own affair — my part is simply the pleasure that you may be able to make use of the action of my story. So I consent most gladly to Mr T[ichý]'s kindly taking it on, and only if it becomes necessary to get Mrs Č[ervinková] will I offer to intercede for you.

Tichý must have set to work quickly, for on 13 May Preissová asked Vladimír Šťastný[1] to have a look at the result. And two days after that, Janáček began composition, as he noted on his 'first draft', written for voice and piano.[2] Originally his one-act opera was to have been a Singspiel, with spoken dialogue, as is clear both from Preissová's next letter and from Janáček's draft, which simply omits the spoken text:

---

1 The author of a couple of volumes of poetry, and a Moravian nationalist who from 1867 gave religious instruction at the newly founded Czech Gymnasium in Brno, the Revd Vladimír Šťastný (1841–1910) was a good friend and adviser to Preissová. Janáček also knew him and in 1897 set his Festival Chorus.
2 BmJA, A23.517; beginning and ending dates (15 May 1891 – 2 July 1891) noted in Janáček's hand.

PR6   **Gabriela Preissová to Vladimír Šťastný**   *Oslavany, 13 May 1891*

Dramatic strength is never essential in opera; in this way one can excuse *The Beginning of a Romance*, in which there is *no* deeper dramatic conflict. Nevertheless I hope that the composer will still be happy with it.

[. . .]

Mr Jaroslav Tichý has a graceful turn of phrase, quite accurate in its folk diction – only here and there would I ask you, as a brilliant poet, if you could kindly change the words underlined to something more apt. I have also tried to do a bit, but I myself am strictly a writer of prose. As written, the text would be long enough for a two-act opera – since a sung sentence takes five times as long as a spoken one. So I suggest cuts – just cut what and where it is possible! I myself have also tried cutting; perhaps the poet won't hold it against me.

For the composer himself would feel it [was too long].

The spoken dialogue [*próza*] is just as I hurriedly drafted it in about two hours, it was naturally more detailed.

[. . .]

God grant that this little opera of Mr Janáček's will succeed – our *first* Moravian opera!

PR7   **Gabriela Preissová to Janáček**   *Oslavany, 4 June 1891*

Don't be cross that it has taken me so long to respond to your kind letter. I wasn't at home.

I am much looking forward to *The Beginning of a Romance*. How far have you got with the work? Mr J[aroslav] T[ichý]'s versification is delightful. That it's a little strange for so many people to come together in one place in one act – don't let that bother you! After all it is a forest with footpaths crossing, where the gentry go for walks and so on; *the entry of every character is justified*. What about those operas where if a chorus is needed a crowd rushes on from the wings! And so on. An opera text does not call for such rigid standards as drama.

If you already have something written, couldn't you make an outing to visit us in Oslavany for instance on Sunday (via Ivančice!)? Later I am going off for a while with the children to my parents in Bohemia. You ought then to play me your studies on the piano and, on the basis of the text, which you would have to bring with you, I would, 'criticize' it.

It seems that this visit took place, judging from a letter from Preissová dated 11 June (**PR8**), confirming that she was expecting Janáček 'on Saturday afternoon in Tetčice'.[1] A little later, on 2 July, Janáček completed his first draft of the vocal score, and Preissová made arrangements to hear the whole opera on the piano.

Gabriela Preissová to Janáček *Oslavany, 5 July 1891* **PR9**

On Wednesday I and the governess will be going into Brno to do some shopping. I would be delighted if I could have a chat with you about your latest work. If it's possible, write to me by return of post to say whether you could kindly come between 12 noon and 1 to the second-class waiting room of the state railway station. We will go home towards about 5 o'clock. If I have enough time you could play through the work to me on your piano in the afternoon.

Gabriela Preissová to Janáček *Oslavany, 7 July 1891* **PR10**

Thus I will be so bold as to visit your home tomorrow, Wednesday, between 12.30 and a quarter to two. I will grant you the half hour from noon for your lunch. We will have lunched at 11.30 with Mrs K[usá].

With the première at the Prague National Theatre of his folkloristic ballet *Rákos Rákoczy* on 24 July 1891, Janáček's stocks were rising. Preissová was clearly supportive but she did have some reservations about Janáček's new opera, which she expressed to one of her Brno friends, Julie Kusá-Fantová (one of the group of four women mentioned in PR3). She nevertheless made use of her connections with the director of the Prague National Theatre, František Adolf Šubert, to provide a recommendation for the opera to ease its passage in Brno, a wise (if unavailing) precaution in view of the rivalries that held it up for a couple of years.

Gabriela Preissová to Julie Kusá-Fantová *[undated]* **PR11**

[. . .] Do you often go to the theatre? Have you seen Janáček's ballet? He is now writing a one-act opera, *The Beginning of a Romance*, but it seems to me that he is composing too massively, in too classical a

---

1 There are railway stations in both Oslavany and Tetčice. From Brno to Oslavany was a journey of 28 km and involved changing on to a branch line passing through Ivančice (the original plan). The journey from Brno to Tetčice was direct, shorter (19 km) and on a faster line (Brno–Jihlava–Prague). Perhaps this is why this route was chosen; it would, however, have involved a drive at the other end.

style – it could be lighter. He has been playing me all his drafts on the piano. All in all I have great hopes for Janáček. [. . .]

PR12   **Gabriela Preissová to Janáček**   *Oslavany, 16 December 1891*

I will mention to the Director [of the National Theatre] Mr Š[ubert] that the scrutiny of *The Beginning of a Romance* should not take long, but you must also impress this on him yourself, for he likes to be forgetful. I should like to have heard some excerpts sung by soloists. Couldn't you invite some singers to your house and I could come and hear them? For at the end of January I must leave for Hirschenau, our estate in Carinthia, and I shall not be able to return until the autumn – I would not then, unfortunately, to my regret, hear the dear work.

PR13   **Janáček to F. A. Šubert**   *[undated, 17–?25 December 1891]*

I have completed a one-act opera, *The Beginning of a Romance*, and I want to bring the score[1] to you in the new year.

However, I ask you respectfully for one favour. Examining [an opera] usually takes a very long time and I would like to avoid this long, embarrassing uncertainty. Could you speed it up so that I might go home with a decision about it? I think it could be done. I would play the work to the conductors and for further study three or four days might perhaps suffice.

I will submit the piece to the Brno theatre only if it stands up to the critical study of your experts. My position in the *Družstvo*[2] of the Brno Theatre obliges me to do this.

There is no reason to doubt the sincerity of the last sentence nor to regard the seal of approval from Prague as a backdoor route to acceptance of the opera by the prestigious and much better equipped Prague National Theatre. According to a brief report in the *Moravská orlice* on 12 January 1892 (**PR14**), Janáček submitted the opera to the theatre in Brno – in the clear expectation of Prague's approval. He certainly seemed to be counting on a Brno première since, even more significantly, he had jotted down in his diary the names of a prospective Brno cast (**PR15**). One of these, Marie

---

1 Presumably the full score (BmJA, A29.920). Thus between July and December 1891 Janáček had revised the vocal score and orchestrated it.
2 = consortium, association. Administration of the Czech theatres in Prague and Brno was managed by especially formed companies, which tendered for a fixed-term franchise to run the theatre. Janáček was a committee member of the Brno *Družstvo*.

Wollnerová,[1] was proposed for the chief soprano part of Poluška. At this time Janáček was writing reviews for the *Moravské listy* and ventured a few mild criticisms of Wollnerová's performance as Santuzza in Mascagni's *Cavalleria rusticana*.

Janáček: review of *Cavalleria rusticana* PR16

[...] In this scene [between Santa and Turiddu] the acting of Miss Wollnerová (Santa) and Mr Burian[2] (Turiddu) was not sufficiently thought through. Their excessive liveliness during Lola's song pre-empted any further climax. But their singing, too, needs more restraint at the beginning. They sang with love and enthusiasm; undoubtedly during further performances they will also acquire artistic calm and discretion. Just a small step is lacking to absolute perfection of the two performances; it is not beyond them. [...]

Moravské listy (9 March 1892)

Marie Wollnerová to Janáček *Brno, 13 March 1892* PR17

As a result of the review about my performance of the part of Santuzza in *Cavalleria rusticana* I am forced, though most unwillingly, to return with my respectful thanks the part which through your kindness was assigned to me in the opera *The Beginning of a Romance*. Because of your attentions, I have come to the view that I would not be able to perform a part such as Poluška to your satisfaction with regard either to acting or singing. I fear that my poor conception of the part would only be to the detriment to the whole opera, and I do not wish to bring any blame on myself should your opera – in every respect no doubt outstanding – not have in performance the success which you, esteemed sir, expect. Perhaps casting the part with another singer would avoid this and satisfy your refined musical taste. Unfortunately my art is not at such a level that I would be able, esteemed sir, to interpret and perform according to your wishes the part assigned to me in your opera. Forgive me therefore that I am forced to decline this honour. I act as I must act.

---

1 Marie Wollnerová (1858–1939) was a member of the Brno National Theatre 1886–98, and sang most of the chief Smetana soprano roles there, as well as other parts such as Pamina, Donna Anna, Amelia (*Ballo in maschera*), Leonora (*Il trovatore*) and Marguerite (*Faust*).
2 The young tenor Carl Burrian (1870–1924), then Karel Burian, made his début in Brno in 1891 before a distinguished international career took him abroad.

It is likely that Wollnerová's reaction to Janáček's review caused embarrassment among the Brno management. This, together with Janáček's unpopularity among some of the theatre management as someone who spoke his mind, created delays in the acceptance of the opera in Brno, as is later confirmed in a letter by the then director of the Brno company, Václav Hübner (PR28).

PR18   Gabriela Preissová to Janáček   *Hirschenau Manor, Griffen,*
                                             Carinthia, 25 March 1892

I assumed that you had already completely forgotten about me, giving me not even a little news about your dear work. While only now you have had something to complain about. Believe me, such protracted dealings would have infuriated and grieved me if I were not all too familiar with these conditions! . . . I will just say this to console you: Bendl has now had an opera, *The Child of Tábor*, submitted for two and a half years – but written even longer ago . . . A piece by a Czech composer can wait, while when Mascagni writes something, they telegraph at once just to get it as quickly as possible. The Brno [Theatre] director [Václav Hübner] is, I suspect, so tied up that he never has a moment in which to answer letters. It has happened to me twice that I have urgently asked for an answer and not received one.

I think I wrote to you that this year until the autumn we have taken over the management of Hirschenau, our estate. So I had to set out for here with my sister-in-law to oversee things and will have to stay here until the autumn. But even the excessive physical work and the worry won't do me any harm. I have run away here into this fabulously beautiful corner of the Alps with such a desire for peace that I am not taking a single political newspaper, so I don't know at all what is going on in the world. Over *The Beginning of a Romance* I recently turned to Mrs Bakešová:[1] I was longing for some news. If your work doesn't get its turn during April, then don't wish for it to be [performed] until the new season in the autumn; they will undoubtedly drag it out for you until then anyway. Dvořák likewise fared no better, as his librettist, Mrs Červinková, told me. And what if I should relate to you my own experiences as a writer – how many times would you cry out: 'Doesn't it take away your appetite for work?' What can we do? – you see I think only of you. Self-awareness – the consciousness of *honest* endeavour, that guiding light of talent! Even if despite all this lack of recognition a hundred obstacles stood

1 Lucie Bakešová (1853–1935), Czech folksong collector and enthusiast.

in your way, believe me everybody talks about your talent with *respect* and much hope is pinned on you.

I was pleased to hear that I would be able to have a chat with you at the ball of the Readers' Club [13 January 1892] – however, you were not at the ball. Mr Hübner has told me that your work needs deep and time-consuming study, and he says that in particular the orchestra must be doubled.[1] He went on to say that the director [of the Prague National Theatre] Šubert wants to come to Brno to see a performance of *The Beginning of a Romance*. I know that director Šubert admires your talent, but I fear that they might conspire against you for being an outstanding Moravian, consequently as a hated celebrity; I'd love to know whether the conductors really think the same as they tell you. I know that you have a proud spirit, one that does not like to ask for something twice and beg for favours; so it is possible that this is holding up *The Beginning of a Romance*. But persistence will triumph! . . .

With the difficulties that he was encountering in Brno, it seems likely that Janáček began to think of the Prague National Theatre not so much as an ally in securing the performance of *The Beginning of a Romance* in Brno, but merely as a venue for the première. Janáček's letters to Šubert are mostly undated, though it is possible to assign PR19 to early February 1892 by its reference to 'Monday the 15th' (February 1892 is the only applicable month in which Monday falls on the 15th). The meeting proposed in it seems to have taken place and the verdict of the conductors at the National Theatre was such that Janáček embarked on revision, and resubmitted the work, judging from the reference to a 'corrected score' in what was probably the next letter (PR20).[2] PR21 was probably written shortly after receipt of Preissová's letter of 25 March (PR18). Janáček, it appears, had come to terms with the fact that the opera would not be performed in Brno that season and, although it is not directly stated, seemed now to be urging its performance in Prague.

Janáček to F. A. Šubert *[undated, early February 1892]* **PR19**

I am sending the score of *The Beginning of a Romance*. I now have the half-year holidays;[3] could you specify a time on Monday the 15th when I might play the conductor my work in its main outlines?

---

1 The orchestra stood at 24 for the 1891–2 season; the following season it went down to 20 (Nováková 1956, 58 and 66).
2 The dating proposed here differs from that in Pala 1955, 89–92, where these letters were first published.
3 A holiday in February between the two semesters of the academic year. In 1892 at the Teachers' Training Institute it would have lasted about a month.

I shall arrive in Prague on Sunday afternoon, if nothing upsets this plan, and I shall be so bold as to look you up.

PR20   **Janáček to F. A. Šubert**   *[undated, ?March 1892]*

I have sent the corrected score to the Directorate of the National Theatre. Please kindly look on my case with favour and notify me as soon as possible about the fate of my work.

PR21   **Janáček to F. A. Šubert**   *[undated, c.?28 March 1892]*

I hoped that I would get from you the answer you promised concerning *The Beginning of a Romance*.

I did not send a reminder as I wanted to invite you to the first performance in Brno. Since it has been drawn out beyond expectation here – at best they will be finished with copying out the parts only on Wednesday – and since the opera company leaves Brno next week [for its regional tour], it will probably not be performed in Brno this season.

On the basis of the conductors' statements recommending the work for performance I ask you to be so kind and send the prompt reply you promised.

The conductor Mr Čech [see PR24+] naturally does not see the work as an *opera* in the modern sense of the word. Then again, that was not how it was intended. Mrs Preissová called it a dramatized idyll and I wrote music to it, aspiring at least to the level of musical expression in Blodek's *In the Well*,[1] which I had in mind.

I enclose the libretto; the score is at your disposal to the end of this week.

Prague was no less dilatory than Brno, as is clear from the increasingly impatient tone of Janáček's letters:

PR22   **Janáček to F. A. Šubert**   *Brno, 3 April 1892*

Forgive my impatience. Will I, during the course of this week, receive the decision of the esteemed Directorate about *The Beginning of a Romance*?

Kindly take steps to bring this about.

---

1 *In the Well*, given in 1867, a year after *The Bartered Bride*, is a one-act village comedy by Vilém Blodek (1834–74) and one of the most successful and durable Czech operas of the nineteenth century. It is written in a style that recalls Nicolai and Lortzing as well as Smetana.

Janáček to F. A. Šubert *[undated, ?mid-April 1892]* **PR23**

Do forgive me please, if I now ask about the fate of my work. The uncertainty is unsettling me and depriving me of the right mood for work, just as, on the other hand, the opinion of the professional experts naturally matters greatly to me.

So please could you ensure that I might know the final verdict as soon as possible.

Janáček to F. A. Šubert *[undated, ?late April 1892]* **PR24**

Hoping that my letter will reach you in Prague, I venture to ask you again about the decision over *The Beginning of a Romance*.

Forgive my impatience, but to wait almost two months despite the promise of speedy action is surely a long time.

When they eventually came, the reports made to Šubert by his chief conductor Adolf Čech and assistant conductor, Mořic Anger,[1] were negative. Anger's is particularly interesting in its linking of the work with the ballet *Rákos Rákoczy*. The ballet is little more than a string of orchestrated folksongs and dances and this technique was, rather more surprisingly, used in many passages in *The Beginning of a Romance*, with the libretto text fitted over existing music.

Adolf Čech to F. A. Šubert *[undated, ?April 1892]* **PR25**

I can do no other than repeat what I have told Mr Janáček in person, that his *The Beginning of a Romance* in no way matches up to our view of operatic works, either in invention or in form. Furthermore, the instrumentation is, so to speak, as 'elegantly' thin as that of the same composer's ballet *Rákos Rákoczy*. I cannot therefore recommend this musical work for performance at the National Theatre in Prague. With this action I will save the *Družstvo* a considerable outlay, and the composer unpleasant disappointment. [. . .]

Mořic Anger to F. A. Šubert *[undated, ?April 1892]* **PR26**

According to your wishes I have looked through the corrected score of *The Beginning of a Romance* of Mr Director Janáček. As far as conception and instrumentation is concerned it is a 'pendant' to

---

1 Adolf Čech (1841–1903) and Mořic Anger (1844–1905) were both experienced conductors. Anger had been taken on at the National Theatre in 1881; Čech had been Smetana's deputy at the Provisional Theatre in 1866 and was chief conductor from 1876 until 1900.

Rákos Rákoczy, and *I cannot recommend this mixture of Moravian and Slovácko songs for performance because it is a manifest failure* – stylistically it is not an opera and cannot be – perhaps a so-called *Liederspiel* (some of those songs we have already heard in *Rákos Rákoczy*); harmonization and instrumentation is again the same. In no way can I recommend this work for performance at the National Theatre.

PR27   **F. A. Šubert to Janáček**   *Prague, 2 May 1892*

I greatly regret that on the basis of the rigorous expert opinion of both the conductors Anger and Čech I can give you no news other than that it is not possible to accept your work *The Beginning of a Romance* for performance in the National Theatre [in Prague]. Returning your score I am with all respect [. . .]

Further disappointments were in store for the composer when he heard more about the background to the delays in Brno from the artistic director and intendant of the Brno National Theatre for the 1891–2 season, Václav Hübner (1857–1920).

PR28   **Václav Hübner to Janáček**   *Prague, 5 September 1892*

Word has reached me that the Committee of the *Družstvo* of the Czech National Theatre in Brno is maliciously stating that it was my fault that your opera *The Beginning of a Romance* was not staged in last year's season, and that you are said to take the view that I am to blame for the fact that the première of the opera did not take place. I know of course that in the theatre people talk a lot and that it is therefore not necessary to take such theatre gossip seriously, though I find it my duty, however, to tell you the unvarnished truth in this matter, and for the reason chiefly that I regard you as the person in the whole Committee of the *Družstvo* most competent in theatrical matters, and because I am convinced that in my difficult position as director I had in you a fair-minded ally.

Whatever you might have already heard, I am writing the whole truth to you and I am ready to prove it to everyone.

If anyone is to blame for your opera not being performed it can only be Mr Jílek,[1] the conductor. As soon as you kindly informed me that you were entrusting the performance of the opera to us, I

1 František Jílek (1865–1911), conductor at the Brno Czech Theatre 1891–3.

definitely said to Mr Jílek that we must perform the opera this season and that it would also be an excellent enrichment of the repertory for the country tour and a welcome piece for the box office too. Then when we first went to your house to hear the opera, I realized from the conductor's comments that he was apparently unhappy to see that your opera was to be rehearsed. Such remarks he did not hide even from Miss Fürstová,[1] who was in hospital at the time and whom we stopped to see on the way to your house.

Then when we heard your opera and, still later, when he was handed the vocal score and full score, I and also doubtless other people frequently heard his fairly caustic remarks, which he did not hide, particularly from the singers, drawing attention mainly to the difficult voice parts and to the problems which the orchestra would have to overcome.

I, however, constantly urged him to have the parts copied out and several times pressed Mr Stross [Štross] myself about when this would happen. Mr Stross himself is undoubtedly a witness to this. I certainly told the conductor in the presence of the general secretary Mr [Jan Josef] Ninger, Mr [František] Syřínek and Mr [Antonín] Chlumský that I and the whole committee definitely wanted the opera to be staged even if it was at the end of the season. He constantly declared that he was unable to prepare it now and on my urging did no more than smile or fob me off with 'So study it yourself if you know so much about it!'

As further proof that I definitely wanted to stage your opera in the last season I cite the circumstance that I wrote to Mr Merhaut,[2] who was working on his scene from Brno life – *The Scoundrel*, [urging him] to hurry up with his work so that we should also have a drama première when we gave the première of your opera.

This is not slander, scandal-mongering or stirring but just an honest plea of my innocence in this matter when I state that the conductor Mr Jílek somehow intended that your opera should not reach the stage. I presume that it was in return for the fact that in his view you did not write favourably enough about him and the whole opera company in *Moravské listy*. I don't even hide the fact that he probably knew well enough – although perhaps was not himself the cause – that Miss Wollnerová gave back to you her part from your opera.

1 Karla Fürstová (*b.*1870) sang in Brno 1892–3, before moving to Munich.
2 Josef Merhaut (1863–1907), from 1885 journalist, critic and editor at the Brno *Moravská orlice*. He is known chiefly for his short stories.

I have felt that it was proper and necessary to tell you this much [. . .]

Please regard this letter as completely private, I was concerned merely to excuse myself, and that only to you, so you should know who the culprit was.

It was two years before these difficulties were smoothed out. One obstacle was removed in the winter of 1893 when the conductor František Jílek left to take up a post in Sarajevo, and Janáček himself conducted the work – the only opera that he conducted personally. Bridges too, had been clearly mended with Miss Wollnerová:

PR29   **Marie Wollnerová to Janáček**   *[undated]*[1]

Do forgive me for thanking you only today for kindly sending material for *The Beginning of a Romance*. Please, dear sir, accept my warm thanks for your kindness; but together with my thanks I make the request once again, dear sir, though most respectfully, if it would also be possible for me to borrow a vocal score and libretto for *The Beginning of a Romance*. It will be necessary to correct the orchestral parts thoroughly since you have, as is clear from the score, changed many places[2] and this would hold up rehearsal too much since we would have to wait until all the parts were completely corrected; and also it is a little difficult to accompany from the full score. [. . .]

PR30   **Gabriela Preissová to Janáček**   *Oslavany, 4 February 1894*

I would like to go to the première of *The Beginning of a Romance*. In case it is not given on the 8th of this month as originally decided, then I ask you if it would not be too much trouble to send me a few words on 6 February. If I don't receive news I will know that I can come towards evening of the 8th.

       [. . .]

1 The letter is undated but would seem to have been written a little before the opera's première rather than in early 1892 (before PR17) because of its references to revisions – which Janáček made probably no earlier than mid-March 1892. More revisions were made later (see PR31).

2 There are a large number of changes in orchestration in the surviving score, mostly affecting the harp part, the woodwind and horns (Janáček made little use of trumpets and trombones in the opera). Many of the changes were omissions, indicating a general desire to thin down the texture.

Janáček to F. A. Šubert *[undated, ?5 February 1894]* **PR31**

I venture to invite you on Saturday the 10th of this month to the first performance of *The Beginning of a Romance*. Some time ago the conductor Mr Čech expressed himself unfavourably about my work. After two years I have again looked over the work, corrected and supplemented it.

I would be most grateful therefore if I could welcome you on that day in Brno.

F. A. Šubert to Janáček *Prague, 6 February 1894* **PR32**

Wishing you and your work every success, I greatly regret that it is not possible for me to leave Prague at this time. For, more than at other times, I am overwhelmed by my work, both routine and exceptional, and cannot therefore allow myself the pleasure of getting to know your work in your theatre. However if it is your wish dear sir, I would be delighted, if you would send your score for examination.

Karel Sázavský:[1] review of *The Beginning of a Romance* **PR33**

With *The Beginning of a Romance* not only has the composer written a work in the spirit of folk music and Moravian music, but also he has directly, and most effectively, used several folksongs whose texts fitted the action of the opera. [. . .] The fact that the chosen songs have suitable texts is proof what an important part folksongs were and perhaps still are in the affairs of our people, how the singing of songs was a natural expression of thought and feeling.

It is self-evident that the composer, writing today for a modern stage, will not employ the old forms. Self-contained arias with regular interludes during which a singer must cross the stage several times and fill in the gaps with various gestures do not exist in Janáček's opera. Such arias of course are gladly listened to, they have their fame, and many their history. If anyone was expecting something similar, he was disappointed: mostly also perhaps by the unaccustomed melodic progressions, which someone with a knowledge of our folksongs was able to follow with understanding. The orchestral accompaniment flows independently along with the voice parts, adjusting itself to the sense of the words and taking account of the situation and the folk aspects of the opera. The opera has been called

1 Karel Sázavský (1858–1930), music teacher, writer and music critic, e.g. for Janáček's *Hudební listy*.

'romantic'.[1] The epithet is justified partly by the action and is also taken into account by the music.

The importance of the evening was understood by everyone. We noticed this in the numerous attendance – the theatre was filled to overflowing in all parts – as well as in the warm reception with which the composer, Mr Janáček, was rewarded. He was given three wreaths: silver, laurel and [one] from national offerings.[2]

Moravská orlice (13 February 1894)

The naive enthusiasm accorded to Janáček's little opera reflects that, ten years after the Czechs opened their own theatre in Brno, Moravian opera was still somewhat in its infancy, and its audiences relatively unsophisticated. (Other reviews criticized the thinness of the action and the lack of drama; see Fiala 1964, 216–18.) The *Moravská orlice* critic Karel Sázavský was right to stress the importance of the folksongs in the work and it was probably this appeal to local patriotism that ensured its warm reception. This reception encouraged Janáček to try again with Šubert for a Prague production:

PR34   **Janáček to F. A. Šubert**   *[undated, ?25 February 1894]*

I will take the liberty of again sending you the full score of *The Beginning of a Romance* but nevertheless ask you respectfully, since you yourself are so busy, kindly to send, if I might ask, the conductor Mr Anger to the fourth performance on the 27th of this month.

PR35   **F. A. Šubert to Janáček**   *Prague, 26 February 1894*

On the receipt of your esteemed letter I told the conductor to prepare to travel to Brno on 27 February. Because I now hear from Mr Anger that the performance of your opera was postponed, I take the liberty of informing you that Mr Anger will travel to Brno on 1 March.

Mořic Anger's prospective arrival for the performance on 1 March was duly noted in the Brno papers (Straková 1958, 161). Suddenly, however, Janáček lost interest or faith in the work. Perhaps Anger persisted in his criticisms, or perhaps Janáček himself realized the work's shortcomings. It was about this time that he decided to set Preissová's second play, *Her Stepdaughter*, and it must have been apparent to Janáček that he was dealing with a very different type of work, with quite a different potential and appeal. Despite the enthusiasm of the Brno audiences, *The Beginning of a Romance* was taken off after

1 On the printed poster; transcription in Straková 1958, 161–2.
2 *z národních obětin*; 'national offerings' were collections for charitable purposes, the contributors rewarded with receipts on cards or stickers. In this case wellwishers probably clubbed together to buy Janáček a third wreath.

four performances and was never revived during Janáček's lifetime. Evidence of his dissatisfaction can be found in the Janáček entry in the Hornovés' book on Czech opera (1903) in which *The Beginning of a Romance* is mentioned as having been performed in Brno, but no plot description is given, as in other entries, 'since the composer was unable to lend the libretto' (PR36, p.144). And when Preissová, in the light of the great success of *Jenůfa* in Prague in May 1916, suggested revising their earlier work, she clearly met with a cool response from the composer:

Gabriela Preissová to Janáček   *Prague, 1 June [1916]*   **PR37**

[. . .] I would like you to try and offer the finely honed comic opera *The Beginning of a Romance* to our theatre. Please send me that text by Mr Tichý. I would arrange it differently, more dramatically and I would wish you from my heart to insert in it very many clear echoes of Slovácko songs. Don't fear repeating them – or, so to say, borrowing them. Just see how nicely the 'Zákolanská'[1] works for instance in Smetana's *The Two Widows*. The whole audience is electrified by it. We would also put some choruses into it. Meanwhile don't say anything to anyone about it, send me Mr Rypáček's text and I will suggest a different construction without your having to discard many elaborated motifs. [. . .]

Gabriela Preissová to Janáček   *Prague, 5 December 1917*   **PR38**

[. . .] Might my daughter Ella, a good musician, ask you if she could read through your earlier setting of *The Beginning of a Romance*? She just wants to have a look at it – not to borrow anything from it! You disown this youthful work, so be it, but you could surely lend it out for a day or so. [. . .]

In fact in the Czech edition (1924) of Max Brod's biography of Janáček, the list of works, prepared with Janáček's co-operation, stated that the opera had been destroyed (PR39), though this was soon denied in a review of the book in *Hudební rozhledy* (PR40, 15 November 1924) by Vladimír Helfert, who wrote that 'a full score and piano sketch survive', and proved it by printing a facsimile. There was something in the 'destroyed' theory – a number of pages had been torn out from the full score and sketch vocal score, though the full score was easily reconstructed from the still extant parts when the work was revived for the Janáček festival in 1954. Despite Helfert's statement, Janáček

---

1 Nejedlý (1924–33, iv, 343) describes the *zákolanská* as a more recent (i.e. nineteenth-century) small-town dance usually given at private balls celebrating the engagement of the daughter of the house. Preissová could perhaps have in mind the polka before the final chorus of the opera (with two couples happily paired off).

still claimed that the work was fragmentary: 'I know, because I burnt a good half of it', he wrote in a placatory letter to Brod (**PR41**, 24 November 1924). His final damning judgement on the work was delivered at about this time in his autobiography:

PR42   Janáček's autobiography (1924)

The Beginning of a Romance was an empty comedy; it was tasteless to force me to put folksongs into it.[1]

And it was after *Šárka*!

Just listen for instance what I had to set! [Janáček quotes a quatrain of doggerel verse from the opera.]

And, somewhere in a drawing room of a house in Prague near the Jungmann statue, I begged for a libretto. Mrs Maturová knows about it.[2]

The Beginning of a Romance holds a unique position amongst Janáček's operas. After the success in Prague of *Jenůfa* he finished *Brouček*, revised *Šárka* and would have revised *Fate* if Procházka, Brod or anyone else had had any ideas for clarifying the libretto. But *The Beginning of a Romance* he left firmly on the shelf despite the pleas of Mrs Preissová. He had burnt part of it, declared it was 'lost', and in this comment virtually disowned it. It was his only opera in which he showed none of the confidence that was to sustain him through the long years of waiting.

[1] 'bylo nevkusno mi vnucovat do něho národní písničky.' The Czech is ambiguous. Other possible interpretations are 'It was tasteless of me to force folksongs into it'; 'I hated putting the folksongs into it'. By his quotation of a bad example from the piece, it seems that he was reproaching not himself but his librettist for forcing in the folksongs. Or perhaps Mrs Preissová, who as late as 1916 (PR37) was urging even more 'clear echoes of Slovácko songs.'

[2] The house in Prague may have been that of Mrs Červinková-Riegrová, assuming Janáček went to see her personally (see PR4+; when in Prague she lived at her father's house which is indeed near the Jungmann statue). It could not have been that of the singer Růžena Maturová, who did not return to Prague until her engagement by the National Theatre in 1893. Janáček's contacts with Mrs Maturová date from 1907, by which time she had married her second husband, František Jílek, the reluctant proposed conductor of *The Beginning of a Romance*.

3 Jenůfa

GENESIS

Gabriela Preissová: letter to editor   JP1

The material of *Her Stepdaughter*[1] is composed of two real-life incidents, though much idealized! In the first a lad wounded a girl, his brother's sweetheart, while slicing cabbage. He wounded her in the face deliberately because he loved her himself. In the second a woman helped her stepdaughter get rid of the fruits of her love (the girl threw the baby into the sewer), but I did not want to have two murderesses. Jenůfa falls through love, but she has enough goodwill and strength to live a better life.

Pražské noviny (30 November 1890)

Gabriela Preissová, who had made a reputation for herself on the basis of short stories celebrating the rural life of Slovácko (see PRI–2), had been encouraged by the director of the National Theatre in Prague, František Adolf Šubert, to turn one of these stories into a play. *The Farm Mistress* was staged with such success in 1889 that Preissová was immediately encouraged to write another: *Her Stepdaughter*. The plot hinges on the jealousy of Laca. He has loved his cousin Jenůfa from childhood, but while he was away in the army Jenůfa fell for his good-looking younger half-brother, the mill-owner Števa. In a fit of jealousy Laca slashes Jenůfa's cheek with a knife. By then, however, Jenůfa is pregnant with Števa's child and six months later gives birth to it in secret. Števa rejects her, but the penitent Laca is still eager to marry her, though dismayed to hear about the child. In desperation, the

---

1 Preissová's play *Její pastorkyňa* will be referred to here as *Her Stepdaughter*; Janáček's opera based on this play, though sharing the same title in Czech, will be referred to as *Jenůfa*. 'Pastorkyňa', a Moravian form of 'pastorkyně', means literally 'not own daughter' and is thus ambiguous – both 'stepdaughter' and 'foster-daughter' are forms of 'not own daughter'. Although Jenůfa addresses the Kostelnička as her 'pěstounka' ['foster-mother'], she is literally the Kostelnička's stepdaughter, as is evident from references in Preissová's play, and particularly in the novel that she later wrote on the subject. Discussing the German translation of the title (JP2: to Universal Edition, 22 September 1917), Janáček insisted on *Stieftochter* [stepdaughter], rejecting *Pflegetochter* [foster-daughter] and *Ziehtochter* [foster-daughter, an obsolete usage], and backed up his claim with an elaborate family tree. The Universal Edition score nevertheless has preferred 'Ziehtochter' and 'foster-daughter'.

stepmother murders the child (by drowning it in the icy mill stream), thus
clearing the way to Jenůfa's union with Laca. This otherwise purely melo-
dramatic tale is transformed by Jenůfa's gradual acceptance of Laca's love
and her comprehension of her stepmother's sacrifice for her.

Her Stepdaughter was performed to popular acclaim at the National
Theatre in Prague on 9 November 1890, but was savaged by much of the
press. The play was attacked as a nasty and threatening example of slice-of-
life realism. On the other hand, few of the 'realists' came to her rescue, being
uneasy about the underlying religious postulates of the play and the glow of
optimism in which it ends. Preissová defended herself vigorously against the
sentimental assumptions that such things did not happen in the country: her
play, she wrote, was based on two real-life incidents which she had picked up
in the local paper (JP1). She was, however, appalled by the notoriety she had
achieved, and never again wrote anything as fine or bold, or anything that
contributed further to the development of Czech drama and literature. The
management of the National Theatre also took fright and withdrew the play
after a few performances, and never revived it. But the publisher Fr. Šimáček
brought it out the next year (Prague, 1891: Repertoár českých divadel,
vol.24) and a production in Brno opened on 10 January 1891. Though no
evidence has survived, it would seem likely that Janáček saw the play there.
His annotated copy of the Šimáček edition is in the Janáček archive.[1]

JP3   Gabriela Preissová: 'My encounters with Thalia'

Shortly after the success of my *The Farm Mistress*, Jaroslav Kvapil
wrote to me saying that his friend J. B. Foerster would like to
compose an opera on the subject of my play. One of my friends
advised me not to decide lightly. An opera, it is said, will oppress,
even quite suppress, a play of the same name: after all the opera *Faust*
is competition for a play as famous as Goethe's. Nevertheless I
determined on the advent of the new opera which the talented composer soon brought into the world [without the aid of Kvapil]. And
after half a century there is still lively interest from our theatres in my
play.

After the composer Foerster, the highly talented, quick-tempered
Moravian Leoš Janáček applied to me. He said that he had fallen in
love with *Jenůfa* and already whole sentences of it rushed into his
mind which he immediately dressed with his music. He did not need
to put anything into verse, the words and sentences apparently speak
with their own music fully in agreement with his. We came to a happy
arrangement.

True to his instincts, Janáček began to dress the action of *Jenůfa*

1 BmJA, L 6.

with his heartfelt efforts. He studied the cries of young men at their folk dancing, he went off to the mill where he listened to and noted down the noises of the turning and rumble of the mill wheel.

[PRI]
Divadlo a hudba, i (1941–2), no. 8

These reminiscences of the aged Preissová, half a century after the event, need to be treated with caution. It is true that on 1 November 1893 Preissová wrote to Janáček (with whom she was in friendly contact over the libretto of *The Beginning of a Romance*, see Chapter 2), for advice on a violin teacher for her eleven-year-old son, mentioning 'Mr J. Foerster (the younger) is writing an opera on *The Farm Mistress*. Mr Jaroslav Kvapil is composing the rhymes [verse]. Perhaps this little bit of news will interest you, although Mr Foerster will need three years for the composition' (JP4). Did Preissová believe that Janáček, after writing *The Beginning of a Romance*, would be interested to hear that another opera composer was working on a text by her, or had Janáček already expressed interest in *Her Stepdaughter*? It is clear from her next letter to him, on 6 November 1893 (JP5), that Janáček suggested that one of his pupils from the Organ School could serve as the required violin teacher, and then had gone on to discuss his own plans to set Preissová's *Her Stepdaughter*. It is impossible to say whether the idea came to him as a direct result of the news about Foerster's setting Preissová's play (and thus in the five days between her two letters), or whether the idea had already been there for some time, and Preissová's letter about Foerster was simply warning him that another composer was now at work on another play of hers. Far from coming to a 'happy agreement' at first, Preissová tried to put Janáček off: 'I think that the material of P[astorkyňa, i.e. *Her Step-daughter*] is not suitable for musical setting – but perhaps in time we'll find something more suitable.'

Marie Stejskalová's reminiscences (1959)   JP6

When I went to [work for] the Janáčeks, the master was beginning to write *Jenůfa*. [. . .] He seldom had time for it during the day, but he devoted all his free evenings to it. He rarely stayed out longer than he had to: at concerts, in the theatre, in the Readers' Club, in the Old Brno Beseda [see Glossary] – he never hung around anywhere, and while others went to sleep when they got home, he sat down to work. In the morning I brought a lamp into his study filled to the brim with paraffin, the next day I took it away empty. The mistress would look at it: 'He's been writing through the whole night again.' Today I find it strange that the whole of *Jenůfa* was written by the light of a paraffin-lamp.

Sometimes it seemed to me that the master was battling with

Jenůfa, as if he went into the study not to compose but to fight. He got up from supper, stood and thought a moment and, really more to himself, sighed: 'Lord God and the Virgin Mary, help me!'

[. . .]

In those happy days when we were still all together, the master would often talk about *Jenůfa*: what he was currently working on, how he thought it might continue, whether the work was going well for him or not. He said this with such fire, that he convinced us all what a great work it would be. We were quiet as mice whenever he played through on the piano what he had written, often we crept up on tiptoe to the door of his room, and all three of us would listen. Little Olga wouldn't play about, she wouldn't even laugh aloud when her father was working.

He wrote *Jenůfa* for nine years – he also wrote other things in between – and much changed during that period. Olga became a young woman, she began to seek her place in the world, then came her illness, death[1] – and all that overlaid *Jenůfa*. The more sick Oluška [Olga] became, the more obsessed she became with her father's new opera. And sensitive as he was, he put his pain over Oluška into his work, the suffering of his daughter into Jenůfa's suffering. And that tough love of the Kostelnička[2] – that's him, there is much of his own character in this part.

When Oluška got typhoid fever for the second time in Russia and the mistress was there with her, the master once came to me in the kitchen:

'Mářa, do you know "Zdravas, kralovno"?[3] I know "Hail Mary", but this one I've forgotten'.

I went to get my prayer book, and looked up 'Zdrávas, královno', the master took the book into the study and after a while I heard the beginning of the song which has now gone round the world. People

---

1 Olga went to St Petersburg in March 1902 to stay with Janáček's brother František to improve her Russian. She fell ill in May with typhoid fever, made a brief recovery, but in June had a relapse. She returned home in July with her mother, and despite occasional improvements never fully recovered, and died on 26 February 1903, not quite twenty-one.

2 Female sacristan, sexton; Jenůfa's stepmother is generally known by this name, deriving from her office.

3 *Zdrávas královno!* [Hail, Queen!], a Czech version of the well-known Marian antiphon *Salve regina*. Stejskalová's spelling represents the short vowels of Janáček's native dialect. Jenůfa offers up this prayer to the Virgin Mary shortly before the distraught return of the Kostelnička from her mission to murder Jenůfa's baby (Act 2 Scene 6 of the opera). Quite why Janáček would have needed to see a text is unclear since Preissová quotes the entire hymn in her play. As a choirboy Janáček would have sung the hymn in Latin, possibly also in German, but hardly in Czech. (I am grateful to Dr Jiří Sehnal for this information.)

weep during it. I think this is because the master's heart so wept and bled when he wrote 'Zdrávas, královno.'

Marie Stejskalová's reminiscences (1959) JP7

In the afternoon [Olga] was quite well. We all sat at her bed. During that time the master was just finishing *Jenůfa*. The whole time that he composed it he had to tell Oluška about it; she knew it well. Now she asked:

'Daddy, play me *Jenůfa*, I will never hear your opera in the theatre.'

The master sat and played. If Oluška had asked him to have his hand cut off, that it would relieve her for a moment, he would have done so at once. When the mistress heard the beginning of *Jenůfa*, she clasped her head and ran out into the kitchen so as not to burst out crying in front of Oluška. The latter lay there peacefully, and without moving listened through the whole opera. The master's hands trembled, he was white as death, but he went on to the end. When he got up from the piano, Oluška said to him:

'It's beautiful, what a pity that I won't see it.'

Janáček's autobiography (1924) JP8

I would bind *Jenůfa* simply with the black ribbon of the long illness, suffering and laments of my daughter Olga and my little boy Vladimír.

CHRONOLOGY OF COMPOSITION

The composition of *Jenůfa* is poorly documented. Janáček usually dated his autographs, but in this case he destroyed the autograph, so the earliest dated material is the fair copy of the vocal score by Josef Štross. Marie Stejskalová's reminiscences thus constitute an important source for dating the composition. So do Janáček's own recollections, though written twenty years after the event, and, like Stejskalová's, similarly subject to memory lapses and other distortions.

Janáček to Otakar Nebuška *[Brno,] 22 February 1917* JP9

All that was possible to gather from the old manuscript about the beginnings of *Jenůfa* is as follows:

1. My copyist Josef Štross (in his time an excellent oboist from the

Prague Conservatory during the directorship of D. Weber),[1] noted
only when he finished Act 1 of the vocal score; I then rubbed it out. I
don't know why.

2. Act 2 of the vocal score was completed (by the copyist) on 8 July
1902.

3. Act 3 of the vocal score he completed with the words 'End of
opera', 25 January 1903, 3.30 pm.

It should be taken into consideration that I compose first in full
score and do the vocal score from that; thus work on the full score
was finished earlier. Between Acts 1 and 2 there was a long break. At
that time I was working with Fr[antišek] Bartoš on folksongs published by the Czech Academy.

My maid remembers that in her second year with us I began
composing J. P. [*Jenůfa*]; i.e. in 1896. At that time, composition was
for me something to be done only on the side: being choirmaster and
organist, imperial and royal[2] music teacher at the Teachers' Training
Institute, director of the Organ School, conductor of the Beseda
Philharmonic concerts – to have at home a mortally ill daughter – and
[day-to-day] life. In short it was hard to compose, and thus little was
done. Therefore it's also hard for me to remember.

There might be a date hidden somewhere in my copy of the first full
score; I don't have it to hand. I don't possess the [original] manuscript
of the full score.[3]

This account can be supplemented and to some extent corrected by dates in
Janáček's copy of the play (end of Act 1: 18 March 1894; end of Act 2: 17
January 1895; end of Act 3: 11 February 1895),[4] and by brief references to
the work in Janáček's correspondence. Another date to take into account is
31 December 1894, when, according to the last page of his copy of the play,
Janáček completed the Prelude 'Jealousy'. This was intended as the overture
to *Jenůfa* and was written into the original Brno parts (though, from the
absence of performance markings, apparently never used in the early performances). A comment in the play at the beginning of Act 2 is especially
interesting: 'dne 16.II.1895 zap.[očata] instru.[mentace]' – 'instrumentation

1 Friedrich Dionys [Bedřich Diviš] Weber was the first director of the Prague Conservatory, from 1811 to his death in 1842. Josef Štross (1826–1912) studied at the conservatory from 1840 to 1846, thus coinciding with Weber's directorship for two years.
2 A standard title for state employees of the 'Austrian' part of Austro-Hungary.
3 Janáček had destroyed his autograph full score; Štross's copy was by then in Vienna with
Universal Edition. It contains Štross's signature at the end of Act 1 near a scratched-out
area, perhaps originally a date.
4 These are the chief dates; see Štědroň 1965, 327–30 and Štědroň 1968, 59–63 for a more
detailed account of this material.

begun 16 February 1895'. Although Janáček wrote his first two operas in vocal score and then orchestrated them, we have his word (in the above letter to Nebuška) that he wrote *Jenůfa* straight into full score – his practice in all his subsequent operas. However, it is clear that at least some of the score was worked out in a very rough two-stave version. A single page has survived with decipherable fragments of Act 1 Scene 2.[1] This suggests that Janáček made sketches in this fashion, possibly finishing them on the dates noted in the play at the end of each act. If this is so, then this stage would have been completed by 11 February 1895 (taking in a full version of the overture on the way), with Janáček's beginning detailed work on the full score a few days later, on 16 February 1895. This appears to be in conflict with Janáček's statement, 'My maid remembers that in her second year with us I began composing J. P.; i.e. in 1896.' But Janáček got Stejskalová's starting date wrong: she entered the Janáčeks' service on 27 August 1894,[2] so that her second year would have been 1895.

A date for completing the full score of Act 1 may be 1897, if the comment in the Brno programme (JP28) is to be trusted, that by 1897 'the score of *Jenůfa* already existed in fair copy' (from all other information this could refer only to Act 1). 1897 was also the year that Janáček composed his largest-scale non-operatic work to date, the cantata *Amarus*, which would have meant stopping work on *Jenůfa* for several months at least.

Quite why Janáček should have interrupted the composition of *Jenůfa* is not clear, though if he felt he had somehow lost his way on the opera, as Stejskalová may be suggesting ('Sometimes it seemed to me that the master was battling with *Jenůfa*'), then it was sensible to give it a break. The huge advance on Janáček's style that is evident in *Amarus* indicates that in the long pause between Acts 1 and 2 of the opera, developments were taking place which were to have a marked effect on the remainder of the opera. In many ways Act 1 of *Jenůfa* is not so far from a number opera. There are choruses and dances, a large-scale concertato ensemble, several well-shaped solos, 'secco' recitative sections (i.e. to differentiate numbers), and even short duets and trios. The extent of such 'numbers' was substantially modified in the revisions Janáček incorporated in the first published vocal score (1908); it is quite possible that in its 1897 form Act 1 might have been even more evidently a number opera, and that extensive revisions were made after this long thoughtful pause, perhaps taking into account the speech-melody theories that Janáček occupied himself with intensively in 1897. The loss of the autograph score (destroyed, according to Stejskalová, in a large bonfire when the Janáčeks moved house in 1910)[3] is a tantalizing gap in our knowledge.

It seems that Janáček did not pick up *Jenůfa* again for several years, until he had seen through the press (1899–1901) the huge folksong collection

1 BmJA, A30.380; there are also rough, non-continuous sketches in Janáček's copy of the play and in his diary for 1896–7 (see Štědroň 1970, 293).
2 Trkanová 1964, 21.
3 Trkanová 1964, 93.

mentioned in his letter to Nebuška (JP9), *Moravian Folksongs Newly Collected* (a volume of over 1200 pages), and had written the cantata *Our Father*, completed in May 1901. The first indication that his thoughts were returning to the opera was on the envelope of a letter sent to him in Hukvaldy by his daughter Olga on 30 December 1901 (**JP10**), on which he jotted down a voice part to the words from Act 2 Scene 3. This is corroborated by a brief reference to the work in a letter to Olga: 'I am working very hard so as to finish the second act before the [summer] holidays' (**JP11**, 17 April 1902). Act 2 thus seems to have been written, apart from preliminary sketching in 1894–5, between late 1901 and the summer of 1902, and was copied by Štross in vocal score (apparently after the full score) by 8 July 1902.

Presumably Janáček went straight through into Act 3, which was finished early the next year. There are a confusing number of dates offered for its completion. There are two in Janáček's hand at the end of the play: '18 January 1903 Sunday'; '18 March 1903, the third week [after] the terrible mortal struggle of my poor Olga. Completed', and one in the copyist's hand at the end of the vocal score: 'End of opera 25 January 1903, 3.30 in the afternoon. J. Štross, copyist'. In the absence of Janáček's autograph, it is not possible to tell whether the copyist was merely copying Janáček's date for completion, or adding his own. Were it the former, then 18 March 1903, three weeks after Olga's death on 26 February, might represent a date when Janáček had looked through Štross's copy, corrected and authorized it.

PRAGUE I

The administration had changed at the Prague National Theatre since Janáček's previous dealings over *The Beginning of a Romance*. The franchise held by the *Družstvo Národního divadla* (Consortium of the National Theatre), with Šubert as administrator, had expired in 1900 and the new franchise had been awarded to a different company, the *Společnost Národního divadla* (Company of the National Theatre). The administrative director was an architect and would-be theatre-director, Gustav Schmoranz, and the balance of power was substantially changed, in that according to the new contract, artistic direction of opera and ballet was now the preserve of the chief conductor. From 1900 until his death in 1920, this was Karel Kovařovic, the composer of several operas including the popular *The Dogheads* (1898), and an able conductor. Some of his experience was gained by a year in Brno, where he had introduced an earlier opera of his at a time when Janáček was a regular reviewer.

Janáček: review of Kovařovic's *The Bridegrooms*   JP12

The theatre bill of 8 January 1887 reads as follows:

= An original novelty =
First performance
THE BRIDEGROOMS
Comic opera etc. set to music by
☞ Karel Kovařovic ☜
(performed at the National Theatre with huge success)

'Which *tune* stayed in your mind?'
'___'

'At least which *theme*?'
'___'

'Is it the reason why the opera is dramatic?'
'___'

'I would not have written "set to music by" but "Macháček's comedy[1] etc. *staged simultaneously with music*".'

Both libretto and music are independent. Write a new *operetta* to this *libretto* and to this *music* some sort of *play*: full of horrible gloom, desperate screams, bodies stabbed by daggers.

Thus the *strange phenomenon* that it was *Macháček's and not Kovařovic's 'The Bridegrooms'* which made one burst out laughing several times.

[The composer's] *musical talent* is attested by the overture, with its floods of chords and keys: which accordingly deafened one.

Hudební listy (15 January 1887)

Marie Stejskalová's reminiscences (1959)   JP13

Soon after Oluška's death the master took *Jenůfa* to the National Theatre in Prague. They had already refused his *The Beginning of a Romance* there, but he hoped that they would nevertheless take his new opera, since they had previously performed his ballet *Rákos Rákoczy* at the Jubilee Exhibition [of 1891]. The head of the opera, Kovařovic, told him that he would let him know once he had finished studying *Jenůfa*. But time went on and nothing came from Prague. The master wasn't himself, he kept on waiting for the post. When he came back from somewhere, the first thing he asked was if something

---

1 Kovařovic's opera was based on the play *The Bridegrooms* (1825) by Simeon Karel Macháček (1799–1846).

had come from Prague. Then he could stand it no longer and wrote to
Kovařovic to ask him what was happening with *Jenůfa*.

JP14   **Janáček to Karel Kovařovic**   *[undated, postmarked Brno, 27 April*
1903]

I fear writing to *you*; and it is so unsettling waiting in this way.
    Forgive me for asking about the fate of my work.

JP15   **Gustav Schmoranz to Janáček**   *Prague, 28 April 1903*

I sincerely regret that we cannot accept your opera for performance.
We would wish your work to meet on the stage with complete success
for you and for us, but we fear that your work would not have this
type of success.
    We return both the full score and the vocal score.

JP16   **Marie Stejskalová's reminiscences (1959)**

The master read the letter in the study. He sat at the writing desk. He
buried his head in his hands and began to cry terribly that he didn't
know how to do anything. The mistress ran to him, embraced him
and, also crying, comforted him until he grew quieter. That time at
home it was just like the return from Oluška's funeral. If our master
had been a better judge of people and paid more attention to the ways
of the world, he might have expected something like this as soon as he
offered *Jenůfa* to Prague. A few years earlier he wrote a bad review of
Kovařovic [JP12] and since that time had done nothing to be reconciled with him.[1] Kovařovic then paid him back. – Soon after, a parcel
from Prague arrived. The mistress and I were alone at home. She
stood there as if someone had plunged a knife into her heart. When
she recovered a bit, she kept on repeating:
    'How will I tell him? How could they do that to him? He knows
that it's a good piece . . .'
    In the end she hid the parcel, and we said nothing to the master. So
a few days passed until once during lunch the master said:
    'They haven't returned *Jenůfa* to me, perhaps they have accepted it
after all.'

1 This is not quite true. Janáček had reviewed the vocal score of Kovařovic's latest opera,
The Dogheads, in the periodical *Hlídka* in 1899 (see Janáček 1899b). In comparison to the
little squib on *The Bridegrooms* this is a long, serious review with fifteen music examples,
some quite extensive. Much of it is taken up with points of interest in the harmony; the
general tone is both respectful and admiring.

I was just clearing the plates from the table. My hands put them down again, I looked at the mistress, who began crying. I followed suit. The master stopped short, for a moment he was beside himself, then he said sadly:

'So they returned it . . .'

The mistress went to fetch the parcel, undid it, and herself read the enclosed letter that *Jenůfa* was not suitable for performance. The master just kept on nodding his head.

JENŮFA IN BRNO

Marie Stejskalová's reminiscences (1959)   JP17

But then it brightened up again. In Brno everyone was angry with Prague for returning such a work to the master, and because in Prague they always looked down on everything which came from Brno. In the *Družstvo* of the Brno theatre, the master had friends who believed in him, the Directorate of the theatre was also on his side. Earlier they had wanted the master to offer *Jenůfa* to Brno, and now they suggested it again. But the Prague refusal had so humiliated him that he did not believe in himself and did not want to let *Jenůfa* go out at all. Once the surveyor [Rudolf] Kallus from the *Družstvo* met our mistress on Rudolfská ulice[1] and began to talk her into persuading the master to offer the opera to the Brno theatre. She was glad to do so, seeing it was the only way to put the master back on his feet again. It caused her much work before he agreed to do so. Then it all went quickly: straight after the holidays the conductor Hrazdira[2] began studying *Jenůfa*. Although as his former pupil from the Organ School he understood the master's music, it wasn't at all easy for him. It was a tough nut for both singers and orchestra; the master came back from the theatre rehearsals quite exasperated.

The prospect of a Brno performance resulted in Janáček's making last-minute revisions of the work, which he mentioned in a letter of 3 October 1903 (**JP18**) to Kamila Urválková (with whom he was then in frequent correspondence over his next opera, see Chapter 4). Official negotiations over royalties proceeded in a friendly way. The representative of the Brno *Družstvo*, Alois

---

1 Now Česká ulice, a main street in Brno leading almost to the former Czech theatre.
2 Cyril Metoděj Hrazdira (1868–1926), conductor at the Brno Theatre 1903–7. Later he worked in Croatia and Slovenia.

Doubravský, was one of Janáček's admirers and, as the tenor who created the part of Laca, he was closely involved with the production.

JP19   Alois Doubravský to Janáček   *Brno, 8 October 1903*

In answer to your kind letter allow me to inform you that I agree to your requirements regarding orchestral forces and it would be very pleasing for me if you were not only to hear the first act when we have finished rehearsing, but were also to be present at the preliminary rehearsals and be of assistance to us with advice and suggestions according to your intentions. I will let you know the rehearsal schedule in good time.

As regards royalties allow me to observe that we pay either per performance or as a percentage of the receipts. For performances of Czech works we pay, for instance for all the Smetana operas, K10 in Brno and K6 outside Brno, for [Kovařovic's] *The Dogheads* 7 zl. (K14) in Brno and K10 outside Brno. For foreign works we pay Eirich[1] 6% royalties though we get the complete musical material for our use. It depends then on your kindness what terms you make and at what level.

At the same time I ask you kindly to hand over the vocal score and the full score to the messenger [to give] to me. I will endeavour to devote the greatest care to your work, so that it receives the very greatest success, as it deserves.

JP20   Janáček to Kamila Urválková   *[Brno, 9 October 1903]*

Yesterday at least was one of the joyful days. I have had few of them in my life. Perhaps that 'Highest Justice' has after all turned to me with a smiling face?

The Directorate of the National Theatre in Brno sent for the score of my opera *Jenůfa*.

When they took it away, the servant had something to carry on his shoulders! At the same time it seemed to me as if they had taken away my soul from so many sad years.

Copying still needed to be done (Janáček mentions it taking 'another fortnight' in an undated letter to Kamila Urválková, **JP21**). The orchestra did not begin rehearsing until after Christmas, three weeks before the première:

[os6]

1 Oskar Friedrich Eirich (*b.*1845), Austrian lawyer, dramatist and translator living in Vienna. He represented French, German and Czech stage rights.

Janáček to Kamila Urválková *[undated, Brno, around Christmas* JP22
1903]

Everything of the best, and many, many presents for the holidays!

I received a *madonna* from my wife: a little medallion of my poor daughter; and also an embroidered cushion; I am working all day long; so [the cushion] comes in useful when for a moment it's necessary to put down one's pen and sit back.

These are sad holidays at our house: the first time left all alone. I will go off to my native village for at least two or three days.

Only the soloists and chorus know their parts from the opera and know how to perform them! The orchestra has not had rehearsals yet.[1]

The première was originally set for 14 January, according to Janáček's announcement to Mrs Urválková (JP23, 3 January 1904), but was postponed by a week, presumably because of the difficulties of the score for the tiny opera house. Invitations to critics went out a few days before (see JP25). Janáček, however, set most store by a personal appeal to Kovařovic to come and see *Jenůfa* for himself, and went especially to Prague to invite him, only to find him away sick, resting his nerves on the French Riviera.

Janáček to Karel Kovařovic *Prague, 17 January 1904* JP24

I came to invite you to the first performance of *Jenůfa* and have learnt here that you are in poor health. I regret the fact that I cannot extend the invitation to you personally – and perhaps ask you once again, if you couldn't after all make a place for my work at the Prague National Theatre as well.

I wish you a speedy recovery and I invite you to come to us in Brno – if your condition makes it at least a little bit possible.

Em. Bayer to ?Dr Jan Branberger JP25
for the National Theatre in Brno *Brno, 18 January 1904*

On Thursday, 21 January 1904 the première of Leoš Janáček's opera *Jenůfa* will be given at the Czech National Theatre in Brno. In its general conception, tendency and manner of composition the work goes beyond the present style of music for the theatre. Apart from the use of elements of a specifically Moravian nature, the work will pave the way for a particular type of word-setting, based on the melodic

1 In fact some of the parts had not yet been copied out: the first trombone part is dated by the copyist 30 December 1903 (BmJA, A49.883).

elements of everyday speech. – In so doing it will achieve a special importance and this is why we take the liberty of inviting you, sir, most politely, to visit the Brno National Theatre and hear the work.

We have similarly taken the liberty of sending an invitation to the editorial board of *Čas* [of which Branberger was music critic].

JP26   **Janáček to Kamila Urválková**   *[undated, Brno, ?19 January 1904]*

Today I returned from the first full rehearsal of Act 1 completely fed up. There was such a wretched argument between the director [of the theatre] and the conductor that I was on edge because of it. The 'trumpet player', ticked off during the rehearsal, took it so much to heart that he got dangerously drunk. He did not recognize any 'authority.' He swore at everyone like a trooper. That was like the pebble that is thrown and brings down the avalanche with it – which would badly have damaged my première.

With difficulty they managed to sort out and reconcile everything in order to finish the rehearsal. You poor thing, who longed for the theatre! Be glad that you are in your present state.

I'm dead tired. Emaciated, pale[1] like a paschal candle. My eyes keep closing, but yet I am happier in *this* life.

Again I enclose something printed for you, and invite you to this celebration of mine.

[...]

I was in Prague for the day, as you learnt from the picture postcard [JP27, 18 January 1904].

God grant *that all goes well on Thursday*!

The unique qualities of the work were emphasized by an unsigned note in the programme, if not written by Janáček then evidently based on information supplied by him:

JP28   [?Janáček:] 'On the significance of *Jenůfa*'

The work which is played on our stage today has an unusual significance not only for theatre music in general but specifically for Moravian music. For the former in its use of a prose text and the principles on which it was composed, for the latter because it is the first work in this field which consciously attempts to be Moravian. – Prose was first used in opera by the French composer Alfred Bruneau

---

1 *žlutý* [yellow], the traditional colour of the candle which burns from Good Friday until Easter day; Janáček wishes to convey that he is tired and ill, but not cowardly or jaundiced.

in 1897. Karel Stecker writes of this in his history:[1] 'His operas are becoming key works in history, being the first, and certainly interesting, experiments in operatic composition to a prose text.'

One must now say the same of the work of Janáček, who was the first to do this among Czech composers, not at all after the example of the French, but on his own initiative, drawn to this direction by the principle of truth in recorded speech melody. The French composers anticipated him only in performance, since in 1897 the score of *Jenůfa* already existed in fair copy.

The principle on which *Jenůfa* was written is the following: Janáček recognized that the truest expression of the soul lies in melodic motifs of speech. Thus instead of the usual arias he used these [speech] melodies. In so doing he achieved a truthful expression in places where this is surely one of the most important things.

Driven by the attempt at truthful expression, not just in mood but also in situation, he has employed a realistic expression of the locality, especially in the choruses. In characterization he has deviated from the usual leitmotifs; his orchestra characterizes the mood of the whole scene.

The speech motifs and the appropriately used style of folk music have stamped his work with the nation's spiritual seal.

Programme leaflet for the première (21 January 1904)

Jan Kunc's reminiscences of the première of *Jenůfa*[2]　　JP29

[...] Immediately after the first act there was great applause and Janáček, who had stayed in the wings during the performance, had to take a bow. He was pale and agitated. [...] The Kostelnička of Mrs Hanusová-Svobodová[3] was excellent. The deeply felt music of the second act with its mood-evoking lyricism made a similarly deep impression on the audience. [...] The success was still greater than in the first act. Called to the stage again, Janáček was already more cheerful and was smiling, a clear sign that he felt his success.

The dramatic crisis of Act 3, the wedding day ending with the discovery of the murder of the child [...], then the characteristically

---

1　*Všeobecný dějepis hudby* [General history of music] (1892–1903), ii, 299.
2　Janáček's pupil Jan Kunc recounted his impressions of the première several times. Later versions are fuller, but of little more substance. The omissions here are mostly generalized comments about the plot and the names of the individual singers.
3　Leopolda Hanusová-Svobodová (1875–1941) was a leading soprano in Brno from 1898 to 1915, taking both lyrical and dramatic Smetana roles (Mařenka in *The Bartered Bride*, and Libuše), and other parts such as the title roles in *Rusalka*, *Šárka*, *Tosca* and *Aida*.

Slav confession of the Kostelnička and then the ending, in which
Laca acknowledges his love for Jenůfa,[1] brought the success to a
climax. The applause was unending. Janáček had to take bows again
and again. So did the librettist, Preissová, from her box. [...] The
student population cheered and accompanied Janáček right up to
the Besední dům [see p.21, fn.2], where a convivial evening with
many toasts took place which ran on into the early hours.

Divadelní list, ix (1933–4)

These impressions are confirmed by those of another pupil, Václav Kaprál
(1889–1947), who adds that 'Janáček was presented with laurel wreaths
and after the performance was taken on the shoulders of the soloists (I
think that they were even still in their costumes) to the Besední dům' (JP30).
The success had been gained by a devoted and generally excellent cast and
conductor, and despite an orchestra of just twenty-nine which lacked the
harp, bass clarinet and English horn that Janáček specified.[2] (The orchestra
was further depleted later in the season, see JP39.) Reviews from Brno were
favourable and respectful: hardly surprising since, as Janáček later wrote to
Rektorys (JP31, 21 March 1908; BR7), they 'were mostly by my former
pupils'. The Prague reviews were fewer and generally disappointing. Dr
Branberger of *Čas* (24 and 26 January 1904), who had been carefully
invited (JP25) and later carefully thanked (JP32; Janáček to Branberger, 1
February 1904), compared Janáček unfavourably with Vítězslav Novák,
dismissing him as a composer of purely local importance. Janáček fared
even worse in the inevitable comparison with Smetana, who allegedly had
folksong in his inner being and wrote music naturally imbued with it while
Janáček had to slave away first 'with ant-like industry collecting Moravian
– Slovak folksongs and with an anatomical scalpel dissecting their most
secret components. [...] We must therefore not be surprised that the child
of such long, arduous preparations carries traces of this.' Branberger concluded by praising Janáček's 'great dramatic talent and feeling for the
theatre. Such passages arouse hope that after overcoming his teething
troubles in further works the composer will not be hampered by his theories
and will never be weighed down by them in his musical flight.'[3] Emanuel
Chvála, writing in *Národní politika* (26 January 1904), was warmer in his
praise. While stressing the novelty of the opera and its potential lack of
accessibility to an audience , he noted its 'success, which was all-pervading
and increased from act to act'. In particular he singled out the 'powerful
scenes of Act 2 (the Kostelnička's humbling of herself kneeling before Števa,

1 i.e. despite the revelation that the Kostelnička murdered Jenůfa's child. Laca has been
acknowledging his love through most of the opera.
2 See Němcová 1971, 117–18.
3 Substantial parts of Branberger's and Chvála's reviews are reprinted in Němcová 1974,
142–4.

her decision to dispose of Jenůfa's baby)', which 'visibly excited the audience'.

Janáček to Kamila Urválková   *Brno, 28 January 1904* JP33

I enclose the press reviews for you.

According to them, when you read them, you will see me as nothing less than a wonder. Don't take fright, it's not so bad! If the critic of *Čas*, Dr Jan Branberger, has had a little go at me – I know much better and could list my shortcomings in more detail; I want to put these right in *The Fiery Roses* [a provisional title for *Fate*; see OS8]. One thing is certain – that the work is generally liked, that it's got life in it, that on the stage every word is sharp and effective, just as I emphasized it in the music. They have recognized my talents as a composer for the theatre – and in these times of Wagner, Charpentier, Dvořák, etc, etc, this is indeed significant and extremely flattering for me. As for the ovations which I experienced it's hard to talk about them; I had no idea that something like this could happen. But let me be frank, you might have remembered me with at least a note – I waited – and nothing at all.

Well you must put that right if it's given in Prague. Though that's hardly likely, for the papers attack the administration of the theatre too much – and people with a conscience are touchy! [. . .]

Janáček: letter to the editor   JP34

Allow me a few words to defend and justify the logic behind the chorus 'Každý párek si musí svoje trápení přestát' ['Every couple must get over its problems'] in Act 1 of *Jenůfa*. Whoever hears this motif of the Grandmother, as I have witnessed many times, not only sighs in spirit with the same words, but also agrees out loud: 'Yes, that's so, every couple must get over its own problems.'

From the heart the Grandmother prompts everyone with the well-known truth. From the heart all on stage agree with her.

The Foreman can mention it to Laca with [good] reason, *Laca* can repeat it bitterly, *Jenůfa* in desperate fear, and every young lad urges it to his girl depending on the fate of their mutual love: so the web of the ensemble is woven more and more thickly, and intensifies.

Why, however, are just these few brief words repeated?

Because I had no more to hand but nevertheless felt that it was necessary *to linger here* not only to allow the closely matched musical motif to be taken up by all eight parts naturally, but also naturally to swell and then die away in the faintest *pianissimo*, as if the thought faded into oblivion. However, the chorus and soloists should know their parts so perfectly in this scene for them not to have to hang on to the conductor's beat with their whole bodies.

More text, which the writer Mrs Gabriela Preissová was ready to write for this number, would hardly help: rather, a livelier staging for each of the three parts of the ensemble.

Why do the Grandmother, the Foreman, Laca, Jenůfa and four-part chorus begin with the self-same motif? This surely goes against the principle of the specific naturalism[1] of the melody?

First and foremost it is something of a concession to an effective musical motif which I would hardly allow myself today – although there are plenty of examples where we repeat important words of others, together with their speech melody. In such cases we are really living completely through the soul of another person; we are at one with him in his feeling and desires. Therefore in that scene there is the same melodic overlay.

Jeviště, i (1904)

This single official comment by Janáček on an account in the press of his opera – in this case an amplification of a three-part review-article[2] by his former pupil Josef Charvát (1884–1945) – is intensely interesting. It bears witness to his changing attitudes towards operatic conventions ('a concession [...] which I would hardly allow myself today') and also attempts a defence of the repetition by other characters of a musical motif – or speech melody – assigned to a specific person. If a speech melody is a 'window on the soul', what happens when that speech melody is sung by somebody else? Does not that fly in the face of Janáček's particular brand of musical naturalism? Among the chief criticisms used to prevent the opera's acceptance at Prague were the repetitions of phrases (whether by the same or by another character).

PRAGUE II

JP35 Janáček to Karel Kovařovic   *Brno, 9 February 1904*

After the staging of *Jenůfa* at the Brno National Theatre I take the liberty of troubling you with this letter.

I don't want my renewed request that the Prague National Theatre should also grant a hearing to *Jenůfa* to be based on the most

---

1 'naturismu'; Czech distinguishes between 'naturalismus' and 'naturismus'; the second refers to the French literary movement at the end of the nineteenth century which, as an antidote to decadence, proclaimed a return to the natural life.
2 Josef Charvát: 'Její pastorkyňa', *Jeviště*, i (1904), 15–17, 76–9, 103–110.

flattering Prague reviews, let alone the local ones – my only complaint is that it was unjust to turn down *Jenůfa*.

I appeal over this as a Czech composer to whom no-one wished to grant a hearing.

Because of the Moravian character of the work? So it has, mistakenly, been said. More perhaps for the all-important principle of the specific naturalism ['naturismu', see p.58 fn.1] of the melody – which, as it has turned out, has not been without effect or comprehension.

Can I once again offer my work for performance?

All sorts of corrections were of course necessary in the score – ; I think that many of the criticisms that were made have now fallen away in the corrections.

I ask you for your kind reply.

Gustav Schmoranz to Janáček   *Prague, 11 February 1904*   **JP36**

A decision about the acceptance or non-acceptance of an operatic work is a matter for the head of opera, Mr Karel Kovařovic, who at the moment is out of Prague. Please therefore kindly wait for his return.

Karel Kovařovic to Janáček   *[Prague,] 4 March 1904*   **JP37**

Director Schmoranz has given me your letter of 9 February 1904. Forgive me, but your complaints that the refusal of *Jenůfa* had been unjust and that there was an unwillingness to grant a hearing to you, a Czech composer, are not correct. Precisely because I had very serious reasons in mind and considered the matter most maturely, I became convinced that we could not accept your opera for performance. My fears continue that your work, at least on *our* stage and before *our* audience, would not meet with the complete success that we would wish both for you and for us. This is not however because of the Moravian character of the work (where do you get that impression?).

I am, however, willing to be present at a repeat performance in Brno and would be sincerely glad if the performance there taught me otherwise.

Janáček to Karel Kovařovic   *[Brno,] 10 March 1904*   **JP38**

I don't know myself when there will be a repeat performance of *Jenůfa*. Here it's all coughs and colds in the theatre.

If you were yourself to pick one of the last days of next week, then I am convinced that on your account they would place a performance on any day you suggest. Please however let me know by card at least before Sunday [13 March] a suitable day for you.

I have myself twice wanted to visit you in Prague; I am therefore glad that you have decided on a visit to Brno.

But Kovařovic did not answer. So Janáček tried his contacts in Prague, such as Hana Kvapilová (1860–1907), a prominent actress married to the poet and playwright Jaroslav Kvapil, then serving as dramaturg at the Prague National Theatre. Janáček knew Kvapilová from her time in Brno (1886–8), when her performances were reviewed in Janáček's journal *Hudební listy*.

JP39   **Janáček to Hana Kvapilová**   *[undated, Brno, between 15 April and 9 May 1904]*[1]

Advise me, advise me what to do?!

In less than two weeks the season will be over here. *Jenůfa* will be given at the most once more – for the ninth time – the Directorate is inviting Mr Kovařovic – I now don't even dare to write to him – he simply doesn't answer – and yet he informed me officially that he will come up for one of the performances.

Is he poorly perhaps?

Do you have, Madam, any advice, how I can gain his favour?

Even before now, the orchestra of the local theatre has been incomplete to an alarming extent: the new director has given notice to the horn player, the trumpet player – they are apparently not needed for the summer season.

I myself don't even go to the theatre now – I don't want hear my own work in such a broken-down state.

And think of a guest, who hasn't much goodwill towards me, at a final performance like that!

It's all sickening.

And after all I'm not asking for any more goodwill than was shown to the composer of *Vij*, Mr Moor.[2]

Perhaps I deserve that as well.

I'd much rather deaden the pain with work, but then I've got

---

1 *Jenůfa* was given nine times in Brno that season, the last on 15 April. This letter would have been written some time between then and 9 May, when Janáček wrote to Kvapilová again.

2 Karel Moor's opera was given at the Prague National Theatre on 14 July 1903, with a mere two repeat performances. It is based on the Gogol story about Viy, the chief of the earth spirits in Ukrainian folk mythology.

problems with a libretto [see OS22, ff]. So my soul is torn apart at the moment. [. . .]

Janáček to Hana Kvapilová *Luhačovice, 9 May 1904* JP40

I arrived from Warsaw[1] and, tired, sank from sight straight into Luhačovice. On the way I learnt about the death of Dvořák. I didn't suspect that I would be speaking to him for the last time when the rehearsals for *Armida* were going on. He said in the theatre at the time: *Jenůfa* will be given! I believe in those half-prophetic words – and don't think more about it. The head [of opera] Mr Kovařovic has been told nine times that on such and such a day there will be a repeat performance – without answering. [. . .]

When Kovařovic did not go to Brno that season to see *Jenůfa*, Janáček seems to have made no further attempt to interest him in the work. Kovařovic may have attended a performance in the next season;[2] he certainly asked to see the score again (see JP41), though without any result.

František Lacina to Janáček *[undated, postmarked Brno,* JP41
for the Czech National Theatre in Brno *3 October 1904]*

I was asked in a telegram today by the head [of opera], Kovařovic, to send him the vocal score of *Jenůfa* for about a week. May I inquire whether I can comply with his request?

That Janáček now believed that nothing was to be gained by more invitations to Kovařovic in Prague is perhaps attested by a request to a more eminent composer – conductor in Vienna.

Janáček to Gustav Mahler *Brno, 5 December 1904* JP42

The enclosed Prague reviews (Chvála, Dr Branberger) of the première of my opera *Jenůfa* at the Brno Czech National Theatre speak more clearly than I would be able to briefly about myself.

I wanted even earlier to take the liberty of inviting you, sir, to a performance of this opera, though to be honest – I had no confidence in myself.

---

1 Janáček had been in Warsaw at the invitation of the Governor to consider the offer of the Directorship of the Conservatory.
2 The only evidence for this, first offered in Kašlík 1938, 6, is a comment in the first horn part of the original Brno parts (BmJA, A49883): 'First time in the new season. Gala performance, Kovařovic present'.

Urged on by others, I am inviting you now for the sole purpose of hearing your valuable judgement.

I therefore ask you, sir, whether it would be possible for you to make a trip to Brno to a performance of the opera, which will take place on Wednesday, 7 December, or perhaps to a later performance.

I hope that a similar invitation from Dr Baron Ott[akar] Pražák will have reached you.

Baron Pražák, as president of the Brno theatre *Družstvo*, wrote a similar letter to Mahler on the same day (JP43). Both received courteous replies:

JP44   **Gustav Mahler to Janáček**   *Vienna, 9 December 1904*

As I have already informed Baron Dr Pražák, it is unfortunately not possible for me to get away from here in the near future. But as I would certainly be interested nevertheless to get to know your work I ask if some time you could send me a vocal score with a German text.

This initiative thus came to nothing. The vocal score was not published until 1908, and then only with a Czech text. The performance to which Mahler was invited, on 7 December 1904, was the first in the new season (it was given again on 7 February 1905). Before then it had been given twice on tour in southern Bohemia, in České Budějovice (11 May 1904) and Písek (30 May 1904). The Brno theatre, too, decided to revive it in 1906 (once in Ostrava, 25 September, and twice more in Brno, 6 and 9 October). A request by the new director of the Brno theatre, Antoš Josef Frýda (JP45, Hranice, 5 July 1906), for permission to borrow the full score and vocal score elicited a reply from Janáček which provides details of payment: K 10 for the use of the score in the 1906–7 season and K 8 for every performance (JP46, Hukvaldy, 36 July 196), conditions to which Frýda readily agreed (JP47, Hranice, 28 July 1906). This revival is significant in that it prompted the conductor Hrazdira to suggest cuts (JP48: Hrazdira to Janáček, 11 July 1906). Whether these were carried through then is not known, but the next year Janáček made a thorough revision of the opera (a note by him 'corrected 10.1.1907' survives at the end of Act 2 of the Štross full score). The changes were then incorporated into the printed vocal score of 1908.

Bringing out the vocal score in 1908 was a big event for Janáček since this was by far his most substantial composition to be published. It was largely on his initiative that the Club of the Friends of Art (Klub přátel umění) began to engage in modest publication activities, a suggestion brought to the committee and accepted on 2 December 1907. Striking while the iron was hot, Janáček proposed as the first publication of the music section a vocal score of *Jenůfa*.[1] This went ahead surprisingly quickly. Within a couple of weeks the

1 For further details see Kundera 1948, 55–61.

Leipzig engraving firm of Engelmann & Mühlberg, to whom the production of the score had been assigned, was asking for a printed libretto to help clear up dubious words (JP49, 19 December 1907). First proofs began to arrive even before the end of the year.

Zdenka Janáčková to Janáček   *[Vienna,] 31 December 1907*   JP50

Mářa [Stejskalová] wrote to me today that you are home and in a good mood because the proofs have arrived. I'm pleased. You've got pleasant work, and I am lazing away pleasantly – but I know that you wish me that.

So write to me soon, and a Happy New Year.

Janáček's corrections of the proofs were completed by mid-February (JP51: Janáček to Rektorys, 5 March 1908), and by 18 March Janáček was able to send out printed copies (JP52: Janáček to Rektorys, 18 March 1908). Six hundred copies were printed at a cost of K 3684, thus exceeding the budget by K 684. Three hundred copies were distributed to members of the Club of the Friends of Art as a free gift (*prémie*) for the years 1907 and 1908. The remaining copies were intended for sale,[1] and on 15 April 1908 the Prague publisher Mojmír Urbánek, who had published Janáček's male-voice choruses in 1906, acknowledged a consignment of 227 copies for retail on commission (JP53).

Janáček to Zdenka Janáčková   *[Luhačovice,] 28 August 1908*   JP54

Marie Calma – such a hard name[2] [–] belongs to my latest acquaintance. But don't faint before you finish reading!

She sang *Jenůfa* to me beautifully. Now I've received her *Povídky*[3] and *Nálady*. Aren't you amazed?

A gentle creature – only she has a mother – brr! – who praises her darling all the time. We ate on the cosy veranda: coffee – ice cream – grapes – peaches – *buchty*[4] – well, useless to talk about it. It was only at the end that Dr Veselý introduced [her as] his fiancée! You're amazed? [. . .]

---

1 At K 15 each (as announced in a brief report in *Lidové noviny*, 21 April 1908).
2 Marie Hurychová (1881–1966) took her literary pseudonym from the song 'Ridonami la calma' by Pier Francesco Tosi (*c.*1653–1732). For Czechs, who pronounce 'c' as 'ts', it must have seemed odd.
3 Janáček muddled the name: Calma published *Pohádky* (Fairy stories) in 1906, but no *Povídky* (Stories). Her *Nálady* (Moods) was her first book, published in 1905.
4 Traditional yeast-raised cakes, usually with a sweet filling (curd cheese, poppyseed, jam).

JP55   Marie Calma-Veselá: 'From my recollections of Leoš Janáček'

My recollections of Janáček are linked with Luhačovice and Brno. I
got to know him in the home of Dr František Veselý, where we were
invited together. On the upright piano lay a vocal score of *Jenůfa* with
the pages uncut, published by the Club of the Friends of Art in Brno.
Janáček cut open a few pages and sat down at the piano. 'They say
you sing nicely – so show us what you can do.' He was surprised that
I could sight-sing Jenůfa and the Kostelnička.

Hudební výchova, xix (1938)

Dr František Veselý (1862–1923) was already well known to Janáček. A
medical doctor with an interest in spa treatment, he was the main force
behind the development for public use of the Moravian spa of Luhačovice
and was director of the spa from 1902 to 1909. It was here that Janáček used
to spend a few weeks each year and gained the inspiration for the setting of
his next opera, *Fate*. Janáček soon made use of his new friend. Marie
Calma-Veselá was not only a writer, but a trained musician, a pianist and a
singer who had successfully auditioned at the Munich Hofoper under Felix
Mottl for Wagnerian parts such as Senta and Elsa, though parental pressure
led to her declining the engagement and turning instead to concert work and
to literature.[1] The following March (1909) Marie Calma-Veselá came to
Janáček's rescue by singing, at short notice, the solo soprano part in
Gounod's oratorio *Mors et vita*, which he had to rehearse and conduct in
place of a sick colleague.[2] In the autumn of 1909 the Veselýs moved to Brno,
where they had more frequent contact with Janáček and became more aware
of the injustice of Prague's refusal of *Jenůfa*.

In 1911 the Brno Theatre revived *Jenůfa* for five performances, the first
since 1906. During the revival Dr Veselý, now chairman of the Club of the
Friends of Art, proposed the motion (on 18 February) that they appeal to the
committee of the Prague National Theatre company to stage the opera at the
better-equipped theatre in Prague: 'We see in *Jenůfa* a work of such artistic
significance that it deserves wider national attention' (JP56). The motion was
carried, despite Janáček's objection that he wanted *Jenůfa* 'to be left to find
its own way',[3] and Dr Veselý wrote to the chairman of the National Theatre
Company committee, Dr Jaroslav Hlava, who happened to be an old friend
from university days.[4]

1 JA viii, 6–8.
2 JA viii, 19–22.
3 Kundera 1948, 78.
4 JA viii, 26.

Professor Dr Jaroslav Hlava to Dr Veselý   *Prague, 25 February 1911*   JP57

In answer to your *private* (?) letter concerning Janáček's opera I am unable to give you a satisfactory answer.

Mr Kovařovic at that time did not accept the opera – a decision in which the financial aspect also certainly played a part. For rehearsing an opera takes at least four to six weeks' hard work, and if it is not popular with the wider public, the theatre makes an irrecoverable loss out of it. Kovařovic is quite ready to meet the younger generation half way but from a practical point of view we cannot allow him more than one or two experiments a year. [Hlava then lists some of the new Czech operas performed or about to be performed at the National Theatre.]

The subsidy from the province brings in K128,000; the theatre needs one and half million crowns a year. On top of this the city of Prague has lowered its subsidy from a miserly K15,000 to K10,000. Where are we then to find the money? Look in Moravia for some rich patron, as the Germans have for the sets of Wagner's operas, and then it will be possible.

Mr Janáček has revised his original opera, and would be willing to do so again – I think that is proof that it is not such a masterpiece as you imagine. Rather let Mr Janáček write something new; I will then endeavour to do something for him in the foreseeable future.

I write to you quite openly – my letter is not of course meant for the public – it is merely a commentary on the answer which you will receive from the administration if I learn from you that the letter sent to me was an official one.

Jenůfa was revived once more in Brno, in 1913 – for a single performance (25 March). A letter from Janáček at the end of that year sums up his despair over the work. He was now on the eve of his sixtieth birthday:

Janáček to Dr František Veselý   *Brno, 28 December 1913*   JP58

[...] Do not think that it would be possible to smooth the path for *Jenůfa*. I know very well that I stand alone in my musical feeling. I cannot attach myself to anyone. I am difficult to understand and – in Prague [–] there is no need for anyone to exert himself over it.

After all, in Brno I sit like a magpie alone in my own nest. Dr Elgart from Kroměříž is perhaps one other who is favourable to my work.

I know who decides whom to allow higher and whom not to have his place in the sun. [...]

Janáček was realistic about his chances in Prague. Further evidence of the attitude there towards him and *Jenůfa* is provided in a seventieth-birthday tribute to the composer, written some years later. This tribute by František Mareš, who had known Janáček from the Teachers' Training Institute in the 1880s, also includes a familiar account of what happened next:

JP59   **František Mareš: 'For Leoš Janáček's seventieth birthday'**

[...] In Prague for several years previously *Jenůfa* was the high point of New Year's Eve revels for the group intimately connected with the National Theatre. A parody on it was played with the subtitle 'Pálená kostelnica'.[1] Mr X apparently used to have rag dolls in his pocket and when Mr Y as Jenůfa lamented the death of her son, he pulled a child from his left pocket, then one from the right: 'Don't cry, here you are, I will give you more of them ———'. Perhaps that is enough to make clear that with these views around, *Jenůfa* could not have got to the stage. In 1915 Director Schmoranz came to Bohdaneč, where Dr Veselý was then the spa doctor. Peška-Šípek,[2] a native of the spa, a friend of both Schmoranz and Kovařovic, knew *Jenůfa* and liked it. And he took it into his head to get it to the National Theatre. He went to Schmoranz with a ruse. Mrs Calma-Veselá had to sing *Jenůfa* at an open window and he would go for a walk with Director Schmoranz in the park so that they could hear her singing. The first day Schmoranz was surprised that he didn't know what was being sung, though it was – interesting. The second and third day his curiosity mounted, having found the singing extremely dramatic. Peška said nothing. Then finally Schmoranz could hold out no longer; he let himself be conducted to Mrs Calma and learnt that this was the title part from the derided *Jenůfa*. He was a little thrown, but he was captivated. And won over. [...]

Hudební rozhledy, i (1924–5)

The open window story is charming but untrue. In her own reminiscences of the event published the next year Calma-Veselá gives a rather more sober account of the 'captivation' of Schmoranz.

1 This laborious pun depends on the phrase 'páleník kostelník'. A 'kostelník' is a (male) sacristan or sexton; a 'páleník' is an obsolete word for a distiller; the combination of the two is used to describe a man who is artful and wily. The 'joke' here is to put the phrase into the feminine using not the normal feminine form 'kostelnice' or its diminutive 'kostelnička', but a made-up Moravianism, 'kostelnica'.
2 Josef Peška was the real name; Karel Šípek his literary pseudonym. His friends were inconsistent about how they addressed him or referred to him; the forms used here correspond to whatever was used in the Czech.

Marie Calma-Veselá: 'From the battle for Janáček's *Jenůfa*' JP60

All this lack of success did not frighten off my husband, Dr František Veselý and myself. In 1915 a new opportunity to draw attention to *Jenůfa* was offered to us. In Bohdaneč, where my husband had settled as chief medical officer of the spa,[1] we became friendly with the writer Karel Šípek (Josef Peška), a friend and librettist of Kovařovic and a friend of Schmoranz, and we tried to win him over for Janáček and for his *Jenůfa*. After an evening in which I sang Jenůfa's solos to my accompaniment and at which Karel Šípek was among the enthusiastic and deeply affected audience, he began to get genuinely interested in the matter. And that meant a lot.

We agreed that I would sing *Jenůfa* to Schmoranz when he came to visit Šípek. I remember vividly how it went.

Just at that time I was busy with the installation of an exhibition of paintings in the spa colonnade. In this way we helped painters during the wartime poverty; the spa guests, mostly rich farmers, were good customers. It was there that Schmoranz and Šípek met me. Schmoranz remarked that I would scarcely have time to be able to sing to him. Understandably, I dropped everything and took him into the house.

I sang all of Jenůfa's solos – all the way through – and Schmoranz was delighted. He then definitely pronounced that *Jenůfa* would be given at the National Theatre and asked for a vocal score to be sent.

Šípek thought that all was won. But disappointment followed. The Directorate of the National Theatre returned the score to me and Schmoranz announced briefly that all his efforts were in vain and that he would write about it to his friend Peška at greater length [**JP61**: Schmoranz to Calma-Veselá, 29 September 1915].

Šípek sent me Schmoranz's letter [JP62] and his answer to it, [JP63] written in a fighting mood.

[JP66, JP75, JP84]
Listy Hudební matice, iv (1924–5)

Gustav Schmoranz to Josef Peška — Prague, 29 September 1915 — JP62

[...] I tried to interest anyone I could in *Jenůfa*, finally even Kovařovic himself, after he returned for good. He took *Jenůfa* with

1 In the edition of Janáček's correspondence with the Veselýs (JA viii, 40) Mrs Calma-Veselá makes clear that their permanent address after moving from Brno was Karlín, Prague; they were in Bohdaneč only for the spa season, from April to September.

him to scrutinize it afresh, when I had truthfully described my impressions. But the result is still negative. The prayer and some of the monologues are, as he said, of course successful – everything which can keep to the form of Slovácko songs.

But the dialogue, on the other hand, is absolutely wrong, he says. The composer doggedly follows the principle [of reproducing] the aural impression of the spoken language of Slovácko, while at the same time however, contrary to all real-life speech, he makes the singers repeat individual passages of text countless times.

Where, then, is there any sort of stylistic principle here? According to Kovařovic, it is a strange mixture of striving for something quite 'novel' with extreme primitivism (bordering on compositional impotence) and long since out-dated oldfashioned practices. Kovařovic's new examination of the work merely confirmed his original view of the matter. And he said that he was pleased that in his verdict given some time ago, he had in no way done the work an injustice.

You cannot doubt he was glad to do this on your account. But he is unable to recommend the thing against his own artistic convictions.

JP63   Josef Peška to Gustav Schmoranz   *[Bohdaneč,] 3 October 1915*

This time you have betrayed yourself. If in August you had said: I like it, but without Kovařovic I can't do anything, I would have answered:

So let's give up all hope of that. It's a waste of postage to send the vocal score to Prague. His current expert opinion I could have written myself in August including the phrase that he is glad that the 'new scrutiny' has confirmed his former opinion.

Our dear Maestro made a mistake then, and he's making a mistake today.

I remember what he said about *Rusalka* when he rehearsed it, about [Novák's] *Imp*, when he knew it from the piano.[1] This is why he has an empty repertory, an incomplete ensemble.

You will play *Die Walküre* without a Valkyrie, just as you played

---

1 Kovařovic seems to have been too discreet to have said any of this publicly. Dvořák's biographer Otakar Šourek, however, reported (Petr 1940, 85) that as a pupil of Fibich, Kovařovic had no great interest in Dvořák. Though at the start of his new post at the National Theatre he was unable to wriggle out of conducting the première of *Rusalka*, he offloaded the première of Dvořák's next opera, *Armida*, on to an assistant. Novák himself had nothing but praise for Kovařovic's preparation of *The Zvíkov Imp* and *Karlštejn* under Kovařovic (Petr 1940, 47–8).

Libuše without a Libuše.[1] You are like the Catholic church. You mumble over the bread and the wine, proclaiming: this is the body, this is the blood – and people have to believe you.

[There follows a list of what Peška considered serious repertory mistakes at the National Theatre – works such as *Madama Butterfly*, on which the theatre had first option but allowed to let go to the opposition, and others which had been staged at the National Theatre which should never have been accepted.]

I return from where I left off: if the Maestro had heard *Maryčka Magdónova* sung by the Moravian teachers, he would not have dismissed Janáček as a run-of-the-mill beginner. He would not have dared the tactlessness of scheduling the opera of the young prophet Jeremiáš,[2] an opera whose libretto you have wrung your hands over; and refusing a man of sixty with a drama of Moravian people, composed, tried and tested. But of course: infallibility above all.

With the Maestro two things decided it: personal and principled distaste, and a misunderstanding of the matter.

I have nothing against your giving Kovařovic this letter to read.

Josef Peška to Dr František Veselý   *[Bohdaneč,] 15 October 1915*   JP64

[...] [PS] Schmoranz has not replied so far. Perhaps he'll get his housekeeper to reply to me. Her spelling and style are murderous, but she cooks a gracious cabbage dumpling.

Peška heard from Schmoranz a few days later, though only about Novák's opera *The Imp of Zvíkov*: 'he didn't react to my letter with a single word' (JP65: Peška to Calma-Veselá, 20 October 1915). So Peška decided that his main target was Kovařovic, whom he knew well, since he had provided him with the librettos of his three last operas:

Marie Calma-Veselá: 'From the battle for Janáček's *Jenůfa*'   JP66

Šípek acted in his decisive, energetic way. He let rip angrily at Kovařovic and it's a wonder that he didn't put an end to his friendship

---

1 Both Brünnhilde and Libuše in 1915 were sung by the Croatian Gabriela Horvátová, who although originally a mezzo had increasingly to take over dramatic soprano roles at the National Theatre. It could not have pleased anyone that the title part of such a 'national' opera as *Libuše* was thus in the hands of a foreigner.

2 A reference to a recent *cause célèbre* at the National Theatre; *The Old King* had been submitted in 1912 by the twenty-three-year-old Jaroslav Jeremiáš, accepted by Kovařovic in 1913 despite objections to the libretto. Because of a series of mishaps it was not staged until 1919, shortly after the composer's death.

with him. He extracted at least a promise that Kovařovic would talk
both with me and my husband about his objections to the work.

A meeting in the theatre was agreed. All we could say for Janáček
and his work – we said. At times Kovařovic was moved.

His objections were legion. The chief one, the unvocal character of
Jenůfa, I offered to disprove by singing [sections of] both Jenůfa and
the Kostelnička. A new meeting in the theatre was agreed. I gave
Janáček news of this, and invited him to send the score to Kovařovic.

[JP60, JP75, JP84]
Listy Hudební matice, iv (1924–5)

JP67   **Marie Calma-Veselá to Janáček**   *Karlín [Prague], 10 November 1915*

Director Peška returned the day before yesterday and already today
Kovařovic met him. So I am to go to the theatre on some drama
evening [i.e. when the opera is not playing] and there sing through
Jenůfa to Kovařovic. I will do so the very next week.

Kovařovic's objections are growing weaker and perhaps will disappear altogether. I believe that early in spring we will see the
première of *Jenůfa* at the National Theatre and that it will be a great
success.

[...]

If I get a binding promise from Kovařovic that *Jenůfa* will be
performed in the spring, it would perhaps be better to give up the idea
of the evening [concert]. What do you think? Or simply give an
informative evening for invited critics where you would talk about
your opera? [...]

The evening concert to promote *Jenůfa* was an idea of the Veselýs. Dr Veselý
had written to Janáček on 20 October 1915 (**JP68**) suggesting that the
Moravian–Silesian Beseda in Prague might hold a Janáček evening where
parts of *Jenůfa* would be performed and where Janáček would speak about it
to an audience which would include invited critics. Janáček had readily
agreed the next day (**JP69**), suggesting singers and, to fill out the evening,
performances of his piano pieces *In the Mists* and the Violin Sonata.

JP70   **Janáček to Marie Calma-Veselá**   *Brno, 12 November 1915*

That was a letter which really surprised me!

So it's going to go the right way. To help a composer with a special
evening of compositions – that is something I would not have agreed
to. [...] I would have agreed only to the theme Janáček–*Jenůfa*. But if
by singing you will disarm Kovařovic and get him on our side, this

will be a true victory. There will be no need then for an evening [concert].

[...]

I have looked through the score of *Jenůfa* again and tidied it up. If every act were copied out by a different person, copying the parts would be finished within a month. It's also possible to rehearse it using the vocal scores. So good luck!

[BR57]

Dr František Veselý to Janáček *Karlín, 17 November 1915* **JP71**

Yesterday's conversation with Kovařovic had the following result: K. wants to see the full score. After receiving it he will ask my wife to sing through the parts noted in it within the week.

In principle he is not now against performing it – at the moment he is giving the war as an excuse – [and] on the contrary he shows a willingness to perform *Jenůfa*, but later on. I think that after my wife's singing he will soften even more and in the spring of 1916 – as we wish it – he will direct *Jenůfa himself*. He doesn't want to make this retreat suddenly.

He has mentioned that some places are exquisite, especially the final scene; even without the singing, he says, it's musically beautiful. And he said: 'Why in fact should I not give Janáček although I don't agree with some things, when I am giving modern things, with which I don't agree at all?!'

Send the full score by return of post, so that the matter won't be held up. He would be glad to see – perhaps it won't in the end be necessary – some willingness on your part to change certain places. It seems that only *insignificant sections* would be affected and it would be more a show of goodwill.

It is well known that K. has even corrected Smetana.

The overall impression from the discussion was very favourable and Peška must have worked thoroughly on him.

Jenůfa will certainly be given; our task now will be to get it into the spring schedule. I'm delighted that I can give such favourable news. Of course we will then abandon organizing that evening.

Janáček to Karel Kovařovic *Brno, 20 November 1915* **JP72**

Dr František Veselý is the reason why yesterday I sent you the full score of *Jenůfa*.

I have two requests for you should you want to perform the work in the National Theatre: don't delay it, and take on the conducting yourself.

JP73   **Dr František Veselý to Janáček**   *[undated, postmarked Karlín,*
5 December 1915]

My wife has been invited by K. on Wednesday the 8th in the evening, or possibly on the 9th. I'll give you word immediately about the final outcome.

JP74   **Janáček to Marie Calma-Veselá**   *Brno, 7 December 1915 [telegram]*

Now break through!

JP75   **Marie Calma-Veselá: 'From the battle for Janáček's *Jenůfa***'

After I had sung Jenůfa's solos and also some of the Kostelnička's part, Kovařovic thawed. He liked some of the solos so much that we 'gave' them two and even three times. *Jenůfa* broke through!

But the worst wasn't over. Although Kovařovic promised that he would study *Jenůfa*, he didn't want to start studying before he had obtained the composer's consent to any essential revision of the work in regard to orchestration, cuts etc. On no account, however, did he want to negotiate over this with Janáček himself. Thus the role of intermediaries fell again to me and to my husband.

[JP60, 66, 84]
Listy Hudební matice, iv (1924–5)

JP76   **Marie Calma-Veselá to Janáček**   *Karlín, 9 December 1915*

So I sang last night – Jenůfa['s part] and an example of the Kostelnička. Kovařovic was *very* satisfied – he said that some passages were marvellous.

He has only a few small objections – less as a composer, more as an experienced man of the theatre.

They are tiny things. He will note them in his vocal score (he asked for one as a present) – and then will send it to me. I think – within a fortnight.

If you then agree with these small changes, which originate, let me remind you again, more from a producer's point of view (some cuts mainly in Laca's part) – and were you to make them immediately – *Jenůfa* would be given *for certain* early in spring.

Kovařovic is convinced that with his suggestions he would not harm *Jenůfa*, just as he undoubtedly helped Dvořák's *Dimitrij* and *The Jacobin*.[1]

One thing is certain, that he likes *Jenůfa* – that yesterday he came to like it even more and that he himself would be the best person to prepare it and cast it.

For the part of Jenůfa he wants me, saying that others would not be able to sing it like that – they have, in his words, 'brittle' voices. Horvátová would sing the Kostelnička, Schütz Števa [see JP86+].

Now it's entirely up to you, Mr Director, to win Kovařovic over to *Jenůfa* once and for all with a show of goodwill.

Kovařovic has definitely promised me that when these small corrections are done [in the full score], naturally by you, the première will be at the beginning of April *at the latest*.

So within a fortnight I'll send you the vocal score. It would then be best if you could come to Prague and meet with Kovařovic either at our place or in the theatre. If of course you should agree with his comments – there would be no need for any meeting and it would be sufficient if you were to carry them out and send them here. He would have it copied out here by his people.

Are you satisfied? I hope so.

To this Dr Veselý himself added his own letter, with much the same message: 'Kovařovic fully recognizes the beauty of the music and its individual character but as a man of the theatre he requires certain changes *"for the work to achieve momentum and flow, and gain in dramatic impact"*' (JP77, 9 December 1915).

Janáček to Dr František Veselý   *Brno, 10 December 1915*   JP78

I've already torn up a second letter – thus one makes mistakes and does silly things when joyful.

I want to thank you and your wife – but what's going round in my head is all too much, and thus I can't find the words. Well, you know – it's like a prisoner should the gates to life and freedom open. Will he be able to speak?

I will now write to Mr Kovařovic telling him to arrange cuts as he thinks fit. I will accept all gratefully – and then at once travel to Prague.

So see you soon!

1 Both operas were given at the National Theatre in Kovařovic's versions; it was only in the 1990s that Czech companies began to restore Dvořák's original version of *Dimitrij*.

JP79 Janáček to Karel Kovařovic *Brno, 10 December 1915*

Mrs Calma-Veselá sent me a letter which certainly cheered me.

How could I not accept suggestions from you for possible cuts!

You can be assured that I will accept them thankfully.

Whatever you think fit will hold good. Moreover, I ask you kindly to make these corrections.

Mrs Calma Veselá gives me to hope that you yourself would rehearse and conduct the work – if so I don't know how I would be able to thank you enough.

JP80 Dr František Veselý to Janáček *Prague, 12 December 1915*

We take sincere pleasure in your pleasure and, as a former chairman of the Club of the Friends of Art, I also went first thing in the morning to thank Director Peška in the name of Moravian art for his precious and selfless support with which he helped us in our attempt.

Were it not for his great influence on Schmoranz and Kovařovic as well as his continual, daily contacts with the National Theatre I don't know whether our action would have come off.

Therefore don't forget to show him your thanks with a few appreciative words. You know his address: Jerusalémská ulice 12.

Last night Kovařovic spoke with Peška and said that he had received your letter and that the première could be in the first week of April. In view of the fact that Easter comes at the end of April, this is still quite early. It's possible, however, that the première will be even sooner.

Who would have said, when I decided on Bohdaneč this year, that there we would plot for the acceptance of *Jenůfa* at the National Theatre? In such a way are the fates of men tangled up.

I said to Kovařovic then that the Club of the Friends of Art will give him as many copies of *Jenůfa* as is needed. That is also the duty of the Club.

JP81 Dr František Veselý to Janáček *Karlín, 15 December 1915*

Yesterday I sat in a café with Kovařovic and Director Peška. Both send their greetings and K. sends word that he has his hands full with *Der Rosenkavalier*, which is being given tomorrow. After that he will make his changes in the vocal score and send it to you to carry them out in the full score.

Then he will probably have the score copied here and, when it is finished, get on with rehearsals so that the première could take place at the end of March or possibly the beginning of April.

Should you not agree with some of Kovařovic's changes, you would then have to get here to [come to] an agreement. Otherwise there would be no need for the journey.

If you like, have the news published in the Brno papers that *Jenůfa* will be given at the National Theatre. Or should I do it from here?!

Janáček to Dr František Veselý *Brno, 17 December 1915* JP82

If Mr Kovařovic could speed up his proposal for cuts by Sunday, 26 December, it would save time and would save sending the score to Brno. Either way, I will be coming to Prague on Sunday, 26 December.

I have all sorts of other work there. I will stay there for two or three days: I could then carry out the revision of the full score according to the proposal. There would be time for consultation and it would be settled quickly, more quickly than by letter-writing.

The parcel post in the Brno–Vienna direction is also very much held up, particularly now towards the holidays. Be so kind and mediate in this.

I will be in Prague on Sunday 26 December after 3 o'clock in the hotel in Na Poříčí [street], the Imperial, I believe. If I could have the vocal score there with the suggestions for cuts – everything else could be done quickly.

If Mr Kovařovic agrees with making it public – then kindly inform the papers briefly. At least I would not be accused of self-importance and impatience.

Dr František Veselý to Janáček *Prague, 20 December 1915* JP83

I passed on your greetings to Director Peška, who wrote to you himself yesterday [see BR57]. Kovařovic is said to have piled into the score industriously and will apparently write to us when my wife should go to him.

He wants to show her possible changes in the part of Jenůfa and for her then to sing the two versions to him. By your visit everything will probably be ready and prepared.

On your way from the station, do make a detour via the hotel to see us. If there should be a meeting that day with you, then I will let you know perhaps at the hotel.

On your return from Prague Director Peška wants you to visit him in Bohdaneč, where he went today. We'll put the news into the papers promptly at the New Year, as a New Year surprise.

JP84   Marie Calma-Veselá: 'From the battle for Janáček's *Jenůfa*'

In the morning at 7.30 Janáček sent the servant from the hotel for the vocal score with an apology for disturbing us so early [JP85: visiting card from Janáček to Dr Veselý, undated]. Half an hour later he came himself with the vocal score and the full score, saying that he didn't understand the cuts. I explained to him what Kovařovic had in mind, I saved two cuts by putting a new text underneath.[1]

During this time we worked for the reconciliation of Janáček and Kovařovic. It took place during a performance of *Libuše* which Kovařovic was conducting. Between the acts I sent my husband with Janáček to Kovařovic. It is said that their long-prepared *rapprochement* turned out to be deeply felt. I will let on that I had told each composer only the nice things that they had said about each other. In this way the rough edges were smoothed down.

Janáček returned to his box satisfied and remarked to me in his terse way:

'It's all settled!'

He had no idea how much work had been needed and how many good, earnest words for it be settled.

[JP60, JP66, JP75]
Listy Hudební matice, iv (1924–5)

JP86   Janáček to Dr František Veselý   *Brno, 31 December 1915*

During those few days in Prague it was as if my brain was in a furnace.

In a short time we ended what had long been prepared.

I think that the performance of *Jenůfa* will not just be a splash in the ocean. I feel strongly that the little stone, vigorously thrown by your gracious wife, will pull down with it mountains of prejudice; I'm able to breathe freely. I thank her for it sincerely.

And you? You rushed ahead until it made people uncomfortable.

---

1 Originally the Kostelnička sang four times, 'Mívejte se tady dobře' ['Have a good time here!'], as she left the stage in Act 1, the first three times in a brief ensemble with the Grandmother and Laca. Calma-Veselá saved the ensemble by inventing and substituting the words: 'Zítra ihned dom mi půjdeš, aby lidé neříkali, že se za tím štěstím dereš' ['First thing tomorrow you will come home to me, so people can't say that you are in a hurry for your happiness'] (JA viii, 64).

You awoke them from their ease, which is unpleasant for sleepy people.

THE PRAGUE PREMIÈRE AND ITS PREPARATIONS

Casting the new production had already begun in December. 'For the part of Jenůfa he wants me,' Calma-Veselá had written to Janáček in her letter of 9 December (JP76), 'Horvátová would sing the Kostelnička, Schütz Števa.' The temperamental Gabriela Horvátová (1877–1967) was a Croatian who had joined the Prague National Theatre in 1903 and through her talent as an actress and immense dedication and versatility had become one of the key members of the ensemble, moving from contralto and mezzo parts (such as Carmen) to dramatic soprano (Elektra, Brünnhilde). The Kostelnička was one of her most successful parts and during the rehearsal period she struck up an obsessive and intimate friendship with Janáček. Theodor Schütz (1878–1961), under his own name of Bohdan Procházka, had been the original Števa in Brno. On Janáček's advice (JP87: Janáček to Schütz, 5 February 1916), he sang Laca, not Števa in Prague. This was a sensible decision in view of the fact that as his voice developed after further schooling and experience in Vienna (1907–11), Schütz had taken over much of the *Heldentenor* repertory when joining the National Theatre company in Prague.

But Marie Calma-Veselá did not sing Jenůfa. It was presumably a decision on Kovařovic's part to use one of his company, Kamila Ungrová (1887–1972), rather than an outsider with no stage experience. The Veselýs bitterly reproached Janáček for lack of gratitude in not exerting pressure on Kovařovic. 'My disappointment [. . .] rests solely in the fact that you could not say or did not know how to say: "I want Mrs Veselá to sing Jenůfa because I feel that no one else would sing it like her"' (JP88: Marie Calma-Veselá to Janáček, 25 February 1916). There is some justice in Calma-Veselá's reproach, especially since as a few weeks later Janáček passed on to Kovařovic the name of the wife of his former pupil, the conductor Josef Charvát, as a possible Jenůfa (JP89: Janáček to Kovařovic, 18 March 1916). And Janáček's embarrassment is evident in that the Veselýs were almost his only friends that he did not invite to the première. This is particularly sad in view of the claim by Mrs Calma-Veselá in her 1925 article (JP90, p.144) that in order to smooth *Jenůfa*'s path to Prague Dr Veselý had guaranteed to underwrite the first six performances, if they were not sold out.

For all the past reluctance to stage *Jenůfa* in Prague, rehearsals went ahead smoothly, and with obvious enthusiasm:

Josef Peška to Janáček   *[Prague,] 21 March 1916*   JP91

On the orchestra stands lie the parts of [Montemezzi's] *L'amore dei tre re*. Brzobohatý is rehearsing it. It will be in March. Kovařovic has

Jenůfa in hand. I heard from Schmoranz and others that Horvátová is enraptured with the Kostelnička. When I meet her I will ask her myself. Kovařovic delights in the Slav spirit of the work. They fear, however, that the censorship might find fault with the recruits' songs.[1] Should [Kovařovic] ask for more changes in the repetition of the text, allow him to without hesitation. The main thing is for it to be on the boards. The success will be decisive, perhaps sensational. [...]

JP92   **Janáček to Karel Kovařovic**   *Brno, 28 March 1916*

Dear friend,

I address you in this way because you take such an interest in *Jenůfa*!

Mrs Horvátová has told me so many fine and flattering things that truly I am waiting impatiently for the day when I will hear how the roles are interpreted and performed.

According to Mrs Horvátová's first run-through I already know that it will be outstanding.

Thank you for your devotion. I will remember it gratefully.

JP93   **Gabriela Horvátová to Janáček**   *Prague, 17 April 1916*

[...] *Jenůfa* is being rehearsed *daily* at the piano and is now fully prepared, nevertheless in recent days three circumstances have caused your work to be held up. Above all, it was the death of the brother of Miss Ungrová (Jenůfa); second, the huge difficulties in preparing *Mozart in Prague*[2] for the pension fund; and last but not least, the difficulties with the preparation of Dvořák's *Stabat Mater*[3] for the pension fund – thus, as you see, circumstances which no one could have foreseen. As soon as the holidays are over we will begin at full steam with the rehearsals; the head of opera himself will surely inform you of these in good time.

As far as the Kostelnička is concerned I can assure you, Maestro, the more I get into it the more I like it, and not only I but also Miss

---

1 Their fears were justified; see JP103–5.
2 *Mozart in Prague* was one of the items presented at a 'Mozart evening' – a play by Alois Jirásek incorporating performances of pieces by Mozart. The evening, given on 11 and 14 April 1916, also included several independent orchestral works by Mozart and a performance of *Der Schauspieldirektor*.
3 Given under Kovařovic on Maundy Thursday, 20 April 1916.

Ungrová, Mr Schütz and Mr Lebeda[1] and Mrs Pivoňková,[2] who are singing their parts with love. I have the Kostelnička worked out so far that I think you will perhaps be content. I wish you pleasant Easter holidays and take pleasure that you will soon visit us in Prague for the final rehearsals.

Gabriela Horvátová to Janáček [Prague,] 25 April 1916 JP94

This morning, 25 April at 11 o'clock, we had our first big rehearsal of your opera, at the piano in the hall, before that at 9 the chief held the first orchestral rehearsal. I am glad to tell you that it went *excellently*, to the delight of the chief, and all of us taking part. Tomorrow they will rehearse all the small roles together and in three to four days we will begin to block out movements on stage. This much only briefly. Permit me again to let you know the further course of events.

Karel Kovařovic to Janáček Prague, 28 April 1916 JP95

The piano rehearsals of the soloists for *Jenůfa* have advanced so far that your presence now would be greatly welcome to us.

For this reason allow me to invite you – if it will be possible for you to come to Prague next week – for *Thursday, 4 May*; I ask for a reply by telegram whether I can count on your presence that day in the morning or evening.

Janáček to Zdenka Janáčková [undated, Prague, 4? May 1916] JP96

I'm writing the same day so as still to retain my memories. In the morning there was an orchestral rehearsal. They played to the end of Act 1. With what virtuosity they played in the last scene! I held my breath. It ended at 11 o'clock (having begun before 9) and they went on to rehearse blocking the soloists' movements (at Žofín).[3] First among the performances is again that of Mrs Horvátová. Schütz knows his excellently. Miss Ungrová will be a gentle Jenůfa, but good. Veleba [Lebeda?] a good actor. Act 1 overran to 2 o'clock.

1 Antonín Lebeda (1873–1946) was a member of the Prague National Theatre company 1908–28, singing *Heldentenor* parts and, after the arrival of Schütz, more lyrical tenor parts, including Števa at the Prague première of *Jenůfa*.
2 Věra Pivoňková (1866–1939) created the part of Grandmother Buryjovka at both the Brno and Prague premières of *Jenůfa*. She sang mezzo and contralto roles in Brno (1887–93, 1900–12) and then at the Prague National Theatre until her retirement in 1928.
3 The island Žofín (now Slovanský ostrov, Slavonic Island) in the Vltava near the National Theatre contained a hall seating about 300 people which was used by the National Theatre at the time for stage rehearsals.

I went out at once for a small consolation at Thomayer.[1]

From there for a little ice cream – in this summer heat.

And back immediately for the rehearsal on Act 2. This is heart-rending. Thus in an exalted mood the end was reached, up to the blessing. And then – this unpleasant coarseness of one of the musicians, a coarseness springing from the lower theatrical waters.

A talk with the secretary, with the intendant. Well, so home now! And tomorrow to lunch with Kovařovic. To have a rest and finish the work. I will be sad when everything is over. [. . .]

Amongst them I feel as if at home. They like me.

So much in haste. I haven't eaten yet. The weather is lovely – 34 degrees. I will let you know by telegram when I'm coming. I will teach for a few days in Brno and again, travel to Prague for at least a week before the première. They want me here now, and from time to time it is necessary.

JP97   **Janáček to Zdenka Janáčková**   *Prague, 5 May 1916*

Yesterday after the rehearsal I went for supper to the 'representative' [i.e. Obecní dům, Smetana Hall]; I found Nedbal[2] there. He promised me that he would come to the première.

This morning there was an orchestral rehearsal from 8 o'clock. They got to the middle of Act 1. But they polished it so much that it was a pleasure. Then towards 12 o'clock I still had a long consultation with Kovařovic. He must have *Jenůfa* on his mind waking and sleeping! I announced a visit to Miss Ungrová for the afternoon in order to get her into the right frame of mind during the prayer and during the words 'Tož umřel!'.[3]

She was waiting for me in full domestic finery. And she was very pleased that I came. I got a box for the evening. I took the Janáčeks[4] with me. But they annoyed me. It was [Fibich]'s opera *Hedy*. They

1 Perhaps an open-air restaurant unofficially called after the landscape gardener František Thomayer (1856–1938), who was responsible for the design of many Prague parks. There was an open-air restaurant at the time on Žofín island. I am grateful to Dr Jitka Ludvová for this suggestion.

2 This is more likely to be the composer Oskar Nedbal (1874–1930), who was conductor of the Vienna Tonkünstlerverein 1906–18, than his nephew, Karel (1888–1964), also a conductor, then employed at the Vinohrady Theatre in Prague, but too young and not well known enough to be mentioned simply as 'Nedbal.'

3 'Zdrávas královno' (see p.44, fn.3); 'Tož umřel' ['So he died'], Jenůfa's reaction to the Kostelnička's story in Act 2 Scene 7 that her child died while she was delirious.

4 Josefa Janáčková (née Procházková, 1865–1937), the widow of Janáček's cousin Augustin Janáček (1851–1900), lived in Prague with her daughter Věra (1891–1967).

were continually 'carried away' by the 'beautiful' music. And it's so dry that one's tongue sticks [to the roof of one's mouth]! Of course I kept quiet about my things – although my heart is full and I could almost shout aloud about my joy when I see and hear how my work is enthralling everyone.

They sent me a message to come backstage after Act 2. *How* joyfully everyone greeted me! It was almost like a passionate explosion of joy: the conductors Brzobohatý, Zamrzla, Picka,[1] the producer Polák,[2] 'my' ladies Horvátová, Rejholcová,[3] Maixner.[4] Kovařovic again called me to his office and again he was [engrossed] in the full score. He will be ready this week with the fair copy of Act 1. Tomorrow morning an orchestral rehearsal, at 11 a rehearsal for blocking and movement on stage, in the evening soloists and chorus. As you see, it's all go. I was glad to be alone for supper in the 'representativní' restaurant: but then Kocian[5] ran up to me. Artistic life, this true, creative life which draws human souls together, binding them in pure friendship – this sort of life is beautiful and I am experiencing it. I did not suspect that sometime I would come to Prague for the happiest moments of my musical life.

On Sunday [7 May] I return; I will teach for a few days and then I'll come back here again. My presence drives everything forward.

Janáček to Zdenka Janáčková   *Prague, Thursday, 11 May 1916*   **JP98**

First thing in the morning I was invited by telephone to the theatre for 9 o'clock.

They had orchestral rehearsals for Act 2; those places of madness and insane visions of the Kostelnička and Jenůfa. I think that I have caught it well in the orchestra. Then from 1 o'clock to 5.30 there followed a rehearsal of soloists and choruses. Quite a few suggestions were necessary, both for the acting and the dancing. The Kostelnička

---

1 Bohumír Brzobohatý (1869–1949), Rudolf Zamrzla (1869–1930) and František Picka (1873–1918) were all conductors working at the National Theatre at that time.
2 Robert Polák (1866–1926), bass and the chief opera producer at the National Theatre during the Kovařovic era; he produced the Prague premières of both *Jenůfa* and *Káťa Kabanová*.
3 Marie Rejholcová (1891–1937) was one of Janáček's ladies in the sense that she sang the part of the Mayor's Wife in *Jenůfa*.
4 Vincenc Maixner (1888–1946) was Kovařovic's assistant and repetiteur at the time.
5 Jaroslav Kocian (1883–1950), well-known concert violinist and teacher. Janáček had attempted to interest him in giving the first performance of his Violin Sonata at the 'Janáček evening' at the Moravian-Silesian Beseda, an event abandoned once *Jenůfa* was accepted at the Prague National Theatre (see JP68).

of her own accord undergoes the judgement of the people: this is her moral purgation. This passage brings up solemn peace.

The producer didn't get it right. They would have made a circus of the time-honoured dance and would have detracted from the first appearance of the Kostelnička. That will be put right tomorrow.

The intendant, court councillor Kvěch,[1] was present again; this inspired the last drop of strength. In Act 3 the women members of the chorus wept. In the auditorium there were guests already although it was [only] with piano!

Then Mrs Horvátová and I visited the sick Maixner and stayed with the poor fellow until 9 o'clock. The continual topic of conversation: only *Jenůfa*. What new things I picked up here! I know that you are not, and cannot, be jealous of Mrs Horvátová;[2] only because I know that I write to you that I've never known before such a deeply serious artiste.

She is going to invite Jirásek to a rehearsal so I can meet him. Vítězslav Novák has already asked her to let him into a rehearsal. Here there is a stir from all this such as has not been seen for a long time – especially amongst professional musicians there is much excitement.

You already know from the papers that the première is on the 25th of the month. They want me to remain here till then, but those devilish young people in the Organ School cannot be trusted. Tomorrow there is Mozart's Requiem [in memory of] Smetana;[3] at 10 o'clock a rehearsal in the theatre again. In the evening Mrs Horvátová has invited me into the intendant's company at Žofín. I didn't sleep the whole night – my eyes are already closing up with tiredness; it's only 11 o'clock in the morning.

JP99   **Janáček to Zdenka Janáčková**   *Prague, Friday, 12 May 1916*

Where to begin – there is so much to tell.

In the morning I went to the requiem for the late Smetana; they performed Mozart's at Vyšehrad.[4] It sounded powerful. Having not waited for the end I ran off to see the poet Procházka [over *Brouček*, see JP100] and arranged a meeting with him on Saturday evening.

1 Otomar Kvěch was intendant at the Prague National Theatre 1913–18.
2 Zdenka became extremely jealous of Mrs Horvátová. There is some indication of this in JP100.
3 Smetana died on 12 May 1884.
4 According to legend, the site of the fortress of the first Czech dynasty, now a part of Prague with a cemetery where distinguished national figures are buried.

Then I jumped into a tram and [went] to the theatre. They were rehearsing the chorus, soloists, backstage music, and the clatter of the mill [Act 1]. It's good that I am here: now the recruits will come from *the distance* and everything will develop magnificently. The clatter of the mill will be on stage – [coming] from the mill. Tomorrow there is an orchestral rehearsal and then [work] on that dance. I have chased up Úprka[1] and Lolek[2] to teach the steps and the movements. If only they come! A premonition then drove me to see Preissová – and she had gone off to meet her husband *this* morning to Hungary! That saddens me. I wrote a note and had it sent to her.

They have planned the first rehearsal of the orchestra for Monday [15 May] and everything on stage *without action*, i.e. they will just *sit* on stage. This is how they perfect it! I have to stay, and I will go off on Monday by the afternoon express to Brno – simply because of my worries with the Organ School! Otherwise I would stay here on St John's day [St Jan Nepomucký, 16 May] to have a little rest. On Wednesday there is already the first full rehearsal and I wonder whether they will be ready at all by then. And so two journeys still await me!

But like bees from the hive so from the theatre reports are flying around from those taking part that it will be magnificent.

If only I now had the second and third opera, one finished, the other corrected. Wretched librettos![3]

I will send you a telegram tomorrow: *put it up on Monday morning before 9 on the blackboard in the Organ School.*

Janáček to Zdenka Janáčková   *Prague, Saturday 13 May 1916*   JP100

Today my head is going round again. The orchestral rehearsal was wonderful. 'Jako by sem smrť načuhovala'[4] – you know that place where one gets goose pimples – they played it in such a way that one trembles. After the rehearsal Kovařovic and I embraced; we were both overcome. The sculptor Úprka will take over demonstrating the dance from Act 1. So everything will be stylistically pure and perfect.

---

1 František Úprka (1868–1929); like his brother the painter Jóža Úprka (the model for the painter Lhotský in *Fate*), he had strong ethnographic interests in Moravia.
2 Stanislav Lolek (1873–1936), painter; see LB2+.
3 See Chap.5 and Chap.4 for the current states, respectively, of *The Excursions of Mr Brouček* and *Fate*.
4 The final words of Act 2, delivered by the tormented Kostelnička: 'As if death is peering in here!'.

Here it's already known that *Jenůfa* will be an event. For the afternoon I was invited to Mrs Horvátová for tea. I made the acquaintance of him [her husband], Mr Noltsch, a good-natured, vigorous fellow, nice and affable. He sat with us until the evening, then had to go to a meeting and the three of us remained in discussion only about *Jenůfa*. We thought of you kindly; after all I know that now perhaps you also believe in my musical calling and save my strength for my work. I went through the whole flat – fourteen rooms and how [richly] furnished! *Carpets to the value of 60,000 zl.!* [. . .]

Tomorrow on Sunday I have a discussion in the morning about the libretto [of *Brouček*] with Procházka. After noon I have to divide up my time: in the theatre Schmoranz has invited me for the afternoon; Kovařovic for the evening.

On Monday there is already the big rehearsal. Therefore I'll only leave after it. I think my telegram[1] surprised you, but it wasn't possible otherwise: I am now making my future. Today in the *Národní listy* there was a feuilleton with a nice bit on me at the end.

You know, [this is] a fairytale – about which I never dreamed. [. . .]

PS   I almost forgot! I also have to go tomorrow to the Janáčeks for a snack. Dr Rosenberg[2] will be there with his mother. Is there perhaps going to be an engagement![3]

JP101   **Janáček to Zdenka Janáčková**   *Prague, Sunday, 14 May 1916*

This morning [I was] with the writer Procházka; we came to an agreement about *Brouček* and discussed *Fate* – Langr.[4] Then with Věrka at the exhibition of folk costumes. I met up there with the sister of Dr Veselý. Calma has apparently got the whole family up in arms.[5] After Vinohrady we looked for Slovácko women to demonstrate the dances in the theatre, and found them. I had lunch at the Janáčeks and ran off to the afternoon theatre [session]. Schmoranz told me then about the stupidity of the censorship: it has forbidden 'Zdrávas'

1 See JP99. The telegram presumably announced his delayed return to Brno for classes at the Organ School. In his letter of Thursday, 11 May (JP98), Janáček wrote that he really ought to stay on in Prague until the première but feared that his students could not be left unsupervised. In the end he remained in Prague until after the rehearsal on Monday, 15 May, returning to Prague again on Thursday 18 May.

2 Viktor Rosenberg (1876–1932).

3 There was; Věra [Věrka] Janáčková married Dr Rosenberg on 2 December 1916 (Janáček was a witness at the wedding). They were divorced in 1921.

4 Possibly a reference to Dr František Langer (1888–1965), writer and military doctor.

5 Janáček was no doubt looking for reasons for distancing himself from Mrs Calma-Veselá; see JP87+.

[Jenůfa's prayer in Act 2] – that has really gutted *Jenůfa*. Somebody will go to the Governor tomorrow.

Dr Rosenberg is nice; just let her marry him!

The evening at the theatre. Gorgeous sets for *The Bartered Bride*. They so like it here yet it is – with the exception of the final act – dramatically impossible. From this viewpoint Act 2 is downright bad.

Tomorrow will be a decisive day. The orchestra will finish Act 3 and then the orchestra and soloists Acts 1 and 2. In the words of Mrs Horvátová, tomorrow will be a 'battlefield'.

Then I will just jump on to the express.

Is the new suit in Brno?

Janáček to Zdenka Janáčková   *Prague, Thursday 18 May 1916*   **JP102**

After the orchestra rehearsal I went to visit the press agencies. Mrs Horvátová made me do it – and I don't regret it. Ostrčil[1] was glad to see me. He told me that he wanted to give *Jenůfa*, but the National Theatre beat him to it. This is important and interesting. Chvála was also pleased at my visit – but when he had been in Brno at that time he had not yet believed in my style, he said.[2]

Dr Šilhan from the *Národní listy* will already have a preview article. The intendant was again at the rehearsal.

There are also things to laught at; [foolish] to write to you – better when I tell you in person.

The première is *outside the subscription series*;[3] Novák's thing[4] was in the subscription. [. . .]

Kovařovic said yesterday, [']*I think* of it as *if it were* <u>my</u> *work*[']. And also, with what love and dedication he is working on it! The other day he sat over the score until 5 in the morning!

An unusual stir!

There have been as many as twenty-three orchestral rehearsals.

---

1 See JP109+; Ostrčil was then chief conductor at the Vinohrady Theatre.
2 Emanuel Chvála was one of the few Prague critics who reviewed the Brno première; see JP32+.
3 The significance of this remark is that it indicates the management's confidence in filling the house without resort to the subscribers (whose four groups could guarantee four reasonably attended performances, see Tyrrell 1988, 47).
4 i.e. Vítězslav Novák's first opera *The Zvíkov Imp*, given its première at the National Theatre on 10 October 1915. It was more popular than the management thought it would be and was given eleven times in the 1915–16 season.

More than for *Louise*.[1] That had only twenty-two. And for [my opera], on top of those twenty-three, there will be another five!

Yesterday I didn't have a pen and ink in the night. I am writing, Friday morning – and I overslept. It's 7.30.

Today there is an orchestral rehearsal at 9 o'clock, and a *general* rehearsal for Acts 1 and 2 with stage action as well.

Do you perhaps have the suit now? It was sent only on Wednesday!

So, now count the days until you arrive!

How will that evening end!

[PS] Mrs Preissová has already invited me; she's here [in Prague].

JP103   **Janáček to Zdenka Janáčková**   *Prague, Friday 19 May 1916*

Today was a rush. From 8.30 the orchestra 'polished' Acts 1 and 2; then there was a full rehearsal, singing, solos, chorus, orchestra for Acts 1 and 2. In the auditorium Úprka, Kalvoda[2] and the conductors and the intendant! He told me that the police have allowed talk of 'God' and the singing of the 'Zdrávas'! So wise, aren't they?

Today I was at the police (the official, Dr Martyn) in the afternoon. He suggested to me that Laca should go to – America, instead of to the army!

I explained to him that it wasn't possible now, but they will sing 'já neboráček *rád* budu vojáček' ['I poor fellow will *gladly* be a soldier'].[3] His face immediately brightened up.

Then I went to see Mrs Preissová. She took pleasure that 'our baby' is doing so well, growing.

During tea we talked frankly. Her son [is] a good-looking, nice fellow. She brought up the financial question. I said that we will arrange things as is customary in the theatre.

Then to Mrs Maturová; she wasn't home. Then to the theatre. I found Kovařovic there – again working on my score. I brought up Mrs Preissová's question with him. He responded that they are

---

1 Charpentier's *Louise* (1900) was one of the great successes of the Kovařovic era. It received its Czech première at the National Theatre in February 1903 and made a profound impression on Janáček when he saw it there on 21 May 1903.

2 Alois Kalvoda (1875–1934), landscape painter, the designer of the National Theatre's 1915 production of *The Bartered Bride*. From his correspondence with Janáček in late 1915 it seems he was considered as a designer for *Jenůfa*. Janáček turned to him again in August 1916 when trying to get modifications to the Act 1 set of *Jenůfa*.

3 Part of the recruits' chorus when they enter in Act 1. The actual words are 'musím být vojáček' ['I must be a soldier']. Any show of reluctance for soldiering was naturally unacceptable to the censorship at the height of the First World War.

waiting for me to sign a contract. K 600 as a composer's fee, and then 8% for each performance.

I will talk with Peška to push them up to K 1000 for the fee. I'd like to offer one sixth to Preissová. Now I am going among 'countrymen.' They want to get up an evening after the première. The première is on Friday the 26th. *But come as arranged.*

Janáček to Zdenka Janáčková   *Prague, Saturday 20 May 1916*   **JP104**

Premières are all the same, but one has to know about these [Prague] social contacts and manners. A fellow cannot be churlish here.

Here my adviser, and admittedly an energetic and crafty guide, is Mrs Horvátová.

She took me off willy-nilly to pay a visit to the intendant, Court Councillor Kvěch.

From there at once to Councillor Šafařík, from there to Mrs Kovařovicová [the wife of Karel Kovařovic].

Now I have come home and already they have passed to me the visiting card of the Court Councillor, who was in the hotel to repay my visit.

Now [Mrs Horvátová] wants by hook or by crook to contrive an introduction to the Governor. I have problems with the police; do you think that even frightened her? She went with me and like an advocate successfully buttered them up. The censorship is cutting the recruits; again they have called me for tomorrow. She [Mrs Horvátová] is grateful to me for the role, which elates her, and because by right I singled her out in front of everyone during the rehearsal.

In the afternoon there was a photograph session for [the newspaper] *Český svět*. In the evening I was in the director's box for *The Kiss*.

So the day approaches which is talked about through all of Prague. [...]

Janáček to Zdenka Janáčková   *[Prague,] Sunday 22 [21] May 1916*   **JP105**

I wanted to go off by steamer to Zbraslav;[1] but it wasn't possible – they called me as early as 9 o'clock to the police because of the censorship. But the police official goes day in day out to mass, confession and communion! Isn't he a terrible sinner! I didn't catch

---

1 A town a few miles downstream from central Prague (now a part of Prague), with a former Cistercian monastery in which the last of the Přemyslids, the first Czech dynasty, are buried.

him; once more to him at 10. With people of that sort it's altogether impossible to talk sensibly. It even began to look as though it wouldn't be possible to give *Jenůfa* at all. Imagine such perversion of the human spirit! It will probably be decided tomorrow morning. You will come as planned. I will wait for you on Wednesday morning. After a long consultation with Kovařovic we patched up the words for the recruits out of all recognition.

Mrs Horvátová then continued to take me to the chairman of the *Družstvo*, Court Councillor Dr Hlava, and the wife of the Councillor Mrs Šafaříková. Visits are returned here. She then invited me to her place for lunch. In the evening in the theatre I had a box at my disposal, but I invited Mr Maixner to share it with me; you know, in order to be left in peace. There was *Tannhäuser* in the theatre; I found that the theatrical ground here is hot. If I penetrate all that brilliant mist which in the atmosphere of the theatre veils the actors and the audience, which they are all accustomed to breathe here, in which they get enthused and carried away, if with my *Jenůfa* I break through all this and win – I don't even want to think where it will end.

I've got on my side everyone who is performing the work from Kovařovic – down to the stage hands, who also give me a friendly greeting. I have booked two rooms at the same prices as mine.

Tomorrow they rehearse Act 3, on Tuesday and Wednesday there are dress rehearsals. So you won't receive any more letters.

JP106   Zdenka Janáčková to Janáček   *Brno, 21 May 1916*

We will be coming only on Thursday morning, I can't travel alone on Tuesday night.

I just wish it was all over; I'm very agitated.

[PS] Should I bring the new suit?

JP107   Janáček to Zdenka Janáčková   *[Prague, Monday 22 May 1916]*

Impressions of Monday, 22 May 1916:

The morning orchestral rehearsal: they went through Act 2 and completed the rehearsing of Act 3. The ending sounds like a hymn, the victory of pure love!

At 11.30 the rehearsal with soloists and chorus of Act 3 began. Mrs Horvátová ran up [to me] after her scene, grippingly performed, of the confession to the people. She drew my attention to the presence of Mrs Kovařovicová; I approached her from the back and *she was in tears*. She could not leave the theatre she was so red in the face. On the balcony Director Schmoranz with Maixner, Schmoranz delighted; they clapped after the end of the rehearsal.

At lunch (U Ježíška,[1] a bad lunch) Maixner told me that yesterday Kovařovic said to him: '*After fifty years of "The Bartered Bride" it will be Janáček's "Jenůfa" which will similarly delight [people].*' I *already believe in its success.*

[...]

Should Hercka [Dr Emil Hertzka] from Vienna perhaps be invited? He is a music publisher. I hope they will invite him.

The Police have now given permission! In truth that was something that *I* achieved. Today at [Smetana's opera] *The Secret* in the theatre I was an object of interest. Now I'm sitting at home with your card in my hands. I'd love to see you here, but on the other hand I have at least more peace of mind. To let you wander here round Prague alone, get lost – that would hurt me. And I myself again must serve those who are serving me. I would be as if torn in spirit – and in this great strain and excitement I need at least a few peaceful moments.

I will wait for you then, as you write, on *Thursday* morning. I'll be at the station.

Don't bring the suit. Every moment I'm paying calls; I have to be dressed in a long coat.

Calm down, now! Everything is going to turn out well.

PS I really wrote this letter only for myself.

Janáček's postscript gives a clue to all these letters to Zdenka. He knew how important the Prague première of *Jenůfa* was to his career and his future creative plans and needed to record his impressions day by day. He did not keep a regular diary, preferring to confide his thoughts in letters. But after their days of courtship, he was not in the habit of writing long letters to his wife, partly because they lived together, making letters redundant, but partly also because he did not feel the desire to communicate in this way with her: from his remark in JP100, it seems that he felt that she did not really 'believe' in him. These letters describing the preparations for the première were his last group of such long and detailed letters to Zdenka. He was already writing more enthusiastically to Mrs Horvátová (who told him constantly how much she believed in him), and within a year his voluminous correspondence to Kamila Stösslová would begin.

---

1 Former beer-hall at Spálená ulice, no.32 (now the site of the department store Máj on the Národní třída).

JP108 Marie Stejskalová's reminiscences (1959)

The première was on 26 May 1916. The master saw it as the happiest day of his life. He wanted all his friends to be present at this victory of his, and invited them in person or by letter. A good number of them also travelled to Prague from Brno. *Jenůfa* was completely victorious. It was well prepared and also happened at the right time, during the war, when the whole nation became united and the Bohemians began to draw closer to Moravia. Prague again began to prize folk art highly[1] and therefore was enthusiastic about life in a Slovácko village, as depicted in *Jenůfa*. The master, Mrs Horvátová, who accompanied him everywhere, as well as Kovařovic, were overwhelmed by glory and congratulations. The master was so overflowing with happiness and joy that when he returned home after the première with the mistress he gave me money for the journey to go and see the Prague *Jenůfa*.

JP109 Otakar Ostrčil to Janáček   *Smíchov [Prague], 28 May 1916*

Your *Jenůfa* made a huge impression on me. Seldom have I left the theatre so taken by a work as on Friday's première. You know how to keep the listener as if in a vice for the whole evening. I have been living for the past few days in continual memories of your work, I go over individual scenes, I page through the vocal score, in short I am yours. I can't go to tomorrow's performance, I am working that evening and believe me – I am almost glad of it. On Friday at least I went from the theatre with the impression that I would not be able in the immediate future to expose myself again to such an overwhelming experience. But rest assured that the next performances of *Jenůfa* will find me the most faithful follower. I had pleasure from the tremendous success of the work and from the first-rate performance. It was in truth the duty of the theatre to make every effort to redress the wrong. Accept from me, Maestro, my sincere congratulations on this well-deserved success and my wishes that the ice now already dispersed will open the way for all your works into the hearts of people.

Janáček received many letters of congratulation. Ostrčil's was the most important to his career. As Kovařovic's successor, Otakar Ostrčil (1879–1935) was to conduct the next four Janáček premières at the Prague National Theatre, including the world première of *The Excursions of Mr Brouček*. It

---

[1] There had been a wave of enthusiasm for folklore in Prague in the early 1890s, stimulated particularly by two major exhibitions (see Tyrrell 1988, 243–4)

was crucial that Janáček had someone at the theatre who was clearly on his side. Ostrčil was also one of the most substantial Czech opera composers of his time; his admiration for Janáček, a quarter-century older than himself, is all the more touching in the context of Ostrčil's usually careful and restrained utterances. Janáček's response to another letter of congratulation, from Josef Bohuslav Foerster, one of the most distinguished Czech composers of the period, provides further evidence of how much Janáček regarded *Jenůfa*'s success in Prague as a turning point. Foerster's recognition must have been particularly welcome. It was possibly following Foerster's example that Janáček had turned to *Her Stepdaughter* in the first place (see JP4), and in 1910 he had sent him an inscribed copy of the published vocal score (**JP110**: Foerster's letter of thanks, 2 November 1910).

Janáček to Josef Bohuslav Foerster   *Brno, 24 June 1916*   **JP111**

You don't know what pleasure I took from your letter! To me it seems as if I am in a fairytale. I compose and compose because something is driving me do to it. I no longer valued my works – just as I did not value what I said. I did not believe that sometime someone would notice anything [of mine]. I was overtaken – my own pupils had begun to advise me how to compose, how to speak through the orchestra. I smiled at it; I could do nothing else. I am beginning to believe in my life and its mission. You have given me strength.

The opera continued with immense and sustained popular success. It drew packed audiences for its remaining performances that season, and thereafter became a staple work in the Prague repertory. Up to 1924, when this production was put to rest before the 1926 revival, it had been performed sixty-six times.

Once back in Brno, Janáček received accounts from Mrs Horvátová of the sold-out performances and the numbers of curtain calls she received.[1] Janáček sent telegrams back. His friendship with Horvátová aroused considerable comment, and prompted a long and awkward letter from Kovařovic (JP112, 3 June 1916) pointing out that Janáček's 'private telegraphic greetings to the Kostelnička, which were of course well meant' had made the rest of the cast jealous, thus making Kovařovic's task in sustaining morale all the more difficult.

Janáček to Karel Kovařovic   *Brno, 4 June 1916*   **JP113**

I have just got your letter.

How surprised I was at it. No, with my telegrams I did not want to bring about what, according to your words, was achieved by it.

---

1 See JA vi, 15ff.

I would have addressed the telegrams to you – if only you had answered me sooner with just a word!

In the long days of my stay in Prague it was only at Mrs and Mr Noltsch [i.e. Gabriela Horvátová and her husband] that I found some sort of social notice taken of me. Thus it happened that I asked Mrs Horvátová to hand over the telegram.

I certainly didn't want to insult or humiliate anyone else. A proof of this is that my first letters of thanks, as soon as I began to get over my illness and general stupefaction, I sent to you, to the Director Mr Schmoranz, to Mr Schütz, Miss Ungrová, Mr Lebeda, the chorus and to the most esteemed orchestra.

Next time, then, in order to avoid any sort of misunderstanding I will address my remarks during repeat performances to you, and I ask you kindly to accept them and pass them on as the occasion warrants.

Will it be all right like that? [. . .]

JP114   Janáček to Karel Kovařovic   *Brno, 4 June 1916*

Did you get my first letter?

Days full of commotion, full of excitement, full of fear and again full of hope, full of expectation, full of victory and almost stupefaction – all this had a profound effect upon me. I left Prague but felt at the same time that I would pay for it. I caught your 'flu and, having it far worse, went to bed in Brno. I am going through the recollections of all these events, how it all went, grew, ripened – and always I encounter you and your devoted work. What can I do to reward you? But I come again only with a request to you: stand by me again in my next work. It is *Brouček's Excursion, the True Excursion to the Moon*.[1] It is a *burlesque* opera, in spirit and character the complete opposite of *Jenůfa*. But blowing through it is a whiff of Bohemian pure love which mitigates the emptiness of the wit and the sharpness of the satire. May I dedicate the work to you at the head of the score as thanks for the enormous labour with which you have raised me to prominence? As a consequence I must consider my position seriously, be surprised by its eminence and perhaps believe that I am really so exceptional. Will you accept the dedication?

I have already written to you so many times and it hurt me that you

---

1 At this stage Janáček's next opera, *The Excursions of Mr Brouček*, was conceived only as a single excursion (see Chap. 5). In recommending his opera, Janáček seems to have been unaware that Kovařovic himself had composed a 'Brouček' work, incidental music for *The Excursion of Mr Brouček to the Exhibition*, a light-hearted and topical affair presented at the 1894 Ethnographic Exhibition.

never replied. Will you answer now, when you know that I am convinced of the greatness of your self-sacrificing work, when I will never forget that you came and conducted although you were sick, gravely sick.

I want to come again to Prague during the holidays. I feel happy only in that dear house amongst all those you rule over to the honour and the glory of Czech art.

Accept me again in as friendly a manner as I hasten to you with a pure heart and count the days when I will be amongst you.

I take up my pen only now to thank all those by whose efforts I have grown. I was as if in a state of stupefaction and only now feel myself coming back to life.

Karel Kovařovic to Janáček — *Prague, 8 June 1916* — JP115

I returned yesterday to Prague from a four-day holiday and found your letters.

I see that you take everyday backstage discord among some soloists too tragically.

I regarded it as necessary to inform you about it in order that the matter should not needlessly upset the excellent course of the further performances of *Jenůfa*.

Your letters have warded off that danger for good and there is no need to concern yourself any further with the matter.

From the daily papers you will have already learnt that yesterday's performance of *Jenůfa* was given before a sold-out house. You could not wish for any greater success . . .

On Monday [12 June] the performance will be *outside* the subscription series [see p.85 fn.3].

We are glad that we will welcome you again into our circle.

By the end of the month I hope that we will have given at least *ten* repeat performances.[1] This record speaks most eloquently about the *great success of the work*.

After the holidays it is planned to give *Jenůfa* as a gala performance on 18 August (the day of the Emperor's birthday).[2] Would you not like to *conduct* this performance? *It would increase not a little the glitter of the whole evening!*

1 This was too optimistic a prediction in a theatre which gave drama and ballet performances as well as opera. By the end of the season *Jenůfa* had been given eight times, which is still remarkable considering how late in the season it had been introduced. There were another eighteen performances in the next season.
2 Franz Josef I: it was his last birthday; he died in November that year.

Think about it and on Monday tell me in person how you have decided.

The dedication of *Brouček* I accept with joy and thanks as a rare gesture from the composer himself intended for all members of the company for performing *Jenůfa*.

On Monday I firmly hope that we will see one another in Prague.

Janáček did not conduct the gala performance. He replied at once (JP116, 9 June 1916) that the work could not be in better hands than Kovařovic's. Nor, despite Kovařovic's graceful acceptance of the dedication of *Brouček*, was Janáček's next opera dedicated to him (see BR208+, BR209).

PUBLICATION, TRANSLATION AND
FIRST PERFORMANCES ABROAD

The acceptance of *Jenůfa* in Prague encouraged a leading Czech publisher, Hudební matice, under its chief executive Otakar Nebuška, to consider buying out the remaining copies of the 1908 vocal score and publishing a new one. Negotiations over the publishing rights with the Club of the Friends of Art, the owners of the 1908 edition, continued throughout 1916, and were not settled until early 1917.[1] One of the questions to resolve was in what form to issue the score: Janáček's 1908 version, or the Kovařovic version. This particularly affected the end of the work.

JP117   **Otakar Nebuška to Janáček**   *Prague, 11 February 1917*

Today I have been finishing the end of *Jenůfa* and by comparing your version and Kovařovic's I see a difference between them not just in the sound, but also in the composition itself. I ask for your decision by return of post which version you would like in the vocal score. [...]

Nebuška made a compromise suggestion: to use Kovařovic's version to figure 66 (i.e. the final Maestoso, after the voices), then Janáček's. They settled for Kovařovic's: in his next letter (JP118, 16 February 1917) Nebuška described making a piano reduction of Kovařovic's ending, which is what was printed in the new score. Apart from such passages, the Hudební matice score used the old plates. It was published in May 1917 (JP119: Nebuška sent a copy to Janáček on 5 May 1917).

Negotiations for a German edition were going on at the same time. During December 1916, Schott of Mainz had shown an interest in acquiring the

1 Kundera 1948, 59–60.

work (**JP120**: Jan Löwenbach to Janáček, 5 December 1916), but by the end of the month the Schott negotiations had been abandoned in favour of those with Universal Edition in Vienna (**JP121**: Löwenbach to Janáček, 27 December 1916), with whom Janáček signed a contract on 10 December 1916 (**JP122**).

Janáček's negotiations with Universal Edition came immediately into conflict with those over the second Czech edition. Essentially, Hudební matice attempted to prevent a Czech text being printed in the Universal Edition score (e.g. **JP123**: Janáček to Universal Edition, 2 April 1917), and Universal Edition tried to limit Hudební matice to a single edition of 1000 copies and nothing further (e.g. **JP124**: Universal Edition to Janáček, 24 January 1917; **JP125**: Janáček to Universal Edition, 5 May 1917). Both plans failed. Universal Edition issued a dual-language edition, and Hudební matice and its successor companies have continued to issue a Czech vocal score. At first Universal Edition planned to use the Hudební matice plates, but soon decided that Hudební matice was being too difficult and secured Janáček's agreement to a new edition 'according to the full score' (**JP126**: Janáček to Universal Edition, 8 February 1917). By 12 March 1917 (**JP127**) Universal Edition reported to Janáček that it was negotiating with 'the best Viennese arranger, [Josef] von Wöss' to do a new piano reduction, certainly more pianistic than the 1908 reduction (which seems to be Janáček's own work).

The Universal Edition score went ahead quickly. By 3 May 1917 Janáček had received Act 1 and commented that the arrangement had been done in an expert fashion (**JP128**). He returned the Act 2 proofs on 10 May 1917 (**JP129**); part of Act 3 got lost in the post on the way to Brno, but Janáček was finally able to send the proofs back on 9 June 1917 (**JP130**). The edition was thus ready to print except that no agreement had yet been reached on the Czech text. Eventually it went ahead without any agreement. According to Janáček's wish to emphasize the central importance of the Kostelnička, the opera was entitled *Jenůfa-Její pastorkyně/Ihre Ziehtochter* (**JP131**: Universal Edition to Janáček, 26 September 1917) and a front cover made based on a drawing of Mrs Horvátová as the Kostelnička (**JP132**). Four copies of the vocal score were sent to Janáček on 4 December 1917 (**JP133**). The full score appeared less than a year later: on 9 September 1918 Universal Edition sent two copies (**JP134**).

Janáček was fortunate in the author of the German translation printed in the Universal Edition score. Max Brod, a cultured Prague German, was a novelist and writer, the friend and later biographer of Kafka. As a part-time composer himself with an interest in opera and a good understanding of Czech, he was ideally placed to translate Czech opera texts into German, and already had experience with translating two of Novák's operas. He went on to translate most of the texts of Janáček's works that Universal Edition issued. He also became one of Janáček's most fervent advocates in the German-speaking world, his first major biographer, and a much-valued, frank-speaking adviser, whose friendship with Janáček continued to the end of the composer's life. Brod himself described how the association with Janáček came about:

JP135   Max Brod on the translation of *Jenůfa*

One day the great composer Suk wrote to me quite out of the blue
that I ought to go and listen to the opera *Jenůfa* at the Prague Czech
Theatre. I listened and had my greatest artistic experience since the
beginning of the war...

The house was sold out, and with some trouble I found a place for
standing in the top gallery. I saw nothing, only listened. Suddenly
there pounded up to me the primary sounds of a recruiting song, of a
peasant dance. Tears of happiness, long missed tears, welled up into
my eyes... Oh, it was simple and good once again to be in the world!

My heart awoke!

A few months later. An unknown old man stood in my room. It
was Sunday, still quite early. A moment before, I had been sleeping
deeply. Was I still dreaming? – This head with its high, beautifully
domed forehead, twinklingly serious big open eyes, and curved
mouth: it was Goethe's head, as drawn by Stieler,[1] but transposed
here into softly Slavonic lines . . . A name sounded in my dream. 'Leoš
Janáček.' It was the composer of *Jenůfa*.

In between I had written a report in *Schaubühne* about the effect
Jenůfa had had on me.[2] Was this not indeed an extraordinary case,
that an operatic masterpiece lies around mouldering twelve years in
the offices of theatres, and then is discovered by accident, suddenly
sees the light of day, and immediately enthrals and stirs everyone
through the boundless musical forces contained in it? So that one asks
with amazement: why not earlier? Why did a generation have to die
without this emotional shock?

[. . .]

I did not want to take on the translation, I had already written a
letter of refusal to the publisher.[3] Several plans for stage works were
nearing completion. Having urgently drawn attention to Janáček's
work in a Berlin newspaper, I thought that I had done enough... Then
the Maestro came to me himself, undaunted by the long journey from
Brno. His glance bewitched me. Still more his words, whose holy

---

1 Karl Joseph Stieler (1781–1858), German painter, famous for his portraits of Goethe and
Beethoven.
2 'Tschechisches Opernglück', *Schaubühne* (16 November 1916); reprinted in Brod 1923,
17–30.
3 Lost, see Janáček 1988, 17.

naivety moves me still today.[1]

When I saw Janáček sitting in front of me, I felt: this is the sort of man that God wanted. Strong, kind, upright. And what have we made of ourselves!

Without long deliberation I gave him my promise.

Sternenhimmel: Musik- und Theaterlebnisse (1923)

Brod's charming description of the event omits to mention that he had actually invited Janáček to come that Sunday, though not specifying a time. From Brod's letter to Janáček of 28 November 1916 (**JP136**), it is clear that Janáček had already written to him expressing his pleasure at Brod's article about *Jenůfa* and suggesting a meeting. The very Sunday of their meeting, 3 December 1916, Brod and Janáček sent Universal Edition a joint telegram, stating that Brod would now do the translation (**JP137**). It took him just three months. Janáček had a copy of the 1908 vocal score sent to him (**JP138**: Janáček to Universal Edition, 21 December 1916). Brod sent back his translation act by act, and on 20 March 1917 Universal Edition reported to Janáček (**JP139**) that Brod had announced that it was finished. The translation, however, did not turn out entirely according to Universal Edition's satisfaction, and correspondence on the matter dragged on until publication and after.[2]

Much of the problem with the translation was caused by Hugo Reichenberger (1873–1938), a conductor at the Vienna Hofoper, which was now showing an interest in *Jenůfa*. Brod had translated into standard German; Reichenberger wanted an Austrian equivalent of Janáček's Moravian dialect. In the end, both got their way, with the Vienna performance adapting Brod's printed text. This probably coloured Brod's view of the Viennese première and his suggestion that Janáček had not liked it either. They had sat in a box together, with Janáček allegedly digging him in the ribs when he disliked something, and Brod coming back with very sore ribs.[3] But this is hardly the impression one gets from Janáček's own account of the rehearsals to the Prague Kostelnička, Gabriela Horvátová:

Janáček to Gabriela Horvátová   *Vienna, 12 February 1918*   JP140

How much I would have liked to have you here! You can't imagine what I am experiencing.

---

1 In a later memoir ('Jenufa Reminiszenzen', *Prager Tagblatt*, 27 October 1926) Brod recalled some of these words: 'You have made me known abroad, now you must also translate me.' When Brod tried to excuse himself through pressure of work, Janáček responded: 'I arrived today at 6 o'clock on the morning train from Brno and from 6 I have been walking to and fro in front of your house and thinking to myself all the time: "If Dr Brod takes on the thing personally, then everything will turn out well. If not, it is the end".'
2 JA ix, 16–40 provides a detailed account.
3 Susskind 1985, 51 gives Brod's description of this incident.

Today the rehearsal was already in costumes. Sets, lighting, everything as at the performance.

[I wish you could see] this magnificence of colours – 150 folk costumes – the wonderful deep stage: everything new, sparkling! The mill and that long view into magnificent mountain scenery. In the sun so that the spectator almost sweats. Recruits, with the lad from the mill on a garlanded horse – it was a set for which I longed in Prague – in vain.

Mrs Weidt[1] acts outstandingly – as directed by the producer. She is a soprano, and so she doesn't have *your* silky, dark voice, so appropriate to the action – but *she acts outstandingly. You must see her!* There are moments when one is horror-struck.

And then just think, the Jenůfa [Maria Jeritza][2] is ideal. How those two ladies vie with one another! It can't be described in words. The director [of the Vienna Hofoper] Gregor said to Mrs Weidt that she is singing a part the like of which she has never sung or known in her life.

The rehearsal went well. Tomorrow there is another just for memorizing, and the day after tomorrow the dress rehearsal.

The Czech Quartet is passing through Vienna tomorrow; they asked to be allowed in to the rehearsal. Well, they won't see much, they will just be 'marking.'[3]

Reporters are after me; but every day the local newspapers are also full of *Jenůfa*.

Do you remember how Prague was silent before the première in the National Theatre? The papers did not breathe a word about it until the very evening before the *Národní listy* carried a feuilleton by Dr Šilhan. We really know how to do ourselves down!

Director Schmoranz is coming here. Representatives from theatres in Strasbourg and Zagreb are also here already.

Today in the evening company in the Hotel Post there were also Mayor Groš and a councillor from Prague.

---

1 Lucie Weidt (1876–1940), Austrian soprano. She was one of the famous members of Mahler's ensemble in Vienna, where she sang from 1902 to 1927 and created parts there such as the Marschallin and Kundry.

2 Maria Jeritza (Marie Jedlitzková, 1887–1982), Austrian soprano. She was born in Brno and made her début in Olomouc. A member of the Vienna Staatsoper 1913–32, she also sang at Covent Garden, London, and at the New York Metropolitan Opera (the first American Jenůfa and Turandot).

3 i.e. not singing at full voice (or not at all); this rehearsal 'for memorizing' was presumably also without sets and costumes.

I just hope I can keep calm in my soul! I think I will. I go to bed early and get up at 8 o'clock.

Rehearsals last from 10 o'clock to 2.

František Mareš: 'Reminiscences of Leoš Janáček' JP141

A year and a half after the Prague première there followed the première of *Jenůfa* at the Vienna Hofoper. This was yet another big success. It was on 18 [actually 16] February 1918. It was said that the acceptance of the opera was due to the outstanding opera singer Jeritza, who urged it on the young Emperor Karl. She wanted to sing Jenůfa. Another version had it that the protectress of *Jenůfa* at the court was the Empress Zita, herself a fine musician, who came to like Jenůfa's Act 2 aria 'Zdrávas Maria' [sic]. In continual agitation Maestro Janáček awaited the news from Vienna and when rehearsals began after the New Year, he went down there frequently. He was positively excited by Jeritza's Jenůfa. The première had an unusual gala atmosphere. The court and aristocracy were present, in the orchestra a hundred musicians, a very beautiful completely authentic décor, faithfully taken from Slovácko [models], everything correct. Jeritza's voice, acting, beautiful appearance and magnificent folk costume – the finest Jenůfa Janáček had ever heard. The success was enormous. Called on after the second act by the audience, Janáček took a bow. It was arranged that after the show a group would meet up in the Hotel Post, where the Maestro was staying. I went with Janáček after the theatre, on the way to the hotel he *fainted*. In the hotel – when we finally got to it – Janáček's friends and admirers were waiting in a cheerless room. The Maestro sat amongst us glowing with joy, happy, and we really felt how after this success his work was reaching out to confront triumphantly new musical challenges.

Lidové noviny (17 February 1940)

Neither of these accounts gives any idea of the difficulties that needed to be sorted out in Vienna before the work was performed: over the text, Jeritza's illness (resulting in a delayed première), and, most seriously, a protest by German nationalists which needed court intervention for the opera to go ahead.[1] But with the success of *Jenůfa* in the Austro-Hungarian capital, the opera's and the composer's international reputation began. Before the end of 1918 Otto Klemperer had taken up the work in Cologne. A particularly successful production in Berlin under Erich Kleiber in 1924 opened the way to virtually all the smaller German opera houses. By Janáček's death in 1928,

1 See for instance Vogel 1981, 226–8.

the work had been produced sixty times outside Czechoslovakia.[1] But the pleasure in this success which the elderly composer should have enjoyed in his last years was embittered by the name that had blighted the early years of *Jenůfa* – Karel Kovařovic.

KOVAŘOVIC'S REVISIONS

The changes that Marie Calma-Veselá urged Janáček to allow in order to facilitate Kovařovic's acceptance of *Jenůfa* were cuts. Although he had used a prose text for his libretto, Janáček had not jettisoned the notion of a regular phrase structure and had often achieved this by straight repetition, either in the orchestra or in the voice part (where it was easier to repeat a verbal phrase than to adapt another to match it). Many of these 'rhyming repetitions' disappeared in Kovařovic's version: one phrase remained where Janáček had two or more.

Cuts were not new to the opera. Janáček had made them himself when he came to prepare the score for publication in 1908. The long 'explanation aria' that the Kostelnička gave after stopping the dancing in Act 1 was not printed in the 1908 vocal score. Several numbers were shortened (notably the 'Každý párek' and 'A vy muzikanti' ensembles in Act 1; and the Jenůfa and Laca duet at the end of Act 2). Nor was Janáček too proud to take advice from others. Many of these cuts had been suggested by the conductor Cyril Metoděj Hrazdira when preparing the score for its revival in October 1906 (see JP48).

The other respect in which Kovařovic's version differed from Janáček's was in its orchestration. By woodwind doubling, by the substitution of horns for Janáček's rougher trombones, and, most strikingly, by augmenting the final scene with a grandiose canonic apotheosis, Kovařovic skilfully smoothed out and expanded Janáček's roughcast orchestration to approximate to the sophisticated expectations of an audience acquainted with Strauss and his Czech imitators. While it was the cuts which the Veselýs thought might be the stumbling block in Janáček's acceptance of Kovařovic's revision, Kovařovic's revisions to the orchestration – which went through on the nod – were the source of much bitterness later, right up to the end of Janáček's life. It was a question which Janáček eventually saw as a slur on his own ability as a composer.

After its successful run of performances in Prague *Jenůfa* was now played everywhere in Kovařovic's version, even in Brno, where new parts had to be made. The second (Czech) edition by Hudební matice (1917) printed the complete score, though indicated the cuts. (Even remaining copies of the 1908 edition were offered for sale with an errata page[2] listing possible cuts and printing a handful of the altered passages.) The German–Czech vocal

---

1 Přibáňová 1984, 11–15.
2 See Simeone 1991, 21.

score (1917) and full score and performance materials (1918) published by Universal Edition simply omitted the passages cut by Kovařovic, and the full score included Kovařovic's revisions without comment or even announcement, hence perpetuating a version of the score which supplanted Janáček's own. For Kovařovic's work Universal Edition paid a flat K300, a sum which at Schmoranz's suggestion was deposited in the National Theatre's Widows and Orphans fund (JP142: Universal Edition to Janáček, 3 January 1917).

Kovařovic also took performance royalties. On 27 October 1919 (JP143, to Schmoranz) Janáček queried a payment slip: from his 10 per cent royalty of K758.65 he had received only K556.35. He knew that Mrs Preissová should receive '1 per cent' (in fact the contract specified one sixth of Janáček's royalty); where had the rest gone? According to Schmoranz's reply (JP144, 2 November 1919), it had gone to Kovařovic, who received 1 per cent of the gross takings, even before Mrs Preissová had had her portion.

At this stage Janáček may not have been clear what the 1 per cent was for, though his surprise later (see JP147) that money was being paid to Kovařovic's widow suggests that he assumed it was for his conducting rather than for his revisions. Apart from Janáček's obvious exasperation that Kovařovic was making money out of *Jenůfa* (on Schmoranz's reply above he scrawled 'I call this villainy and robbery'), there is no indication at this stage that Janáček was not happy with what Kovařovic had done to his score. In his letters to his wife during the rehearsals he had continually praised Kovařovic's dedication to the score and the wonderful sound of the orchestra. A former Organ School pupil employed in the National Theatre orchestra, Pavel Dědeček, recalls how when hearing the ending of the opera in Kovařovic's much-altered arrangement, Janáček was evidently moved and 'almost incapable of speech, saying only to himself "L-l-l-like that, please"' (JP145). Some commentators, beginning with Václav Kašlík (1938, 12), have even argued on the basis of a sheet of corrections, some in Janáček's hand, that Janáček participated in the most far-reaching of Kovařovic's changes, the canonic finale to Act 3. Janáček's hostility to Kovařovic's revisions dates from 1923, three years after Kovařovic's death. It was triggered by a strong letter from Mrs Anna Kovařovicová, widow of the conductor.

Anna Kovařovicová to Janáček   *Prague, 28 May 1923*   JP146

I notify you, reluctantly – but with every justification – that today in the National Theatre I was not paid the 1 per cent royalty from the last performance of the opera *Jenůfa*.

Allow me to remark that should this royalty not be paid by Wednesday this month [30 May] – I forbid, I will not allow the opera *Jenůfa* to be performed in the arrangement by my late husband.

In 1922 Schmoranz had retired from the National Theatre and was replaced as director by Jaroslav Šafařovič. While Schmoranz had participated in

creative decisions such as repertory, Šafařovič's post now became purely administrative and concerned with finance. It seems he took a fresh look
at the company's commitments; stopping the 1 per cent payment to
Kovařovic's heirs may have been one of his ways of economizing.[1] Janáček
turned at once to Ostrčil, now head of opera at the theatre:

JP147   **Janáček to Otakar Ostrčil**   *Prague, 29 May 1923*

I was today surprised by the enclosed letter. I would have answered
Mrs Kovařovicová, but I don't know her address.

I ask you therefore to tell her the following:

Mr Kovařovic asked a fee from the publisher for his 'retouching.'
If I'm not mistaken[2] it was K 500; I think that the publisher paid out
that sum, otherwise it would not have got printed.

At the same time I will ask for confirmation from the publisher of
this sum. The matter was surely settled by that [sum].

In the few last performances of *Jenůfa* I saw in the accounts 1 per
cent to Mr Kovařovic. I was not able to explain it in any way –
[since] he was no longer conducting *Jenůfa*.

It was inexplicable also for the following reasons, that he did the
retouching of his own free will, without any sort of agreement,
whether verbal or written.

It's possible that the publisher discharged the K 500 through some
special agreement with the late Kovařovic.

I don't know about this.

I am curious about the answer of the publisher.

As far as her ban is concerned then, let Mrs Kovařovicová kindly
wait it out until the matter is cleared up.

I was in agreement with the request for K 500, but I don't know
any reasons why they should go on paying 1 per cent for work that
has already been paid.

I will come to Prague on Thursday morning [31 May] and will
look for you in the theatre around 10 o'clock.

PS   I ask for Mrs Kovařovicová's letter [JP146] back.

Ostrčil presumably made his response to Janáček in person on 31 May
(there is no record of any reply to Janáček's letter). Universal Edition
responded briefly to Janáček's inquiry with the comment that they were not

---

1 Němeček 1968–9, ii, 86, fn.165.
2 He was; K 300 was paid (see JP142).

in any direct business contact with Kovařovic and had looked through their correspondence from the early years without finding any reference to such a sum (JP148, 30 May 1923; they overlooked JP142, see JP161–). Janáček's first tactic was to bargain with Mrs Kovařovicová:

Janáček to Anna Kovařovicová   *Brno, 21 June 1923*   JP149

You must surely acknowledge that two people cannot make a contract at the expense of a third – without the knowledge of that third. If up till now the administration of the National Theatre paid the sum of 1 per cent from its own [funds] that was its affair. But to pay it from mine without my permission is unheard of!

    You, Madam, are in the right, but I am also.

    In order to avoid a quarrel with the administration of the National Theatre – the consequences of which surely would serve neither you nor me – I will voluntarily and without prejudice to my legal position and only for your person permit half a percent to be taken off from every performance of *Jenůfa* at the National Theatre.

This ploy, however, seems not to have worked.

Janáček to Otakar Ostrčil   *Luhačovice, 21 September 1923*   JP150

Fourteen years he refused my *Jenůfa* and twenty-one years later Mr Dvořák (son of Dr Antonín Dvořák) and Mrs Kovařovicová are continuing this work.

    To defend my honour as a composer there remains nothing but for me publicly to reject the orchestral additions of Kovařovic to *Jenůfa* as unnecessary, undertaken arbitrarily by Kovařovic – for whatever reasons.

    Kovařovic himself never asked for any fee from me for his 'bandmasterish' work for performances, even when these additions of his were published with his knowledge, and now the appetite of Mr Dvořák and Mrs Kovařovicová is growing.

    It is necessary for me to repudiate these additions particularly for the reason that gossip is now circulating in Prague that Kovařovic did all the orchestration of *Jenůfa*, just as in Brno stories are being spread that *Káťa Kabanová* was orchestrated by God knows who!

    Do you think that such orchestral additions in which there is not a chord apart from mine, in which there is not a motif apart from mine, which are simply a consolidation of the orchestral impression – are the creative work of a composer?

For fourteen years[1] *Jenůfa* was given without Kovařovic's orchestral additions – let it go on being given like that. And anyone who wants them let them buy them himself from the greedy Mrs Kovařovicová.

On the same day Janáček wrote both to Universal Edition (JP151) and his Brno lawyer Dr Jaroslav Lecian (JP152) pronouncing a ban on performances of *Jenůfa* in Czechoslovakia which used Kovařovic's orchestration. Abroad it was a different matter. As he wrote to Lecian, these performances 'are given on the basis of the *printed* score which contain Kovařovic's orchestral additions. [...] This is something which Universal Edition will have to sort out.'

A month later Janáček drafted a letter (apparently unsent) to the Prague National Theatre asking formally for Kovařovic's revisions to be omitted from performances of *Jenůfa* (JP153, 1 November 1923), and the day before, to Lecian (JP154, 30 October 1923), itemizing his reasons. Most are familiar from his earlier letters, but the seventh and final point was new: 'The reasons why he used so much red ink in the score will lie elsewhere than in compositional necessity: it is the fourteen-year[2] refusal of *Jenůfa* on Mr Kovařovic's part and his ultimately unavoidable capitulation.' A couple of days later, Janáček consulted a Prague lawyer, Dr Leopold Katz.

JP155   **Janáček to Dr Leopold Katz**   *Brno, 3 November 1923*

On the recommendation of Mr Václav Štech,[3] I wish to turn to you for advice. It concerns purging the libel from my work *Jenůfa*.

Would you kindly receive me on Monday, 5 November?

I would come towards 10 o'clock.

Whatever the threat of damages that may have been contained in Janáček's brief explanation, Katz took a more careful line, explaining to the Kovařovics' representative, Dr Otokar Dvořák, that since Kovařovic's work on *Jenůfa* was not creative, it was not covered by copyright law. Kovařovic's estate did not have the right to forbid performances and would, moreover, have to be responsible for any loss to Janáček that would be caused by such a ban (JP156: Katz to Lecian, 29 November 1923). Mrs Kovařovicová's party did not accept this, nor, as it turned out, was it practicable for Janáček to forbid performances of *Jenůfa* without Kovařovic's revisions. So in the new year it was decided to take the matter to arbitration.

1 Only nine years in fact: 1904–13.
2 Thirteen years, counting from the first submission in April 1903 to the first Prague performance in May 1916.
3 See p.150, fn.1.

Janáček to František Neumann   *Brno, 1 January 1923 [1924]*   JP157

You know best what is composition and what is retouching. A pack of strange people wants to place both types of work on the same level – and exploit me.

I wanted simply in future to ban the revisions of the late Kovařovic, but that would create difficulties for the theatres; therefore I have agreed to a peaceful settlement of the whole matter.

As my experts I am asking for you and Mr Ostrčil. Two would also be added from the other side. The fifth you will choose yourselves. I ask that the fifth be knowledgeable in law, either a judge or a lawyer. I draw your attention to Dr Löwenbach.

I have drafted the questions myself. Other questions could be formulated.

See from my questions that I am meeting Mrs Kovařovicová – more than halfway – since I was told that she is in need.

The following questions were sent to Neumann, Ostrčil and the arbitration commission:

Janáček's questions for the arbitration commission   JP158

1. Does the importance of *Jenůfa* and its success on stage depend on the revisions of the late Karel Kovařovic?
2. If *Jenůfa* were given successfully from 1904 to 1916 under the directorship of Doubravský, Lacina, Jiřikovský[1] and under the conductors C. Hrazdira, Winkler,[2] and *accepted in its original form* by the late Karel Kovařovic for performance at the Prague National Theatre, were further, unasked-for revisions necessary?
3. Did these reorchestrations belong in the domain of conductor and head of opera *if he did them of his own free will and got himself paid for them by the theatre management*? And must the composer pay for them although for as long as the late Karel Kovařovic lived he *never asked for anything from him*?
4. If the late Karel Kovařovic came to an arrangement with the theatre administration – *without my knowledge* – for recompense of

---

1 Directors of the Brno National Theatre during this period were: Alois Doubravský (1903–4); František Lacina (1904–5); Antoš Josef Frýda (1905–9); František Lacina (1909–15); Václav Jiřikovský (1915–19).
2 Josef Winkler (1885–1942), conductor at the Brno National Theatre 1907–8, 1909–11 and 1912–19; he succeeded Hrazdira and conducted most of the subsequent performances of *Jenůfa* in Brno until the Neumann era.

1 per cent, which he received, and I now at the time of this dispute would like to give the widow of the late Karel Kovařovic for her person voluntarily 1 per cent of my royalties from the performance of *Jenůfa* at the Prague National Theatre, *are these revisions thereby sufficiently remunerated?*

5. If these revisions were printed in the score with the knowledge of the late Karel Kovařovic and without *any reservations or without a request for any recompense* from the composer and from the publisher am I now obliged to pay the widow of the late Kovařovic anything for them?

Ostrčil, one of Janáček's appointees, dropped out immediately:

JP159 Otakar Ostrčil to Janáček   *Prague, 3 January 1924*

I ask you earnestly not to count on me as an expert in the question of the *Jenůfa* revisions. You know yourself that the job is not an enviable one. Apart from that I have a difficult position as Kovařovic's successor. Any sort of judgement to his detriment from my side would be taken as an attempt to belittle Kovařovic's artistic work. Finally I fear that among the experts named by Mrs Kovařovicová I would meet with one gentleman with whom I do not wish to meet.

Forgive me, then, for my decision to remain outside this delicate affair.

Janáček did not really forgive Ostrčil; relations were cool on Janáček's side for the rest of his life, although Ostrčil continued to conduct Janáček's works, including the Prague premières of *The Cunning Little Vixen* and *The Makropulos Affair*, and a new production (1926) of *Jenůfa*.

JP160 Janáček to Otakar Ostrčil   *Brno, 4 March 1924*

I'm writing in this way, although you left me high and dry in the dispute with the heirs of the late Kovařovic.

But no matter. A letter was found at Universal Edition from the late Kovařovic and Director Schmoranz in which [Kovařovic] asks for K 300 for the revisions and the right to print and play them – for the [pension] fund of the soloists at the National Theatre. And a receipt was found [showing] that the money was paid. In this way I was cleared, for I knew nothing whatsoever about all this action.

For a year and a half the heirs with Mr Dvořák have tormented me, threatening K 60,000 [damages]!

Thus the matter is settled. [. . .]

[KK86]

It seems that Universal Edition had a more thorough look in their files, for on 12 February 1924 Janáček thanked them for 'the Kovařovic–Schmoranz copies' (**JP161** – this is clearly related to JP142). This led to the collapse of the Kovařovic case; as Katz wrote to Janáček on 19 February 1924 (**JP162**), Dr Dvořák pronounced it was no longer possible to defend Mrs Kovařovicová's position, and he now regarded the matter as closed. So it should have been, except that when the Prague National Theatre revived *Jenůfa* in 1926, it now began to calculate an 11% royalty: 10% to Janáček (less Mrs Preissová's sixth) and 1% to Mrs Kovařovicová 'which had been allowed by the Directorate' (**JP163**: Dr Šafařovič to Janáček, 10 July 1926). The fact that Mrs Kovařovicová's 1 per cent now ate into the National Theatre's takings rather than Janáček's was not enough to pacify the composer. As he wrote to Dr Löwenbach in Prague, 'If the Directorate wants to give a free gift to Mrs Kovařovicová let it give it from performances of *The Dogheads* etc. [. . .] I cannot forget the wrong done to me by Mr Kovařovic or the unprecedented torment when Mrs Kovařovicová wanted to squeeze K 60,000 out of me' (**JP164**, 8 September 1926). Despite advice from Löwenbach that Janáček could not stop the National Theatre doing want they wanted to with their own money (**JP165**, 11 September 1926), the matter rumbled on for a further year, with Janáček threatening not to offer any of his new works to the National Theatre (**JP166**: Janáček to Löwenbach, 15 September 1926), a threat which turned out to be empty since *The Makropulos Affair*, which Janáček clearly had in mind, was duly presented in Prague in March 1928.

Though Mrs Kovařovicová dropped her case, Janáček lost this argument. The Kovařovic version was played exclusively since the sole publisher of the full score and performance materials, Universal Edition, issued only this version. Even in 1969, when a new edition was issued, changes by later conductors were carefully footnoted, and apart from adding the Kostelnička 'explanation aria' (which Janáček himself had excluded from the 1908 vocal score) Janáček's own version was ignored. Furthermore, the Kovařovic family took up the case again and in 1963–4 secured a ruling from a specially appointed commission that the Kovařovic revision was a creative collaboration which had contributed to the work's success worldwide.[1] Although Janáček's pupil Břetislav Bakala, using the original Brno parts, gave a performance on Brno Radio in 1941 of excerpts in Janáček's version and was one of the few experts of the time who claimed that Janáček's version was perfectly usable at it stood,[2] it was not until Charles Mackerras's Decca recording of 1982 that it was possible to hear *Jenůfa* as the composer intended it.

1 Němeček 1968–9, ii, 86 fn.136.
2 Article in *Rytmus*, viii (1942–3), 85; reprinted in Štědroň 1946, 172–3.

4 Fate

OS1 Marie Stejskalová's reminiscences (1959)

After Olga's death and the Prague refusal of *Jenůfa* [the master] went for a cure to Luhačovice. He was sitting there at a table alone, sad and ailing, when suddenly an unknown beautiful woman sent him a bouquet of crimson roses. He went to thank her, and so they got acquainted. This was Mrs Kamila Urválková, whose husband was a forestry official in Zaháji u Dolních Kralovic in Bohemia. She was in Luhačovice for heart treatment. Mrs Urválková had a strange penchant: she always carried three roses in her hand. She told the master about her life, and that she wanted to become an actress, and about her unhappy love for the conductor Čelanský. The master decided that he would write an opera about it.

OS2 Janáček's autobiography (1924)

And she was one of the most beautiful of women. Her voice was like that of a viola d'amore. The Luhačovice *Slanice*[1] was in the scorching heat of the August sun.

Why did she walk about with three fiery roses and why did she relate the story of her young life?

And why was its end so strange?

---

[1] Local name for the the spa, a reference to the salty earth out of which the curative salt waters come.

['and soon there came the melancholy echo of everything;
the love-story incomplete']

Why did her lover disappear as if the earth had swallowed him up?
No sign of him at all.

Why was the conductor's baton more like a dagger to the other
man?

And the work, sighing in tone, feminine in its diction, was called
Osud-Fatum.

Janáček met Kamila Urválková in August 1903 at the Moravian spa of
Luhačovice, where she was on holiday, apparently with her husband and
five-year-old boy.[1] She was twenty-eight years old. Janáček was captivated:
'The most beautiful lady I have ever met', he wrote on her fan.[2] He was
particularly taken by her low, melodious voice which he compared to a viola
d'amore, and thereafter smuggled this archaic instrument into his scores as
an erotic symbol. Janáček himself was alone in Luhačovice, his life empty
after the death of Olga in February that year and the refusal of *Jenůfa* in
Prague. But he was not so obsessed by his own sorrows that he ignored the
holiday society around him.

Janáček to Kamila Urválková   *[undated, ?October 1903]*   OS3

[...] I have written a feuilleton for the critical journal, *Hlídka*. It is
entitled 'My Luhačovice.' You know: just notes, just snatches of
tunes from speech and overheard talks. People will be amazed that I
have noticed them! Mrs Koťátková, the Jewish women, the booksel-
ler's wife, 'broken umbrella', the nightwatchman, the bakers, servant
girls and so on.

---

1 Janáček arrived about 12 August 1903 (Štědroň 1939, 23). As Theodora Straková (1956,
212) has pointed out, it is not clear from Janáček's correspondence whether Mrs Urválková
was together with her family at Luhačovice. Janáček's notations of their speech in his
notebook, and in his article in *Hlídka* (OS4) imply that they were with her.
2 Štědroň 1959b, 160.

Do you think that you're missing there? Far from it! You are there with your husband's three Our Fathers [as penance] after confession before the wedding, and your little boy with the classic answer to the question: 'What is love?'. *Enthusiastic admiration is devoted to the musicality of your voice.* And that theatrical air with which you know how to talk sometimes is documented by many examples. [...]

[JP21, OS7]

OS4   Janáček: 'My Luhačovice'

The speech melodies of the *violetta d'amour* [viola d'amore] imposed their strange fascination. They were brought alive with an almost theatrical power.

They fell like evening shadows suddenly turning into unhappy memories and then immediately began to laugh with the golden lightness of heartfelt merriment. Let's look at several tunes of this type [...]

['I am an excellent actress! Applaud me, applaud me!']

And there followed straightaway a heart-rending, tearful laugh, which broke into new melodies before one became aware of the first one.

'What is love?', they ask her five-year-old boy. I hear the well-mimicked reply:

['When Nana and Johan love one another!']

'He set me three 'Our Fathers' as a penance', remarked the future husband:

['Me too; do we have the same sins!?']

childishly inquired the happy bride.

Hlídka, xx (1903)

Several elements from this extract found their way into Janáček's next opera. The nightwatchman, the bakers, the servant girls and other minor characters disappeared during revisions to the first libretto, but the answer given by Mrs Urválková's little boy survived into the final form of the work. And there are other parallels such as the sudden intrusion of 'unhappy memories' in Janáček's article and the 'bitter memories' ['trpké vzpomínky'] aroused by the red roses the heroine is given soon after the beginning of the opera. Both result in a sudden change of atmosphere.

Many of the questions Janáček posed in his account of *Fate* (OS2) cannot be answered today, but we can guess at some of the characters, whose names were only thinly disguised in the opera. The conductor, for instance, called Lenský in some scenes of the opera, was Ludvík Vítězslav Čelanský (1870–1931). Čelanský's one-act opera, written to his own libretto and given nine performances at the Prague National Theatre between 1897 and 1899, was called *Kamila*. Its title role was alleged to be an unsympathetic portrait of Mrs Kamila Urválková. Depicted as attractive though superficial, the operatic Kamila conducts an ostentatious flirtation with a visitor, causing her faithful, if sensitive, poet–lover Viktor to abandon her. Was 'Viktor' Čelanský's portrait of himself? His middle name was Vítězslav, the Czech equivalent of Viktor, and by 1903 he had certainly 'disappeared', in the course of an itinerant career, to Lwów, Kiev and Warsaw. If his baton (Čelanský was a well-known conductor) was more of a 'dagger' to the other man, this may indicate that Mrs Urválková regarded his opera as a character assassination of herself and her husband. And perhaps she suggested that it was Janáček's chivalrous duty, as an opera composer, to write a sequel which would clear her name. 'The Star of Luhačovice' was Janáček's response. This provisional title was a reference to Kamila Urválková's dazzling appearance in Luhačovice society and suggested that hers would be the leading part.

OS5   Kamila Urválková to Janáček   *2 October 1903*

[...] Are you working hard, how is 'The Star of L[uhačovice]', is it finished yet? Will you dedicate it to me? At least I will have a constant reminder of those unforgettable days at Luhačovice. My God, how time has flown! [...]

This is part of a long, rambling and self-absorbed letter from Mrs Urválková, which shows signs of the mental problems that began to cloud her life. But one sentence stands out and provided the future title of the work: 'It is fate which pets you, spoils you and then casts you aside into the trap from which there is no escape.' Janáček took up this reference to fate in a later letter. His interpretation, however, was characteristically positive – 'We make our own fates ourselves' – and immediately he shed some of his teaching duties in order to compose a new opera.

OS6   Janáček to Kamila Urválková   *[Brno,] 9 October 1903*

[...] As an imperial and royal music teacher, I am applying to be retired, so that I can devote myself wholly to composition and literary work. There are times on the horizon for which I have waited all my life. Shall I live to enjoy happier ones? Will my spirit be capable of more splendid work? I think so – though who knows what's going on in my brain. Things are happening so feverishly in my whole body that it seems only guesswork or a miracle can explain it. It's up to God and to fate! We make our own fates ourselves. I know that I have painted black upon black in opera; gloomy music – as was my spirit. What I'd like now is a libretto that is fresh, modern, bubbling over with life and elegance – the 'story of a child' of our time. Oh, but who will write it for me? I have many details for it myself; I'm told that I know how to handle words – but I am frightened among literary people. And those who offer their services to me know only the coarse life of the tavern; and have no notion of the spirit which blows through all of life, that it can be found quite near at hand, in ourselves, in the society well known to us – so charming, so piquant, with such surprising songs and amazing scenes. They have no notion of this, these literary people, because they don't know this life. Oh, who will write me a new libretto? [...]

[JP20]

Janáček to Kamila Urválková   *[undated, ?October 1903]*   OS7

[...] But I have no peace. I drive myself on further – just as if I felt this: do it, do it while there is time, there is so little of it!

You know that I am looking for a libretto. A modern one. I don't know a writer who would suit me. Everything is artificial, nothing is natural, completely true to life.

I know my own inner life best; unfortunately my life does not have as many romantic adventures as the stage demands.

And imagination? Let it dream up the necessary scenes!

I want to have Act 1 completely realistic, drawn from life at a spa. There is a wealth of motifs there!

Act 2 is to be actually a *hallucination*. No more reality, instead the mind, provoked almost to a nervous breakdown, propels the action further to the point where it is hard to say whether is it real or a hallucination, a delusion.

While the setting of Act I is magnificent spa scenery, Act 2 ought to reveal the extravagant interior of ladies' boudoirs, the scenery of southern landscapes.

Act 3 will be strange.

It is the great hall, the ceremonial chamber of the Conservatory. The students assemble – ladies and gentlemen. The usual student high spirits, pranks. On a wall hangs a poster of an opera – its name? I don't know yet. Perhaps 'The Three Roses' or 'The Angel's Song'.

The students argue about the opera. Whether real or imaginary, the second act was downright psychopathic. It is drawn from the life of the artist. Smetana heard a *single* note with elementary force in his brain – and he was ill. With my artist it will be worse. He ends his opera, with far greater agitation, at the second act. The professor asks his students: 'Suppose you were to plunge the white-hot passion of love's real pain and bliss into that frothed-up blood?'

'He might go mad', replies a student.

'They say that he went mad', points out the professor. 'His life story is not even well known – he was a mediocre composer.'

Thus would end the opera.

I am beginning work with the aid of the writer *Fedora Tálská*. [...]

[JP21, OS3]

This is the earliest scenario of *Fate*. It is striking that even in this letter to the person who inspired the work, there is no sign at all of her operatic counterpart: only of the composer. While the first two acts are described only in terms of setting and atmosphere, with Act 2 bringing about an unstated and possibly imaginary crisis, Act 3 is surprisingly specific in its plot, which remained with only a few changes in the final version.

In the course of the next couple of months Janáček fleshed out his scenario. The results were dramatized and versified by Fedora Bartošová (1884–1941), a young schoolteacher, and friend of the late Olga.[1]

OS8   **Fedora Bartošová to Vladimír Helfert**   *Bratislava, 4 December 1933*

It was at the beginning of November 1903 – about a week after All Saints' Day, when Leoš Janáček invited me to his house. As a teacher, I had come from Sudoměřice near Strážnice to see my mother in Brno for three days, into the old house of Mrs Kusá-Fantová in Klášterní náměstí [Monastery Square],[2] where at that time we lived and were neighbours with Janáček and his wife Zdenka. (Olga, their daughter, was already dead by then.)

It was not the first time that I had been into the Janáčeks' flat, for while she was alive I had visited Olga quite frequently. As children we had played together. Later we used to discuss serious things, especially when Olga returned ill from Russia, which country she talked about a lot, and with enjoyment. But – by then poor Olga, always delicate and translucent, was marked out for death – and everyone guessed it only too well.

So, we all went into the Janáčeks' flat respectfully and with bated breath. Behind the large dining room was Leoš Janáček's study, where he escorted me that time in November. I had not known in advance the real purpose of the invitation; I knew only that it would be a 'literary' conversation. At that time I had written and published a few poems and by a roundabout way I had somehow learnt that Janáček liked their form. I thought the visit would be about some song or other. But – Janáček came with a much greater matter – quite grandiose for me. He told me that he planned to work on an opera to be called either 'The Crimson Roses' or 'The Fiery Roses'. He was already thinking about the overall effects and the main characters:

1 Bartošová's modest and brief career as a poet is mentioned in Miloslav Hýsek's posthumous memoirs of literary Brno (1970, 95–7). She published her earliest poems in school magazines; Janáček may have noticed the three poems published in the *Lidové noviny* on 16 February 1903, ten days before Olga's death. But he muddled her name. Her earliest poems were published under the pseudonym of Kamila Talská (after the maiden name of her mother, Josefina Talská). Bartošová seems also to have had musical talents, composing possibly both music and words of an ode in honour of Franz Josef's sixty years as Austrian emperor (1908). She married Dr Josef Lavický in 1915, taught for a while, and moved with her husband to Bratislava (1924–36). I am grateful to Dr Eva Drlíková for this information.
2 Now Mendlovo náměstí [Mendel Square].

about Živný the composer (right from the beginning I fancied that Živný and Janáček were one and the same person), about Míla Válková (this was the beautiful lady whose photograph [see Plate 5a] he had on his writing desk), about the spa scenery of Luhačovice, which played a big part in his life. There he relived his musical inspirations, cured his physical ailments, and strengthened and stimulated his nerves, which were overwrought as is often the case with a choleric person. He talked about a musical conservatory – I knew that he had in mind the Organ School, which was his joy and the field in which, like the ploughman, he sowed his seeds. As he talked, his eyes sparkled and I knew that his imagination was filling out scenes from his life that he had lived through – but where the boundaries were was difficult for me to determine.

I went away enthusiastically from this first 'consultation' with Janáček, promising that I would try my best to understand him, and comply with his wishes and give form to his thoughts. He himself would write the action and the individual scenes and I would put them into verse.

And so Janáček's scene sketches trailed after me to Sudoměřice; they were quite detailed and on the whole I did not change them, but simply put most of them to verse. In the letters that supplemented the scrolls he sent Janáček explained his characters, described them, justified their entrances and their actions. But he also sometimes dealt in his letters with characters and details that later dropped out of the work altogether. [. . .]

[os22, os28]

On 9 November 1903 Janáček stopped teaching at the Teachers' Institute in Brno on the grounds of ill health[1] and set to work immediately on the libretto. He sent Bartošová his scenario in four batches: Act 1 (12 and 17 November), Act 2 (29 November) and Act 3 (8 December). Bartošová did her part equally quickly: 'I had the first act finished on 25 November 1903, Act 2 Scene 1 on 4 December 1903. Later I wrote Act 2 Scene 2, and Act 3 was written up, copied and finished on 21 December 1903 – thus before my departure for the Christmas holidays.'[2] Additions and corrections however continued into the new year. One thing that emerges from the correspondence is how fluid and changeable was Janáček's scenario: he was basically

---

1 Štědroň 1959b, 179. Janáček's application for leave was granted on 12 January 1904; he was permanently retired in October 1904.
2 Dates for Janáček's work are taken from his letters printed below; dates for Bartošová's work are stated in her letter to Vladimír Helfert (os8), and corroborated by dates on the libretto itself.

making up the story as he went along. Even when sending Act 2 on 29 November he did not know the ending (OS15) and several months after Bartošová's work was finished he was making radical changes affecting the motivations and mutual relationships of the chief characters (OS23 and OS24). Janáček's piecemeal scenario has not survived, but it is possible to form an impression of it from the surviving correspondence printed below and from Bartošová's original libretto.[1]

OS9   **Janáček to Fedora Bartošová**   *Brno, 12 November 1903*

I am sending you a part of the sketch – until the appearance of the main characters.

First therefore, I ask you to provide a *general stylization*.

Second, to develop [the sketch], filling it out, *where necessary making complete changes* in those scenes based on *real life* which I have sketched with a few words. I have marked this with red pencil, 1., 2., 3.

The scene [marked with a wavy line] could close with a combination of those various voices all over the promenade: I would say a 'festive hymn' to the godlike beauty of nature.

Into this brilliance the main character, *Mrs Míla Válková*, would enter.

The form of verse that I have in mind is that which Pushkin uses in *Onegin*. e.g.

> *Já na formu již myslil plánu*
> *a jak by rek as nazván byl*
> *a prozatím jsem do románu*
> *již první hlavu dokončil; atd*
>
> [I've drawn a plan and a projection,
> the hero's name's decided too.
> Meanwhile my novel's opening section
> is finished, and I've looked it through[2] etc.]

You know of course the overall contents, as I explained it to you in person; I think, therefore, that you will be able to work in stages. I would like to get on now with composing the music and therefore am

---

1 Bartošová's libretto and the fair copy sent to Janáček are held in BmJA, L10 and L11, and are described in Straková 1957, 133 ff.

2 The opening of the final canto (LX) in Chap.1 of Pushkin's *Eugene Onegin*, in the English translation by Sir Charles Johnston, reproduced by permission of Penguin Books Ltd. Janáček quotes from the Czech translation by V. A. Jung (Prague: Otto, n.d.), a copy of which survives in his library (BmJA, J123). The metre and verse form of both closely match those of the Russian original.

sending you this section in the hope that in the stillness of your village you will soon have it done.

Please fit the underlined sentences, questions, answers to the metre.

The music of this part is carried by a quiet conversational melody; it gets quieter during the Angelus and builds up and grows to ceremonial strength. [...]

Fedora Bartošová to Janáček   *Sudoměřice, 16 November 1903*   OS10

I will set to work with joy. I aim to send off what I have done at the end of the week.

I won't launch into any excessive changes of scenes. It depends on what you yourself will decide. Some figures I see vividly before me. It is only perhaps Živný I don't know where to place. Perhaps in that category of spa guests who observe life and are thus in the most direct contact with the audience?

Is he not perhaps the *main* character?

The verse is coming on well – it happens to be my favourite metre. I hope it won't be amiss if mixed rhymes occasionally occur (*abba* instead of *abab*)?

I am worried also about making scenes tediously long.

I think it would be better to compress *more* action into a *shorter* time-span. One, two, let the puppets play . . .

Here and there throw in a little humour – something to amuse people and make them laugh. [...]

I am putting the words for the hymn to godlike nature into the mouths of four people with artistic thoughts and feelings (perhaps divided somewhat symmetrically: two gentlemen and two ladies; or can I add more people?).

Do forgive me please, Mr Director, if I have not quite understood some places. I neither disown my work in advance, nor praise it.

If you like I could perhaps rework the beginning some time later once I am more experienced (they say that the very opening ought to arrest and excite one!). At the beginning of the holidays I could take a look at some spas – perhaps Luhačovice – which we have in Moravia.

Živný – the Czech word means 'life-giving' – was of course the main character, as Janáček explains in his next letter. His comments on the 'hymn to God's nature' for mixed quartet helped turn this into the joyous chorus in praise of the sun that opens the opera (in its final form).

OS11   Janáček to Fedora Bartošová   *[undated, postmarked 17 November 1903]*

From this continuation you will probably guess who is at the centre of the action.

[...]

In the spas, especially in Luhačovice, a beautiful sunny day is a joy to all the guests. There are few such days. When the sun appears there is no other topic of conversation. Everyone praises it: it's from those cries of joy, sometimes muted, sometimes loud, that the hymn must finally sound as a chorus.

Thus *many* people can take part in it – everyone in fact who is on stage.

The method of rhyming will not get in my way at all.

The first act takes place during the *day*.

The beginning: into the quiet of the morning, words spring up only here and there among the groups of people who have recently appeared.

The wave of spa life now rises – and at night sinks strangely.

I look forward to your work. I will start composing at once.

OS12   Fedora Bartošová to Janáček   *[undated, Sudoměřice, before 25 November 1903]*

So I am sending you Scene 4 with its additions and the completed scenes 8, 9 and 10.[1]

If you would like me to make corrections to some of the previous ones, do please tell me. I would be glad to give complete satisfaction.

I am aiming again to work on steadily during the evenings, when I write most happily and most easily.

OS13   Janáček to Fedora Bartošová   *[undated, postmarked 25 November 1903]*

I won't send you Act 2 in stages; I want you to have it whole and judge it in its finished state; [to see] whether in Act 2 there will be enough drama, strength and interest.

---

1 Scene 4 became the opening of the opera after Janáček jettisoned the first three scenes (see OS18); scenes 8–10 comprise the choir rehearsal scene and reactions to it by the rest of the company, Dr Suda's satiric song followed by the departure of most of the company on an excursion, and the important central dialogue between Míla and Živný.

Tomorrow I am going off to Prague, partly to see the doctor,[1] but also to see *Tosca*, the latest opera.[2]

I praise your flowing verse and thoughts. Dr Suda, however, he is a dry, dapper solicitor.

Poetry is as far from him as the sun. His excursion song should express this.

How on earth would he be able to conjure up those pictures about the 'golden eyelid'?

> *V paprsků tvých deští zlatém –*
> *smích k tobě chvátá!*

[In the golden rain of your rays – laughter hurries to you!]
He [would use] the sort of Prague verse that's in [the humorous magazine] *Švanda dudák*.

However, I know you understand me. (You know, there was enthusiasm about the sun at the beginning – Dr Suda [expresses this] with rather frivolous merriment.)

[PS] Scene 4 is now good.

Accordingly, Dr Suda's poetic verses were discarded in favour of another strophic song ('Ty zlaté naše sluníčko' – 'Our dear little sun') about how the all-seeing sun was aware of the goings-on on earth. Set for soloist and chorus of students and girls, this attractive number accompanies their departure on an excursion leaving the stage to Živný and Míla.

Janáček to Fedora Bartošová   *[Prague,] 26 November 1903*   OS14

You are working so splendidly that I am getting down to sketching *Act* 2 with relish.

I want to be finished with the music to Act 1, let's say by June – and with the whole opera in one year's time.

But that's a lot of work.

Janáček to Fedora Bartošová   *[undated, postmarked 29 November*   OS15
1903]

Reading quietly through Act 1, I am, frankly, amazed by your work. I like it.

1 Probably Dr Emilian Kaufman (1852–1912); see Sajner 1982.
2 *Tosca* was first performed in Czech at the Prague National Theatre on 21 November 1903. Janáček's programme for the performance of *Tosca* on 26 November 1903, conducted by Karel Kovařovic, survives in BmJA (Racek 1955, 21).

I am now sending you also Act 2 Scene 1.[1]

Tell me if, in your judgement, this sketch has enough dramatic force?

News has appeared in the *Moravská orlice* – it gave me a fright.

We don't know the end – everything has not been thought through – and already the nosy parkers won't leave me in peace.

I explain the psychology of the second act to myself in this way. Quite naturally, Mrs Míla V. *refuses* Živný in Act 1. She did not know him.

She knows of course about his love and observes it – unhappy [as she is] herself. In so doing her own sympathy for him *grows*. When she is a witness to *Živný's purging of his guilt* it is natural, psychologically speaking, that she will also openly express her feelings.

The brutality of her husband is the climax of everything.

The artistic process ends with this, that Živný's fantastic notion is backed up by the truth.

Or only a *shadow* of truth?

Act 3 will have to explain this.

[PS] If only the newspapers would be quiet until everything was finished!

In its final form, the story of Acts 1 and 2 is as follows. The composer Živný meets with a former lover, Míla, at the spa town of Luhačovice. Their relationship, which had resulted in the birth of a child, had been terminated by Míla's ambitious mother. Živný and Míla decide to leave together, to the consternation of her mother. By Act 2 the couple and their five-year-old son Doubek are living together. Míla's mother, mentally deranged, lives with them too and provokes the final crisis of the act when she accuses Živný of stealing her money. When Míla tries to restrain her, they both fall over a balustrade to their death. Another important feature of this act is Živný's remorse over the opera he has written depicting Míla's faithlessness: he attempts to destroy the score.

At this early stage, however, it is clear from Janáček's comments (corroborated by Bartošová's libretto) that there were important differences. The first is that Živný had not met Míla before Act 1 (or only briefly) and she refuses his advances, because 'she did not know him.' Furthermore, she is married to a husband whose violence provides the climax of Act 2. There is no sign of the mother.

---

1 A scene in Míla's boudoir where she is seen reading a letter; a servant announces the arrival of the author of the letter, Živný, who has a short monologue. The pair begin speaking to one another in Scene 2. This scene was later cut (see OS23) even before the act was substantially revised (see OS24+).

Fedora Bartošová to Janáček   *Sudoměřice, 1 December 1903*   OS16

You allow me kindly to give my verdict on the scenes of Act 2 and on their dramatic force.

This force cannot be denied. The drama of the second scene [see OS18+] is particularly gripping.

And above all I am taken by the whole modern atmosphere of the second act – or rather the modern atmosphere of Živný's eccentric soul.

But a quite different tone is needed here and different colours in the diction. I am only now catching and breathing the mood – I look for it in the soul –

Later on the words will come –

Would you forgive me, then, esteemed Mr Director, if my work comes a little later? I do want you once again to be able to say with satisfaction: I like it – or at least: it will do –

I do not read the *Moravská orlice* here – so I didn't catch that piece of news. But it is unpleasant when newspapers anticipate everything which is still being planned or is in the first stage of work.

So I am looking forward once again to my work. I was really sorry that it was a long while before the second act reached me. Now I still have to feel my way into the atmosphere of the artist's soul – and afterwards I still have to find at least passable words for your beautiful thoughts!

If both scenes get finished soon, I will perhaps send them together.

Janáček to Fedora Bartošová   *[Brno,] 3 December 1903*   OS17

Good! In Act 3 there is still more gradation – a tangle of laughter and surprise – so perhaps we have got it! – human life is like that!

I won't however send you Act 3 now – so that you can concentrate on Act 2. Even I didn't know where the blow from the first act would fall or let alone from the second. I will need a short quotation from Act 2 Scene 1 – but I will simply leave it out for the moment.

Janáček to Fedora Bartošová   *[Brno,] 8 December 1903*   OS18

I am sending you Act 3 now without any introductory words. You will understand it yourself.

I have started the composition of Act 1. I have shortened the first scene; it begins immediately on the full spa grounds. It will be more striking. But I will insert little episodes into it. Here and there you will correct the odd word for me.

I like the first scene of Act 2. I am already looking forward to working on it.

In Act 2 Scene 2 let Lhotský intervene in the shooting!

Janáček's shortening of the opening scene meant the exclusion of a whole number of subsidiary characters – servants, a baker, an old woman selling herbal cures, a nightwatchman, cleaners, a gardener – all bustling about in the very early morning to get the place ready before the first spa guests begin circulating. This reduced the opening four short scenes to just one and resulted in the present striking opening scene with the chorus to the sun instead of an opening reminiscent of *La bohème* Act 3 and Act 2 Scene 2 of *Louise*. The painter Lhotský (thought to be a reference to Janáček's contemporary Jóža Úprka from Hroznová Lhota)[1] had originally a greater part than the episodic figure who is seen greeting Míla and commenting on Živný near the opening of Act 1. In Act 2 Scene 2, in a scene set on the Dalmatian Riviera, he is portrayed as Živný's sparring partner in debates on art and life. Živný believes in the creative vision, in the spirit and in truth. Lhotský is more cynical: he paints merely to make money and thus believes in giving the public what they want. However, when Míla's husband returns to find her embracing Živný, Lhotský attempts to defend the lovers from the husband, who has a gun and fires at them. It is Míla who dies.[2]

Bartošová took rather longer over the final act. Janáček's brief reminder (OS19, postmarked 17 December 1903) got an immediate response:

OS20   **Fedora Bartošová to Janáček**   *Sudoměřice, 19 December 1903*

Somehow it has taken me a long time – the ending in particular – but today, yes today, I have now finished with *everything*. I have only still to *copy* it. Something was always lacking for me to be completely in the mood ... but perhaps after all I have got to the right moment, so that today I am now finished!

You will perhaps kindly forgive me for not sending it. For – on Tuesday [22 December] I will be in Brno – (of course in the evening) – and so it would now make almost no difference. (To send just a part copied out is hardly worth it.)

Besides, we can then deal with the corrections in person.

These last days were somehow a bad time for thinking and writing (the children's school reports had to be written ... and there weren't any of those 'festive moments' of creation in my soul).

1 See Straková 1957, 140; Jóža Úprka (1861–1940).
2 Straková 1957, 136 and 144.

So please kindly excuse me. Otherwise – have no fears! The work is done; now we – or rather I – will begin to polish it a little and trim it according to your wishes.

I am greatly looking forward to the holidays in Brno – naturally!

Janáček's comments written on Fedora Bartošová's letter OS21

1. Flowing melodious lines
2. Fit for printing
3. So new, new!
4. Not just the main characters are clear but also the episodic ones
5. So much life before and after the big monologues – they can take it – Act 1! This Luhačovice!
6. For a big, even a Prague public.

From Janáček's comments above there was no hint at this stage that he was not completely satisfied with his collaborator and with his opera so far. In fact he was beginning to see the work as something with which he might at last conquer Prague.

Fedora Bartošová to Vladimír Helfert   *Bratislava, 4 December 1933*   OS22

[. . .] At Christmas a change took place. Up to now Janáček had kept quiet about his work. And now he sought critics, he sought advisers. At first they were perhaps friends from Tebichova búda[1] in Brno who read through and criticized Janáček's libretto (my verses). And various criticisms persuaded Janáček to make changes. There began rearrangements of scenes and acts (I know that once Janáček even suggested that the last act should be the first), a change in the contents of scenes, cuts, looking for effects – and also – a change of name of the opera to 'Osud' [*Fate*].[2]

---

1 A wine cellar created by the architect Dušan Jurkovič in Moravian peasant style for the Brno builder Antonín Tebich. It became a meeting place for an artistic circle interested in exploring a Moravian dimension to Czech culture ('búda' is the Moravian dialect equivalent of 'bouda', a booth, cabin, den, etc.). Regular visitors included the architect Dušan Samo Jurkovič, Dr František Veselý, the school director František Mareš, the painter Jóža Úprka, the writer Josef Merhaut, and Janáček (Kožík 1976, 25).

2 These changes are recorded in a third libretto, this time in Janáček's hand, with additions and corrections written in by Bartošová (BmJA, L 14). It was probably written out to record the text that Janáček had actually set; Bartošová's additions seem to have been made much later than their other recorded contacts. The title is *Mummy, do you know what love is?* (a quotation from the scene for Míla and her child), corrected on the next page to *Fatum (Blind Fate)* (cf OS34). The whole of the Conservatory act (Act 3) is placed first, with Acts 1–2 renumbered as Acts 2–3.

After Christmas I worked on changes to the libretto. Even then I wrote gladly. I remember that prose began to appear among the verse. Janáček was more or less content with the work and gave me the impression that the opera was ripening. [. . .]

[os8, os28]

Janáček's original intention had been little more than an operatic depiction of his encounter with Mrs Urválková at Luhačovice. The composer Živný (= Janáček) and Míla Válková (= Kamila Urválková) had met before only fleetingly, if at all. He (like Janáček) had a daughter, to whom some misfortune had occurred, which has cast a shadow over the opera he has just composed. He now hopes to write some great new work. She tells him of her love for a composer (= Čelanský), from whom she had to part because of opposition from her parents. The composer, she asserts, wrote an opera named after her (= *Kamila*) and based on their affair. He then went off to make his living as a conductor. Míla is now unhappily married to someone else and has a young son. She (like Mrs Urválková) gives Živný three red roses and departs; he wonders whether his attraction to her will turn to love. Act 2 Scene 1 was to have been a scene in which Míla, in her boudoir, reads a letter from Živný, as perhaps Janáček imagined Mrs Urválková reading his letters before the correspondence was terminated by her husband. Act 2 Scene 2, set on the Dalmatian Riviera, provided the crisis when Živný and Míla, increasingly drawn to one another, encounter the fury of her jealous husband.[1]

Janáček's revisions affected this central relationship and in particular its manifestations in the second act. What if the child (known here as Dubek Urva[2] and later as Doubek, and who appears in Act 3 as a young conservatory student) was in fact fathered not by Míla's husband, but by Živný? This change opened up a whole prehistory to their meeting at the beginning of the opera. Furthermore, the idea that Janáček was writing an opera as a corrective to Čelanský's treatment of Mrs Urválková in his *Kamila* became somehow transformed into the notion that Živný had written an opera in which he had shamed his wife and son (perhaps because of the way the relationship had been forcibly ended). This is the opera which Živný now remorsefully wishes to destroy: he is seen musing about it as the second act opens. The original boudoir letter scene was dropped, as was the Dalmatian Riviera setting of the second scene.

Other changes included juxtaposing Míla's narration against the return of the excursionists. Fortunately, however, Janáček thought better the next day of his plan of beginning Act 1 with the schoolmistress (i.e. the choir-rehearsal scene). This would have meant omitting the infectious opening waltz chorus

---

1 Straková 1957, 135–6.
2 The similarity between 'Urva' and 'Urválková' provides another clue to the original identity of the boy's mother.

in praise of the sun, and the initial meeting between Míla and Živný, now charged with the embarrassment of an existing and embittered relationship.

Janáček to Fedora Bartošová *[undated, Brno, ?10 April 1904,* OS23
postmarked Strážnice,[1] *11 April 1904]*

Consider this further correction by which the whole action would be sharply heightened.
Act 1, Scene 10[2]

What if Mrs Míla said:
'No sooner had the horses taken him away from us -
I travelled *with* my secret' – etc.
and at the end:
'Above the cobweb of my memories something plays about [like a child] – The laughter of *our* boy.'

What if at this moment Živný recognized that this boy is in fact *his* own?!

What if the thread of Mrs *Míla's* narration were to be snapped by Živný's cry – by those returning from the excursion?

Thus the whole *first* act would be shortened; it would probably begin immediately with the words of the schoolmistress: 'To the rehearsal, please, my ladies!'

This, however, would effectively give a lift to the act.

Always better to leave out than not to be up to scratch.

In Act 2 the first scene would now be dropped completely. It would begin straight away with the second scene, *Živný's monologue*: 'The child is mine!'. Thus with his work, the opera, he wanted to pillory his own child and its mother; because of this he burns the score.

This justifies the outburst of his fury, in which he asks Mrs Míla, who has just entered, for *his* child.

How this scandal will be resolved and ended it's not necessary to bother with now.

How about if you were now to work up Act 1 Scene 10 with the chief thought that Dubek Urva from Act 3 is thus the real child of Mrs Míla and Živný?

Mrs Míla of course marries her husband against her will.

How does that seem to you?

---

1 The Strážnice postmarks date the receipt of letters at Bartošová's local post office, usually the day after sending.
2 i.e. the scene of central encounter between Živný and Míla.

OS24   **Janáček to Fedora Bartošová**   *[undated, Brno, ?12 April 1904,*
postmarked Strážnice, 13 April 1904]

I've now been spending time on the libretto too!

I am working further on Act 1; when it's ready we will then sit down together revising it. The climax of Act 1 will be when Živný hears that Urva Dubkův [i.e. Dubek] is his. Thus don't change *anything* in Act 1.

It's mainly about Act 2.

Válek [i.e. the husband of Míla Válková] took from *Živný* not only his wife but now his child; whether consciously or not is no matter. In his opera Živný tore the veil from the life of Mrs Míla – that would still have passed: now however he pillories his own child and its mother!

The painter [Lhotský] draws back a little the veil over Živný's own conscience – because of all this Živný burns the score! In his anger he betrays the secret.

Voices from the company: 'It's his child and hers – !' 'What a scandal!'

The *fate* of Mrs Míla is *de facto* sealed – it's unnecessary to see more or hear more about it; every one will work it out for himself.

In Act 3 it is suggested that the child, Urva Dubek, has nevertheless come under the influence of the father. He tries to instil his soul into Dubek etc.

Now we can get by without the passive character of *Válek*! Instead we must take the young Dubek into the end of Act 1.

Dubek will also be in Act 2.

From the present Act 2 let us cut the short-lived first [boudoir] scene.

Act 2 we will leave in the piano salon in the same spa [i.e. not on the Dalmatian Riviera].

In this act there is Živný with the score – he pages through it and in the monologue he bares his own soul: (which I mentioned on p.2 above). Scene 2 begins with Lhotský; Scene 3 Mrs Míla with Urva; spa society assembles and witnesses the *episode of the romance* uncovered *in the spa* (Scene 4). Thus, please get down to Act 2.

Bartošová wrote a new Act 2 along these lines, in which the character of Míla's husband Válek was omitted. It is undated, but a date later than the rest of the libretto is suggested by the different size of the paper and the fact that the verse is unrhymed. In the same style was a further variant, set in the Conservatory, and designated as 'Act 3, Scene 1.' This is an eight-page monologue for Živný on the eve of the performance of his opera. Janáček seems to have ignored Bartošová's new Act 2 (there are no markings by him on the libretto), and instead adapted the Conservatory monologue to serve as the basis for the Act 2 that he finally composed. Válek is naturally absent, but so is Lhotský and the spa society mentioned in his final paragraph (Scenes 2 and 4), though Janáček took the incident with the child (Scene 3) from Bartošová's original Act 2 libretto. Doubek (i.e. Urva, Dubek etc) does not appear in Act 1, as Janáček suggests earlier in his letter that he might, but the family relationship between the young conservatory student Doubek and Živný is made apparent in the final version of Act 3.

Janáček to Fedora Bartošová   *[undated, postmarked Brno, 22 April*   OS25
                                                        1904]

I have not written to you because I have been finishing off Act 1. It is finished and the rest could grow out of it. We can 'polish' Act 1 only in the full score.

On 2 May I am travelling to Luhačovice. Could you make a trip there? You have good [rail] connections: Strážnice, Veselí, Kunovice, Újezd.[1] From there a coach to Luhačovice. We would be virtually finished with this work in a day.

And also the second act would now fall to us.

So I invite you – you also will get to know the 'atmosphere' of the whole novel-like episode.

Janáček to Fedora Bartošová   *[undated, postmarked Brno, 28 April*   OS26
                                                        1904]

You have given me so much nice material that now it really will be possible to make a fine opera of it.

I will certainly await you on the 11th and 12th in Luhačovice.

Really not even the first work was poor; I see that now.

Of course it was merely not completely *ripe*! Ripening always needs time.

I will already be in Luhačovice on Thursday [5 May]. It's possible that I'll write to you again before then.

I have taken the best passages from the first and the second versions.[2]

And about the rest by word of mouth.

1 Until 1905, when the railway reached Luhačovice, the nearest station was Újezd (now Újezdec u Luhačovic), 12 km away.
2 This would seem to refer to Janáček's compilation in Act 2 of the new Živný monologue with the child scene from Bartošová's first version.

OS27 **Janáček to Fedora Bartošová** *Luhačovice, 9 May 1904*

The agreed day draws near.

Unfortunately is it still fairly deserted, no sign of any spa *life*. If you would like to come as late as the Whitsun holidays so that you would get some pleasure out of it, decide that for yourself. It makes no difference to me. So kindly let me know when I should expect you.

OS28 **Fedora Bartošová to Vladimír Helfert** *Bratislava, 4 December 1933*

[. . .] In Luhačovice on 11 and 12 May 1904 we went through one scene or other – and that is the last of my recollections of my work with Janáček on the libretto. I saw Luhačovice for the first time then, the scene of some of the action of the opera *Fate*. It was cold and rainy there at the time, but the young green was awakening, spring was peeping through the branches. There were only a few guests. Dr Veselý, the director of the spa at the time, with a smile gave me – the author of the libretto in which 'his' Luhačovice would live and sing – a posy of lilies-of-the-valley, and with a proprietorial gesture kept us company – Janáček, my mother and myself.

I don't know the definitive fate of *Fate*. I don't know what form the libretto had in the end, how many acts and how many scenes, who worked on the text after me, what was omitted and what was added. [. . .]

[os8, os22]

REVISIONS: THE PROPOSED BRNO PRODUCTION

After his Luhačovice meeting with Bartošová, Janáček seems to have got on with the opera by himself. Just one impatient postcard, asking what was happening with the libretto (OS29, postmarked 3 July 1904), suggests both that Janáček was expecting more, and that he did not receive it. Janáček must have finished the score in the early part of 1905 since the fair copy by Josef Štross, the earliest extant version of the work, is dated 12 June 1905.[1] Janáček had overrun his original estimate of completing the opera by a few months.

Janáček seems not to have submitted *Fate* immediately to any theatre, as he had done with *The Beginning of a Romance* and *Jenůfa*, but instead made a thorough revision of it. Some changes could be written into the full score, but others needed the replacement and insertion of new pages. Almost a third of the pages were new and after Štross's retirement (at the age of eighty) as

---

1 BmJA, A23.464.

Janáček's copyist, these had to be written out by a new copyist.

In his earliest scenario (OS7), Janáček expressed the need for some crisis in Act 2. This was supplied originally by the conflict between Živný and Míla's husband. But Míla's husband was eliminated in the April 1904 revisions (OS24) and a new source of conflict was eventually found in Míla's mother. Like Míla's husband, though in a quite different manner, she stands in the way of any union between her daughter and Živný. Míla's mother is introduced towards the end of Act 1 looking for Míla, and is horrified to hear that her daughter has gone off with her old flame, the impoverished composer Živný. In Act 2, some years later, the old lady lives with the now reconciled couple, but has lapsed into madness. Just as many of the characters in his earliest scenario seem to have been taken from life, so Janáček sought a model on which to base this new character.

Janáček to an unknown doctor[1] [undated] OS30

Permit me to ask whether you would arrange for me to listen to the patients in the women's section of the Prague Institute [for the Insane].

I have two aims. I am interested in the speech melody of the insane in general; secondly I am looking for a particular case where miserliness was the cause of the illness.

A wealthy widow did not want to marry her daughter to a 'beggarly' artist.

When a marriage nevertheless took place, she went mad. She feared that she might be robbed even of her jewel box.

One day, when running away, she jumped from a staircase and killed herself.

This, briefly, is the type – possibly rare; I failed to find one, even in the Brno Institute for the Insane.

I will be staying in Prague until Tuesday and ask you whether before then I might be able to observe the mentally ill women.

I am living in the hotel Archduke Štěpán and ask you for your kind answer.

From an undated postcard sent to his wife from Prague (OS31, probably December 1907), it is clear that Janáček realized this aim: he has been 'in the institute where the good Lord has extinguished the clear light of the soul'.

---

1 This letter was probably never sent and thus remained with Janáček's correspondence, the identity of its intended recipient still a mystery. It is not possible to date it precisely from internal evidence. Dr Svatava Přibáňová, who has looked into the matter very thoroughly, believes that Janáček's visit to the Brno institute (Mährische Landes-Irrenanstalt) took place in 1905–6, but the Prague visit may have been later, particularly in view of OS31.

Janáček's only change from the synopsis he outlined to the doctor was to make Míla also fall to her death, when trying to restrain her mother. This new crisis for the end of Act 2 was now grafted on to a version of the act which was quite different from Janáček's original scenario. In his letter of 12 April (OS24) he had described a new plan starting with a monologue for Živný and ending with a scene in which, to the humiliation of Míla, the true meaning of Živný's opera is publicly revealed. In between, two other scenes are mentioned: one with the painter Lhotský and another between Míla and her son. The last scene, based on Janáček's speech-melody notations from 1903 (OS4), became a transition to the final crisis of the mother and her jewel box. Lhotský was dropped, as indeed were all the spa guests and the spa setting. The idea of Živný musing on his opera the day before its performance did however attract Janáček, and his first musical setting of Act 2 was simply this.[1] In his later revision he included a few spectators – Míla and Doubek onstage, the mother offstage – whose reactions were simply added to the existing score. The setting for this act, which had varied from Míla's boudoir and the Dalmatian Riviera in Bartošová's first libretto to a 'piano salon in the same spa' (i.e. Luhačovice) in Janáček's first revision (OS24), was now definitively located in the studio of Živný's home. A year after Stross completed the first fair copy of the full score, Janáček's revised version was now ready for Stross's successor. The composer was confident enough about the work to announce its completion.

OS32   ***Družstvo* of the Czech National Theatre**   *Brno, 16 June 1906*
       in Brno to Janáček

The Committee of the *Družstvo* of the Czech National Theatre has heard the news that you have finished your new opera. It goes without saying that we regard it as a duty to ask you to entrust it to our National Theatre in Brno. We hope that it is as important to you as it is to us that our theatre should become the representative Moravian theatre and that this consideration will speak in our favour when you make your decision. Should you grant our request, the *Družstvo* will do everything to ensure that you suffer no material loss and that your work receives the very best performance warranted by your kind advice and suggestions.

---

1 The exact text of Janáček's first musical version is impossible to establish since many pages of the Stross score were replaced with new ones by different copyists. The original vocal score was similarly revised. But the original, unrevised, voice part for Živný, without accompaniment, has survived (BmJA, A7545) and a study of this and the revised vocal score indicates that Act 2 consisted mostly, if not entirely, of a monologue for Živný.

Družstvo of the Czech National Theatre in Brno to Janáček

The Committee of the *Družstvo* of the Czech National Theatre in Brno thanks you most warmly for your particular goodwill and the favour which you have shown us with your kind communication of 22 June 1906 that you will entrust your new opera to our theatre.

It will be our endeavour that the opera will be staged according to your wishes and we look forward warmly to its première.

Janáček's letter of 22 June 1906 has not survived. Despite the theatre's enthusiasm, Janáček seemed in no great hurry with the opera. He replied to the *Družstvo*'s letter only in October (OS39). During the next few months he supervised the copying of the revised sections of the score, spending his summer holiday in Hukvaldy checking and supplementing the copyist's work. He also reconsidered the title.

Janáček to Jan Branberger

When we were on the embankment I said to you that I would tell you the title of my new opera.

Now, when I am quite finished, I keep my promise.

I think the best title is

Fatum.

I would emphasize it, if appropriate, by the addition: *Slepý osud* [*Blind Fate*].

It is a novelistic event [*příhoda románová*][1] which I set to music.

Janáček to Antoš Josef Frýda

[...] I will give you my thoughts on the opera *Blind Fate* (Fatum) as soon as I receive the vocal score and full score from the copyist.

I will look through it once again.

He's due to deliver it to me on 7 August.

In fact the vocal score came on 30 July, and Janáček, in his letter that day to his pupil Jan Kunc (OS36) announced that he would begin 'the final corrections' of the copyist's score. It was Kunc, in his reply, who was responsible for the near-final title of the opera.

---

1 'Novel' cannot adequately express the Czech word *román*, which (like its French root) also has older connotations of romance, romantic adventure. When Dr Suda and the others comment on Míla's elopement with Živný they use the same word ('A romance [román], a Luhačovice romance!'; see OS62).

OS37   Jan Kunc to Janáček   *[Brno,] 13 August 1906*

[...] If I may make a request to you then leave the title as *Fatum* rather than *Blind Fate*. There would certainly be jokes about it: Lame Fate, Deaf Fate. And the word 'Fatum' says it all well. I also ask you, as soon as you are finished with corrections, to send me the score so that I might make a proper analysis of it whilst still on holiday. I will take great care over it and publish it in some leading Czech journal with music examples and a substantial study. In the holidays I will have much more time for it all than in the school year. [...]

By the end of August Janáček had completed his final revision, except for the metronome marks (he had no metronome in Hukvaldy), and was ready to hand over the opera to the theatre.

OS38   Janáček to Jan Kunc   *[undated, postmarked Hukvaldy,*
27 August 1906]

I am arriving in Brno on Friday [31 August] (before 1 September). When will you be there? I will have the material bound and will indicate the tempos with metronome marks; then you can have a look at it.

OS39   Janáček to the *Družstvo* of the Czech   *Brno, 9 October 1906*
National Theatre in Brno

I have finished my new work and have informed the director, Mr Frýda, that he can send for the full score and piano practice score.[1] In answer to your esteemed letter of 9 July [OS33] I ask that if the work is performed it should have new sets.

This concerns especially the scene at the Luhačovice spa in Act 1, the elegant study of Act 2 and great hall of the Conservatory in Act 3. I have indicated minimum orchestral forces in the score.[2]

The third condition which I express in the case of performance is that I be reimbursed for the actual expenses incurred in copying out the score: it comes to K 167.

---

1 *klavírní cvič[ebni]* part. This is how Janáček's vocal score of *Fate* is described on the score. This unusual formulation implies that it was a rough score for rehearsal purposes, and not for publication.

2 Janáček did this by sticking in tiny slips of paper into each act giving his minimal forces as 4 first violins, 3 second violins, 4 violas, 2 cellos, 2 double basses; 2 flutes, 1 oboe, 2 clarinets, 2 bassoons; 3 horns, 2 trumpets and 3 trombones. The score itself has parts for 2 oboes, English horn, 4 trombones, Glockenspiel, harp, timpani and triangle.

These conditions were met (**OS40**: Frýda to Janáček, 11 December 1906), and consultations proceeded with the painter Zdeňka Vorlová-Vlčková (1872–1954), and a producer, Karel Komarov.[1]

Zdeňka Vorlová-Vlčková to Janáček   *Prostějov, 3 January 1907*   OS41

After your letter of 12 December 1906 I waited for the letter you mentioned from the director, Mr Frýda, so that I could then write back to tell you more about the matter. – So far his letter has not arrived, and so I don't know how the matter stands.

I am of course willing to make a drawing of Luhačovice for your opera, but I have done only sketches and studies of buildings [see Plate 4]; for any future designs Mr Jurkovič[2] would have to lend me his drawings. He has, it seems, already designed the spa house and the new colonnade.

As for costumes for the conservatory students, I will have to think more about this. It's true of course that they will wear town clothes, strikingly fashionable, if possible. For the ladies I would suggest some sort of head ornament, flowers perhaps or some type of hat, especially where the action is set in the spa.

The men are more difficult; I don't know what you, Mr Director, had in mind yourself? The sort of cap that academics wear? It is difficult to think of anything different to go with the men's costumes.

Or do you see the men and women students at the Conservatory in the same costumes? i.e. a special costume like a uniform for the women, and the same for the men?

I also don't know the action of your opera and if you wish for my collaboration please give me a brief description of the action and the characters.

When will you need the designs to be ready? It will also be necessary for the director Mr Frýda, or whoever will be making a firm order for the designs, to send me the *dimensions of the stage*, i.e. the back wall and wings, and [to let me know] how many wings you need.

---

1 (1870–1928), baritone and producer. He sang in Plzeň, Olomouc, Ostrava and from 1899 to 1915 in Brno, where he was also an opera producer. From 1915 to 1928 he worked as singer and producer at the Vinohrady Theatre in Prague.
2 Dušan Samo Jurkovič (1868–1947), architect, influenced by folk architecture, especially of the Valašsko region, where Luhačovice is situated. In Luhačovice he designed or adapted many of the chief buildings in the spa. Among these was the Janův dům, where Janáček stayed in the summers of 1907 and 1908.

OS42   Antoš Josef Frýda to Janáček   *Brno, 16 January 1907*

The vocal material for *Fate* has just been delivered to me. Allow me
please to raise the question whether at some moment convenient to
you we could talk a little about the casting.

As regards the design for the Luhačovice spa sets I am writing to
Mrs Vlčková-Vorlová [sic].

OS43   Karel Komarov to Janáček   *[Brno,] 26 March 1907*

Lacking an opportunity for personal contact, I make so bold as to
turn to you through this method of communication.

It is about your *Fate*. I will have the honour of accompanying it
into the world (God willing, actually into the world!) as producer of
its première. I value your reforming principles too much for me to
have on my conscience a production given in a routine manner. It is
important to me that your beautiful work should receive everything
from us that is in our power. And according to your intentions.
Therefore I make so bold as to ask for a few moments of your
valuable time so as to come to an understanding both of the external
features of the work (that type of stagecraft to which our critics
confine their production comments), and of its psychology, its soul,
so that by the summer I might have some influence in this sphere on
its rehearsal, i.e. on the theatrical staging and the fine tuning.

As for the scenery, I believe that given the dimensions of our stage it
is impossible to set the first act in Luhačovice if the delightful genre
picture of spa life, full of charming episodes, is not going to suffer by
making the stage too narrow. For this reason allow me to make
another proposal. It will however be necessary to solve these things
soon if the sets are really going to be painted in Prague. In any event I
must emphasize the requirement that I be taken into consultation
during the making of the sketches. I have already informed the
director and the *Družstvo* of this and regard the matter as virtually
self-evident.

And for the casting, mainly of the numerous episodes, and arrangement [on stage] of the choruses, it will be necessary to have your
consent. And many other things – for which excuse my boldness in
intruding on you in this way.

NEGOTIATIONS WITH PRAGUE I: FINAL REVISIONS

Although Komarov's letter suggested that the tiny Brno stage would have trouble accommodating Janáček's new opera as the composer had conceived it, there was no indication that the work would not come to performance just as its predecessor *Jenůfa* had three years earlier. His modest conditions accepted, negotiations with designer and producer had begun. That the work was never produced in Janáček's lifetime was indirectly the result of a suggestion from Artuš Rektorys.

Artuš Rektorys to Janáček   *[undated, Prague, 12–14 May 1907]*   OS44

[...] Allow me to ask at the same time whether you have submitted yet any opera of yours to the Vinohrady Theatre? If not, I am most willing to take the necessary steps, and ask you kindly for news of this.
[...]

[PS] A *fifty-piece* orchestra has already been engaged for the Vino-hrady Theatre!

Janáček's contacts with Artuš Rektorys date back to the year before when Rektorys, as editor of the Prague journal *Dalibor*, had printed a short feuilleton about Janáček. Eager for allies in the generally hostile Czech capital, the composer welcomed Rektorys's friendly overtures and over the next few years he became Janáček's chief correspondent and confidant. Though employed as a bank official, Rektorys had many useful musical contacts in Prague and Janáček took up his offers of help in many matters, and readily acted on his advice. Rektorys's letter is the first suggestion in the correspondence that *Fate* could be submitted to the new Vinohrady Theatre in Prague, but it nevertheless echoed Janáček's own thinking (see OS21).

Janáček to Artuš Rektorys   *[Brno,] 15 May 1907*   OS45

I have not offered myself to the Vinohrady Theatre.

I was frightened off by *the joke about the flood* [of applications] in *Humoristické listy*.

I think that they are truly inundated with new works which have never found a home anywhere.

I would be grateful if you would kindly inform me about these matters.

At the time there were three permanent opera houses in Prague: two German ones (under a single management), serving the substantial German minority in Prague, and the Czech National Theatre. In 1907, however, a second, independent, Czech opera house opened, the Town Theatre in the Royal Vineyards (Městské divadlo na Královských Vinohradech, situated in the Královské Vinohrady [Royal Vineyards] district of Prague). Like the Czech National Theatre it put on a mixed repertory of plays and operas. A stroke of irony, of which he was seemingly unaware, was that its first chief conductor was the composer Čelanský, the original model for *Fate*'s main character.

OS46   Artuš Rektorys to Janáček   *Prague, 17 May 1907*

I went at once to Čelanský and I beg you not to delay but to send the score of your new opera immediately to the Vinohrady Theatre.

Čelanský assured me that it goes without saying that the opera will be accepted as soon as you submit it and it would be a joy for him if its première could be earlier than in Brno.

I can dispel any fears you might have about performance and ensemble. The ensemble will be very good, so that [I think] you will be satisfied with it, and the orchestra – said to be excellent – has (already) fifty members.

I wish you much happiness and the best outcome from this action. Please kindly inform me of your decision.

OS47   Janáček to Artuš Rektorys   *[Brno,] 29 May 1907*

I'm about to send the score of *Fate* to Director František Šubert – I don't know Mr Čelanský's address.

In the letter – please fill in the address – I ask Mr Čelanský to look through the score at least by Monday [3 June], and I further ask him for a consultation – perhaps on Monday.

I'm coming to Prague early by express train (perhaps towards 10).
Where could we meet?

Of course if there's an opera on at the National Theatre I'd like to go and see it. [. . .]

NB   I only hope that Mr Šubert passes on the score immediately to Mr Čelanský!

OS48   Artuš Rektorys to Janáček   *Prague, 31 May 1907*

I gave the letter to Čelanský personally so that at the same time I could give you news how the matter turned out. I doubt – judging from Čelanský's words – that he would be able to look at the score by Monday (he is too busy now), however that makes no change to the matter, because the opera was accepted the moment you submitted it.

A visit by you would be welcome to him, though since Čelanský has (chorus) rehearsals just at the moment he asks you kindly to look him up in the morning at Vinohrady (Národní dům [National House], theatre room). I fixed up a meeting with him on Monday evening since I assume that you won't be going to the theatre to see [Smetana's] *The Devil's Wall* (you probably know it well).

[...]

If you have anything you want me to take care of for you please advise me without embarrassment – I am willingly at your service.

I'm writing to you at once so that you'll have the chance to write to me again by Monday.

The Monday evening meeting indeed took place, at Čelanský's home. Rektorys was there (as was Čelanský's wife) and reported that the impression the work made on him and Čelanský was so strong that both 'burned with enthusiasm'.[1]

Janáček to Artuš Rektorys · [Brno,] 8 June 1907 · OS49

Director Šubert has requested the libretto for scrutiny.

It exists only in the full score; I therefore asked him if he would kindly have a libretto written out from the full score at my expense.

Do you know anyone who could make a professional job of it?

I fear the critical spirit of 'the writer Šubert'!

I know that the characterization of people and action in *Fate* ought to emerge clearly from the excellent acting of the singers – *and by analogy with real-life relationships*.

There are so many ideas in these three novelistic scenes [see p.131, fn.1] – for the listener to be able to fill out from his own [experience] what is merely suggested on stage by the situation or perhaps by word and movement.

So for example *Živný* and *Mrs Míla* (Scene 1) are unable in the spa grounds – where they are observed and followed – to talk openly (in as much detail) as in a book where their situation would have to be expressed in all its turns.

As much as is suggested – that much is necessary for understanding them.

For such places I have chosen gossamer orchestration so that each word might be intelligible and its mood complemented.

1 JA iv, 41, fn.

*Those introductory words written on the title pages of each scene
also belong to the text.*

Won't a literary man of such serious mettle as Director Šubert be
narrow-minded in his attitude?

It was a pity that I could not talk about it with Director Šubert, as I
could with Mr Čelanský about the music.

Are you not in contact with Director Šubert? [. . .]

Janáček had had dealings with Šubert sixteen years previously, in his attempt
to interest the Prague National Theatre in *The Beginning of a Romance* (see
PR13ff). After a distinguished career as the first administrative director of
the National Theatre, Šubert, now aged fifty-six, had moved into a similar
post at the Vinohrady Theatre. Though his literary career has long been
eclipsed by his administrative achievement at the National Theatre, his
writings include historical novels and half a dozen plays, one of which (*Jan
Výrava*, 1886) was revived at the National Theatre as late as 1937. Janáček's
sudden panic at Šubert's possible reactions to the text of *Fate* resulted in his
firmly pasting over the 'introductory words' in the score as well as another
revision of the opera.

OS50   **Artuš Rektorys to Janáček**   *Prague, 11 June 1907*

I got your letter only yesterday morning because I went off on
Saturday to my family in Dobřichovice. In the evening I called on
Čelanský and learnt from him that he had already given instructions
for a libretto to be written out from the full score.

I myself also wanted to ask you to give the libretto first to someone
to look at, and on Wednesday (5 June) I spoke with Dr Skácelík[1] (the
literary and stage critic of the *Radikální listy*, an excellent fellow,
sensitive, he knows you very well, he even stayed near you) to see if he
would be willing and kind enough to do this for me. He promised me
he would. I ask you therefore to allow me to lend the score to him for
his perusal – if it is not needed at the moment. A new copy of the
libretto would produce an unnecessary expense. Dr Skácelík will give
you (me in fact) a reliable expert opinion, and will possibly help with
advice.

I gave your letter to Čelanský to read. I think that the introductory
words prefacing the full score are quite in order and could not appear
trivial even to Šubert. I don't come into contact with him, but should
you wish it, I would be willing to call on him.

1 Dr František Skácelík (1873–1944), a doctor by profession, also active as a journalist,
critic and writer.

If you have anything at all on your mind do please tell me without any anxiety – I willingly put my services at your disposal. Just straight out: no.1, no.2 etc. [. . .]

Janáček to Artuš Rektorys *[Brno,] 12 June 1907* OS51

I'm grateful to you. In any event it will be necessary to have an expert to write out – and possibly slightly correct – the libretto.

Do please therefore ask Dr Skácelík in my name.

Mr Čelanský will be so kind as to give the score for this period to Dr Skácelík.

If necessary I could perhaps hop over to Prague to talk to Dr Skácelík.

Artuš Rektorys to Janáček *Prague, 13 June 1907* OS52

I have arranged the whole thing – taking your agreement for granted – in the following way:

As soon as Nademlejnský[1] has copied out the libretto from the full score (which needs no great skill), he will give me the libretto and I will get it to Dr Skácelík with the request that he look over it, make his comments and possible corrections, and then I will send his work to you for your comments and for any use you might make in the score of the new insights.

And only then will you give it to Šubert.

In any event don't travel to Prague on account of this if you have no other reason; it would be a waste of money! [. . .]

František Skácelík to Janáček *Prague, 18 June 1907* OS53

I received your esteemed letter only today. I was out of Prague for a few days.

I am honoured by your trust and I will very gladly revise your libretto. It will be necessary to exploit first and foremost the dramatic nature of the material, to prepare the crises, to motivate the catharsis and to unify the whole composition, which of course as a musical drama must not lack lyrical passages.

I will think the matter over in the light of my experience and abilities. It would be necessary to have a talk of course when I have read the libretto and have thought about it; tomorrow I will speak to Mr Rektorys and will perhaps learn more about it.

1 Josef Nademlejnský (1865–1935), archivist at the Vinohrady Theatre.

OS54 'The Town Theatre in the Royal Vineyards'

The following new works have been bought for the Opera and the Operetta: K. Weis's opera *The Polish Jew* and operetta *The Inspector General*, Malát's comic opera *The Old Fools*,[1] Puccini's opera *Madama Butterfly* and Giordano's opera *Fedora*, the French operetta *Les filles de Jackson* [Justino Clérice's *Les filles Jackson et cie*] and the German operetta [by Joseph Hellmesberger] *Das Veilchenmädel*. The acquisition of four further new works (three operas and one operetta) is being negotiated.

Národní listy (22 August 1907)

OS55   Janáček to Artuš Rektorys   *Luhačovice, 23 August 1907*

I know that if you could have given me favourable news about *Fate* you would have done so long ago.

Today's [actually yesterday's] *Národní listy* containing the operas accepted at the Vinohrady Opera is evidently preparing me for the fate of *Fate*.

I ask, haven't I had enough of this torturing uncertainty over the whole holiday period?

Please find out for certain how the matter lies and write to me as soon as possible about it.

I will still be at Luhačovice (Janský dům) [= Janův dům, see p.133, fn.2] up to 1 September.

OS56   Artuš Rektorys to Janáček   *Prague, 26 August 1907*

I understand your uncertainty, but I think that you are giving yourself unnecessary worries. *It is impossible* – in my opinion – that your opera was not accepted, and it is surely only because of its relative simplicity that Malát's opera, *The Old Fools*, which was officially accepted, has an advantage.

I did not catch Director Šubert in the theatre on Sunday [25 August] and so, after mature consideration, I decided to await the arrival of Čelanský. I can have some effect on him and I also want to know in advance what the situation is before I turn to Director Šubert. So please be patient for a few days.

---

1 Karel Weis (1862–1944) and Jan Malát (1843–1915) were minor Czech composers of the period. Malát is best known today as a theoretician and collector of folksongs. Weis was a more committed opera composer; *Der polnische Jude* and *Der Revisor* were originally given at the Prague German Theatre in 1901 and 1907 respectively.

Čelanský is due to come after 1 September.

I assure you that I will do everything I can, conscientiously and with all my powers, though I have no doubt that my intervention will not be necessary.

Do not paint the situation blacker than it is. I repeat: *it is impossible* that your opera was refused. These gentlemen are surely aware of this! And so just be patient for a few more days.

As soon as I learn something positive I will tell you at once.

[PS] Dr Skácelík's work also nears its completion, so he told me, at the same time referring to the thoroughness of his suggestions for revisions. He has been completely taken with the idea. He only regrets that the libretto did not fall into more professional hands.

Janáček to Artuš Rektorys *Luhačovice, 28 August 1907* OS57

I heartily thank you.

Director Šubert has also informed me about the acceptance of *Fate* and asks now for the libretto.

I'm curious about Dr Skácelík. [...]

Janáček's curiosity, if not impatience, with Dr Skácelík is apparent in several more exchanges with Rektorys, who did his best to chase up his dilatory recommendee. A month later, Janáček got his verdict, the first clear exposition of the sort of criticisms that the libretto of the opera has faced ever since.

František Skácelík to Janáček *Prague, 27 September 1907* OS58

I have gone through the libretto of your new opera *Fate* several times, I have made several attempts to rework scenes, to make it a more realistic work for the stage so that the fundamental plan as supplied by Miss Bartošová would remain unchanged – but I have failed in this attempt.

Nothing would remain on the basis of the given material, which is entirely made for the theatre, other than to create *a priori* something quite new. You were good enough to mention that the subject is taken from real-life events. I drew up a series of questions necessary to get further details and wanted, according to your response, to try for myself to make a complete dramatization of the sequence of events. (The questions were also sent by me to your address, but I could not know whether a complete reworking would suit you. And then it would have needed at least half a year's work, all of which in the present circumstances, when the music has been written, has perhaps no practical value. And just as I was considering this circumstance I gave up the attempt at a complete reworking.)

Perhaps, however, it would be possible to make some smaller changes which would not disturb the overall framework, and perhaps the author of the libretto would be happy to make them at your suggestion.

All the acts suffer because the locale is depicted on a scale disproportionate to the action of the persons taking part, i.e. the main characters, who must stand out and must themselves somehow fictitiously evoke their setting. If one is concerned with the dramatization of an idea, then the locale must have a dramatic relationship to it and must itself lead the hero to catharsis or to his fall. This does not occur here and all sorts of things could be changed.

To liven up the action the young lady [Bartošová] made use only of subsidiary elements, which is impossible because the audience would then naturally be more interested in these secondary matters. I think that the action ought to be extended to that of the main characters, that they really ought to have something to do and, as far as possible, something detailed. It is mainly conversations which tell the story, but they themselves afford little opportunity for action.

The first act, for example, begins very nicely, but the end is unclear and I am sure that the audience will not know what to make of it. The uncertainty of the first act is the curse of the others, chiefly the beginning of the third, which comes *out of the blue* and is in no way motivated by the events of the past.

The ending could stand. It is psychologically motivated, but there ought to be more action in the third act. The parallel occurrence of the storm and Živný's narration needs to be resolved by something other than pure chance. Živný's tortured inner being could *deliberately* seek *the storm*, but a broader action would of course be necessary.

Then the diction should be more concentrated, less lyrical; more drama is needed, more life, less decorativeness.

I would suggest quite a different plan for these interesting events. It would perhaps be impossible to carry it out given such a lengthy draft, but then I would realize it in scenes possibly similar to those in Tchaikovsky's *Eugene Onegin*. And perhaps planning and executing it in short scenes would be the way to preserve as much as possible of the libretto in its present state and carry out necessary changes in the best possible way.

That is generally what I have found. We are concerned now only with the weaknesses I have mentioned. And the libretto is full of good things. Best is the material itself. What it needs, however, is a poet and a practical man of the theatre.

I have spoken about the work to Mr F. X. Svoboda,[1] an experienced playwright. He would be willing to read the piece. If needs be, write to him (Prague, Městská spořitelna [Town Savings Bank]). Perhaps he would be able to make a more realistic proposal. If there is time for it, I could if needs be work on it myself, although I don't know whether I would come to grief again.

Though Skácelík had done his tactful best to wriggle out of any further involvement with the piece, Janáček was persistent, and now asked for help in revising specific sections. Skácelík contributed virtually nothing, but Janáček's letters to him, mostly unanswered, provide a vivid picture of the final revisions of the work:

Janáček to František Skácelík   *[Brno,] 10 October 1907*   OS59

I come with help!
  I already have the music for the end of Act 1 in mind. [...]
  The music is woven out of the motif of *Mrs Míla's Mother*. Lights come on in the hotel, they turn them off on the promenade. Dance music on the piano is heard from the hotel; the orchestra continues further with the motifs of *Mrs Míla's Mother*. She appears hurriedly, peering into the illuminated rooms – she runs here and there.
  Meanwhile Fanča runs out from the hotel.

Janáček then quotes in dialogue form two incidents now found in the final version: the short scene between Fanča (a young girl, also referred to as Miss Pacovská) and a student, who wants a kiss from her; and the scene where Míla's Mother, looking for her daughter, is told that she went off with Živný. He then leaves four lines of dots for Skácelík to fill in:

Put into her mouth now an outburst of desperate cries! She stumbles in her haste [originally: 'flight', crossed out] after her daughter ——
  A question on the faces of the others.
  So, that's what I suggest, it would fit my music excellently. Will you do this for me, at least this, terribly soon?

---

1 František Xaver Svoboda (1860–1943), poet, novelist and dramatist.

OS60   **František Skácelík to Janáček**   *[Prague,] 16 October 1907*

I'll be finished by Sunday. Last week illness kept me completely from work. I have already studied your instructions.

OS61   **Janáček to František Skácelík**   *[Brno,] 22 October 1907*

I can hardly wait. I'm on tenterhooks.

At least please send me your plan for the change to the end of Act 1. There will be time enough for the rest.

Just so that I can work, otherwise I will not be ready.

If I can have your suggestions then we can come more quickly to an agreement.

So now I am waiting with certainty at least for the changes to Act 1!

OS62   **Janáček to František Skácelík**   *[Brno,] 28 October 1907*

I have done the ending of Act 1 like this: [. . .]

Quoting dialogue, Janáček now reverses the incidents. Míla's Mother is seen looking for her daughter (suddenly renamed 'Mína'), and hears from the Councillor's Wife that she has gone off with Živný. Míla's Mother disappears into the dark while everyone else goes into the hotel leaving the stage clear for the Fanča-Student incident. When, in trying to get his kiss, the Student threatens to tell Fanča's parents that she spoke to 'Mrs Mína', the Mother interrupts and demands to know why this should be regarded as a threat. The Student tells her that her daughter has gone off to Újezd (the nearest railway station) with Živný. As the Student runs off, calling for Fanča, Dr Suda, Konečný and Lhotský comment softly together: 'A romance, a Luhačovice romance!' (see p.131 fn. 1), and the full force of Míla's Mother's horrified reaction is heard. This, apart from minor cuts, became the final version of this scene.

This arrangement thus follows on nicely from the previous section, because the delayed excursionists – and the young people in particular – give away [Mrs Míla's] departure.

Miss Pacovská was ordered by her parents not to speak with Mrs M., who was sympathetic to her. The 'bad' reputation of Mrs M. had already spread through the spa.

Mrs M's Mother searches for her daughter among the excursionists, she peers into the illuminated windows – she overhears the insulting warning – parents punish their children, young girls, if addressed by or if they address her daughter!

No wonder she clutches the Student convulsively – when she learns such things about her daughter who, with grim forebodings, she has been seeking the whole afternoon!

She learns more! Her daughter has really gone off with Živ[ný]!

The Student runs off after 'Fanča' into the darkness – Fanča runs into the hotel, surely she will now tell the young men what has been going on outside –

As mute witnesses to the sight of the crushed mother they characterize the situation – with their remark: A romance – a Luhačovice romance.

Somewhere in the dark the Student's calling is still heard: Fanča!

My addition has also developed well musically – it doesn't have the effect of an afterthought.

Do you approve it?

Will you correct it?

What was I to do – when you didn't reply even with a single word?

I think that I shall succeed more quickly with these corrections; they suit my music.

You, I think, have been led astray too far by the text?

I am now thinking about the end of Act 2.

The worst will be Act 3.

Do you have any plan for it yet?

How to get an open stage for the beginning?

Put in a change of scene?

It seems too short to me.

Do advise me.

Janáček to Artuš Rektorys   *[Brno,] 3 November 1907*   OS63

At the time of my departure from Prague I informed you that Dr Skácelík, with every sign of good will, promised me to do the suggested text changes within three days.

Today a month has elapsed – and I have nothing.

But I am not waiting for anything now since I am convinced that further changes could grow only on and out of the motifs of the music.

I have done the corrections briefly myself, together with the music.

I'd just like to know what to make of Mr Skácelík! Should I think he's ill?

Janáček heard from Skácelík a few days later (**OS64**, undated [Prague, 4 November 1907]), when he received his reworking of the end of Act 1 with changes in text and in metre to show 'the beginnings of the mental derangement of the mother'. They came too late to be of use, but his request for instructions about the next two acts prompted Janáček to describe his vision of the rest of the opera:

OS65   Janáček to František Skácelík   *[Brno,] 14 November 1907*

I was not able, unfortunately, to use many of your additions – they came too late; but amongst them was one highly dramatic moment and I am grateful to you for suggesting it.

I see the end of Act 2 like this:

1. It is necessary to know that Mrs Mína [= Míla] is dead. That was unclear until now.

2. It is however necessary to make a link with the storm [in] Act 3:

I think that it would be possible to express both briefly and succinctly.

Živný carries in the lifeless Mrs Mína in his arms.

Doubek (cries out): Mami, mami!

Živný (certain that his wife's life is slipping away, is beside himself and can only whisper): Quiet, quiet! (convinced of the death of his wife). This is a bolt from the blue (his grief breaks out).

Thicker and thicker, your pallid lightning-flashes!

Where are your thunderclouds?

(People can be seen on the staircase carrying away the corpse of Mrs M.'s mother.)

Živný (gazing steadfastly into the open doorway repeats): Where are your thunderclouds! (falls on Mrs M.)

                    (The curtain falls.)

The thunderclouds from which fate strikes Živný are his own work (he seduced Mrs M.) – which now begin to resound in his conscience as the reason for his misfortune.

He calls God's thunderbolts upon himself: in them he sees his only purgation – ; Mrs M. must forgive him – but she could not; in them there can only appear to him (in his confusion of the senses) the face of his wife, paler than the silver flashes of lightning – in forgiveness.

In this vein I have also corrected the text of Act 3. I opened the scene immediately. Something like this: [. . .]

Janáček then quotes a substantial section of the opening of Act 3. It resembles the final version of the opera in that it is a description of a storm, sung by a chorus of male students and which culminates in a solo voice (Hrázda) telling of his mental torment which recurs during such storms, and as at the end of Act 2, the soloist invites the lightning flashes to rain more heavily upon him. In a second section Janáček explains that 'Verva managed in the theatre to get his hands on sheets torn out from the final act; he displays them and plays from them.' Then follows the solo quotation of the 'Do you know what love is' scene between Míla and young Doubek, followed by a love song for Živný, not set in the final version.

I think that in this way it will be more intelligible.
Would you agree?
I ask for your expert opinion.
At the same time please send me also the copy of the libretto – it will be necessary to write some tiny changes into it.

Five days later, on 19 November, according to Janáček's letter to Rektorys (OS66, 20 November 1907), Janáček sent off the opera with additions to Šubert. At the same time as sending the score Janáček suggested to him that he might be invited to the opening of the Vinohrady Theatre, on 24 November. Janáček received no invitation however and, despite Rektorys's advice, he huffily refused to go there without one (OS67: Janáček to Rektorys, 23 November 1907). Nevertheless, the next contact with Šubert was encouraging.

F.A. Šubert to Janáček *Královské Vinohrady, [Prague], 1 December* **OS68**
1907

Please note that your opera *Fate* is already being copied. As soon as the copying is completed, steps will be taken towards the first preparations for its performance.

But however hopeful things may have sounded then, four months later any production of *Fate* seemed no nearer, and Rektorys spent much time in his correspondence trying to explain the delays in staging a work that had been 'accepted the moment it was submitted':

Artuš Rektorys to Janáček *Prague, 8 April 1908* **OS69**

[...] I can at last tell you something sensible about *Fate*. It will be given *for certain*. It is necessary before then, however, for the ensemble to be somewhat played in so that it can overcome the enormous obstacles which lurk for it in the work. All the [performing] material is written out and Čelanský firmly hopes that he will be able to perform the opera at the beginning of the autumn. [...]

This explanation seems to have come directly from Čelanský. It is corroborated by a newspaper interview he gave several years later when he
returned as music director of the Vinohrady Theatre:

OS70   Anon: 'With the conductor Vítězslav Čelanský'

[...] Leoš Janáček belongs among the unrecognized [Czech] composers. [...] This is why his opera *Fate* was accepted although at first
glance it gave the impression that it would not be a box-office success.
Since the opera is very interesting, *it was worth a try*. Six years ago
the *Družstvo* of the Vinohrady Theatre agreed to stage the work on
my recommendation.

In my first year I could not proceed right away with the rehearsal of
such a difficult opera. [...] If the *Družstvo* is to stage such an opera,
and is not to bleed to death, the conductor has to allocate his time. I
wanted to rehearse the opera *Fate* between the preparation of other
operas, not wanting to narrow the repertory and wanting to be
thorough. So I postponed rehearsing *Fate* to the next year, when the
members of the theatre would be played in. [...]

Národní obzor (27 June 1913)

Rektorys's reassurances, together with an earlier, disturbing report to Janáček from Komarov about the conditions in Brno (**OS71**, 3 June 1907), were
enough to prevent Janáček from returning to the original plan of a Brno
production in spite of the most earnest entreaties. In a letter of 8 July 1908
(**OS72**) Janáček had categorically instructed the Brno *Družstvo* not to ask the
Vinohrady Theatre to send them the full score or vocal score of *Fate*. Even
Brno's willingness to do the opera after a Prague production was of no avail
since the performance material remained in Prague awaiting some sort of
action there.

OS73   Dr Jaroslav Elgart to Janáček   *Brno, 29 July 1908*
for the *Družstvo* of the National Theatre in Brno

Forgive me that only now is it possible for me to answer your kind,
but also unwelcome letters. The committee meeting was only the day
before yesterday. [...]

Director Frýda has guaranteed to bring the orchestra in *all* operas
up to 34 men; from his side this is a sacrifice and [a gesture of]
goodwill worth recognizing. The conductors Messrs Moor[1] and

---

1 Karel Moor (1873–1945), composer, second conductor at the Brno National Theatre in
1908.

Pavlata[1] (from Plzeň) say they will do all they can to have good players in the orchestra. You can see that we are trying gradually to raise the musical level.

All the harder I take your news that you will not allow [us] to perform *Fate*. I'm happy to believe that you – an artist ordained by God – set little store by Brno. Your future is still to come and it is not necessary for great men to depend on the recognition of today['s public] and Brno. – But why on earth shouldn't we, lacking a large theatre, want to appease our musical hunger in our humble conditions at least with illusions? Fair enough, you don't think it important that *Fate* is given in Brno – but we long for it! [. . .] *I earnestly beg you to allow us to perform 'Fate.' Mr Moor will surely take every possible care for it to turn out as decently as possible* and we would like to have it as the highlight of the spring season. By then it will be possible for the Vinohrady Theatre to lend us the score for copying, since it is quite certain that it will be given there in the autumn.

Answer me, I earnestly entreat you, as soon as possible.

Janáček to Dr Jaroslav Elgart   *Hukvaldy, 31 July 1908*   OS74
for the *Družstvo* of the National Theatre in Brno

[. . .] And now about *Fate*. My esteemed friend, if I could have heard at least a rehearsal of some part of *Fate*, for instance the storm in Act 2 or anything else, and thus be convinced of the effect of at least some parts – a work one has imagined and its actual sound are sometimes far from one another – then I would say yes or no. [. . .]

By the autumn Janáček was becoming impatient. In a letter to Rektorys (OS75, 25 [26] September 1908) he complained that Šubert had said that *Fate* would be performed that autumn, but nothing was happening, and he asked Rektorys to give Čelanský a nudge. Rektorys seems to have failed in this and instead suggested more drastic action:

Artuš Rektorys to Janáček   *Prague, 28 October 1908*   OS76

[. . .] I have another piece of advice for you. Write a letter to the Directorate of the Vinohrady Theatre saying that it should begin rehearsing *Fate*: it was accepted now a year ago, and its production has been promised. Please don't mention any of the officials (i.e.

---

1 Rudolf Pavlata (1873–1939), cellist (the first performer of Janáček's *Fairy Tale* for cello and piano) and conductor. He worked as a theatre conductor in Plzeň (1906–8) and Brno (1908–11).

neither Čelanský nor Šubert) in your letter. Just write a general *complaint*. Please inform me of the theatre's answer. I will print it in *Dalibor*.

OS77 **Jan Hebrle to Janáček**   *Královské Vinohrady, 4 November 1908*
      for the Vinohrady Theatre

Allow me to inform you that in today's meeting, which drew up the repertory for the period to the end of January, the opera *Fate* was not included.

The staging of your work can therefore take place only after January 1909, about which, assuring you of my respect, I will give you news.

NEGOTIATIONS WITH PRAGUE II: THE LAWSUIT

Two years later Janáček was still waiting. In the meantime there had been changes at the Vinohrady Theatre. Šubert, whose artistic ambitions for the fledgling company were in conflict with the more money-conscious Executive Committee of the *Družstvo*, resigned after a prestigious, but loss-making tour to Vienna in September 1908. The strike that broke out on 24 September in support of Šubert resulted in the formation of a new ensemble under a new administrative director, Václav Štech,[1] with a well-defined brief of satisfying the financial requirements of the *Družstvo*. A less adventurous repertory was dominated by conversational comedies, farces and operetta.[2] Worst of all for Janáček's hopes was the departure of Čelanský.

OS78 **Janáček to Artuš Rektorys**   *Brno, 29 June 1911*

You know how it began with my *Fate* and the Vinohrady Theatre.

At the time I made a contract with Mr František Šubert; the piece was accepted for performance.

It is well known how afterwards it faltered at the Vinohrady Theatre. But a period of three years passed and it wasn't performed.

It seems to me that the compact with Šubert isn't even legally binding – according to what Štech has said.

I would like to have some assurances about this. Could you acquire

1 Václav Štech (1859–1947), writer and administrator. He was director of the Vinohrady Theatre 1908–13.
2 *DČD*, iii, 306.

for me the statutes of the *Společnost*[1] which administered the Vino-hrady Theatre – during the time of Šubert?

Did he have the right to sign papers, agreements for the *Společnost*?

I don't want to insist on a legally enforced performance of any of my works – God forbid! – but I would like to have some light [on the matter] to see whether composers here were cheated. I am surely not the only one affected. [. . .]

Despite this statement, Janáček now began to use lawyers rather than private persuasion to secure a performance of his opera. In this he was at first represented by Dr Adolf Stránský (1855–1931), later by Dr František Pauk (1880–1957).

Janáček to the Vinohrady Theatre   *Brno, 9 August 1911*   OS79

I ask you to settle the affair of the opera *Fate*, which was accepted for performance. I wish to defend my author's right if necessary by legal means, not in order to a compel a production of the opera, but simply to ensure the law can take its course.

Dr E. Miřička to Dr Adolf Stránský   *Prague, 4 October 1911*   OS80
for the Vinohrady Theatre

In the case of Mr Janáček the Directorate of the Town Theatre of the Královské Vinohrady passed on to me your esteemed letter of 13 September and I am able to inform you of the following:

In the entire theatre no-one is aware that the opera *Fate* was bought from Mr Janáček, no contract was found in the files, and also Mr Janáček, despite the fact that he was invited to, has not divulged the terms of the contract.

Thus the director was not even entitled to perform the work and there can be no talk of any compensation.

Should Mr Janáček wish for any agreement to this end, i.e. that the work might be performed, let him communicate his conditions and I will then ask for the decision of the Executive Committee.

Štech, however, hoped to settle the matter out of court:

---

1 Janáček was here confusing the *Společnost* [company] which was granted the franchise for running the National Theatre in Prague in 1900 with the *Družstvo*, which it replaced and which then went on to run the Vinohrady Theatre.

OS81   **Václav Štech to Janáček**   *Královské Vinohrady, 10 November 1911*

This letter is a purely private expression and has absolutely no official connection with the actions of the Executive Committee of the United *Družstvo*.

I would like to talk privately with you before the meeting on Thursday [16 November] where your case will come up. I am not very well. I caught a cold on the way to Vienna and I am afraid of undertaking the journey to Brno.

As a writer I feel the need to tell you my opinion in confidence and to hear your opinion, also without preconditions. I think that as two authors we will be able to deal with your case in a quite businesslike way, without merely regarding the various legal positions.

I am especially concerned that we two should reach an agreement. Allow me to suggest therefore that you should kindly visit me at home any time before next Thursday. I am willing to reimburse your travel expenses from the theatre fund at my disposal.

I ask you kindly to send your answer to my home address.

Janáček took legal advice (**OS82**: Dr František Pauk, 11 November 1911) on whether to meet Štech. There is no evidence that he did except that a few weeks later, and, for the first time, Janáček had a legal contract with the Vinohrady Theatre for the performance of his opera.

OS83   **Václav Štech to Janáček**   *Královské Vinohrady, 6 December 1911*

I ask you kindly to return the attached contract signed in your own hand. Whereupon we will send you the text of the same contents signed by the Directorate.

I am delighted that it was possible to settle your case easily in this way.

Štech sent Janáček the signed contract on 20 December 1911 (**OS84**). The contract itself (**OS85**), signed and dated 18 December 1911, specified that the Vinohrady Theatre would perform *Fate* in the winter of 1912–13. But once again things did not run smoothly. In a brief letter of 4 February 1913 (**OS86**) Štech intimated that things were not going well and that he would come and see Janáček 'within the next few days'. Any unpleasant news that Štech gave at the meeting, postponed by Štech to 4 March (**OS87**, 3 March 1913), was not quite a bolt from the blue. Since the previous November Janáček had been in touch with Vojtěch Ševčík (1881–1955), about copying the latest version of *Brouček*. Ševčík was originally a horn player in the Brno theatre orchestra and as such had taken part in the Brno première of *Jenůfa*.

Now orchestral secretary at the Vinohrady Theatre, he was able to supply Janáček with frank reports on the progress of *Fate* at the Vinohrady Theatre:

Vojtěch Ševčík to Janáček   *[undated, postmarked Prague,*   OS88
                                       20 February 1913]

[...] Your *Fate* has not been handed out even to the soloists and after those two operas [d'Albert's *Die verschenkte Frau*, Malát's *The Old Fools*] there will be another operetta, so I don't know for the time being when it will be given.

In the last few days we were with director Štech and he told us that with the exception of the chairman Mr [Dr František] Marek, the *Družstvo* was in favour of reducing the orchestra by six members, that apparently it costs a great deal. There would therefore be only thirty-two of us; you have as large an orchestra in Brno. [...]

Vojtěch Ševčík to Janáček   *[undated, ? soon after 3 March 1913]*   OS89

[...] Holeček[1] has stated that so long as he is conductor here your *Fate* will not be given; whether this possibly arises out of some personal animosity, I have not ascertained.

However I am convinced that he is scared of it because there is a great difference between rehearsing a new work, never given before, and a work which has already been performed and which can be cribbed, as they say. That's one reason.

Another reason is that there is public talk about the work, that it's not up to much, and so on, and this is creating an antipathetic mood in advance; so you can imagine with what distaste they are applying their efforts to the work, and there is talk about it among the audience. Thus these people will later go to the theatre convinced by the insinuations that they must condemn the work, repudiate it in fact...

In your place I would not insist upon a definite performance under any circumstances, but I would wait until someone else came along who would take up the work with love, and who would not damn it in advance.

Also the circumstance must be taken into account that the

1 Bedřich Holeček (1882–1942), conductor at the Brno National Theatre 1902–4, 1907–8 and at the Prague Vinohrady Theatre 1908–13.

director Mr Štech is not musically educated and leaves all musical things to his [Holeček's] judgement. [. . .]

OS90 Václav Štech to Janáček   *[Královské Vinohrady,] 22 March 1913*

I have been almost a week on my travels. Before I left I took measures for there to be one further attempt to see if it was possible to rehearse your opera *Fate*. I entrusted this task to the conductor Piskáček,[1] who should report to me about it after the Easter holidays. I shall inform you of the result on Tuesday or Wednesday [24–25 March].

Janáček now consulted his lawyers.

OS91 Dr František Pauk to Janáček   *Brno, 5 April 1913*

In connection with your opera *Fate* I have obtained from the director, Mr Štech, the news that it is impossible for the Directorate to stage your opera *Fate* since during the rehearsals undertaken by the second conductor all the soloists proclaimed that the opera puts such demands on them that they are unable to cope with it.

Kindly let me know whether you wish me to proceed with an action against the Directorate.

OS92 Artuš Rektorys to Janáček   *Královské Vinohrady, 6 April 1913*

I delayed [writing] so that I should not be the first who had to give you such unpleasant news.

Now, when you already know it, I can thus only recapitulate that *Fate* will not be put into rehearsal at all since the members of the Vinohrady Theatre have declared that it is quite impossible to study these parts and that the director Mr Štech, anticipating a lawsuit, had these declarations from the soloists noted down.

I regret that I cannot give you more pleasant news and be assured that at this moment I truly feel for you.

If it comes to a lawsuit – Štech told me that he has already received notification from your solicitor – I can only advise you to be very careful in your choice of expert advisers.

I think that you will possibly consider either Kàan[2] or Čelanský. I would not advise the latter in view of his former relationship to the

1 Rudolf Piskáček (1884–1940), composer, conductor at the Vinohrady Theatre 1908–18, 1921–5.
2 Jindřich z Albestů Kàan (1852–1926), director of the Prague Conservatory 1907–18.

Vinohrady Theatre, and the former is again too set in his ways [*příliš strnulá pagoda* – 'too stiff a pagoda'] although his judgement on the performability of the work would of course carry weight in the trial.

Please inform me without fear of any wishes you may have; I will be of service to you wherever and however it is in my power.

Only forgive me that I am not a happier intermediary . . .

Janáček to Artuš Rektorys   *Brno, 14 April 1913*   OS93

Forgive me for not answering you any earlier. You know what a mood I am in – three years I compose the work – five years it lies around in the theatre with a contract binding them to perform it for me.

I still don't know what I'll do. If there is no certainty of convincing the soloists of their dishonour to their profession I will not launch into a lawsuit, for on top of all this to pay out expenses, which could amount to K 1000–2000, that would be too much.

And to gamble the thing on the expert opinion of 'specialists', that I won't do. This is really a personal matter – I won't be instructed in such things – by anyone.

I will let you know when the thing becomes a little clearer.

But Janáček did seem prepared to 'gamble'. A letter from the first Kostelnička in Brno, Leopolda Hanusová-Svobodová, dated 16 April 1913 (OS94: to the tenor Alois Doubravský) is interesting both in that it reveals that she studied the part of Míla (the Brno rehearsals must have got further than other documents suggest) and that Janáček really did consider going ahead with the court case and assembling witnesses. According to a letter to Janáček from his legal adviser Dr Pauk (OS95, 27 May 1913), the hearing was set for 9 a.m. on 4 June 1913 in Prague. An undated press-cutting describing the hearing (OS96: 'From the courthouse', *Národní politika*) mentions Janáček's demands: that within fourteen days after judgement the *Družstvo* begin preparations for the performance of the opera and that it be performed on the stage of the Vinohrady Theatre within six months. It noted with interest that 'Mr Janáček expressly refuses financial compensation from the *Družstvo*'.

At its request the defendant was given until 27 August 1913 to prepare its case (OS97: Dr Pauk to Janáček, 10 July 1913). And by this time an unexpected development had occurred, the return of Čelanský as chief conductor at the Vinohrady Theatre. This meant that the opera was no longer in the hands of the hostile Holeček or the inexperienced Piskáček, but instead with the man who had accepted the opera in the first place. Moreover he was prepared to defend his choice in public (see OS70). Shortly after his return he energetically began trying to come to an agreement with Janáček:

OS98   **L. V. Čelanský to Janáček**   *[undated, probably 18 July 1913]*

[...] I ask you please to let me know when you are passing through Prague so that we could have a chat about your *Fate*. I would like in some way to repair your relationship so that neither the Executive Committee nor you felt at all hard done by.

You, after all, as I have heard from Dr Pilař,[1] are concerned only with the performance of your opera. On the other hand you know that it was I myself who accepted your opera – as an example of a new artistic direction and of your own individuality. I was never led to this by any possible financial success in the theatre, and you yourself cannot surely believe that the theatre could make any financial gain through the performance of your opera – rather the opposite. Just think how many rehearsals I will need if I want to give your opera even half decently. And I don't want to do it badly. By doing so I would not be helping you.

If you now insist, given the current changed situation in the theatre, that the opera is performed *as quickly as possible*, it would mean an artistic loss for you and this, as your good friend, and as a man who has the success of a certain new Czech opera at heart, I cannot advise.

I write to you therefore privately for the time being and give you this advice:

Withdraw your suit and announce this to the Executive Committee, mentioning that you will submit your opera once again for performance.

In this way you will ease my position to the point that I will be able undisturbed to spread out my work [over a period of time] on your opera.

I advise you sincerely as your friend, and as a man who wants to help you.

If you were perhaps to pass through Prague it would be better if we could have a chat about this, for the situation in the Prague theatrical world during the past two months has greatly changed to the benefit of Czech music, and I would be sorry if you too were not to profit from this.

I await your visit or your letter.

---

1 Dr František Pilař, legal representative of the *Družstvo*.

Janáček to Dr František Veselý   *Mšeno, 8 August 1913*   OS99

[. . .] [PS] Čelanský has not put *Fate* on the programme. This is now a
spiritual torment for me!

Janáček was suffering from severe rheumatism at this time and had been in
Karlovy Vary (Carlsbad) for spa treatment, to where Čelanský's letter was
forwarded. By the time the letter reached him, he was back in Brno and in no
state to travel again. Judging from Čelanský's next letter (OS100, 26 August
1913), along much the same lines as the above, Janáček insisted that he was
concerned only with a performance of his opera, and that he would secure this
by legal means if necessary. Čelanský continued to have faith in gentle
diplomacy, backed up with an out-of-court settlement.

Dr Karel Marek to Janáček   *Královské Vinohrady, 1 September 1913*   OS101
for the Vinohrady Theatre

As the director of opera, Mr L. V. Čelanský, has informed us, you are
withdrawing your suit concerning the performance of your opera *Fate*,
submitted to our theatre five years ago.

Allow us to inform you in this matter that we are willing to pay
expenses up to K250, i.e. two hundred and fifty crowns, arising from
the dispute to this time; with this addition that it will be our endeavour
to perform your opera in our theatre at a time when circumstances in
the theatre allow.

Requesting that you kindly sign the enclosed letter [. . .]

Janáček, however, did not sign the letter. On 14 September 1914 Čelanský
wrote him a pained letter (OS102), in which he complained that Janáček was
not behaving in as friendly a manner as he hoped he might since he was
continuing to deal with his legal advisers, whose interests, he assured him,
were other than purely artistic. 'Why do you trust solicitors more than a
fellow-artist who knows well what it means to write a big three-act opera and
then to have to beg for its performance somewhere?' But even this letter did not
do the trick though Janáček, through his advisers, had the case adjourned
(OS103: Dr Pauk to Janáček, 20 September 1913). The adjournment did not
satisfy the Vinohrady Theatre, and Čelanský wrote again, this time more curtly:

L. V. Čelanský to Janáček   *Prague, 24 September 1913*   OS104

I put your last letter, addressed to me, before the Executive Committee.
The Committee, at its last meeting, voted that I should write to you
[asking you] either to sign *that document* in which you must withdraw
your suit etc – or to act as you think fit.

OS105 **L. V. Čelanský to Janáček** *Královské Vinohrady, 18 October 1913*
for the Vinohrady Theatre

The Executive Committee of the Town Theatre of the Královské Vinohrady takes note of your last statement, confirmed by your signature, concerning the performance of your opera *Fate*, whereby the whole matter is concluded.

The Directorate of the Opera regrets only that on your side matters did not rest with the first pronouncement suggested by the Directorate.

OS106 **Dr František Fuksa,[1] to Janáček** *[undated, Prague, 2 March 1914]*
for the Vinohrady Theatre

Re your letter of 28 February allow us to return to you the score of your opera *Fate* and note that you no longer have an interest in its performance.

And so ended the long, fruitless tale of *Fate* and the Vinohrady Theatre. Janáček's withdrawal of the score speaks of his bitterness and exasperation, but also of the possibility of a production in Brno, suggested by a letter from the producer-designate of the first, aborted Brno production:

OS107 **Karel Komarov to Janáček** *Německý Brod [now Havlíčkův Brod],*
3 July 1914

[...] Director Lacina[2] and I have agreed for the time being about my return to Brno as opera producer, and so I will have the honour of the first staging of your *Fate*, with which you have graciously favoured the Brno Theatre for this year's [i.e. 1914–15] season.

No further documentation has survived about this proposed production in Brno, but the outbreak of the First World War seems to have delivered a body blow to the small Brno Theatre's attempt to perform the opera. Moreover, within a couple of years Janáček's circumstances were to change dramatically with the success of *Jenůfa* in Prague. This meant that he took up the abandoned *Brouček* and completed it. But he also began to reconsider his earlier works. The libretto of *Fate* had always appeared to be the problem, and he turned to his current librettist, F. S. Procházka, with a new idea for *Fate*:

1 Fuksa replaced Štech as administrative director of the Vinohrady Theatre in the summer of 1913, remaining in the post until 1935.
2 See p.105, fn.1.

Janáček to F. S. Procházka   *Brno, 9 January 1917*   OS108

Would you write me, in verse, a nice love story on a common theme? Just an everyday one?

There were two young people, he, she, who burned with violent love for each other. She was rich, he poor – *an artist* – a composer. They didn't marry; she was married off to a rich farmer.

He took revenge on her for her lack of trust: he depicted her in one of his works – an opera – as a naked lie; he tore off from her what was honest in her. Her husband rejects her. And the simple end: the young people meet up again at a certain spa.

The event is an actual one, a Vinohrady one[1] – with serious consequences.

I would need this story, gently flowing, as a scene-setting introduction for my opera *Fate*.

Would you kindly sketch it for me? [. . .]

In his reply (OS109, 15 January 1917), Procházka did not exactly refuse, but pointed out that he first needed to know much more about the project. Janáček thought of other help. A letter to him from Jaroslav Kvapil (OS110, 26 March 1917), the librettist of Dvořák's opera *Rusalka*, reveals that Janáček also approached him for advice on how the libretto could be made theatrically more effective – without changing the music. The letter is interesting for Kvapil's mention that he had seen the libretto for Act 1 many years before.

A year and a half later, Janáček made one last attempt to salvage *Fate*. Max Brod, the German translator of *Jenůfa*, had shown an interest in looking at the score. His comment was the most devastating of all:

Max Brod to Janáček   *Prague, 8 September 1918*   OS111

[. . .] In confronting your text of *Fate* I am, unfortunately, completely at a loss and in my opinion it would need a miracle, an inspiration of genius, to give *after the event* some sense to this impossible drama. Forgive me that I say so openly what I feel. [. . .]

After this Janáček abandoned any further thoughts about *Fate*. A year later at the age of sixty-five, he began writing a new opera, *Káťa Kabanová*, and with it a new phase of his career began. *Fate* was his only opera, apart from his final one, that he never saw performed.

---

1 A Freudian slip that gives some indication of the hurt that his negotiations with the Vinohrady Theatre left; Janáček means a Luhačovice one.

OS112   Fedora Bartošová to Zdenka Janáčková   *Bratislava, 15 March 1934*

I have just thanked Professor Vladimír Helfert for drawing my attention to Tuesday's broadcast[1] of the Brno Radiojournal [the Czechoslovak broadcasting company] in which we heard the performance of
Fate, thirty years old – and yet so beautiful. Then as a twenty-year-
old girl I *collaborated* on your husband's libretto. I cannot help on
this occasion writing to you also – and being transported in spirit into
the atmosphere of your flat, especially the one in Klášterní náměstí,
where we once lived as neighbours. How enthusiastically I worked at
the time! To Sudoměřice, where I travelled to, I always took with me
new ideas and appetite for work from my holidays. – And how sorry I
was when the composer was sometimes out of humour – and changed
his work on the various advice of his friends.
   [. . .]
What would the Maestro say today of the performance of his
work? [. . .]

---

1 This first broadcast performance (13 March 1934) under Břetislav Bakala was not
complete; a complete version was given later that year on 18 September. The first staged
performance of *Fate* took place in Brno on 25 October 1958.

5 The Excursions of Mr Brouček

THE EXCURSION OF MR BROUČEK TO THE MOON

'Significant words' (reprinted, with kind permission of the author, Mr BR1
Svatopluk Čech, from The Excursion of Mr Brouček to the Moon)

I.

Finally it ought to be added that everything simply teemed with endless caryatids, sphinxes, winged lions, griffins, statues, monstrous gargoyles, bosses, fantastic vases, weather-cocks, so that colourfully shining frescoes covered every inch of plaster, and that the whole of this Babylon appeared to vibrate madly with the sounds of unheard music. You might even think that the town itself was one colossal musical instrument.

The solemn tones of the organ resounded, gigantic bells tolled, here from a balcony the strains of a lute, there from a window a flute pined, elsewhere castanets clacked and a tambourine jingled; again elsewhere a tamtam thundered, one could hear shawms and cymbals, harps and bagpipes, glockenspiels and drums – every house contributed richly in its own way to the stupendous concert amongst which chorales sung by choruses could be heard and heart-rending arias. [. . .]

Hudební listy (1 February 1888)

It was into this cacophony that Mr Brouček intrepidly ventured during his *Excursion to the Moon*. This extract from Svatopluk Čech's recently published novel found its way into the February issue of Janáček's journal, *Hudební listy*, taking up two pages out of sixteen. It comes as something of a surprise. The journal, which Janáček had founded three and a half years earlier, usually provided a diet of theatre reviews, opera reviews (by Janáček), long theoretical articles (by Janáček) and historical articles published in instalments, and a few news items. The extract was chosen for its musical connections: at the end Mr Brouček flees from the concert hall during a performance of *Storm*, a composition by the lunar composer Harfoboj Hromný.

Whether this passage and the novel itself lodged in Janáček's mind as a potential opera subject can only be a matter of speculation. Janáček was working on *Šárka* at the time, and was soon to be engulfed in his rediscovery of Moravian folk music. The next year, 1889, he turned to Čech, unsuccessfully, for his collaboration on a cycle of folksong arrangements *The Little Queens* and in 1895 he contemplated a setting of Čech's *Slave Songs*. Svatopluk Čech (1846–1908) was a prominent literary figure of the time, known more for his poetry than for his prose, but he scored a success with his *Brouček* novels, which have remained popular to this day in Czechoslovakia. The first in particular, *The True Excursion of Mr Brouček to the Moon* (1888)[1] proved such a hit that Čech quickly brought out a second, *The Epoch-making Excursion of Mr Brouček, this Time to the Fifteenth Century* (1889) plus a couple of later, rather slighter sequels. In all the works the mechanism is the same: the comic confrontation of the resolutely philistine, middle-aged, middle-class Prague landlord Mr Brouček (Mr Beetle) with other worlds that are quite beyond his experience and comprehension. Mr Brouček finds the 'moon' inhabited by an ethereal breed of creatures who neither eat nor drink but live off the scent of flowers and devote themselves entirely to artistic pursuits. This was a send-up of extreme trends in Prague artistic society of the time. In comparison, the unpretentious, down-to-earth Mr Brouček comes across as more sympathetic. But in Mr Brouček's next venture, to the fifteenth-century Hussite Wars, a famous period in Czech history when the Czechs beat off armies of crusaders drawn from the whole of Europe, Mr Brouček's cowardice in the face of national peril is set in sharp relief to the stern heroism of the time.

The death of Svatopluk Čech on 21 February 1908 may have served to remind Janáček of him and his *Brouček*. Less than three weeks later, in the middle of his voluminous correspondence with Artuš Rektorys over *Fate* (OS44 ff), Janáček let slip the first indication of his renewed interest in *The True Excursion of Mr Brouček to the Moon*: he asked if, during his coming visit to Prague, he could be introduced to Čech's publisher (**BR2**, 12 March 1908). The meeting presumably took place: five days later Rektorys wrote to find out whether Janáček had 'gained a libretto' (**BR3**, 17 March 1908). As it becomes clear later in the correspondence, permission for the use of Čech's novel needed the consent of all seven members of the Čech family. This permission was obtained through their legal representative, Dr Ladislav Klumpar (**BR26**: Rektorys to Janáček, 28 October 1908). Janáček energetically set to work meeting two senior members of the family (**BR4**: Janáček to Rektorys, ?18 March 1908). Shortly afterwards a family conference was held where it was decided to allow Janáček to use the text, on condition that the libretto made from it was 'artistic work' (**BR5**: Rektorys to Janáček, 26 March 1908). Janáček had already heard the good news in a telegram from Rektorys on 21 March (**BR6**), just nine days after his inquiry about Čech's publisher. A letter written shortly before the telegram arrived

---

1 An early version appeared under a pseudonym in 1886 in *Květy*, the literary journal which Čech edited. This original version was considerably different, essentially a literary parody of the fashionable utopian novels of the period. Čech considerably strengthened the element of social satire in the 1888 version.

bears witness to his haste, impatience and passionate absorption in the project.

Janáček to Artuš Rektorys   *[Brno,] 21 March 1908*   BR7

The Čech family were to have a meeting on Tuesday [17 March] – and I still haven't had a line!

I beg you, I would be abundantly grateful if you could manage to get the Čech family to give me the rights for *Brouček*.

I am so taken with the material that it is difficult to write about it.

I have reminded both Dr Klumpar and Miss Zdenka Čechová again about the matter by letter – and all in vain.

I fear that they are at a loss [what to do] – and I don't know how to urge their acquiescence!

Perhaps you will succeed!

[. . .]

So I beg you – I am waiting for news from you [saying]:
                    You have Brouček!!
                                                              [JP31]

Janáček to Artuš Rektorys   *[undated, postmarked Brno,*   BR8
                                        21 March 1908]

You're a dear man! Thanks for the telegram. I will write in detail tomorrow.

Rektorys not only helped Janáček with negotiations over the rights for the libretto; he also proposed (in BR3) the opera's first librettist, Karel Mašek (1869–1922), librettist of Ladislav Prokop's opera *The Dream of the Forest*, produced in Prague in June 1907. In the same letter he asked for Janáček's ideas on the piece as a guide for the librettist. Janáček's response is an important document giving his first thoughts on the opera. Considering the long period of composition, it is surprising how closely Janáček adhered to his original plan:

Janáček to Artuš Rektorys   *[Brno,] 22 March 1908*   BR9

I hold on to the words: libretto permitted!

[. . .]

So you suggest Fa Presto [the pseudonym of Karel Mašek]?

We will thus agree the matter. I don't know Mr Mašek; forgive me then if I ask you again for your good offices.

Tell him that I therefore ask him for his work as a librettist.

In its basic outlines I see the whole like this:

Please have a copy of *The Excursion of Mr Brouček to the Moon* to hand.

1. Four acts[1] naturally suggest themselves:
 I. (pp.18–32)[2]
 II. (–p.96)
 III. (–p.168)
 IV. to the end.

2. On stage (a view from the castle steps to the entrance of the street leading to the Vikárka)[3] *the first act* takes place late on a moonlit night;

The second act takes place on the fabulously beautiful lunar landscape with *Lunobor*'s quaint summer house in the background (pictures on pp.63 and 67 [see Plate 6a]).

The third act is in the centre of the palace of All Arts: a vestibule with corridors radiating out to the poets, painters and musicians (partly shown on the picture on p.126).

The fourth act, again on the earth, I don't want to locate yet: perhaps in the landlord's [Brouček's] room, just as they are bringing him home and he is babbling on and addressing everybody in the style of his moon adventures!

3. It will be necessary to work out in more detail:

a) In the first act we will have to bring Würfl and his staff on stage; [depicting them] quite realistically as they close the pub and Mr Brouček's earthly life that day.

b) The fourth act is likewise not sufficiently worked out.

Could a foil to Etherea be introduced, perhaps some buxom barmaid or 'domestic servant'?

c) In the third [= second] act Brouček would have to be more affectionate to Etherea – *until he recognizes the flimsiness of her body.*

---

1 The four-act division of the excursion survived until the later revision of the opera when the first two acts became two scenes of Act 1. The relationship is shown as follows:

original plan	final version
Act 1	Act 1 Scene 1
Act 2	Act 1 Scene 2
Act 3	Act 2
Act 4	Act 3 (Epilogue – later omitted)

2 These, and all subsequent page references, are to the 1888 edition of the novel, illustrated by Viktor Oliva. Janáček's working copy, with numerous annotations and re-bound with alternating blank pages, is in BmJA, JK 9.

3 A well-known and still surviving pub, opposite St Vít's Cathedral in the precincts of the Prague castle.

For her part, Etherea would have to become noticeably inflamed by the portly Brouček, *pursuing him from that moment.*

The convulsive outbursts of Blankytný (a sonorous alto) (p.93) would be a splendid end to that act!

d) The fourth [=third] act: the moving force would be Etherea as she flies in after Brouček; a catastrophe occurs when from one side of the door Etherea calls out 'Jsi můj! jsi můj!' ['You're mine! you're mine!'] and from the other Brouček is driven away by the noise of *Storm* [the composition described in BRI+].

He blows her away – a tragic death!

In the moon acts (2 and 3) all the people involved are in continual rhythmic – *i.e. balletic* – movement.

Acts 1 and 4 with their naturalism would make a superb contrast.

These are my general observations on the libretto.

By this of course I don't rule out good ideas and another arrangement and conception of the whole!

Please therefore place these lines before Mr Mašek. Let him make a proposal, let it all then be settled with a contract, *but soon, as soon as possible!*

I would then come to Prague.

Much of this was preserved in the final version. The few changes that do occur affect only details. Blankytný for instance (not the *travesti* alto as suggested but a typical Janáček high tenor) is joined by Lunobor in bringing Act 2 to an end. Etherea's part, although an important element of the third act, does not constitute its main 'moving force'. Janáček discovered, a year later, a more ingenious solution for her 'foil' than the 'buxom barmaid' (see BR32+). The biggest departure from this initial conception was the omission of the *Storm* symphony. Originally this loss was partly compensated for by the final moon chorus with its references to noisy instruments (see BR48+), but when Viktor Dyk (see p. 192, fn.2), in the final revision, rewrote František Gellner's verses for this moon chorus (BR80–81), even this association fell away. Janáček's emphasis on the realistic aspects of Acts 1 and 4 and on the necessity to fill them out was crucial; these were the main points of variance between him and his first librettist, Karel Mašek.

ACT I

Karel Mašek to Artuš Rektorys   *[undated, Prague, 29 March 1908]*   **BR10**

Although at the moment I am largely occupied with my own work – and besides I have 'manufactured' just about enough librettos 'from materials brought to me'[1] – nevertheless I would like to be further acquainted with the proposition concerning *Brouček*, since this material happens to be very dear to me and years ago I made a libretto from it; at the time of course it remained unused. If it is your wish to discuss the matter further with me, I will expect you.

In his letter written to Rektorys the next day (**BR11**, 30 March) in response to an abortive visit by Rektorys to his flat, Mašek stated his financial conditions (an advance of K250 and a quarter of the composer's royalty) and suggested a meeting with Janáček. He warned him that he could not promise a complete libretto before November. No letters from Janáček to Mašek survive, but it is clear from Mašek's next letter that Janáček had written back, proposing to visit Mašek in Prague. Even before the matter of the librettist had been settled, Janáček had begun work on the introduction (**BR12**: Janáček to Rektorys, 27 March 1908).

BR13   **Karel Mašek to Janáček**   *Prague, 4 April 1908*

I was delighted to receive your letter and it will be an honour for me to meet you personally; surely only then will it be possible to come to a definitive agreement and decision; I will also tell you then frankly of the circumstances that might hold up the work from my side.

I ask only that I should know in good time the actual days of your stay in Prague, for I am due to spend part of the holidays in the country.

My original libretto, made years ago, was written with a small, domestic production in mind, which then did not come off; it was divided into three acts (arrival on the moon – at Lunobor's – in front of the Temple of All Arts and departure), and written for only four characters.

How I would visualize it today – that will become clear during our verbal negotiations.

One point that emerges from Mašek's description of his earlier *Brouček* scenario is that he was not concerned with the earth scenes. Admittedly they are not an important part of Čech's novel, their function is merely to acquaint the reader with Brouček's character by depicting him in home surroundings: the core of the novel lies in the conflict between the philistine Brouček and the Moon Artists. Mašek nevertheless accepted Janáček's four-act division and overall conception of the opera (**BR14**: Mašek to Janáček,

---

1 Mašek is quoting from typical tailors' advertisements of the time.

2 May 1908) and a fortnight later sent off what he had written of the libretto so far – six pages mostly devoted to the first act.[1]

Karel Mašek to Janáček *Prague, 17 May 1908* **BR15**

I am sending what I can like the poor widow; I leave on Wednesday, as I told you some time ago – and before my departure I had an awful lot to do to get everything in order. So please don't be angry with me – I refer you again to my original remark [that he would not be able to do the work before November].

I am working very uncertainly, trying to get round similarities in diction and to catch something of the [original] character; and then I'm not happy with it – perhaps there is not enough time for 'maturing' and for revisions.

I'm sending Act 2 only in its main outlines, I think that changes will be necessary here. The first [act] in a little more detail – and the earth scene expanded.

I will change things or put them into verse according to your wishes (the drinking-songs?) But I observe once again that I will withdraw, renouncing all rights, should you find a suitable person to help you sooner.

Perhaps Mr Mrštík[2] could recommend someone to you? I heard that he greatly praised Mr Kurt[3] (and as a writer of verse).

I know that you are in a hurry for the thing and that the continual delay rests with me, and I have a bad conscience on account of it.

On 20 May Janáček wrote to Rektorys to say that he had received 'the beginning' of the libretto and was now immersed in 'joyful work' (**BR16**). Mašek's libretto for Act 1 consisted of a short parting conversation on the steps of the Vikárka between Brouček and the innkeeper, Würfl, interrupted by a drinking-song from within the inn. Brouček finally says goodnight and hurries away. This is followed by Brouček's address to the moon, to be taken straight from Čech (Mašek merely quotes the page number of the passage). During this eulogy on the manifold advantages of a moon which lacks all the sordid complications of everyday life, Brouček finds himself drawn higher

1 Virtually all libretto material for this opera is held in BmJA. A full list with shelfmarks can be found in Tyrrell 1968–9, 120–2.
2 Mašek presumably had in mind here the Moravian playwright Vilém Mrštík (1863–1912). Together with his brother Alois (1861–1925), he wrote *Maryša*, which Janáček considered for an opera libretto in July 1908. Janáček did approach the Mrštík brothers for a *Brouček* libretto, as is clear from BR39.
3 Janáček had connections later with Maximilian Kurt (pseudonym of Maximilian Kunert, 1877–1960), since in 1911 he composed the cantata *Čarták on Soláň* to Kurt's text, but seems not to have turned to him on this occasion.

and higher by some inexplicable force until (in the second act) he finds himself on the moon. Mašek was clearly reluctant to introduce new elements: the drinking-chorus is the only incident not to be found directly in the original.

BR17   Karel Mašek to Janáček   *Capri, 4 June 1908*

I have seen Naples – now I must die – and I won't be able to finish the libretto, but if I don't die, I will return to Prague on the 15th.

BR18   Karel Mašek to Janáček   *[Prague,] 4 July 1908*

Forgive me that I didn't reply immediately; after my return I had a lot of work that had accumulated, and also I became a little ill from the fatigue of the journey.

I would gladly fit in with your plans, since your intentions for your work are, naturally, the deciding factor. But it seems to me that there is a fundamental conflict between us in how we regard the original, i.e. Čech's *Brouček*.

You place the main emphasis on the realistic earthly side, while I would rather suppress this as much as possible and instead emphasize the poetical and satirical moon scenes.

I acknowledge your standpoint and would gladly accommodate you – but it won't work with me, for it goes against my own view.

Indeed I like the character of the Young Waiter very much, it is certainly most apt – but, however nice, I can't bring myself to add this part to Čech's work in addition to Mazal at the Vikárka. Čech's Mr Brouček would never have fraternized with Mazal and sat with him in the same pub.

Mazal (the word means 'dauber') is fleetingly mentioned in Čech as one of Brouček's more difficult 'Bohemian' tenants. On p.19 of the novel, Brouček is described as being 'in a gloomy mood caused by one of his tenants, a painter by profession; the details of this affair would scarcely interest the reader and therefore I shall pass over them in silence.' To this Janáček laconically added in the margin – 'pity'.

I will make one more attempt – and so today I ask once again for your indulgence. I must satisfy you somehow as soon as possible. If you have any further plan concerning the scene on the moon, please send it to me so that we could take it at the same time.

A few days later, in response to Rektorys's inquiry about *Brouček*, and whether Janáček was satisfied with Mašek (**BR19**, 7 July 1908), Janáček commented that Mašek was too overawed by Čech, but believed that they would reach an agreement since they both wanted the best for the work (**BR20**, 8 July 1908). Janáček's optimism was unfounded.

Karel Mašek to Janáček   *[Prague,] 21 July 1908*   **BR21**

I thank you for your kind notes and ask your pardon for not writing for so long. But after your last letter it seems very difficult to me; of course, putting the thing off only makes it worse – and so I must go at it.

I am not 'afraid' – but your writing reveals an even more fundamental difference between our views, the conflict of musician and writer. For me the original work, out of which one has to create, is sacred and as far as possible inviolable; I allow only for the conversion to a stage setting – from Zeyer's novel (for Ostrčil)[1] I retained everything to the fullest extent as far as possible, course of action, scenes, diction, and did not admit foreign elements.

Having an affection for *Brouček*, I wanted to take on its adaptation only 'out of love' although – as you know – at the expense of other works which I had decided on earlier, and which are more important to me.

But now I simply cannot accept your views – we are completely at odds. [. . .]

The letter ends with a further proposal for a new librettist (Josef Vymětal)[2] and a refusal to continue work. Even then Janáček seemed undeterred. In answer to another inquiry from Rektorys about the progress of *Brouček*, he replied on 26 September (**BR22**) that since Mašek had not sent his libretto, he was getting on with smaller things: 'If you see Mr K.M., remind him of me, and my longing to have his work right now.' It was only on receiving Mašek's next, even more strongly worded, letter that Janáček at last accepted that Mašek would not give him a libretto.

Karel Mašek to Janáček   *[Prague,] 28 October 1908*   **BR23**

I assure you that by letting myself be drawn into making a rash promise which I was unable to fulfil, my difficulties have been made much greater. But however I try, I'm unable to produce a single line,

---

1 Ostrčil's opera *Kunála's Eyes* (1908); for Zeyer see Chap.1.
2 Josef Vymětal (1872–1935), writer and translator into Czech of some forty operas (including the *Ring*).

and I doubt that I shall be able to do so in the foreseeable future; I am living in terrible spiritual depression.

It's not through my efforts that the matter got into the newspapers – nor you into your [present] situation [–], for as early as the spring I begged you to relieve me of this obligation and I suggested to you two other ways forward; you completely ignored my request.

This doesn't of course excuse my fault that I am unable to refuse energetically when something is asked of me.

I think that it is not too late for another hand, quicker and more competent, to take up the work now, and I will send the manuscript immediately for this purpose.

I cannot excuse myself, nor can I ask for forgiveness.

By now a further complication had arisen. The composer Karel Moor had written to Rektorys (BR24, 25 October 1908) demanding to know whether there was any truth in the report that Janáček was composing a *Brouček* opera, because Moor himself had received express permission to use the work from Vladimír Čech, the younger brother of the late Svatopluk Čech. Though Janáček and Rektorys established in their next flurry of letters that Moor was working on incomplete and thus invalid permission (BR25: Janáček to Rektorys, 27 October 1908; BR26: Rektorys to Janáček, 28 October 1908), Moor went ahead with his work, and his operetta *The Excursion of Mr Brouček to the Moon* was performed in 1910, ten years before Janáček's opera reached the stage. At this point Janáček called it a day with Mašek.

BR27   Janáček to Artuš Rektorys   *Brno, 1 November 1908*

[. . .] Mr Karel Mašek did not behave well. When I called at his house after the holidays – actually in the holidays – I was told 'that I would receive a continuation in two days'.

Now I am negotiating about a continuation with the writer Holý and Dr Janke. [. . .]

With Holý, however, Janáček had no success at all.

BR28   Josef Holý to Janáček   *Brno, 8 November 1908*

I wanted to speak personally with you about *Brouček*, but perhaps it's enough if I write a few words in this way, since you aren't here.

I don't like the material and I have no inclination to do a libretto. If there is not the will or the right mood, it would not turn out well, however I tried, and so I ask you to count me out.

But allow me to advise you to turn to Mr K. St. [sic] Neumann,[1] a writer in Bílovice near Brno, who might perhaps take the thing on.

Josef Holý (1874–1928) may have been more interested than this letter suggests, since two years later he published in the literary magazine *Lumír* (xxxviii, 1910, 193–202), a 'ballet with songs in three parts' entitled *The Moon*, loosely connected to Čech's novel (see BR38).

Dr Zikmund Janke (1865–1918) proved more amenable. He was a medical doctor, a ear, nose and throat specialist working both in Prague and in the spa of Luhačovice, where Janáček had got to know him during several summer holidays. From 1903 to 1912 Janke edited a journal for singers, *Věstník pěvecký a hudební.*

Dr Zikmund Janke to Janáček   *Luhačovice, 15 November 1908*   BR29

I have been held up a little with my reply – do forgive me. I have just had some necessary and urgent work!

So let me tell you: I will at any rate have a go at the text [you] mentioned. There is only the question – if I will be up to it. I will however do all I can to make it so. I therefore intend to do a section as soon as possible and give it to you to look at – [to see] if it corresponds with your intentions. If you should wish some other approach do tell me your opinion quite openly, for I would want to satisfy you.

Would you perhaps have a preliminary sketch *of your own* of the whole work?

In how many acts do you see it?

Do you know already *from where to where* each individual act should go?

If you would then like perhaps to give me similar information or wishes – please do – I will try to satisfy you. Perhaps there will soon be another meeting of the Luhačovice administrative committee and then we could see each other in Brno in person and have a talk about the matter.

Two weeks later Janke sent off his libretto for the first scene:

Dr Zikmund Janke to Janáček   *Luhačovice, 16 December 1908*   BR30

I am very curious to hear your judgement since it will indicate to me whether I should, and if I can, continue *more or less in this vein.*

For this reason I have not even begun Act 2.

---

1 Stanislav Kostka Neumann (1875–1947), poet and communist publicist.

BR31   Dr Zikmund Janke to Janáček   *Luhačovice, 22 January 1909*

I was somewhat unpleasantly surprised by your esteemed last letter, because I see that the time that I have devoted to *Brouček* up till now has been for nothing. I had got started with 'composing' the second act and already have a 'nice pile' of lines ready – when your esteemed letter 'shot' into this, and in such a way that it completely shot my work to pieces. While, on the one hand, it is unpleasant for me, I appreciate that, on the other, the plan you have done is *indeed more effective and more suited to the theatre* – I only regret that it was not made known to me earlier. I still see too much lyricism and simple narrative in *Čech*'s work, and I completely recognize that elements *must* come into it which would give it theatrical life and an ability to succeed in the *theatre*!

I had in no way kept this opinion from you when I wrote to you the very *first* time on this matter, asking you if you had some definite plan drawn up ... And for this reason I now regret that the plan, which you have now kindly proposed to me, was not put at my disposal right at the *beginning of work*, since meanwhile much time has elapsed, and I have my hands full of all sorts of other essential work. The plan would have very much appealed to me – I acknowledge it to be very good (although considerably different from Čech's work – but that must be so) – but it is now a question of whether there will be enough time for me to be finished with it in the way you want. I am very much taken up with all sorts of functions which I cannot get out of. For this reason I advise you most sincerely: if you have someone else to whom you could and wanted to turn, please do this completely according to your inclination. I would not be offended in any way! If not, then I will continue to keep my word to you, but I would have to be given a decidedly longer period in which to finish my 'product.' [...]

Janáček's 'last letter' mentioned at the beginning of BR31 has disappeared and its contents can only be inferred. Janke's next communication, apart from a précis of this letter a week later (it seems that Janáček mislaid BR31), was a short note on 9 February (**BR32**), in which Janke 'gladly agreed' and hoped 'that it would work very well in this way'.

Two things seem to have happened. One was that Janke had mistaken his instructions as far as the first act was concerned. By the time he got in touch with Janke, Janáček had completed a rough draft of Act 1, made a revised version of it and copied out the words in a libretto. It is clear that Janke saw this copy. It was probably made for him as the guide he had asked for in

BR29 as his subsequent libretto closely followed it in its action: Mašek's chorus, which Janáček incorporated, is actually quoted. Janáček himself had added a few details, including Čech's Young Waiter (the character that Mašek, in BR18, could not bring himself to add), who runs after Brouček with the sausages that he forgot. Unless Janáček intended rewriting every note of the sung portions, it is clear that what he needed from Janke was not a new libretto but merely verbal additions for passages where he had overrun the available words and written in textless voice parts. Such places were indicated in the libretto he sent to Janke with red-pencil signs (e.g. words for the Waiter calling after Brouček; for Mazal's mocking of Brouček). Janke did a great deal more. He produced a completely new piece of work full of rhyming couplets in a breezy, drinking-chorus style. Janáček was not taken with it. He underlined only two passages that appealed to him: a couplet for Mazal, where he makes fun of Brouček, and the following couplet:

Svatá pravda, to je malvaz!
Člověk by ho vypil naráz!

['Sacred truth, that's Malmsey! A fellow could drink it up in one go!']

These lines originally were also to have been sung by Mazal. By a strange chance they remained in the opera as a fragment of a drinking-chorus heard from the inn just before Mr Brouček emerges (VS10–11) – Janke's sole contribution to the final score of the opera.

However, both from the tone of Janke's letter (BR31) and from the reference in it to a new plan, it is also clear that Janáček had had an entirely new idea which was going to affect the whole work.

Opposite the first page of his revision of the score, Janáček jotted down the following words in pencil: *Málka* (like 'Málinka' and 'Máli' a diminutive of 'Amálie'), *Sakristán*, and *valčík* (waltz). Here, in just a few words, were the remaining characters in this scene and an important new element of the plot. The new characters added are the Sacristan and his daughter, Málinka. Málinka is in love with the painter Mazal; her father would prefer her to marry the well-to-do Mr Brouček. The final version of the opera begins with a quarrel between Málinka and Mazal over a waltz he is alleged to have danced with Brouček's housekeeper. The significance of the extra two characters is shown in the cast list that Janáček quoted in his first surviving letter to Janke:

Janáček to Dr Zikmund Janke — Brno, 8 March 1909 — BR33

I missed you – and I would so much have liked to have settled all this with you.

I enclose a sketch of Act 1.

I would be glad if there was some *Prague dialect*, slang expressions such as are common in this sort of company. Would it be possible?

At 1) it could be put into verse. [. . .]

At 2) the Sacristan[1] *hates* Mazal,[2] who is courting his daughter.
    Mr Brouček
    Würfl (Čaroskvoucí)
    Mazal (Hvězdan Blankytný)
    Sacristan (Lunobor)
    Málka, his daughter (Etherea)
    Waiter from the Vikárka
    Painters, musicians, police, moon-beings

I need here a *few* juicy two- or three-syllable terms of abuse.

Scene 3. The drunken Brouček *curses everybody*, in this way he relieves his feelings and goes – to the moon.
The Sacristan proffers his daughter to him [as a bride].
Scene 5 is in Čech's original.

That is my sketch. You can change it, correct it, improve it with ideas, just as you wish.
    I expect it as soon as possible.
    In Act 2 you will have more work.
    There, verse will be necessary throughout – except for Brouček.

What Janáček did was not merely to add characters to fill out the action of this first act: he took the relationships between the characters from Čech's moon scenes and mirrored them in earthly terms. Lunobor and his daughter Etherea became the Sacristan and his marriageable daughter Málinka. Both Málinka and Etherea enjoy flirting with Brouček, mainly to arouse the jealousy of Mazal-Blankytný. The parallel does not always fit; the Sacristan is not prepared to accept the impoverished painter Mazal as his prospective son-in-law, while on the moon Lunobor thinks highly of the poet Blankytný.

    The other parallel that Janáček made was the identification of the moon patron, the 'Maecenas' Čaroskvoucí, basking in the adulation of the moon artists, with Würfl, the innkeeper of the Vikárka, celebrated by the earth artists for his beer. Čech suggested that Brouček, on his return, talked to people as if he were still on the moon, but the idea of Brouček's earthly acquaintance being parallelled by the moon-beings of his dream, is Janáček's alone.

---

1 In this letter and other early documents Janáček uses the word *kostelník*; later versions give *sakristán*. Both denote a man who looks after a church in some way. A *sakristán* (sacristan) is more concerned with its contents; the term is associated with larger town churches and cathedrals. A *kostelník* (verger, sexton) is a broader term which might include bell-ringing, grave-digging etc, and is more likely to be found in the country. That Janáček intended *sakristán* is corroborated by the added location ('at St Vít's', i.e. the cathedral).
2 For the final list of characters in the opera and explanations of their names see notes at the end of this chapter, pp.246–7.

Janáček's response to Janke's hints of delays (BR31) has not survived, but it can be inferred from later correspondence that he suggested that he would sketch the libretto himself and then send it to Janke for corrections and additions. Janke agreed in his note of 9 February 1909 (BR32); Janáček sent off the sketch on 8 March (BR33), and had it back ten days later (**BR34:** Janke to Janáček, 17 March 1909). As it was, there was little that Janke changed or corrected. This libretto contains only a few tentative pencil suggestions, none of which was incorporated into the musical setting. Janke appears to have given only moral support.

By 19 March Janáček was able to report to Rektorys: 'I have the *Brouček* libretto at last. I think it will be good' (**BR35**).   Some months later, in a letter to Rektorys complaining about the amount of work he had to do in the wake of various crises at the Organ School, Janáček let slip the following remark: 'and on top of all this I had to compose *Mr Brouček's Excursion*, [just] the first act, four times' (**BR36**, 26 September 1909). This is an exaggeration, unless Janáček was counting the eleven pages he wrote before receiving Mašek's libretto as a separate version. Altogether he composed two very early versions (the second simply a revision of the first) without the Sacristan and his daughter. From the original novel only Brouček's mono-logue to the moon and a basic framework of four characters (Brouček, Mazal, Würfl, the Young Waiter) could be used. Mašek's libretto had vir-tually no effect on the course of the opera, apart from a drinking-chorus and a few lines where Brouček is mocked. Neither did Janke's, apart from the two lines quoted above. It was during his correspondence with Janke that Janáček filled out the action with extra characters and extra action and produced a new libretto, to which he composed his third version of Act 1, presumably complete by the time he wrote to Rektorys on 26 September 1909.

ACT 2

Janáček to Artuš Rektorys   *Brno, 18 February 1910*   **BR37**

[. . .] I have not progressed further than Act 1.
Why?
Last year's drudgery almost cost me my health.
In the holidays I got a heart murmur.
Now it's quietened down again, but I no longer look happily at the world!
I've just written a sort of *Fairy Tale* for piano and cello.
And now I'll make a start on Act 2 of *Brouček*.   [. . .]

BR38   **Artuš Rektorys to Janáček**   *Prague, 28 March 1910*

[. . .] In *Lumír* I saw Holý's ballet *The Moon*, i.e. that material which you told me about some time ago as an independent concept based on [Čech's] *The Excursion of Mr Brouček to the Moon*. I assume it's not possible to get Holý for any further adaptation that you might require?

BR39   **Janáček to Artuš Rektorys**   *[undated, postmarked Brno,*
                                                        29 March 1910]

[. . .] When, in what number of *Lumír*, did Holý's *The Moon* come out?

I've got troubles with the libretto.

For a whole year Mr Mašek – did not have a single idea; the Mrštík brothers, and Elgart Sokol refused; Holý wrote something other than *Brouček* – he wanted to flood me with a sea of quantitative 'feet'[1] – and even has the nerve to publish it!

[. . .]

Next in order was a lady, and also Dr Janke.

I am going to stick to Svatopluk Čech's *Brouček* as faithfully as possible – just let all these other poets of ours leave me in peace.

Everyone is buried in the mist of a narrow horizon and can never reach the sun of a new idea.

This letter provides evidence that the circle of potential librettists that Janáček approached was even greater than his correspondence so far has indicated, with Janáček turning to the Mrštík brothers (whom Mašek had suggested in BR15), as well as their associate, the Moravian writer Karel Elgart Sokol. It would also seem that Holý's contact with Janáček was greater than that suggested by the few surviving notes they exchanged. As Janáček had not yet seen the published ballet scenario by Holý his entirely accurate comments on its character indicate that Holý must have shown it to him earlier, in manuscript. Its chief idea is that the publican's daughter Bětuška is transformed into the moon-being Luneta during the hero's brief sojourn on the moon – a flight of fantasy induced by his nearly drowning in a pond in which he sees a reflection of the full moon (and like Brouček apostrophizes on the better life on the moon). This may have given Janáček the idea of doing something similar in his libretto, but on a wider scale, i.e.

---

1 *'stop' časoměrných*; early nineteenth-century Czech prosody havered between quantitative and accentual verse, settling for the latter towards the end of the century. It is unlikely that Janáček is making a precise comment on the prosody; more that he considered it oldfashioned.

finding parallels between all the characters on the earth and on the moon (see BR33+).

The identity of the 'lady' is mysterious. That it could be Fedora Bartošová, the librettist of *Fate*, as Jiří Mahen asserted,[1] is hardly plausible. Despite his earlier enthusiasm for her verse, Janáček went to Skácelík rather than back to Bartošová for a revision of the *Fate* text. No correspondence between the two survives after 1904, and Bartošová's letter to Helfert (OS28) suggests no more contacts between them after then.

Janáček's first thoughts on Act 2 can be pieced together from the 1908 scenario he sent to Rektorys (BR9), from three letters he wrote to Janke in March 1909, from his comments and annotations in his copy of the original novel, and from a single sheet, a remnant of a longer scenario.

In his letter to Janke of 8 March 1909 (BR33), Janáček commented that Janke would have more to do than in the first act as 'verse will be necessary throughout – except for Brouček'. This notion was apparently based on Čech's remark in the novel that the moon-beings spoke mostly in verse, a custom, however, rarely observed in Čech's dialogue. In the event, except for special set-numbers, Janáček contented himself with moon dialogue in prose most of the time. Another request (BR40, 21 March 1909) was that Janke should include allusions to the parallels between earth and moon characters.

The single sheet (numbered '4')[2] was part of a longer sketch of a scenario for at least the first two acts. The fragment starts in the middle of a discussion of the relations between Brouček and Etherea and continues with a dialogue between Blankytný and Brouček: Brouček refuses to kneel in front of a woman, a stance that Blankytný recommends as appropriate to the occasion. This is straight from Čech. The sketch continues:

Fragment of Act 2 scenario (undated) BR41

The scene will climax in 'where do the children come from?'. Blankytný stops his ears – but Etherea is already head over heels in love with Brouček. After a nice duet, trio (pp. 72–30 [these pages in Janáček's 1888 edition of the novel refer to the verse that Blankytný sings while he accompanies Brouček to Lunobor's house]), the procession advances, moving in balletic motion and singing, *to the Cathedral of All Arts.*

Etherea will not leave Brouček now – and Blankytný is shaking with jealousy. Brouček bounds along with them.

This scenario complements Janáček's annotations to his copy of Čech's novel,[3] which were written mainly in the margin but also occasionally on the

---

1 In *Venkov* (24 April 1917), reprinted in JA v, 30, fn.23.
2 BmJA, L 32 (e).
3 More fully described in Tyrrell 1968–9.

blank pages that he had had bound into his copy. Certain interests predominate. One of these is the dance element that follows from a remark in Čech's novel, underlined in red by Janáček, that owing to the lighter air-pressure on the moon Brouček finds himself actually dancing. This is constantly alluded to: the word 'dance' occurs four times in these annotations. A related concept is the ceremonial march of the moon-beings mentioned at the end of the sketch and twice in the novel annotations. Another of Janáček's preoccupations here is the allocation of voices. Etherea is to be a soprano, her father Lunobor a bass, and Blankytný, as suggested in the 1908 scenario, is marked in at his first appearance as an alto. They were certainly made before Janáček had the idea of linking the earth and moon roles early in 1909 (with the result that Blankytný had to be a tenor like his earthly counterpart Mazal).

Janáček's decision to stick as closely as possible to the original Čech determined the nature of the versions of libretto for both Acts 2 and 3. His first libretto for Act 2 (written on a huge, folded sheet of poor-quality wrapping paper), when compared to pp.34–96 of the novel, reveals that Janáček added nothing new: almost every word can be traced back to Čech, except for the earth-moon parallels and the operatic compression of the end of the act into a trio by collating relevant passages from pp. 92–4. The motivation here is a little different, too. It is Etherea's 'eloping' with Mr Brouček to the Cathedral of All Arts, hotly pursued by her lover Blankytný and father Lunobor, which brings the act to a conclusion, rather than Blankytný's escorting Mr Brouček to the Cathedral for a cultural tour. More changes, mostly omissions, were made in the course of composition. According to his letter to Janke (BR42), composition was complete by April 1911.

ACT 3

The substance of Act 3 in both Čech and Janáček is that Mr Brouček finds himself at Čaroskvoucí's Cathedral of All Arts and is shown round the three main wings, devoted to Poetry, Painting and Music. In desperation both at the posturings of the moon artists and at Etherea's advances, Mr Brouček takes off on the winged horse, Pegasus, on which he had arrived with Etherea; he finds himself flying back to earth. In this act Janáček introduced rather more changes. Brouček is soon detached from his original mentor, Blankytný, whose role shrinks accordingly. On the other hand the parts of Lunobor and his daughter Etherea are expanded. In Čech they appear only at the beginning and the end of this section while in Janáček they chase in and out of the main action.

Janáček's earliest annotations in his copy of the novel and the passage he reprinted in *Hudební listy* suggest that he was originally drawn to *Brouček* by its musical references. He made a point of underlining passages that dealt with the sounds or appearances of instruments. He marked the description of the composition *Storm* approvingly and suggested an 'infernal row' to accompany Etherea's song. Music was also needed for Mr Brouček's home-ward journey ('Music of the spheres', he noted). Čaroskvoucí was to be a 'baryton'. But it was only the two last elements, Čaroskvoucí's voice type, and the splendid interlude music, that survived. A major departure from the very first libretto was the omission of most of Mr Brouček's encounters with moon musicians. In Čech the last of Brouček's lunar experiences occurs when, running away from Etherea, he finds himself in a concert hall listening to *Storm*: he has entered the musicians' sector. This was cut, and instead Janáček introduced a single musician into the poets' sector (where the action starts), an 'ugly, lanky fellow', who comes on crying 'Ooooh, E flat, E flat!'.

Janáček's first libretto for Act 3 was written in ink on the blank pages opposite the printed text of his copy of Čech's novel, the first act to be written out in this way. A second libretto, written on separate sheets, shows a considerable reorganization of the material, for instance the introduction of the flower banquet scene, which in Čech occurs earlier, at Lunobor's house, and which Janáček now copied out word for word. In this new libretto certain passages were marked with red pencil, Janáček's usual sign that he needed outside co-operation. The passages concerned are:

1. Čaroskvoucí's song
2. The arrival of Mr Brouček at the Cathedral of All Arts
3. Oblačný's recitation of a 'hundred ghazels'[1]
4. Brouček's enforced adoration of Duhoslav's picture.

For help with Čaroskvoucí's song Janáček turned again to Dr Janke and Josef Holý. Janáček's letters to both, and the two replies, all survive, though of these four letters only one is dated – Janke's of 16 April 1911. The letter that prompted it reveals something of Janáček's original conception of the piece:

Janáček to Dr Zikmund Janke   *[undated, Brno, April 1911]*   BR42

I come again after a long period. I'm finished with Act 2 and enclose a sketch of Act 3 [probably the second libretto described above].

The red dots show you where I lack text.

In particular I desperately need the song: 'O a patron's vocation is hard'; just in the form of Čech's sonnets.

Perhaps you *also* know some sort of 'patron' from real life?

Particularly as Čech conceives him – so long as he is a patron they celebrate him – and the results when this no longer happens!

---

1 ghazel: an Arabic word for love-making, also applied to a form of lyrical verse (usually a love-poem) in which the first two lines and all even lines end with the same rhyme or word. The Czech poet Jaroslav Vrchlický, one of the objects of Čech's satire, wrote ghazels in imitation of fourteenth-century Arabic and Persian models. Oblačný's 'hundred ghazels' exaggerates the form by having every line end with the same word or words: at first 'od věků', then 'zánikem', finally 'vnedohlednu' (VS109–16).

Thus please read through the sketch and send it to me as soon as possible.

Janke's reply (**BR43**, 16 April 1911) came from Switzerland, where he was on holiday. Although he was unhappy with the song, he enclosed it as requested, to show his goodwill. Janáček exercised his judgement and, ignoring Janke's rollicking couplets, turned instead to Holý. This time he sent his own idea as a guide:

BR44   Janáček to Josef Holý   *[undated, Brno, April 1911]*

Song: O how hard is the calling of a patron! In this the publican Würfl has in fact to show through the Maecenas Čaroskvoucí.

A few ideas have occurred to me, but of course I don't want you to be bound by them.

O how hard is the calling of a patron (to a composer):

O nightingale – that melody – but only on the bombardon [a bass tuba]. I hear that melody only from the bombardons.

– and in those nimble rhythms (he hums a polka tune).

That's it!

O how hard is the calling of a patron (to a painter):

But why do you paint that ragamuffin! You should paint (conspicuously indicating himself) that collection of nobility and ideal proportions –

and that black spot, there under the nose (a painter somewhere at the back, rudely)?

That's a shadow! – but put it somewhere else!

O how hard is the calling of a patron! (to a poet):

Well, good! Say Aurora, and not eye, say locks and not hair. And never water! – just dewiness, crystal, mirror!

May I ask you for this!

Holý's reply (**BR45**, undated), written on the back of Janáček's note, was brief: perhaps Janáček's ideas would be better left in prose, not put into verse.

It would seem from the abrupt style of Janáček's letter that he had already been in contact with Holý (who also lived in Brno) over the proposed contribution, and that Holý thus had some idea what it was about. The conception of this song, involving the three artistic wings of the Cathedral of All Arts, is a development of the idea noted in the sketches, of collecting all the artists together at the beginning of the scene. The instructions to the painters and to the musicians are Janáček's inventions, those to the poets

were from Čech. The opening idea of the song – the hard lot of a patron –
comes from Čech as well.

The only part of this version of the song that was ultimately worked into
the opera was the instruction to the musicians. Janáček eventually got his
song for Čaroskvoucí from elsewhere, but it is introduced with virtually the
same words ('Tuto melodii – ale do bombardonu') and a short tuba solo
(VS82).

Janáček's next collaborator proved more helpful. There is no clue as to
who this could be; the handwriting belongs to none of the other librettists.
The contribution consists of three unnumbered sheets written in pencil. The
first, dealing with Mr Brouček's arrival, offers lines of horror for Čaroskvoucí and the artists. It is evident that the line which Janáček eventually
set as chorus reaction to Brouček's arrival, 'Příšera z dálavy!' ['Monster from
faraway!', VS86] was inspired by one of the exclamations of the artists here:
'Příšera vzdálených temnot!' ['Monster from distant darknesses!'].

The second page was concerned with the problematic patron song, and the
third page with Oblačný's recitation. This is written in a tight metrical form,
each line consisting of two groups of six syllables, each group ending with a
stressed monosyllable giving a pompous effect, well suited to the pretentious
recitation in mind. Although the recitation itself was not used in the opera,
one of the lines was taken over by Harfoboj just between Čaroskvoucí's song
and Brouček's arrival:

Ústa zamkněte již, zpívati počnu já!

['Mouths shut now, to sing begin I!', VS85]

Mr Brouček's arrival was the reason for Harfoboj's not carrying out his
intention.

Janáček's failure to find someone to undertake the patron song and other
Act 3 insertions held up work for a year. Unlike in Act 2 he could not 'stick to
Čech' completely; he was unable to begin composition before he had the
song with which the act was to open.

Other literary figures that Janáček approached included the poet S.K.
Neumann, whom Holý had suggested as early as 1908 (BR28). Neumann
wrote back on 29 April 1912 (BR46), declining to contribute to *Brouček* and
suggesting instead the poet and translator Josef Mach (1883–1951). It is
possible that through Mach Janáček got into contact with Mach's friend, the
satirical poet František Gellner (1881–1914).

Gellner provided more than all the previous *Brouček* librettists. His contri-
butions to the opera survive in the final form of the patron song, Oblačný's
long recitation, and the musicians' chorus at the end of the act:

František Gellner to Janáček   *[undated, before 17 June 1912]*   BR47

I'm sending you that patron [song]. I don't know if it's going to suit
you, but you will see my goodwill at any rate.

This accompanied four stanzas of which Janáček ultimately used three, somewhat modified, in the final version of the song (vs83–5).   Gellner next sent the recitation for Oblačný. With only minor differences the words correspond to the present text (vs109–16). Janáček set this as a melodrama recitation against a musical background. Near the end, in the flight of his poetic fancy, Oblačný breaks into song, a device Janáček indicated in Gellner's original copy with a red pencil line. Janáček also added in pencil 'čichej! můj nos' ['smell! o my nose!'], which gives the final context for the song (recited while the artists apply themselves to Čaroskvoucí's 'banquet' of fragrant flowers). Janáček's only change in the setting was to shorten the last stanza by four lines and give some of the key words to the chorus.

BR48   František Gellner to Janáček   *Prague, 17 June 1912*

These lines are a sort of continuation of the previous three stanzas that I sent you last time.

Forgive me that I've made you wait so long, but I had lots of work.

This is the first dated letter from Gellner and refers to Oblačný's recitation. Janáček also made use of the continuation; most of it became a further song for Oblačný in praise of Čaroskvoucí. However, in his 1916 revision Janáček omitted it, and today only a single line remains as Oblačný's welcome to Brouček: 'Buďvítán, muži osvícený!' ['Welcome, enlightened man!', vs91].

Gellner's final contribution to Act 3 was a chorus which was obviously intend to have much the same effect as Čech's *Storm* symphony:

> *Tlučte paličkami*
> *bijte poklicí*
> [. . .]
> *Bijte do kláves a*
> *šlapte na měchy*
> [. . .]
>
> ['Beat with the drumsticks, bang the cymbals [. . .]
> Bang the keys and tramp the bellows [. . .]']

Janáček used all but two of these lines as a final chorus in praise of Čaroskvoucí while Brouček made his escape on the winged horse. Viktor Dyk took exception to many of the lines when he helped Janáček revise the libretto in 1916, replacing most of them so that only a few rhymes from Gellner were left in the final score (vs145–51).

Janáček did not date the continuous musical draft that he wrote of the act, but in a reply (**BR49**, 20 February 1920) to Šourek's inquiry about the dating of the work provided a firm date for finishing the act: 12 February 1913. Even before this Janáček was in touch with Gellner about a libretto for the final act.

ACT 4

František Gellner to Janáček   *Prague, 23 October 1912*   **BR50**

I have read your letter and from it it is clear to me that you are asking for a substantial piece of work from me: I don't know whether I shall be able to take on this task immediately. [...]

After his success with Gellner over the satirical songs for Act 3, Janáček was pressing him for a libretto for the final, epilogue, act of the opera. The problem here was rather similar to that in the first act. For the two moon acts (2 and 3; today Act 1 Scene 2 and Act 2), Janáček had been able to use dialogue straight out of Čech's novel and needed no outside help except for the songs. But the two short earth scenes that frame *The Excursion of Mr Brouček to the Moon* had been only scantily treated in the novel, with little direct speech. All that Čech supplied for the final scene was a description of Mr Brouček at home, after he had been brought back in a wheelbarrow by the police who had found him on the castle steps babbling incoherently. Watched over anxiously by his housekeeper, Brouček gradually comes to, and calls for food. He considers telling her about his adventures, and how he left his purse and his watch on the moon, but decides against entrusting such revelations to the misinterpretations of an ignorant and gossipy old woman.

Janáček had been obliged to make up most of the first act himself; for the last act he hoped that his most helpful librettist to date would now relieve him of this labour. Gellner, however, seemed no better than his predecessors. More than six months later he had still done nothing:

František Gellner to Janáček   *Prague, 23 May 1913*   **BR51**

It is getting on for a month now that I have had your libretto at home and I still haven't moved a finger. I don't know what to do with it. Write to me – I could perhaps come over to you some day and then we could write a few words together. Forgive me, but I don't understand the thing myself.

Janáček, it seems, had sent Gellner his own libretto or scenario for Act 4 in an attempt to get him moving. Of this, as indeed of Janáček's letters to Gellner, there is no trace today (the earliest surviving libretto in Janáček's hand is post-Gellner). However, Gellner did now write a libretto for the act, and within a couple of weeks. His final communication to Janáček was to send him four stanzas to be inserted in it:

BR52   **František Gellner to Janáček**   *Prague, 17 June 1913*

The placing of each of the four stanzas you can surely do yourself; from the contents it is clear where and to which situation each belongs.

The first stanza could be sung at the beginning and at the end of the third act [i.e. the epilogue act], but otherwise you will know better than me.

Let me know perhaps with a postcard whether you've received these lines and whether they suit your purpose.

Gellner's letter refers to the four stanzas of 'My máme mnoho na práci' ['We have much work to do'], which were used in Janáček's later versions of the libretto.

Gellner's libretto was set not in Brouček's bedroom, as in Čech, but outside the Vikárka, where Brouček's anxious housekeeper has gone to look for her master. A search party, which includes all the characters familiar from the first scene, finds him after an elaborate processional march (the stanzas that Gellner sent with BR52). A new element that Gellner introduced was a display of jealousy between Brouček's housekeeper and Málinka, the flirtatious daughter of the Sacristan.

Janáček did not care for this as it stood and wrote a revised version which included more of the original Čech (with Brouček himself suggesting that Czechs should be transported to the moon). This incorporated some ideas from earlier acts, such as the revenge motif from the opening scene (VS14, where both Málinka and her father vow revenge on Mazal), and the moon musicians' chorus. The work was to end with Gellner's processional song. No musical setting, however, was attempted at the time. As in the cases of *Šárka* and *Fate*, there seemed then little likelihood of its ever being produced. As Janáček wrote to Dr Veselý a year later (**BR53**, 8 April 1914), 'I would like to finish *The Excursion of Mr Brouček* – but I will begin the last act only really when I'm certain that I'm not working in vain.' Janáček had this certainty only at the end of the following year when Kovařovic accepted *Jenůfa* for production in Prague.

JANÁČEK TAKES UP *BROUČEK* AGAIN:
ADDITIONS AND REVISIONS

BR54   **Janáček to Marie Calma-Veselá**   *Brno, 12 November 1915*

[...] I've been looking through the work on *The Excursion of Mr Brouček*. I think that it's worth finishing. [An idea for] the last act has occurred to me – perhaps Mr Peška will develop it for me after all. I will tell him how we could still steal into Brouček's quiet household and how that real Bohemian love could still be worked into the whole concept. [. . .]

[JP70]

Josef Peška, who had been so helpful in getting *Jenůfa* accepted at Prague, was a librettist himself (for Kovařovic), and Janáček had solicited his help with *Brouček*.[1] His initial reaction, before reading the libretto, was most enthusiastic:

Josef Peška to Janáček   *Prague, 12 October 1915*   BR55

Just send it! I'll be delighted to read it through and do it. I make just one condition: if my revision doesn't suit you, don't set it.

Here it's only [your] eagerness that counts, not courteous regard. As soon as I know what to do, I'll write to you and you yourself will decide: yes – no. That idyll in Act 3 would appeal even to me. It will be necessary to scrape off part of the caricature of philistinism from Brouček. His heart mustn't be completely overgrown with fat. For Štork[2] it would be a part made to measure. [. . .]

Two weeks later Peška had received all the librettos, had read them through, and refused to collaborate.

Josef Peška to Janáček   *Prague, 27 October 1915*   BR56

It's necessary to consider external and internal defects. So:
A) In the 1890s Šamberk's elaboratedly staged farce was played at the National Theatre: *The Excursion of Mr Brouček to the Exhibition*, with music by Kovařovic.[3] 'Tři párky z Vikárky, tři párky z Vikárky' ['Three sausages from the Vikárka'] was a leitmotif, taking off 'Tri karty' ['Three cards'] from *The Queen of Spades*.[4]

---

1 This is evident from BR55. However no letter from Janáček prompting it survives.
2 Mirko Štork (1880–1953), tenor at the Prague National Theatre 1905–36. Despite a full-blooded voice, his small, portly stature destined him for buffo roles, such as Vašek in *The Bartered Bride*. He went on to create Brouček at its Prague première. One of his last roles was an outstanding Mime (1932).
3 This was based on one of Čech's sequels to his Brouček novels, *Matěj Brouček at the Exhibition* (1892), which cashed in on the popularity of the Provincial Jubilee Exhibition held in Prague in 1891. The play by the actor František Ferdinand Šamberk (1838–1904) was given forty-eight times between 1894 and 1897.
4 Tchaikovsky's opera received its Czech première at the Prague National Theatre, 11 October 1892.

In this century Moor's operetta on the same subject was played at Smíchov [Prague; see BR24–6].

Mr Gellner's text stands head and shoulders above both works through its freshness and thrust, one might say artistic stylishness, but:

B) It assumes a knowledge of Čech's humorous tale. It doesn't expound anything. It jumps straight in taking things for granted. What is Mr Brouček like? What is his relation to the Sacristan's daughter, to the housekeeper?

The clash of the two women in the third act is an excellent idea [see BR52+], but not in the least prepared. Much space is devoted to subsidiary things: jealousy at the painter's dance partners, the intrusion of the Young Waiter with the sausages.[1] Act 1 takes place in front of the Vikárka; in night light the spectator sees the characters in vague outlines. How will he know who is who in Act 2 when he sees them in their moon masks?

For Brouček, 'woken up from his hangover', to deliver a moral lecture to the nation is unthinkable. Comic opera, and opera in general, is no place, in my view, for sermons, however well meant. Even in Čech's book I was bothered by the inadequate psychology of the dream. That literary lunar escapade could have been dreamt up by Čech, but not however by a Prague drunkard of the most trivial order.

And I'm filled with amazement that you, a musician, can make do with that scrap of lyricism in the libretto, which is really only an unworked sketch – kitsch, as the painters say. [...]

When Peška next wrote to Janáček, on 19 December 1915 (BR57), mainly in connection with the forthcoming production in Prague of *Jenůfa*, he made a number of suggestions for texts for a new opera. Among his recommended librettists was F. S. Procházka, 'editor of *Zvon*. A Moravian, a shrewd spirit, a brilliant versifier. What about his *King Barleycorn*?'

Peška had not however reckoned with Janáček's tenacity. Before the year was out Procházka was involved, not with a libretto made from his poem *King Barleycorn* (a democratic vision based on the Moravian folk hero, 1906), but with the last act of *Brouček* and revisions for the previous acts. Janáček presumably went to see Procházka in Prague and secured his agreement to help him with *Brouček* (the first letter from the surviving correspondence begins *in medias res*). From his remark (BR58) that composition was

---

[1] These are two incidents from the opening scene of the opera. Málinka accuses Mazal of dancing 'a waltz and a mazurka' with 'that Fanča' (Brouček's housekeeper) – see vs8. The first appearance of the Young Waiter with the sausages is at vs25.

finished 'as far as the text goes' it would seem that Janáček sent Procházka neither Gellner's nor his own version of the epilogue libretto, merely his copy of the text of the earlier acts.

PROCHÁZKA'S ADDITIONS

Janáček to F. S. Procházka   *Brno, 31 December 1915*   BR58

I enclose the text of *Brouček's Excursion to the Moon*.

Composition is finished in fair copy as far as the text goes. The end of the second part of Act 2 lacks only that *Bohemian nocturne between Mazal and Miss Málka*.

In Act 3, in Brouček's flat, Mazal, Málka, the Housekeeper, and Brouček encounter one another.

I ask you thus to take on the completion of the whole work.

I think that it will be to our honour and to that of Svatopluk Čech.

But just terribly soon.

PS As you will notice when reading the manuscript, text is missing on p.7a [Here Janáček quoted the two lines of Janke's drinking-song, see BR32+, and indicated four further lines with dots.] and on p.21:
Lunobor: 'Přečtu mu tři kapitoly' ['I will read him three chapters']: (here it is indeed necessary for him to read them).
He [Lunobor] also appears several times with them on p.26.

In the event Janáček got by without the expansion of Janke's drinking-song (see VS10–11) and it was left to Procházka's successor to contribute the other missing items. About the epilogue Procházka had his own ideas:

F. S. Procházka to Janáček   *[undated, postmarked Prague, 6 January*   BR59
1916]

I have read through the libretto. Filling in the places indicated will not be difficult, but I must go on thinking about the ending, which must be very swift and concise, and it seems to me here that, logically considered, it isn't possible to place the end in the living-room of Brouček's flat. What reason would bring here all those people who have to be there? I think that at the end there cannot be any change of scene; it must be played out in the Vikárka street, where it began.

I would see it like this: Mazal has a lyrical duet with Miss Máli [Málinka], whom he does not succeed in getting on to the street; when he wants to climb up to her through the window, a noise breaks out in the street. Some men and a policeman are carrying Brouček, wet through; he had lost his way, got into the Fürstenberg Gardens[1] and there had fallen into a water butt. He has Würfl's bill in his pocket, which is why they carry him here – to find out who he is. All Würfl's customers also congregate here and the ensemble is complete. The action takes place towards morning – the sun comes out and lights up the scenery. Brouček also comes to and thus the thing closes, headlong and quickly.

What do you say to this? If you have any suggestions, please let me have them.

BR60   Janáček to F. S. Procházka   *Brno, 10 January 1916*

Thank you for reading through the libretto as far as it is ready.

Please kindly take further into consideration:

1. Because of the utter confusion of people *in the dream*, a few could be missing when [Brouček] is sober; it wouldn't matter.

2. But for motivation and comprehension it is essential that the *real story* of the first act should come to its end – in the last act.

3. The Sacristan, Máli and Mazal promise *revenge* for insults [given] in Act 1.

4. In my opinion it would be sweet revenge if Mazal and Máli had Mr Brouček carried off 'in a barrow' to his home. Brouček's housekeeper would be horrified by this, 'v truhle!' ['in a barrow!' – from Čech].

5. The scene – the real action outside the dream – would then be appropriately ended, rounded off.

Do you concede this?

6. All this can take place better in Brouček's home rather than back in the street.

I would also be able to bring a new tone – mood – to the composition, whereas back again in the street, I would lapse into its atmosphere.

7. The sun could peep even into Brouček's room.

That's my view.

But don't take too much notice of the details; just [make sure] the *sweet revenge* be expressed. How? In whatever way will be best and easiest for you to write.

---

1 The Fürstenberg Palace is now the seat of the Polish Embassy in Prague; its gardens would have been accessible to Brouček from the Vikárka since they lie beneath of the Prague Castle.

Janáček had not really answered Procházka's objection that it was difficult to find a pretext for bringing the cast into Brouček's home (whereas on the street it was possible to assemble everyone without too much contrivance). It is clear that Janáček wanted a new scene, not for any logical reason, but for the opportunity it would give him to create a new mood. The disagreement slowed down proceedings. Although there was a steady exchange of letters between the two (over the women's choruses to Procházka's words that Janáček was setting), references to *Brouček* consisted only of Janáček's reminders and Procházka's temporizings until Procházka felt able to confront Janáček with his objections. He particularly resisted Janáček's *idée fixe* about 'revenge':

F. S. Procházka to Janáček   *Prague, 3 April 1916*   BR61

I have done what I could. Judge for yourself if it's possible for a change of scene still to follow, in Brouček's flat. The thing requires a quick ending, no-one is expecting any sort of revenge, because in the first act it is not in any way emphasized. And why would the Sacristan have to be revenged? On whom? That's also a mystery. There would have to be some other complication in the course of the act. I cannot advance with this in any other way without becoming banal.

Please read through what I have patched and knitted together; I see that such work, built up on a foreign structure, simply doesn't suit me.

The end should now, in my opinion, be very brief. Towards dawn they would bring Brouček to the pub, and there the housekeeper would come for him. Brouček would speak in moon-language and with his general ridicule there it would close. If you would like, I could still add on an ending like this, but anything else I just wouldn't know how to do. [...]

Janáček agreed (**BR62**, undated) to Procházka's proposal. He also thanked him for the lines for the lovers, which had 'come off excellently; they are sufficient for the work and fall nicely into the whole'. These were the 'Bohemian nocturne between Mazal and Miss Málka' which Janáček had requested in his letter of 31 December 1915 (BR58) and which he used instead to fill out the opening earth scene (VS28–33).

F. S. Procházka to Janáček   *Prague, 29 May 1916*   BR63

I'm sending you *Brouček* as I promised and do hope that it suits you. I don't know how to do anything else with it. Everything else I have filled in, as you wished. It is really a musical burlesque, a bit of mischief, and it must end mischievously. As you will see, you have 'revenge' in it, as you wished. [. . .]

Procházka's libretto does not depart substantially from his outline. Janáček put a line through all the libretto except for the opening love-duet and, again, wrote his own, based largely on Procházka. But even then, it seems, he was not satisfied.

MAHEN AND DYK

BR64   Jiří Mahen: 'How I did a libretto with Janáček'

[. . .] In June 1916 (in the autumn I had to go to the army) Janáček happened to meet me and lamented about the labour he was having with *The Excursion of Mr Brouček to the Moon.* He said he had a libretto which he wasn't satisfied with, and that he needed something for the final act in which Brouček returns to Prague from the moon, something *warm.* Janáček always made a quick job of everything. I should write him that ending, [and] that he needed it as soon as possible. Understandably, I was a little confused, for I knew nothing about this, I didn't know any libretto to *Brouček,* and so I simply promised that I would deliver the requested verse lines or prose, but I would of course be glad to see the whole libretto. Although this didn't exactly grab the composer, as they say, he invited me one day to his place and gave me the whole libretto to read. It was quite a thick little book and there were various hands in it. I sat myself down beyond the town, at its limits, and read and read. The revision of the libretto was said to have been done by F. S. Procházka; here evidently was his ending in which Janáček wanted something *warm,* but where had Janáček got the rest from? I confess that I was thoroughly unhappy with it. There were things there which were impossibly comic and there were direct quotations from Svatopluk Čech, which naturally did not harmonize one little bit; the framework of the acts indeed staggered about somewhere in the mists, and in between were places which while I read them sent cold shivers down my back. What was this? Surely someone was making an outright mockery of the whole thing! Who?

I went to Janáček and told him directly that this was an incoherent ragbag and that the whole thing ought to be done again. He was clearly surprised by this, but he acknowledged my arguments. 'I hope that you haven't yet set it all to music?', I asked him. 'Of course not',

1 Jaroslav Věšín's picture 'The Beginning of a Romance' (1885), the initial inspiration for Preissová's short story, and consequently for Janáček's second opera (see description, Chapter 2). Reproduced from the framed copy which hung in Janáček's study in his Hukvaldy home.

2 Gabriela Preissová (1862–1946), author of the short story on which Janáček's second opera *The Beginning of a Romance* is based, and the play on which his third opera *Jenůfa* is based (see PR1 to PR12, PR18, PR37 to PR38 and JP1 to JP5). Illustration from the frontispiece to a collection of short stories by Preissová published in 1889.

3 Fedora Bartošová (1884–1941), a young schoolteacher, and friend of Janáček's daughter Olga. Bartošová collaborated on the libretto of his fourth opera for *Fate* (see OS8, OS28 and correspondence OS9 to OS27).

4 Two water-colour views by
Zdeňka Vorlová-Vlčková
(1872–1954) of the Moravian
spa resort of Luhačovice
where Janáček took a
summer holiday in August
1903: it provided the setting
for his opera *Fate*. These
views were reproduced as
coloured postcards and
Janáček stuck them into a
preliminary page of his full
score of the opera.
Vorlová–Vlčková was
approached to make the
designs for the proposed Brno
première (see OS41, where she
mentions her 'sketches and
studies of buildings').
(a) The main promenade in
Luhačovice where Act 1 of
Fate is set (see OS9).
(b) The Mineral Baths
Building, today known as the
Jurkovič House after the
architect Dušan Samo
Jurkovič (1868–1947), who
adapted it to its present form
after the manner of Moravian
folk architecture.

5(a), (b) The originals for the two main characters of *Fate*, Míla (Mrs Kamila Urválková, 1875–1956) and Živný/Lenský (Ludvík Vítězslav Čelanský, 1870–1831). See os2, os2 +, os4 + for explanations of their relationship to the opera. The photograph of Mrs Urválková is that mentioned by Fedora Bartošová in os8; the picture of Čelanský is from 1894, about the time of his affair with Urválková.

6 Illustrations by Viktor Oliva for the first
editions of Svatopluk Čech's *Brouček* novels
(1888–9). Janáček refers to them in his letter to
Rektorys (BR9) describing his initial conception
of the scenario.
(a) The 'fabulously beautiful lunar landscape',
the setting for Act 1 Scene 2
(b) Mr Brouček on his way to the moon
(c) Mr Brouček (centre) conversing with the
Hussite leader Jan Žižka (seated).

7 Kamila Stösslová (1892–1935) in 1927. She was the close friend of Janáček during his last years and the model for the heroine of *Kátà Kabanová* (see KK10 to KK12 and KK90+ to KK96) and other characters in his operas.

8 Set designs by Josef Čapek for the Prague
première (1928) of Janáček's penultimate opera
The Makropulos Affair. Josef Čapek
(1887–1945) was the brother of Karel Čapek,
who wrote the play on which the opera was
based. Janáček wrote (VM81) that Čapek's sets
'weren't a success'.
(a) Act 1, Chambers of the lawyer Kolenatý
(b) Act 2, backstage at the theatre after the
performance by the singer Emilia Marty (Elina
Makropulos)
(c) Act 3, the hotel room where Marty/Elina
meets Prus to regain the Makropulos document
from him.

9 Leoš Janáček and Kamila Stösslová in Luhačovice, summer 1927.

10 Dr František Veselý and his wife Marie Calma-Veselá in 1922. Dr Veselý (1862–1923) was the chief force behind the development of the Luhačovice spa and Janáček got to know him from his annual visits there (see e.g. OS28). Both Veselý and his second wife, the writer and singer Marie Calma-Veselá (1881–1966), were influential in persuading Karel Kovařovic to accept *Jenůfa* at the Prague National Theatre (JP55 ff).

he replied, 'a whole number of people did it for me, finally Gellner, and Procházka did the end, but I am not satisfied. Throw yourself into it! Re-do it!' – 'Let's re-do the ending first of all!', I suggested, and Janáček agreed. I went home and read the libretto again and again. [. . .]

[BR66, BR68]
Panorama, vi (1929)

Jiří Mahen (1882–1939), one of the most substantial literary figures in Brno at the time, went on to describe how he remodelled the epilogue in a couple of days, took it to Janáček, who pronounced himself satisfied, and asked him to carry on with the earlier acts – all this at a time of maximum excitement in the First World War with the Russians losing, and the French only just holding their own. Mahen's story, and the amicable relations between the two are documented by several letters.

Jiří Mahen to Janáček   *[Brno,] 19 July 1916*   BR65

You will get Act 3[1] probably on Saturday [22 July] – it is already almost completely finished. Please, if you get the text of the libretto copied out; have it copied *in typescript* two or three times and kindly send me one (paginated) copy so that we can then easily discuss it if I cannot get to Luhačovice.

I wish you the very best time at the spa – and lots of appetite for work.

PS I very much would like to ask you to do it [i.e. have the text copied out] – in Act 1 I want to change some tiny things and correct something in Act 4. So it's urgent!

Jiří Mahen: 'How I did a libretto with Janáček'   BR66

I then packed it up and took it to Janáček at his house. The Maestro wasn't at home. Before I was received by the lady of the house, I looked around the piano curiously . . . A large fat volume lay open there, full of notes: *Brouček . . . Brouček . . .* Such a fat volume? First scene *completely finished* – according to the old text . . .! Second scene *completely finished* – according to the old text . . .! I didn't look any further. [. . .]

I waited indeed with no little curiosity for his verdict on the libretto. Why didn't Janáček tell me that he had the libretto (the old

---

1 Mahen reverted to the old act numbering. He is thus referring to Act 2 Scene 2.

text), set to music (possibly) *completely*? Surely all that was really needed was some revision of the fourth scene – and that would be that.

[BR64, BR68]
Panorama, vi (1929)

BR67   **Janáček to Jiří Mahen**   *Luhačovice, 10 August 1916*

I looked out for you here, and you are beyond the hills.

What you left for me has made me very satisfied; I will use much from it. You have saved me work.

[. . .].

Keep well. I go to Prague on 17 August and then I will shut myself off from the world.

BR68   **Jiří Mahen: 'How I did a libretto with Janáček'**

Fine, I said to myself, that means that we *both* shut ourselves off from the world, and that *only now will we put the libretto in order.* [. . .] I had to go to the army in October, during August (the remainder of), and September it could all be put together. Although my health was going from bad to worse I was nevertheless looking forward somehow to the cutting and playing it over on the piano. It would be possible to save it!

Suddenly *Právo lidu*[1] brought the news that *Brouček* was now finished and the libretto was written by – Viktor Dyk.[2] How so? [. . .]

[BR64, BR66]
Panorama, vi (1929)

BR69   **Jiří Mahen to Janáček**   *[Brno,] 8 September 1916*

I learn to my amazement that you also gave the libretto for *Brouček* to my friend Mr Dyk to do.

I ask for an explanation. When and where!

---

1 The newspaper *Právo lidu* carried two reports on *Brouček*: one on 5 September 1916 announcing that Mahen was writing the libretto; and a second on 13 September that the words were not by Mahen because, as the composer had declared, the text was partly arranged by himself and partly by Viktor Dyk (see JA v, 30, fn.22). But Mahen's first letter objecting to his treatment was written five days before the second report: he must have heard the news on the grapevine.

2 Viktor Dyk (1877–1931), poet, novelist and dramatist. Dyk describes his contacts with Janáček in BR71.

Janáček to Jiří Mahen *Brno, 13 September 1916* BR70

Why with amazement?

How can I simply throw away my work, the work of three years? In my method of composition, where the tune is created by the word, the whole melody subsequently depends on the sentence; it wouldn't be possible any other way. These composers who can put text underneath any old ready-made tunes of theirs [have it easy]! But that's not the case with me.

I began work on the first sentences in fair copy – but it was all over! On Friday I finished reading your proposal and saw that [even] with the best will I could not use it. Not perhaps because of any superficiality in it, but because I would have to compose it *all* over again.

I ask you, visit me so that you might understand completely that *I would not and could not now in any way do such work a second time!*

Mr Viktor Dyk approved my old text, *he did not change anything,* he only did the ending faithfully according to Svatopluk Čech in Brouček's home.

For this reason also he is not given in any way or any place as a librettist.

I ask thus for a talk so that I can fully convince you that it is not out of ill will that I have not touched your work, but that simply, however excellent it might be, I cannot use it because it is so far at variance with my original work that I would not be able to use even a note from it.

Viktor Dyk: 'A memoir of Leoš Janáček' BR71

It was the time when I had enforced leave as an editor and when my correspondence was shown the rare honour of attention on the part of the Austrian police. I received then a letter from Leoš Janáček [after 15 June 1916]. On four pages, written with a characterful, energetic hand, the composer of *Jenůfa* turned to me with a surprising request. He was composing *The Excursion of Mr Brouček to the Moon.* And it was I, yes I, who could help him. He had tried elsewhere, but none of those to whom he turned was giving him satisfaction. What was needed was me, what was needed was concise speech, trenchant verse, or so Janáček wrote. Half request, half order. And before I got round to replying a reminder came, and then a second reminder: I *must* do it, if his work was not to be killed off and destroyed. And for him, the composer who had had to wait so long, it was impossible to wait patiently. In the end – the reader must not imagine that this all lasted more than four or five days! – he appeared before me.

I tried to wriggle out of it in every way I could. I had not had the happiest experiences as a librettist and in general as a man of the theatre.[1] I pointed this out to Janáček. Why should the fate of his work depend of all things on the fate of a dramatist who had had so little pleasure from his own work. In vain. I must, I must, I must.

Frankly, I was not convinced that it had to be me. But the fate of a composer who had had to wait for success until he was grey-haired had already inspired me as an essayist to write a feuilleton in *Lidové noviny*.[2] And perhaps it was just that feuilleton which drew Janáček's attention to me and awoke his trust in me. I did not lack goodwill. But the material frightened me. As I understood Janáček, his choice was strange to me. Why that *Excursion of Mr Brouček to the Moon*? It seemed to me a very troublesome, perhaps an impossible, subject for an opera. But Janáček was already completely [absorbed] in his material and was horrified at the thought that everything that he had put into the work would be lost. He believed in himself, he believed in the material, he had not a shadow of doubt and it was like my speaking to a brick wall. It will be fine. Only soon, soon, soon. He had waited so long and had no time to wait any more.

And so it began. Even before I had decided, there was a news item in the newspapers[3] that I was writing a libretto for Janáček. And hardly had it appeared in the papers than I received an enraged letter from a Brno author [Jiří Mahen] who had written a libretto before me, like all sorts of other people. He was very angry with Janáček, he warned me and described the previous fates of the *Brouček Excursion* in rather grotesque colours. He appealed to my solidarity as an author, he assured me that everything could end only in a notable disaster.

The author of the letter was a serious person and the letter did not

---

1 Perhaps Dyk had in mind his recent (1915–16) experiences as translator of plays at the Vinohrady Theatre. By this time some nine of his own plays had been produced in various theatres in Prague, though only three at the National Theatre.
2 As Rektorys reported when he reprinted Dyk's article in JA v (61, fn.48), the editorial staff of *Lidové noviny* were unable to trace this feuilleton. It is hardly surprising. The 'feuilleton' (15 June 1916) is a brief report on opera in Prague with merely four lines devoted to *Jenůfa*. However these comments are wholly positive, placed in flattering comparison to Wagner's *Die Walküre*, and was clearly noticed by Janáček, who underlined the passage in red and wrote 'Vik. Dyk' at the end.
3 In *Právo lidu* (13 September 1916).

contribute greatly to the improvement of my mood. I tried to smooth over the matter with Janáček; I pointed out that I was unwilling to appear before a literary colleague – and literary colleagues – in a hardly colleague-like role. I expressed the wish that he should make contact again with the writer of the letter. But again, all in vain, again the request and the command: I must, I must, I must!

I set to work. But soon I struck a greater difficulty than I had supposed at the beginning. While I racked my brains to give the libretto at least some sort of theatrical verve, while after much deliberation I came to the conclusion that it was essential as far as possible to depart from the original Čech text and give *The Excursion of Mr Brouček to the Moon* a slightly different message than in Čech's satire, I found that I racked my brains in vain. Janáček had progressed too far with his composing and to my surprise laid stress with particular thoroughness on the aspect which I would have completely cast out from the libretto as ballast, and the deeper, more human core, which I would have inserted into Čech's fable, did not meet with his especial favour. Very soon I found that I didn't have to write a libretto, but simply to revise it, that my hands were tied by Janáček's earlier work and by his clinging to individual details which were not exactly up my street. I had wanted, if it was now necessary to use the *Brouček Excursion* material, to extract the poetical core from the tale, whereas Janáček was concerned mainly with the grotesque motivations and the genre of comedy which seemed foreign to me.

What to do? I gave up after a vain attempt to convince Janáček and to secure a free hand with the libretto for myself. I couldn't ask the composer to throw overboard work already finished and to change his plan and conception, seen with all of Janáček's clarity. I gave up authorship and tried to preserve what could be preserved as the adapter of foreign material and a foreign text, bound hand and foot. I would have been sorry to cool Janáček in his creative ardour or even break him, and eventually I said to myself that any possible failure would be more the failure of the material than of Janáček's music. If the composer had fallen in love so strikingly with such bizarre material perhaps he would be able to extract from it more than I could imagine.

[...]

And I slaved away in order to extract, at any rate, as much as possible from the set task. I sent my suggestions to Brno. From Brno Janáček wrote me his explanations, principles, objections; patiently I

tried to accommodate him, with of course the precondition that I did
not consider myself – despite his offer (materially more advantage-
ous) – as the author of the libretto.

[BR86]
Lumír (10 October 1928)

BR72   Viktor Dyk to Janáček   *[Prague,] 3 July 1916*

I have read what [you] sent and, according to my promise, am giving
you my opinion so far. The text of the beginning and the end of the
Excursion seem to me frankly a little operetta-ish. Perhaps it would
go down well, but I understand that as a composer it considerably
restricts you.

For music surely works mainly with emotion. And the emotional
side is impoverished. In other ways, of course, the text is not without
wit; I agree with you in this respect, however, that in keeping with
today's fashion of dénouement something from the beginning could
be repeated at the end – milieu, songs; and the finale of the piece, a
burlesque death march with the drunken Brouček, would not today,
at a time of so many *real* deaths, have perhaps the most favourable
effect.

How to revise it all I still don't know for the moment, I will try my
best as soon as there will be a little time to do a draft for you – of
course I don't know if there will be other faults in it.

On Saturday [8 July] I will ask for you in the hotel about 5.30. I
usually go to look at the war news after 5, and so this would
particularly suit me. Of course I don't know if I will be able to say
anything new to you.

In a brief reply (**BR73**, 6 July 1916), Janáček announced his plan to arrive in
Prague with the music on 8 July and asked Dyk if he would have time to
work at least on the first scene. At this juncture Janáček was still in friendly
contact with Mahen. Dyk's first instalment arrived more or less simultaneously with Mahen's entirely new libretto (see BR65).

BR74   Janáček to Viktor Dyk   *Luhačovice, 21 July 1916*

Thanks for what you sent me [presumably revisions for Act 1 Scene
1]; you have given me wings. The main thing is I will not have to
change much. But just write a little more legibly!

Don't be angry.

I wasn't able to read it.

[Janáček quotes for clarification the lines Dyk supplied for Mazal's 'poetic' gesticulating in Scene 1: 'Zřím jak se směje lidstvo', vs15–16.]

I will then send you the first scene on the moon. But first of all that end! A good, hearty end!

During August Janáček seems to have been dealing with Mahen's work and left Dyk in peace. Dyk's next dated letter, on 6 September 1916 (BR75), was full of apologies for inactivity. On 14 September (BR76), a week after the Mahen explosion, Janáček sent Dyk his revision of Procházka's first scene for Mazal and Málinka (vs28–35). Four days later, 18 September (BR77), Dyk sent his additions and corrections to this scene, out of which Janáček carved some lines for the Mazal–Málinka love-duet with which Act 2 closes. Dyk provided, for instance, Mazal's defence to Málinka that his 'flirtation' with Mr Brouček's housekeeper was only a joke: after all he can't dance ('To Málinko, byl pouze šprým;/ já přece vůbec netančím'), which with one slight change can be found on vs161. Five days later (BR78, 23 September 1916) he sent Lunobor's 'three chapters' (vs77–8), which Janáček had asked Procházka for earlier (BR58).

Janáček to Viktor Dyk   *Brno, 30 September 1916*   **BR79**

I am sending you the text of Act 2 just as I have composed music for it.

How will you like it?

I would like to have the character of the Child Prodigy effectively elaborated.

He has to annoy Brouček by giving him flowers to smell, tear-holders [in which to catch his hoped-for tears of emotion] etc.

It is the figure of the Young Waiter from Act 1.

During his introductions Čaroskvoucí must not pass him over and the Child Prodigy would have to reply: I would like to put a flute solo into the refrain of his answer. As a character it would be good.

I have put a blue line where I don't have words. [...]

I will perhaps be in Prague on 4 October; we could then discuss everything.

But write to me *immediately*, I can still 'refine' the beginning of Act 2 as it stands.

In the end the Young Waiter was not 'introduced' but simply enters 'with curiosity from the music wing (always with a piccolo to his lips)' (vs89). Gaps that Janáček noted in this letter, mostly for the opening of Act 2, were *a few cries* of admiration during the creative work of the artists' (see BR80);

an 'expression of fright' for Etherea before she escapes from Lunobor (in the end Janáček repeated what he already had, vs91); 'a few trenchant critical expressions' (for the jealous artists), and in particular more for the Child Prodigy to do. In his response Dyk suggested (see BR81, no. 1) that his ending for Act 2 pre-empted the much-discussed epilogue. It was only after composing it several times and adding an entirely new excursion that Janáček eventually came round to his view. As a whole Dyk's letter is a good example of the last-minute adjustments that he was able to contribute to Act 2.

BR80   **Viktor Dyk to Janáček**   *[Prague,] 1 October 1916*

Some remarks in haste on Act 2, already despatched:

1. Brouček is found towards the end – and with this the dream now ends. The waking up and reality are then really two [different] things. This however makes the setting of scenes in Brouček's house dramatically dubious.

2. With Čaroskvoucí various trivialities are disturbing – I don't know if it has been handled in too operetta-ish a fashion. Čaroskvoucí's very opening song [he quotes some of Gellner's lines]. The lines [he quotes a quatrain] strike me, apart from their triviality, also as unintelligible [. . .]

3. Similarly unclear is the connection between the musicians' song and the following text [here Dyk quotes the 'Bang with the drumsticks' song, BR48+, and comments on its triviality, poor prosody, repetitions and lack of organization]. Do you hold store by these passages? If not, it would perhaps be possible to replace the text at least in part. [He did so, see BR81].

The beginning of Čaroskvoucí's song could perhaps go: [Dyk here provides the final form of the first stanza 'Také prochodil jsem školu . . . ku psaní', vs83].

The second stanza could be dropped. If it was musically necessary I would prefer to write a new text. [He did, see BR81.]

In between this song you want expressions of wonder – are these to be pronounced by the *artists* about the Maecenas? – or by the Maecenas about the artists? [–] and would it not be inappropriate if the artists were to interrupt the text of Mr Maecenas with remarks unconnected with the song?

If these remarks were [to go] between the strophes, expressions of wonder from the artists could possibly be as follows:

First Artist: Light of lights!

Second [Artist]: Spirit of Spirits!

[Dyk supplied seven such interjections, but Janáček used only the above, sung in chorus in between the three verses of Čaroskvoucí's song, vs83–4.]

These short little lines could be an insertion between the individual strophes of the Maecenas's song.

I'm sending these suggestions so far because they concern the very opening. The rest I will do before your arrival.

Viktor Dyk to Janáček   *[Prague,] 9 October 1916*   **BR81**

I would not like you to be held up in your work and so I am sending you my proposals now – of course with one exception: not having the text of Scene 1,[1] I could not revise anything there.

This letter accompanied fourteen substitute or additional passages in Act 2; the letter continues with commentaries on some of these. Janáček used many of the suggestions. Ones that he adopted include a new second verse for the Maecenas song ('Tvorby zavřeny mi říše', vs83–4); the 'trenchant critical expressions' (vs96); a substantial insertion for the Child Prodigy including the moon anthem and the constant invitations to Brouček to listen and to smell the flowers (vs97–100, 102); substitute words for the final chorus (Gellner's musicians' chorus now becoming 'Požehnáni tvoji rtové', vs145–50); and the echo of this chorus by the Vikárka artists when Brouček comes down to earth (vs147–8).

[. . .]

3. To the moon hymn [from Čech] I have added the refrain: 'Vzdychej! Čichej! Čichej! Vzdychej!' ['Sigh! Smell! Smell! Sigh!'].

There is a double point: in the final analysis it is an ironic version of the sentimental text 'Kde domov můj' ['Where is my homeland', the well-known song by František Škroup adopted in 1918 as the Czech national anthem], and dramatically it creates a transition to Brouček's outburst.[2]

4. In the final lines of Harfoboj [i.e. the continuation of the final moon chorus, vs148–50], I used moon speech from Čech. It seemed to me, however, that it was impossible to repeat the text word for word at the Vikárka – they don't used 'moon speech' there. I have

---

1 Dyk had already revised part of Act 1 Scene 1 in July. Either he was to have a look at it again, or he means the first moon scene, Act 1 Scene 2 – for which there are no corrections by Dyk.

2 In the event Janáček used only 'čichejte' (plural form of 'čichej') and interrupted the moon anthem more prominently with Etherea's expressions of love for Brouček (vs98–102).

therefore left the metre and rhymes and slightly changed the words.[1]
[...]

Dyk also had to provide substitute words for the one item of Mahen's text
that Janáček had used, the drinking-chorus of artists in the opening scene. In
September 1916 Mahen had pursued an acrimonious correspondence with
Janáček (see JA v, 28–38) in which he demanded K300 for his work and the
undertaking that none of his words should be used (**BR82**, 15 September
1916). The dispute was brought to an end only by Dyk's tact and a formal
agreement between Janáček and Mahen, in which Janáček agreed to pay
Mahen K80 for his work (**BR83**, 7 October 1916). Janáček had in fact used
just one song from Mahen, the drinking-chorus for the Vikárka artists in the
opening scene. Thus the chorus on vs23–5 ('Láska, láska, čarovný květ') is
by Dyk, fitted exactly to the metre of Mahen's original chorus. Dyk sent a
carefully considered explanation of the metrical problems and provided the
new words on 16 October (**BR84**). In a brief final letter (**BR85**, 11 November
1916) Dyk sent a continuation of the epilogue.

BR86   Viktor Dyk: 'A memoir of Leoš Janáček'

In November 1916 I was arrested and in December taken off to
Vienna.[2] Undoubtedly I had thereby brought about a most unpleasant surprise for Janáček; but unfortunately, there was nothing to be
done about it. I smile when I recall that at first Janáček made an
attempt to continue with me in the work [we'd] begun as though
absolutely nothing had happened. Artistic egoism is not the least of
egoisms. Above all *Brouček*. I must, I must, I must. But I wrote, I
think, to Janáček that I could no longer help him much. The military
censorship was sometimes very slow and even had I been willing to
continue further it would have drawn everything out longer than
Janáček's burning impatience could bear. [...] Leoš Janáček, continually bombarding me with letters and in cases of need always
willing to surprise me with a visit in Prague, lost interest in his
collaborator as soon as he ceased to be a collaborator. Perhaps he

---

1 When Brouček wakes up from his drunken dream, the first sounds he hears are the songs
of the Vikárka artists celebrating Würfl in song – to the melody used by the moon artists
celebrating Čaroskvoucí (vs157–9).
2 Dyk had been under investigation since 1915 on account of his novel *The Secret
Adventures of Alexey Ivanich Kozulinov*, serialized in *Lidové noviny*, 1 June – 21 September 1915; publication was abruptly stopped because its description of conditions in tsarist
Russia were seen as a lightly disguised criticism of local conditions. Both Dyk and the
newspaper's editor were charged with inciting hatred and contempt for the state administration. On 20 November 1916 Dyk was arrested for high treason, incriminated in the trial
of Professor Karel Štěpánek, and from 15 December imprisoned in Vienna. He was released
on 27 May 1917 for lack of evidence (see Med 1988, 189–92).

thought it a little unkind of me that I had slipped from his reach, albeit at the price of bars on the windows of my cell.

[BR71]
Lumír (10 October 1928)

NEW ENDINGS

However, Dyk's task was virtually done. Janáček had completed the revisions of the earlier acts and, according to the dates he noted on the manuscript, had at last begun work on the final act on 25 October 1916, using the beginning of a libretto that Dyk had sent him by that date. What Dyk sent on 11 November (BR85), nine days before his arrest, was the continuation, but it came too late. Janáček had already mapped out his new version, and completed it between 20 November and 5 December. Dyk's libretto owed nothing to its predecessors. The scene was set back in Brouček's house, as in Čech, thus allowing Janáček his 'new tone'.

Dyk's act begins with the housekeeper's lamenting Brouček's behaviour – the scandal of his being brought home so late, drunk, and in a wheelbarrow. Brouček wakes up to find himself unexpectedly back at home. The voices of Mazal and Málinka are heard outside. The reason for their visit is that Málinka wants Brouček to annul Mazal's notice, which in a fit of pique he gave his lodger the night before. Brouček at first refuses but then, recalling his alarming experiences with Etherea (who Málinka reminds him of), he promptly complies and the lover leaves. The next visitor to Brouček's bedroom is the Young Waiter from the Vikárka, with more sausages. From him Brouček learns how he was brought home. Disgruntled, Brouček sends him off and asks to be left alone.

Janáček set Dyk's text up to the annulment but added a new end. The Young Waiter brings in the sausages but does not describe how he found Brouček; instead his appearance provokes a 'sausage ensemble' for the company. Mazal, Málinka and the Young Waiter leave. The Sacristan then enters to inquire whether Brouček will marry his daughter and learns instead that she is to marry Mazal. In this form Janáček set the entire act, had it copied by Václav Sedláček and even had a piano reduction made (by Roman Veselý).

This might have been the end of the story except that Janáček then showed the opera to Max Brod, who gave his verdict on the text of the opera in a long letter (BR87, 17 January 1917). He felt it should be clearer whether the satire was directed against the bourgeoisie or against the artists. To ensure the former Janáček would have to make a 'real Bohemian' out of Mazal, who would have to lose his ironic name (= dauber). There were two practical consequences. One was a new ending to the epilogue, basically a monologue for Brouček, the second was a new ending for the previous act in which, in an attempt to 'sharpen the satire' the figure of the poet and author Svatopluk Čech was brought on stage as a paragon of hard-working artistic endeavour, in contrast to the drunken 'artists' who hang around the Vikárka. Brod even provided copy (**BR88**, undated) for these two extra scenes, which, since it was in German needed to be elaborated in Czech. Janáček's last collaborator was behind bars in Vienna; so Janáček turned to his predecessor, F. S. Procházka:

BR89   Janáček to F. S. Procházka   *Prague, 31 January 1917*

I am coming to Prague on Sunday [4 February] and will look you up at your home in the morning – for you to help me out since they have locked up Viktor Dyk again.

BR90   F. S. Procházka to Janáček   *Prague, 1 March 1917*

I have knocked up and added to what you wanted [for Act 3]. [. . .].

Forgive me that I have been held up, but I was ill for over a week with angina and a terrible cough – there was very little left of me. I would be glad if I have satisfied you with these additions and that they suit your purpose.

I feel that this Svatopluk Čech cannot let out a patriotic tirade here – it would sound banal. If you emphasize his ironic words, that will be enough.

BR91   Janáček to F. S. Procházka   *Brno, 3 March 1917*

Many thanks! It's not knocking up at all – the lines, which I badly need, are excellent; especially Čech's words.

[. . .]

Are you better now?

I waited a long time, and then asked Mrs Horvátová to visit you and give you a little nudge.

It came just at the right time.

When Janáček visited Procházka on 4 February (see BR89) he probably took with him his own rough translation of Brod's additions. For the end of Act 2 Brod had expanded the scene where Brouček is back on earth. In addition to the chorus of Artists celebrating Würfl and his beer, there are now three individual artists, a painter, a composer and a poet, all with creative plans, but all too tired to achieve them. But working in the corner of the Vikárka is Svatopluk Čech himself, a model of integrity and industry, who, once again (as Würfl observes), has been working through the night. He is the positive element that Brod had sought among the artists. In a concluding speech Čech himself laments over the artists of today who all 'could' do something but 'only on the moon'. Characters from the scene that this supplanted, Mazal, Málinka and the Young Waiter, are heard offstage.

Despite the oddness of bringing a recently dead writer on stage, Janáček, in his rough translation, accepted all of this except for Brod's lines for Čech. He translated only two and left Procházka to fill them out. Procházka instead added lines about the desirability of 'lots of work', 'perfect form' and so on. Janáček was clearly pleased with what came from Procházka. Four days after his first, he wrote a second thank-you letter (**BR92**, 7 March 1917): 'You don't know how your additions have helped me. I'm working with relish. [. . .] To bring Svatopluk Čech on stage and not mock him – I want to get this right.' Janáček set most of Procházka's version, expanding the references to Málinka, Mazal and the Young Waiter with the music he had previously written for the end of the scene.

There remained the final part of the epilogue. By now Janáček had had librettos for this act written by Gellner, Procházka, Mahen and Dyk. He had written three himself (only two survive). Janáček had completed the score on 5 December 1916, based mostly on Dyk's version (see BR86+) and had it copied by Václav Sedláček (19 December 1916). An extensive revision was recopied by Sedláček (15 March 1917). However Brod's suggestions seem to have prompted Janáček to revise the ending. He discarded the last twelve pages of the copied score, thus dispensing with the Sacristan (who now does not appear in this act), and adding a monologue for Brouček: he wakes up properly and remembers parts of his 'dream' in words suggested by Brod and elaborated by Procházka.

Janáček to F. S. Procházka   *Brno, 16 March 1917*   **BR93**

I beg another small favour.

Could you still fill out for me, with sketched ideas, the awakening and sobering up of Brouček?

But I beg you: sit down somewhere and just write! You know how to and can. It is your last tribulation.

It wasn't, of course. Procházka sent his version by return (**BR94**, 18 March 1917), Janáček completed a final version, once again copied out by Sedláček (29 March 1917). When, on 24 March, Janáček thanked him he went on to suggest, with all the vigour of a sudden brainwave, that Procházka write him the libretto for a whole new excursion:

THE EXCURSION OF MR BROUČEK TO THE FIFTEENTH CENTURY

BR95   Janáček to F. S. Procházka   *Brno, 24 March 1917*

Thank you for your contribution. 'Manifik'[1] suits me well.
    [...]
    And how about if I were now to ask you to dramatize *The Excursion to the Fifteenth Century*?
    There is so much truth in it. To overflowing. At the same time its thrusts still affect us. A new time is coming, it's just around the corner, and [it would be wonderful] to place before it a pure mirror at Vítkov [see BR103+]!
    Our small-mindedness is embodied in Brouček; it's made for the stage.
    I already clearly see the dramatic impression in scenes.
    If you were to show just a little enthusiasm, I would begin telling you about it.

BR96   F. S. Procházka to Janáček   *Prague, 28 March 1917*

Your new idea appeals to me. It could be done and I would be keen to try my hand at that fifteenth century. But there is a condition here which no librettist will, or even may, avoid in relation to that material, i.e. a free hand in every direction. Today we do not have that free hand. We would forfeit half its effectiveness and would heat the water only to lukewarm. Or do you have a different opinion?
    You're right to say that a new time is around the corner. It is, certainly. But I would not be able to embark on this before that time is here.

BR97   Janáček to F. S. Procházka   *[undated, written on notepaper of the Prague journal 'Zvon', ?4 April 1917]*

Don't put it off!
    It goes without saying that I will give you complete freedom.
    It's true I've sketched a scenario for myself – but do what you want.
    See you then on Sunday [8 April].

With his eye on the political conditions in the country in the latter phase of the First World War, Procházka wrote too cautiously. Janáček took the 'free hand' to concern himself, not what the censor might permit. Procházka was

1 The beginning of one of Procházka's new lines for Brouček's awakening.

going away over the weekend and suggested postponing the visit until after 10 April (**BR98**, 5 April 1917). By 12 April the visit had clearly taken place and some agreement reached.

Janáček to F. S. Procházka   *Brno, 12 April 1917*   **BR99**

So wet your pen soon!

I want only to mention that we will also agree a contract over the fee, which, of course, it goes without saying.

I am writing to the heirs of Svatopluk Čech [see BR106+].

F. S. Procházka to Janáček   *Prague, 14 April 1917*   **BR100**

I am most willing, as I have already told you, and also eager, which is important. Please don't press me, it must ripen within me, the moment will come, but then I will be very quickly finished with it. The whole framework must be ready within me first. You yourself have suggested a great deal; I will stick to it because I must assume that this is how the thing is taking shape in your own mind. But I will allow myself certain changes, especially a greater accent on sarcasm.

We will come to an agreement about the material side when I have begun work [and am] certain that I will carry it out. Meanwhile don't press me, it won't help. You can't pull up an ear of corn from the earth. It's the same with me.

An undated letter (BR102) bears witness to Janáček's impatience and seems to have crossed with Procházka's announcement that he had started (**BR101**, 28 April 1917).

Janáček to F. S. Procházka   *[undated, Brno ?27 April 1917]*   **BR102**

I am not pressing [you]. I am waiting, I only hope I won't wait in vain.

I don't want to get stuck into other work. So I walk around without thoughts – and that's unpleasant.

PS   Couldn't you at least bite into the beginning?

F. S. Procházka to Janáček   *Prague, 30 April 1917*   **BR103**

Don't get stuck into anything. I'm working diligently. I myself am studying Old Czech phrases. It will be appropriately coloured. It's not easy work. I have inserted Svatopluk Čech nearer the beginning, where Brouček emerges from the jewel chamber. Then the burlesque [*karikatura*] begins and runs without interruption up to the end. [. . .]

The action of Svatopluk Čech's novel *The Epoch-making Excursion of Mr Brouček, this Time to the Fifteenth Century* begins with Mr Brouček's falling into the underground passages beneath the Vikárka that he has been discussing with his friends. He lights a match and discovers himself to be in an ancient jewel chamber. From there he makes his way outside – into fifteenth-century Prague on the morning of the Sunday, 14 July 1420, a crucial day in Czech history. Since the burning of the religious reformer Jan Hus at the Council of Constance in 1415 the country had been in a state of rebellion, particularly after the death of the Czech king, Václav IV, in 1419. His would-be successor, the Catholic Emperor Sigismund, attempted to establish his authority by means of a Crusader army assembled from the whole of Europe. Taborites (the militant wing of the Hussite movement) led by a commander of genius, Jan Žižka, and supported by Prague inhabitants, decisively defeated the Crusader forces at the battle of Vítkov (a hill in Prague) and prompted Sigismund's withdrawal. It is these heroic events in which Mr Brouček finds himself an unexpected and reluctant participator.

Čech's invocation to 14 July 1420 begins Chapter XII, and these words were put into his mouth by Procházka when including him briefly as a character in the opera, an idea that clearly came from Max Brod's notion of introducing him at the end of the previous excursion (BR87–8).

BR104   **F. S. Procházka to Janáček**   *Prague, 1 May 1917*

I've got Act 1 completely finished. Do you want it? I could send you a copy and you could say if I should go on. I hope that you will be satisfied.

PS [. . .] Should we not think up some more suitable, more pronounceable title than that lengthy one of Čech's? What do you think?

Janáček's response (BR106) was to Procházka's previous letter, and the question of the long title was not discussed in correspondence. It was easily solved towards the end of the year when Procházka wrote 'If the two excursions were to create a single evening they could perhaps have the common title: *The Excursions of Mr Brouček*' (**BR105**, 20 November 1917).

BR106   **Janáček to F. S. Procházka**   *Brno, 3 May 1917*

That pleases me! I also had Svatopluk Čech nearer the beginning. Good if you now have him there.

I want to be in Prague on Sunday [6 May]. But it's not certain.

If I don't visit you on Sunday morning, then please send me a copy immediately. If I come I will take it myself.

I already have in my hands the permission of Čech's heirs.   [. . .]

Earlier, Janáček had been in touch with Rektorys about securing permission, declaring that he now felt it was his 'duty' to complement *The Excursion of Mr Brouček to the Moon* with the fifteenth-century excursion   (BR107, 24 March 1917). By this time, as he discovered, Dr Klumpar no longer represented Čech's heirs, and permission came instead from Čech's relative, Ladislav Čech, who readily granted Janáček's request and left any consideration of fee to the composer (BR108: Ladislav Čech to Janáček, 1 May 1917).

Janáček seems to have made the journey to Prague to collect the libretto to Act 1. It seems, too, that they discussed the possibility of paralleling Brouček's earthly acquaintances with fifteenth-century characters in the same way that Janáček had connected them to the moon characters (see final list, pp. 246–7). This time it was not quite so straightforward, and not all of Janáček's proposals here were ultimately realized. In particular the association of the young pair Mazal and Málinka with Brouček's fifteenth-century hosts Domšík od Zvonu[1] and his wife Mandalena (Madlena) went awry. Janáček later associated the young couple with Domšík's daughter Kunka[2] and her sweetheart Petřík, so that Domšík became the equivalent of the Sacristan, while the small part of Mandalena was dropped (see BR134). This much more logical arrangement occurred to Janáček only after he had completed Act 1 of *The Excursion of Mr Brouček to the Fifteenth Century*: he had to rewrite Domšík's part, conceived and written for a lyric tenor, for a comic bass.[3]

Janáček to F. S. Procházka   *Brno, 9 May 1917*   BR109

So to take the characters from the excursion to the moon into the fifteenth century!

Málinka is easy to imagine in the dream as the prudent wife of Tomš.

In *The Excursion to the Moon*, *Málinka* and *Mazal* only talked of love, they love one another as Madlena and Tomš in the fifteenth century.

Their love ends understandably in the fifteenth century. They even have a daughter Kunka.

---

1 Domšík from the Bell, referred to sometimes by Janáček as Tomšík or Tomš. In Čech's novel he introduces himself as follows: 'I am Jan, the said Domšík, and they also call me Janek od Zvonu [Janek from the Bell], this is from my house here, on which you see a carved bell.' Domšík's Christian name Jan (Janek) was not included in the cast-list but occasionally referred to in the text (e.g. vs208–9). Domšík was an historical character; his house with the carved stone bell still stands, beautifully restored, in the Old Town Square.
2 A short form of the archaic Czech name Kunhuta (cf German Kunigunda; French Cunégonde from Voltaire's *Candide*). Sometimes in this correspondence the name comes in the form of 'Kuňka', allowing a pun from the verb 'kuňkat' ['to croak'], see BR152.
3 See Tyrrell 1973.

Brouček would have wanted Málinka in *The Excursion to the Moon* – were it not for the housekeeper.[1] Now he would have fallen for *Kunka* – were he not deluded by the similarity in appearance of *Mandalena–Málinka*. Mandalena's Old Czech confuses him.

In *The Excursion to the Moon* Mazal is the most natural man of all the artists: now he is the respectable magistrate *Tomš* at the White Bell; he dies a hero. An honest man.

Where to put Würfl in the fifteenth century?

I think, I think, that psychologically he would appear most properly as the first person that Brouček meets in the fifteenth century: as the *Alderman*, who arrests Brouček and takes him off to the magistrate.

A few words of confusion [over] Würfl–the Alderman will not be amiss in Act 1.

It won't be necessary for Brouček to know and recognize the other people in the fifteenth century.

Though I will compose the Student-Scribe as for the Young Waiter from *The Excursion to the Moon* and the roles of the townspeople visiting Tomš I will allocate to the artists from the Vikárka.

So to the matter.

I, just at the beginning of my work,[2] can make do with whatever needs no changes – I just ask for that single line of Čech's ode.

You, kindly work on Act 2 and even further. When your work is completely finished we will talk about various requirements.

Especially that *war song* from Act 1 ['Slyšte rytieře boží', see BR116] I would like to have when they give Brouček a weapon (in Act 2).[3]

But don't concern yourself with that now.

Ten additional lines for Čech's 'ode' were sent (**BR110**, 18 May 1917) and acknowledged (**BR111**, 19 May 1917: 'I've got to Svatopluk Čech's ode; so now down to it! – I'm working with joy and hope.'). In the event Janáček made do with what Procházka had originally provided. Eight days later Janáček reported 'I'm already at "Tomš's house". As you see, it is going quickly.' (**BR112**, 27 May 1917.)

1 A character who appears only in the epilogue to *The Excursion of Mr Brouček to the Moon*.

2 The beginning of Janáček's work on the score is unclear. The manuscript is dated 5 May 1917, but according to BR106 he did not collect the libretto before 6 May. He could, of course, have started work before receiving the text.

3 In Act 2 Hussite war songs are heard not as Brouček receives a weapon (VS248–9), but a little later (VS254–9), when the men have left for the battle and the women remain at home praying for victory.

F. S. Procházka to Janáček   *Prague, 29 May 1917*   BR113

And I am now finishing writing the second act.[1] I will be done with it tomorrow or the day after. I can write only in snatches. Over both holidays[2] my pen has not left my fingers. I hope that you will be satisfied. I strongly urge you not to change much. It is logically plotted. [...]

F. S. Procházka to Janáček   *Prague, 31 May 1917*   BR114

I have finished writing Act 2. When will you want to have it? Finishing [the libretto] will now be child's play. As for the text Act 3 will move headlong to the end. When are you coming to Prague? I'd like to have a talk.

Janáček to F. S. Procházka   *Brno, 2 June 1917*   BR115

Send me Act 2 just as soon as you are finished with it. Don't be frightened of changes from my side!

I thought at first that they would be necessary in Act 1; but I will get by without them. Perhaps we will just mix in *Kuňka* [Kunka] and the *Student* in the early morning procession.[3]

I'll come to Prague before the end of this month. If only they would give my *Jenůfa*! For two months they leave it on the shelves! But one cannot compel love.

I would like to have the draft full score of Act 1 ready by the end of June. I think I can do it.

I will then collect my strength for Act 2 during the holidays.

Janáček to F. S. Procházka   *Brno, 9 June 1917*   BR116

Did you get my letter?

I think I have succeeded with 'Slyšte rytieře boží'![4]

---

1 The libretto was cast in three acts. Act 2 ended after the men went off to battle. When Janáček came to set Act 3, he replaced the act division with an intermezzo (see BR134, 18 September 1917) so that *The Excursion of Mr Brouček to the Fifteenth Century* was reduced to two acts. Until that date references to the three-act divisions are retained.

2 Presumably the Whitsun weekend; in 1917 Whit Sunday fell on 26 May.

3 It is early on a Sunday morning when Brouček makes his way into fifteenth-century Prague and at the end of Act 1 armed people process slowly towards the Týn church, Panna Marie před Týnem (late fourteenth-century to early fifteenth-century), which dominates the Old Town Square (Domšík's house with the stone bell lies just in front of it). Kunka and the Student do not appear until Act 2 of the opera.

4 'Hear, o warriors of God!', the chorus that the armed people sing as they move into the Týn church, bringing Act 1 to an impressive close (VS193–203).

How from all sides it begins to resound! Ever more and more sublimely!

I think that I will be finished with Act 1 by the holidays.

I would be glad – to have my mind at peace for a spell of rest.

On the 13th and 14th of this month I will be in Vienna [for the première there of *Jenůfa*]. Perhaps if it turns out well there I would travel by express train to Prague.

So I await the promised Act 2.

BR117   Janáček to F. S. Procházka   *Brno, 9 June 1917*

I forgot something else.

How could the 'young gentlemen' of the fifteenth century leave Brouček in peace when the women set them an example with their mocking 'Kmošku, kmošku, nevoďhlésti, etc.'.[1]

The boys would take this up, *but I would still need a line or two of jesting as a continuation of their unruly behaviour.*

And right away. That's possible, isn't it?

BR118   F. S. Procházka to Janáček   *Prague, 12 June 1917*

Four days last week I was sick with a stomach upset; my stomach won't take these substitutes any more.[2] So forgive me that I didn't write back at once. I have been completely finished with Act 2 for some time, it just needs copying. For me that's always worse work than writing it. I will let you have it soon. I am certain you will be satisfied. I will also soon finish off Act 3.

In August I will be leaving Prague for the holidays; I'll be ready with everything by that time. You can make firm plans according to that.

Here are the lines for the unruly boys:

> *Hera, čerte, hera*
> *Pověz, kdes byl včera!*
> *Chacha, chacha!*

['Hey, devil, hey / where were you yesterday! / Ha-ha, ha-ha!']

Is it suitable? If not I'll send you other lines.

In Act 2 you will have many suggestions for evocative motifs. Right

---

1 These lines of mockery were ultimately omitted. Instead both men and women repeat the women's earlier cry accusing Brouček being a spy of Sigismund ('Špehér Zikmundóv!'; vs189ff).

2 Presumably wartime substitutes for food or medicine.

from the beginning Rokycana's mass, organs, and into this Brouček's prosaic dispute in the [dining-]room, then at the end that warlike uproar, alarm bells and Mrs Mandalena kneels before the open window looking on to the Old Town Square and prays for victory, for the life of her husband and for the motherland. I can imagine Mandalena's prayer being heard against the background of the army noises outside. Kunka also will have a spot where during lunch she quotes part of Rokycana's sermon. There will be a heap of things for you.

Act 2 takes place in Domšík's house, where Brouček is entertained as an exotic guest. Procházka's libretto for the act consisted basically of four scenes: one showing Brouček getting dressed in the fifteenth-century clothes provided by his host; a meal with Domšík, his wife and daughter; the arrival of guests, with whom Brouček drinks and disputes; and the news of the beginning of the battle and the departure of the menfolk. Janáček's major change here was to conflate the middle two scenes, eliminating Domšík's wife Mandalena in the process (see **BR131+**). Kunka's description of the mass in the nearby Týn church and the sermon of Jan Rokycana (a popular Hussite preacher) was retained by Janáček, but transferred from the family lunch to the larger gathering of male guests (VS217–23).

At this stage, however, Janáček's only response was to ask for more lines for the boys (**BR119**, 18 June 1917), which Procházka sent the next day (**BR120**, 19 June 1917). In this letter Procházka recommended that Brouček be dressed to stand out from the others 'in an elegant *white* summer suit' in Act 1. He also mentioned that he was copying out Act 2 and beginning Act 3.

F. S. Procházka to Janáček   *Prague, 23 June 1917*   **BR121**

I'm sending Act 2 and wish you good cheer for work and every success. Please keep my manuscripts, the libretto will then be set in type according to them. I will finish writing Act 3 at the beginning of July and you will receive the manuscript at the end, before my departure. This act will be shorter, as I see it, as far as the words are concerned; the music in it, however, will have much to do. All the grandeur of Hussitism and glory to it will be there. I'm very much looking forward to your opera. When will we see it in Prague?

On this letter Janáček noted down: 'Staročeské duch. zpěvy/Melantrich/ Praha/Doležil'. This is a reference to Hubert Doležil's male-voice collection *Staročeské duchovní zpěvy XIV. a XV. stol.* [Old Czech Sacred Songs of the Fourteenth and Fifteenth Century] (Prague: Melantrich, 1917), which had come out in March that year. All the texts of the Hussite chorales in Procházka's libretto were taken from this source, which, for instance, gives the words of the famous Hussite battle hymn 'Ktož jsú boží bojovníci' ['Ye who are God's warriors'] in a more authentic version of the words than Čech used in his novel ('Kdož jste boží bojovníci'). Čech quoted two Hussite hymns; in his libretto Procházka quoted six. Of these Janáček used only part of three and made up his own tunes, with the exception of 'Kdož jste...'(i.e. in its modern form). This tune was so familiar from its use by Smetana (in 'Tábor' and 'Blaník' in *My Fatherland*) and Dvořák (in his *Hussite Overture*) that it was impossible to ignore it.

BR122   Janáček to F. S. Procházka   *Brno, 1 July 1917*

I've played through all of Act 1 to myself. Under the impact of it I'm now writing to you:

  1. The introduction has the *fight motif*[1] and that of *'dne páně'* ['Day of the Lord', i.e. Sunday]![2] It stands out well.

  2. The transition into the fifteenth century (Brouček's) and Čech's prophetic words stand out clearly.

  3. Dawn and the first waves [of people] that gather in the Týn church work naturally.

  4. Tomš's 'začiná se den Páně, komusi v něm bude bieda' ['the day of the Lord is beginning, for some there will be sorrow in it'][3] – is the climax.

But 5., on the other hand, the mocking of Brouček eludes me. *The children have to be the climax of it!*

I have for it only the couplet:

> *Hera, čerte, hera*
> *Pověz, kdes byl včera!* [see BR118]

I would still need another sort of line which would perhaps refer to Brouček's *Mahometanism*.[4]

I have enough exclamations, I simply need a nimble little line like that.

---

1 From the opening bar, VS163: an agitated somtimes 5–note, sometimes 4–note figure followed by a double cymbal clash.

2 The *meno mosso* section, VS165: a grandiose theme with prominent use of harp chords in the accompaniment.

3 VS199: a climax leading to the *fortissimo*, C major version of 'Slyšte, rytieři' which brings Act 1 to a close.

4 In both the novel and the opera Brouček has to account for his poor (i.e. nineteenth-century) Czech and his odd (i.e. nineteenth-century) clothing to his fifteenth-century captors, who believe he is a spy. He seizes upon the explanation that he has been 'far away', in lands held by the Turks, where he has forgotten his native tongue, and where they dress differently.

This scene, so important, is eluding me. Or perhaps to leave out that theme, to have 'Blepci halafance',[1] taken up by the children.

So I still need that for Act 1.

And now I will read through Act 2.

Janáček to F. S. Procházka
Brno, 1 July 1917 **BR123**

I have not yet read Act 2.

I don't want to dissipate my energies until Act 1 is in order. I will be ready with it today.

I ask you in addition for Act 3 and, after a break, I think that the work will go fast.

I go off to Luhačovice perhaps tomorrow. I will send you my address.

F. S. Procházka to Janáček
Prague, 8 July 1917 **BR124**

Good then! I will get cracking with Act 3. I have no doubts about your success with Act 2, but it will take a fair bit of work!!! What a shame that we won't have it this year! Prague theatres are chock-a-block with the right atmosphere for such things.

In his next letter (BR125) Procházka included the requested words for the boys, including references to Brouček's 'Mahometanism' and explained some of the Old Czech words ('hasačert') which he incorporated. Once again they remained unused.

F. S. Procházka to Janáček
[undated, postmarked Prague, **BR125**
10 July 1917]

[. . .] I'm much delighted by your news that you are satisfied with your Act 1. It seems to me that after the animated conclusion to Act 1, the peaceful atmosphere of the beginning of Act 2 will exactly suit you, continually building up with a crescendo. There are many places there which will attract you musically and I am curious what you will write to me after reading Act 2. It will be the climax of the opera. Act 3 will be a rapid little conclusion with an imposing picture of the victorious tumult and rejoicing.

---

1 The Alderman's words when telling Brouček to speak Czech properly (VS195). In the end the children were omitted here.

BR126   **Janáček to F. S. Procházka**   *Brno, 26 August 1917*

I'm looking again now at the work.
     When will Brouček be burnt?
     That's essential! I thought at the end of Act 2. So then in Act 3?
     Even now a man has the urge a hundred times over to burn that sort of double-dealer!

BR127   **F. S. Procházka to Janáček**   *Planá, 29 August 1917*

I'm returning to Prague after Sunday [2 September], then we will finish off the rest. The burning will be in Act 3 at the end, according to your scenario, to which we have been adhering. Or do you want it otherwise? I think not.

At the end of the novel, Brouček is found out by his fifteenth-century hosts to be cowardly in the face of national peril and is accordingly put to death by burning in a beer barrel (his propensity for drink was noted). Brouček later wakes up in the Vikárka mysteriously lodged in a beer barrel. Janáček's scenario, which Procházka has been sticking to, seems to have disappeared. The editors of Janáček's correspondence with Procházka reported that it was not in Procházka's estate (JA iii, 47, fn.51). The only relevant scenario in the Janáček archive is a short draft headed by the word 'Sen' ['Dream']. This can hardly qualify as the 'scenario', which clearly mentions act divisions (BR127). Furthermore it leaves out the entire section corresponding to the second act (the first four numbered sections refer to incidents in Act 1; the remaining three are incidents in what was originally Act 3). That this is a very early draft is supported by the fact that the first part deals in some detail with the transition to the fifteenth century, then follows:

BR128   **Janáček's scenario (undated)**

[. . .]

Fifteenth century

1. Falls down the [underground] passage
2. Climbs out of the jewel chamber into the street (Change of scene)
3. Clashes with the watch
4. 'Sigismund's spy!'
5. 'Go to Satan!'
6. The burning barrel with Brouček
7. The Vikárka courtyard (Change of scene)

Janáček to F. S. Procházka   *Brno, 31 August 1917*   BR129

No changes in the plan.

The first act is ready in fair copy; I just hope that I will also succeed in the following acts.

If only my time was freer. When the labour of teaching begins,[1] I can only steal time for sitting down to composition. And yet I would like to be finished even with the burning – by the end of the year.

I didn't have much of a rest during the holiday; plenty of longueurs.

F. S. Procházka to Janáček   *Prague, 9 September 1917*   BR130

As you know Čech had Domšík die in battle. Shouldn't they bring on the dead Domšík at the beginning of Act 3? Only after that would the victory jubilation develop and Žižka's ceremonial procession. Wouldn't this sad motif be a violent intrusion? Would it suit you for the piece? Tell me your own opinion about it. Please write to me briefly.

You can be sure that you will receive the end in good time. I can only work in snatches, during the holidays I did nothing and had a rest.

Janáček to F. S. Procházka   *Brno, 12 September 1917*   BR131

Do you have my sketch [scenario]?

In her anxiety Tomš's wife sends Markéta [i.e. Kedruta] then Kuňka by turns, to find out about the course of the battle.

She hears only the news, from the street, that Tomš is no longer among the living. That's enough for her collapse.

A corpse on stage, definitely not.

I will come to Prague on Saturday [15 September] and will look you up.

By the time Janáček came to compose this part he had omitted Domšík's wife Mandalena (see BR134); the final shape of this scene is described by Janáček in BR142. For the victory procession mentioned in BR130 Janáček included the sound of an organ (from the Týn church, the destination of the procession, VS270) and bagpipes (VS263). It seems to have been on his trip to Prague on 15 September that Janáček inquired about the authenticity of both instruments in the piece.

---

1 Janáček remained head of the Brno Organ School and its successor, the Brno Conservatory, until its nationalization in 1920.

BR132 **F. S. Procházka to Janáček** *Prague, 17 September 1917*

I advise you to leave [in] the organ. As early as 1255 there was a 'new' organ in the Prague metropolitan cathedral. In the fourteenth century it already had two manuals. In 1470 pedals were added, in addition to the manuals. It can be assumed that there was an organ in the Týn church in 1420, although its sounds would be different from that today. It is a historical fact.

The little bagpiper can also be there. It is a charming musical idea.

A bagpiper features even more prominently in Act 1, providing an accompaniment to the first Hussite chorale (vs198). In a letter written later to the folklorist Čeněk Zíbrt (1864–1932), Janáček explained his motivation for introducing the bagpiper:

BR133 **Janáček to Čeněk Zíbrt** *[undated, 1918]*

[...] I have received from you a book about the bagpiper.[1] Before I read it I already had bagpipes in my new work *The Excursion of Mr Brouček to the Fifteenth Century*. I needed them as a musical, orchestral indication of that period. [...] I value the bagpipes for their softness and for their melancholy tone; they bring with them the refined tone of the organ to the modern orchestra but are nevertheless more spiritual. This is still lacking in the modern orchestral score. [...]

BR134 **Janáček to F. S. Procházka** *Brno, 18 September 1917*

I'm finished with Act 2.

There is not much action left for the third act, which I await from you.

1. Brouček hares in – he runs quickly across in the Old Town Square; Kedruta after him [crying] 'Antikrist!'.[2] The crowd grows.

2. Brouček pushes his way into the group of warriors with banners: 'Maine Herrn!'.[3]

3. Confusion, sentencing – burning. *I would like to link all this to Act 2 with an intermezzo.*

1 Zíbrt's *The Bagpipes Played* (Prague, 1917); a copy with Janáček's annotations and dedicated to Janáček by the author is in Janáček's library, BmJA, H 612.
2 In the novel Brouček lights up a cigar to the consternation of Domšík's servant Kedruta, who sees the flame and the smoke as a diabolic manifestation and proclaims him an 'Antichrist'; this incident is set in vs258.
3 Janáček refined his ideas for this in BR142.

Please as soon as possible.

The announcement of the death of Tomš od Zvonu I have at the end of Act 2.

As soon as I have tidied up the full score I will write out the text of Act 2 as I have drawn it together for musical reasons.

I think you will be happy.

The persons of the two excursions are as follows:[1]
1. Brouček
2. Málinka – Etherea – Kunka
3. Mazal – Blankytný – Petřík
4. Sexton – Lunobor – Tomšík od zvonu
5. Würfl – Maecenas – Alderman
6. Housekeeper – Kedruta

Tomšík no longer has a wife: I left out Mandalena. She was quite wrong for the fifteenth century.

She would suddenly be passive whereas formerly she was aggressive.

Málinka – Etherea – Kunka is a single character.

F. S. Procházka to Janáček　　　*Prague, 22 October 1917*　　**BR135**

I'm into it, but *nota bene*: between the end of Act 2 and the beginning of Act 3, Brouček had a military adventure, in front of the Crusaders,[2] and *this is why* he is condemned *as a deserter and a coward.* The tragedy could not have occurred because of his smoking a cigar [see p. 216, fn.2]. Otherwise it would seem to me insufficiently supported and justified. And after all the judgement of Captain Chval[3] is based on it. Isn't that so?

Janáček to F. S. Procházka　　　*Brno, 24 October 1917*　　**BR136**

Yes of course. *Petřík* is the main prosecutor in front of the captain.

The cigar frightens Kedruta most of all.

---

1 See pp. 246–7 for final list.

2 In the novel Brouček mistakes some horsemen with a Crusader emblem for the foreign forces and begs for mercy as a 'German' and a 'Catholic'. The horsemen turn out to be Czechs, carrying back a Crusader trophy.

3 Chval Řepický z Machovic, a celebrated warrior in the Hussite wars incorporated into Čech's novel; for instance Brouček goes off (briefly) to fight in his division. Procházka had him lead the victory procession and included a scene where Chval (Žižka in Čech's novel) sentences Brouček to death for cowardice; in the opera these lines were eventually given to the Alderman (vs283–5).

It would be good if I could be finished with it all by the end of the year, at least this is what I hope.

Procházka announced finishing Act 3 on 28 October (**BR137**) and on 7 November, after Janáček failed to find time to collect it during a trip to Prague on 2 November, wrote again (**BR138**) to say that he had sent it by registered post on 5 November. Janáček pronounced on 21 November 1917 that 'Act 3 suited [him] well' (**BR139**) and a couple of days later began looking at it in more detail.

BR140 **Janáček to F.S. Procházka**   *Brno, 23 November 1917*

[. . .] I will need Kuňka at *Petřík*'s words: *'že je na pravdě boží'* ['that he is at God's truth'].[1] *Kuňka* hears this news here for the first time. Let her pour out her grief with a few words over the death of her father. I ask you for them.

Another tiny addition: Svatopluk Čech had it and I took it [from him].

Brouček tells of his heroism and at that moment Petřík surprises him, catches out the liar.

Otherwise I am pleased with your Act 3. [. . .]

The scene where Brouček is discovered hiding by two Taborites, who at first think he is wounded and to whom he unwisely boasts of his military exploits, is not in Procházka's libretto: Janáček took it from Čech – his copy of the novel is heavily underlined at this point (pp. 285–7). The chief difference is that while in Čech the Taborites admire Brouček's fighting spirit and take him with them, Janáček combined this scene with Petřík's denunciation of Brouček. Despite Procházka's reservations (BR141) Janáček included it in the final version of the opera (VS272–4).

BR141 **F. S. Procházka to Janáček**   *Prague, 25 November 1917*

You wrote to me that Domšík's death will be dealt with in Act 2; I therefore placed in Kedruta's lips only a reminiscence of it and the accusation of Brouček that he caused the death of Domšík. I did not mention the death any more than that in Act 3. If you want to have Kuňka there – although it is not logical that she should find out only now about the death of her father, when the death has already taken place in Act 2 – I will send you her crying or wailing.

1 Words added by Janáček at the end of Act 2 to Procházka's libretto indicating the death of Domšík and replaced in the opera by 'Bůh mu daj slávu věčnú' ['God grant him eternal glory'] (VS277).

Further I ask you to consider that proposed addition from Čech where Brouček tells of his heroism. To lie and to boast is not a great fault, even Petřík could not reproach Brouček for it – only laugh at it. Brouček must however take upon himself some real guilt, for which he is condemned, and this is his cowardice, for he knelt before a German and begged him for mercy. This in the eyes of those days was a sin worthy of death. [...] Please consider that Brouček's guilt would be weakened by such an insertion. And then, Brouček puffs himself up with his heroism to Mr Würfl at the end of Act 3; there it is in place, this cheap, bragging Czechness of the present day. [...]

Janáček to F.S. Procházka *Brno, 29 November 1917* BR142

This is how it goes:

Kuňka, Domšík's daughter, when the others go off to fight, has to pray *Our Father* in her desperation [vs251].

She does not finish praying, she seizes a sword and runs out after the others [vs253].

Kedruta, the servant, finishes the prayer in anguish [vs253–5].

Brouček returns. There is the well-known scene between the two [vs256–9; see p. 216, fn.2].

Kedruta rushes out after Brouček [vs259].

After a while *Kuňka* returns crushed; the town is empty; she returns helpless [vs259–60].[1]

The music goes on playing without interruption; peal of trumpets; victorious cries [vs260].[2]

Kuňka calls Kedruta and runs to the window [vs260–1].

(The curtain falls) [vs261]

The music continues to play and changes into the noise of victory [vs261–5].[3]

(Act 3)

The victory procession enters the Týn church [vs269].

---

1 Kunka's words here 'Siro, pusto' ['Desolate, deserted'] and the stage directions are Janáček's addition.
2 Janáček introduced an offstage 'peal of trumpets' (trumpets in three parts), though no 'victorious cries' until persuaded to do so by Schmoranz (see BR242–4).
3 The noise of victory is depicted musically (with the curtain down) with cries of 'Hejsasa!' from children and 'Vítajte!' ['Welcome!'] from adults and once again Janáček's bagpipes. Petřík's cry of 'Dítky' ['Children!' – the first word in another Hussite chorale, heard later] comes a few bars before the curtain rises, announcing the beginning of 'Act 3'.

Petřík etc.[1]
Brouček cowers under the arches of the house at the bell [i.e.
Domšík's house]; *he did not run far* [vs271].
Two Taborites notice him: 'Tu jeden raněný!' ['Here is one
wounded!'] [vs272, words slightly changed].
Brouček little by little gets himself into a muddle with his lies.
Petřík overhears the end of his boasts: 'Lháři' ['Liar!'] etc. [vs275].
Kuňka (comes after Petřík's voice): and hears from his lips here the
brief tidings of the death of Domšík, her father [vs276–7].
Kuňka (her lament).
This is where I need a few words...

Petřík (finishes speaking) [vs280–3]: Brouček sentenced [vs283–
5]. *Petřík exits with Kuňka.*[2]
Brouček kneels, etc., etc.[3]
Everything is kept as you wrote it.
Brouček's boast in this place is more timely than at the end in front
of Würfl. Here he only makes a reference to it [vs295–6], but is glad
to be home.

BR143   F. S. Procházka to Janáček   *Prague, 3 December 1917*

Just as you changed it and added to it, so you have it. Your music
demanded it. I am sending you the requested lament for Kuňka,[4]
which you placed in Act 3, where I had put only Kedruta, Brouček's
passionate adversary. Because the text will now be definitive, I ask
you kindly to send it to me so that I can supply the Old Czech
colouring of the language.

PS I wrote to you [**BR144**, 23 November], that I would now place a
news item in *Zvon*[5] about your *Broučkiada*, if I could know something further about it. Or is it premature?

---

1 This probably refers to the chorale 'Dítky, v hromadu se sendĕme' ['Children, we are
gathered together'], sung antiphonally with the chorus (vs266–9). However it comes
before the processions enter the Týn church.
2 This stage direction was omitted.
3 Brouček begs for mercy, pleading that he does not belong, that he is 'a son of the future',
in view of his cowardice the most crushing indictment in the opera of the nineteenth-
century Czechs.
4 'Umřel mi tatíček' ['My father has died'], vs278–80.
5 The weekly literary magazine that Procházka edited.

Janáček to Kamila Stösslová *Brno, 3 December 1917* **BR145**

[...] I worked doggedly from 7 a.m. to noon; I had lunch and again worked up to half-past 9 this evening!

I am finished with the opera *The Excursions of Mr Brouček*!

It was necessary to check in my mind the whole of Act 3 *in one breath*. And thousands of notes! [...]

Janáček to F. S. Procházka *Brno, 4 December 1917* **BR146**

Thank you for the addition.

I did not want to end Act 2 sadly, therefore I shifted the death of Domeš [sic].

I am thus finished with the score of 'The Excursions of Mr Brouček'.

You can now briefly inform the public.

I will supply the text according to the score and send it to you for correction.

Act 1 is being copied now, Act 2 is being held up until the score is copied.

Will the National Theatre respond to the news in *Zvon*?

I am glad that I am finished with the work; it took up as much as five years!

Janáček also announced to Gabriela Horvátová that the work had taken five years (**BR147**, 4 December 1917), a reasonable estimate considering the stops and starts on the work since 1908. He had found it hard work, he wrote: 'Scenes changing at the drop of a hat. And what is most difficult: moods like the delicate rippling of water. Waves beat only as if under a calm surface: a hard cover over everything.' Here Janáček put his finger on the virtually cinematic technique of the succession of short scenes that he had pioneered in *Fate* and was to develop even further in *From the House of the Dead*.

F. S. Procházka to Janáček *Prague, 7 December 1917* **BR148**

Can I give Viktor Dyk as the author of the 'moon' libretto?

Please send me a message by return, I would like to put the announcement into the very next issue.

Janáček to F. S. Procházka *Brno, 8 December 1917* **BR149**

Yes, you can.

This very week I will send you the whole libretto.

Mr Dyk himself wrote as follows:

[']The text after Svatopluk Čech's work of the same name, arranged by Viktor Dyk according to the wishes of the composer.[']

BR150   Janáček to Gabriela Horvátová   *Brno, 12 December 1917*

[. . .] One must be above the writer. They burn Brouček in a barrel; and the libretto did not say *why particularly in a barrel?* There Mr Procházka left out an important bit. Today I have now corrected it.[1]
[. . .]

BR151   Janáček to F. S. Procházka   *Brno, 19 December 1917*

Happy holidays!
I enclose the libretto.
Kindly read it all, both [parts].
I think that it is a good libretto. A lot of us are Broučeks, or were. Just let there be no more of them now.

When you have done the language corrections I will write them into the score.

It is a habit of mine to let finished work lie – until another flood of mood has passed over it. After a time one looks with different eyes. A work should not drown the whole man, all his thoughts.

If there was demand, I would relax this habit a little.

The libretto was not easy work; I will write a few words about it later.[2] I think that it would not be to its detriment.

But even the musical composition itself was hard, not easy: to bend every emotional fibre – in order to penetrate a deep truth; to sharpen it at all times with sarcasm! I am glad that I am out of it.

BR152   F. S. Procházka to Janáček   *Prague, 23 December 1917*

I have taken advice as regards the language and the orthography and have come to the view that it would be better in the theatre if it were written as spoken [phonetically]. Also the inserted passage of the religious argument in Act 2 recommends this; together with other insertions, it would have to be transcribed.

I went according to your plan, I see now that in places you have

1 Janáček expanded Kedruta's lines as the flames soar above Brouček's pyre and she throws on to them his 'hellish' matchbox and 'devilish spice' (Brouček's cigar) to accompany him on his journey to hell.
2 The 'few words' must have been already written. They appeared on 23 December 1917 as a feuilleton in the *Lidové noviny*; see p. 227, fn.2.

departed from it. I wrote for a whole evening. You are counting on both excursions in one evening. In this lay the misunderstanding. But I have the impression that both librettos are fine.

But let me draw your attention on p. 41 [of the manuscript libretto] to the end of Act 3: Würfl asks: 'Kdo to tady kuňká?' ['Who is that croaking/saying "Kunka" there?']. *And no-one is croaking*, the audience does not hear anyone croaking.[1] Why then does Würfl ask this? Please have a look at my manuscript. There is moaning there. Brouček calls out in his final anguish to Kunka for help. In my manuscript it is justified by his erotic ardour, which was there also on the moon between Brouček and Málinka. This motive has been done away with. So Würfl ought to ask it in another way. This is certainly an important point for the action, in which fantasy mixes in with reality, and this is how Svatopluk Čech concludes it too.

I ask for a brief report about what you think of it. I will then return the corrected manuscript to you. As far as the religious insertion is concerned I paused also over this element: writing the libretto, I left it out because I assumed that in the theatre the reason for the quarrel would elude the audience. The religious arguments, so characteristic of the fifteenth century, would have to be introduced to the audience in more detail in order to be understood by them. Because of this I replaced them with the irony of patriotism, which is really the idea of the whole excursion to the fifteenth century. In this way the libretto has been weakened, and I fear that this will be criticized in it. Do you not think so?

Happy Christmas!

PS Jirásek told me that the Hussites had an organ in the Týn church, and even gave me the name of a famous organist. Of course it had a special stop, which you will understand. I continually hear the Týn organ in that part of the action. It seems to me that a bagpipe cannot substitute for it.

Janáček to F.S. Procházka   *Brno, 25 December 1917*   **BR153**

1. It was essential to characterize the fifteenth century with religious argument; only out of it could the quarrel of which Brouček was the

---

1 Janáček omitted to copy out Brouček's groans (VS292) in his fair copy of the text. There is a punning connection between *kuňká* [croaks] and the name of Kunka.

victim emerge. The 'Student'[1] makes it bearable.

2. I also have organs.

3. Brouček also croaks.

4. The fifteenth century itself had little action. Now it is a serious complement [to the first excursion]. Brouček ends his life as he deserves. The picture is completed.

I think also that the libretto is *good*. [...]

The Excursions of Mr Brouček was now ready for publication and production, a long process which tried Janáček's patience even further. Before then, however, he made one crucial adjustment to the piece:

BR154   Janáček to Gabriela Horvátová   *Brno, 18 January 1918*

[...] How sometimes one throws away finished work with relish. I have thrown away all of last year's work with *Brouček in his home.* The two dreams now follow one another: *just as Svatopluk Čech wrote it.* All other peoples' accretions I have thrown out. And with what relish! [...][2]

PUBLICATION AND PRODUCTION

Even while Janáček was revising Act 2 of *The Excursion of Mr Brouček to the Moon*, there were promising signs that the opera, still a single excursion, would be swiftly published and produced in Prague. Since Janáček had worked in full score, a vocal score was needed and Roman Veselý, who had made piano arrangements of works by Novák, Suk and Foerster, was hired to do the work. Veselý dated his vocal score of Act 1 Scene 1 '5 October 1916',[3] and that very day (**BR155**) Janáček acknowledged receipt of the 'beginning of the vocal score' and matching full score, and made arrangements to deliver the next batch. Veselý made rapid progress with Act 1 Scene 2 (his vocal score is dated 26 October 1916), but delays in getting the full score of Act 2 copied meant that by 17 November Janáček was still promising to send him the final part (**BR156**). It was only on Christmas Eve that Janáček planned to collect Act 2 and deliver the epilogue (**BR157**: Janáček to Veselý, 18 December 1916).

1 The Student is almost as irritating in his precocity as his lunar counterpart, the Child Prodigy. He weighs into the doctrinal arguments, arousing universal hostility from Domšík's guests (VS232–8) until the spotlight is turned on Brouček and his views on church ornaments are anxiously solicited.

2 With this laconic statement Janáček excluded an entire act of the opera, twenty minutes of music. It was broadcast by Czech Radio on 22 September 1936.

3 BmJA, A34.446.

The engraving of the vocal score was not far behind. The Czech firm Hudební matice had taken over the Czech edition of *Jenůfa* and seems to have made an early bid to publish *The Excursion of Mr Brouček to the Moon* (see BR162). In a letter of 22 November 1916 (**BR158**) Otakar Nebuška acknowledged receipt of Act 1 and asked a number of questions about it, drawing attention particularly to the paucity and inconsistency of the stage directions. Janáček's prompt answers were solicited since arrangements had already been made for printing by Breitkopf & Härtel in Leipzig, who promised to engrave Act 1 'within three weeks'. Nebuška followed this up with a postcard a few days later with more questions (**BR159**, 27–30 November 1916) and suggestions for a shorter title: *The Excursion of Mr Brouček to the Moon* (the Čech novel is entitled *The True Excursion...*). Janáček must have satisfied Nebuška sufficiently to proceed, since when Nebuška wrote on 25 December (**BR160**) he announced that he had 'more proofs' for him and awaited the vocal score of Act 2. On 22 January 1917 (BR166) Nebuška was able to announce that Breitkopf had already engraved all of Act 2 and Veselý was working on the proofs. Nebuška also made his usual practical observations, here (now Act 3) about the difficulty of some of the stage directions. It may have been such comments coming on top of Max Brod's critical comments (**BR87**) that set Janáček thinking about revising this act. It was not engraved (Janáček withdrew Veselý's vocal score from Hudební matice), and on 18 February 1917 (**BR161**) Janáček wrote to Veselý telling him that he had 'done it differently', tightening it and 'unifying it with the motif of the housekeeper's indignation'. The score was ready and he would receive it shortly, a premature announcement, since the score still needed copying, and Sedláček did not complete this until 15 March – by which time Janáček was working on a new ending with Brouček's sobering up (see BR93–4).

Janáček was careful to keep Kovařovic informed about the progress of the work. A few days after the première of *Jenůfa*, Janáček had written to him describing his 'burlesque opera' briefly and asking if he might dedicate it to him (JP114). There must have been further talk about it: by the autumn he made a progress report which mentioned the possibility of 'rehearsals':

Janáček to Karel Kovařovic   *Brno, 26 October 1916*   **BR162**

You know that the vocal score of the first act of *Brouček* is being finished. Umělecká beseda [i.e. Hudební matice] will print it immediately; so the rehearsals will be comfortable and fast.

But I am already also finishing Act 2; I have now almost got to the climax[1] and can therefore now look round a little at the effect of

---

1 Janáček reached the end of his revision of this act on 5 November 1916, according to his date in the score (BmJA, A 7450).

the whole. The first part of the full score of Act 2 is in fair copy, and I will take it to Mr Veselý on All Saints' Day. [. . .]

BR163   Janáček to Karel Kovařovic   *Brno, 16 December 1916*

[. . .] During the holidays I will come to Prague for about a fortnight. The vocal score of Act 2 will be delivered to me and I will give you the full score of it. The full score of Act 3 is now in fair copy.

I will send the libretto to Director Schmoranz tomorrow [Schmoranz acknowledged receipt on 19 December, **BR164**].

I only hope that the work is [long] enough for two hours! This occurred to me, and I am fearful [what would happen] if it weren't enough! [. . .]

Thus by the end of 1916 the National Theatre had had sight of the full score of two acts of *The Excursion of Mr Brouček to the Moon* and a complete libretto. That discussion had got as far as commissioning set-designs is evident from a reference in a letter from Nebuška to Janáček on 16 January 1917 (**BR165**): 'Has the administration of the National Theatre already informed you that it considers Wenig's lunar decorations financially and technically unrealizable in wartime?' This theme was developed in Nebuška's next letter.

BR166   Otakar Nebuška to Janáček   *Prague, 22 January 1917*

[. . .] Don't be too quick to take the crisis over *Brouček* so much to heart. [. . .] The first thing is to get someone who could design suitable and realizable sets for the lunar landscape and the Cathedral of All Arts. Wenig's[1] proposals for the sets are barren; the second one, moreover, needs a huge amount of material, and is furthermore unsuitable since Čaroskvoucí's throne takes up the whole stage and there is no room left for the corridors of the sunbeam room [i.e. 'the vestibule with corridors radiating out', see BR9] or even a view into them. They are generally overfull. This someone will be found either in the theatre or outside it. [. . .]

But if the production was temporarily halted by difficulties over stage designs, Janáček himself upset the course of events initially by revising the end of Act 3 (which meant that it was not set up in type and not submitted to the National Theatre for consideration) and, more crucially, by adding a whole new excursion. A year later, with the new excursion completed, he

---

1 Josef Wenig (1885–1939), a designer who worked chiefly at the Vinohrady Theatre, but from 1913 also designed a number of forward-looking sets for the National Theatre.

began to take up the matter of publication and production again. But now the whole affair had become infinitely more complicated.

Originally, publication had been a local matter fixed up informally with Nebuška acting for Hudební matice. In the meantime, however, Universal Edition had published the German edition of *Jenůfa*, which had come out in December 1917. Janáček's international stocks were rising and Jan Löwenbach, acting in effect as Janáček's agent, managed to interest the Berlin publisher Drei Masken-Verlag in *The Excursions of Mr Brouček*.

Jan Löwenbach to Janáček   *Prague, 27 December 1917*   BR167

About a fortnight ago Drei Masken-Verlag from Berlin, one of the largest and most active theatrical publishers, wrote to me saying that they are very interested in your new opera. I had informed them about *Brouček*, and at the same time of *Fate*, whereupon they wrote to me saying that they would like to have a look at both works, and asked for translations of the texts. At the same time [as this letter] I am sending them the brush proofs[1] of the first and second acts of *Brouček* to look at and telling them the contents of the work in its original guise. From your feuilleton in the *Lidové noviny*,[2] I learn that you have revised *Brouček* and extended it and I would therefore be grateful if you could send me the new text to look at. In the next few days I will get together with Dr Max Brod, whose work has also come out with the above-mentioned publisher, and will discuss with him whether he would take on the translation.

I ask therefore if you would kindly inform me whether you would be willing to enter into negotiations with this publisher and whether it would be possible to send them vocal scores of both works to look at. If you have new texts of *Brouček* and *Fate* to hand, kindly send them to me.

In his answer (**BR168**, 30 December 1917) Janáček mentioned that he had also approached by Universal Edition and needed to know what Hudební matice's intentions were: so far he had had no contract (and any verbal understanding concerned only the *The Excursion of Mr Brouček to the Moon*).

Janáček thus had three publishers with an interest in *Brouček*, two foreign

---

1 Rough proofs or 'pulls' taken by hand, in this case from the Hudební matice plates.
2 Four days earlier, 23 December 1917, Janáček had published a feuilleton in the *Lidové noviny* entitled 'The Excursions of Mr Brouček: one to the moon, the other to the fifteenth century', a rather fanciful account justifying his choice of material, and in particular that of the added excursion. The Czech text is reprinted in Janáček 1958, 52–5, an English translation in Janáček 1989, 92–6.

and a local one that had already set up part of the opera in type. Despite prior claim and ownership of the plates for two acts, Hudební matice never stood much of a chance. They were virtually out of the running once they had agreed to pass its rights on to any foreign publisher that would pay for the plates and make available to Hudební matice a number of copies with a Czech text that it could sell locally (**BR169**: Dr Šilhan, for Hudební matice, to Janáček, 8 February 1918).

Drei Masken-Verlag flattered Janáček with a telegram expressing 'lively interest', as he reported to Löwenbach (**BR170**, 16 January 1918), and he responded with a forthright letter suggesting a first edition of 2000 copies to be sold at K300 each and asking how much they would offer him for this (**BR171**, 5 February 1918). Löwenbach supplied a rough translation at the end of April (**BR172**: Löwenbach to Janáček, 13 May 1918), but once Drei Masken-Verlag got down to reading it, they turned down the opera on the grounds of its 'local colour' (**BR173**: Löwenbach to Janáček, 21 June 1918).

This left Universal Edition firmly in the ring. Hertzka had seen some of the brush proofs early in March (**BR174**: Universal Edition to Janáček, 13 March 1918). Two and a half months later (**BR175**, 28 May 1918) Janáček announced to Universal Edition that Kovařovic had asked for the score and that the work might be put on at the Prague National Theatre 'in the autumn, it was hoped' – a year and a half too early, as it turned out. On 5 June 1918 (**BR176**) Janáček wrote to Universal Edition asking for a 16% royalty on the first edition with an advance, a condition Universal Edition accepted (**BR177**, 7 June 1918), though stipulating that the advance could be paid only on 500 copies. Universal Edition also asked what rights Hudební matice had in the matter, what costs had already been incurred, and what agreements they had made with the National Theatre.

Janáček's need to keep up Universal Edition's interest without actually signing a contract faded once Drei Masken-Verlag had turned down the work; Universal Edition's contract was on his desk a month later (**BR178**, 8 July 1918). Its signing, however, was a protracted process. At first he took umbrage at what he regarded as the low royalty paid him by Universal Edition for 'ten sold-out houses [of *Jenůfa*] at the Court Opera' in Vienna (**BR179**: Janáček to Universal Edition, undated ?11 July 1918), and threatened to withdraw from further negotiations with Universal Edition over *Brouček*. He was only slightly mollified to discover that there was more money to come (**BR180**: Janáček to Universal Edition, 12 July 1918), and when he finally sent back the contract, now dated 15 September 1918, he had added many amendments; Universal Edition returned the contract to him asking for their deletion (**BR181**, 17 September 1918). Though Janáček conceded some of his points, he stuck to others so that by 30 September negotiations broke down completely and Universal Edition advised Janáček to find another publisher (**BR182**). After a couple of weeks of cooling off, tentative feelers were put out from both sides, and Janáček climbed down. On 24 October 1918 he sent the contract finally signed with the contested clauses deleted (**BR183**).

Some corrections were necessary for the existing plates, but essentially only half of the opera needed setting. This took place just as the First World War was coming to an end, with the consequent change in relations between the Czech lands and the Austrian capital, and the disruption of mail. It is hardly surprising that it was only on 11 April 1919 that Universal Edition could announce to Janáček that the vocal score was finally ready for printing (**BR184**).

Matters were held up further by the choice of a cover. Originally Hudební matice had planned to put some of Viktor Oliva's illustrations (see Plate 6) on the cover, but once Nebuška had investigated them he had thought them far inferior to Janáček's music (**BR185**: Nebuška to Janáček, 10 December 1916). Two years later, rather grander plans were afoot involving the Czech painter Alfons Mǔcha (1860–1939), known internationally for his pictures of Sarah Bernhardt. In his letter to Janáček of 20 April 1919 (**BR186**) he expressed willingness to do the cover (he had done such work before, the 1911 cover design for the vocal score of Oskar Nedbal's ballet *Princess Hyacinth*). However, the K100 offered by Universal Edition seemed to have been a sticking point (**BR187**: Universal Edition to Janáček, 23 April 1919), and another designer was found, Láďa Novák (1865–1944), who produced a cover without any knowledge of the opera or its libretto ('I wanted to give a picture of Mr Brouček's visions, and not knowing precisely the text of your libretto, I chose the figures of characters (according to the original Čech) who could hardly have remained unnoticed in your work'; **BR188**: Láďa Novák to Janáček, 20 May 1919). Novák's multi-colour cover was so elaborate that its printing held up matters further (**BR189**: Universal Edition to Janáček, 1 August 1919); and a postwar strike in Leipzig where the vocal score was being printed meant that Universal Edition announced that the vocal score was finished and copies were on the way only on 24 September 1919 (**BR190**).

The second complication for Janáček was over Procházka's royalty. *The Excursion of Mr Brouček to the Moon* had a libretto which, when it came down to it, was largely the work of Janáček himself. But *The Excursion of Mr Brouček to the Fifteenth Century* had a specially written libretto by Procházka, who naturally wanted remuneration for his pains. Janáček proposed a 1% royalty from the gross takings of each Czech-language performance and a lump sum for foreign-language performance (**BR191**, undated, before 16 July 1918); Procházka stuck out for 2% for Czech and 1% for foreign perform-ances (**BR192**, 16 July 1918), but eventually had to settle for 1% for all performances and an advance of K200 (**BR193**, 5 August 1918). Part of the problem was that the contested 1% or 2% had to be divided among five claimants: Čech's heirs (who, Janáček informed Procházka, would take whatever he gave them); Dyk (who had settled for a fee of K500, of which Janáček had already paid K300); Procházka; Gellner; and Janáček himself, for his 'scenario' (BR191). Procházka's share was calculated as two fifths of this, and he eventually received K381.94 as his share of the ten National Theatre performances.[1]

1 JA iii, 81, fn.87.

A final complication came with the production of the vocal score. Janáček was pleased with Veselý's score, but once Vincenc Maixner, whom he had got to know during the *Jenůfa* rehearsals (see JP97), had offered to do the piano reduction of *The Excursion of Mr Brouček to the Fifteenth Century* gratis, Janáček gladly accepted his proposal, as he later told Löwenbach (**BR194**, 19 February 1918); he had already paid out K900 on the opera to Veselý and Dyk. Janáček announced Maixner's offer to Gabriela Horvátová on 29 December 1917 (**BR195**) and thereafter sent regular letters to instruct her to go and badger the dilatory Maixner (e.g. **BR196**, 20 February 1918).[1] In the end Janáček had to make his peace with Veselý and pay his charges, at first suggesting he do merely Act 2 of the new excursion (**BR197**, 28 February 1918). Veselý was in no hurry to finish the work (he was in the middle of Suk's *Ripening*), and had furthermore to apprise Janáček that Maixner had only managed to do four pages from Act 1 (**BR198**, 13 April 1918). It was not until late August that Janáček was able to send the final part of Veselý's vocal score to Universal Edition (**BR199**, 22 August 1918).

Janáček had intended to play through the vocal score of the whole work to Kovařovic once Maixner and Veselý had finished it (**BR200**: Janáček to Procházka, 5 March 1918). However when Kovařovic brought up the topic in conversation, Janáček hastened to take him the complete libretto (**BR201**: Janáček to Horvátová, 23 April 1918, in which he states he will take the libretto to Prague on 27 April). Within a few days Janáček was pestering Löwenbach with demands to visit Kovařovic to find out how he liked it (**BR202**, ?2 May 1918). Despite reassurances from Löwenbach (BR172, 13 May 1918) that he believed that Kovařovic thought, as he did, that the text was now much better and more effective, Janáček had to wait, most impatiently, until 17 May for the arrival of Kovařovic's telegram (**BR203**) asking him to send the full score. It needed another prompting from Janáček (**BR204**, 9 June 1918), this time pointing out to Kovařovic that the contract with Universal Edition over the proposed edition needed some commitment from the National Theatre, to squeeze from Kovařovic a written assurance that the opera really would be performed:

BR205   **Karel Kovařovic to Janáček**   *Prague, 11 June 1918*

It goes without saying that we will very gladly give you a statement about the production of *Brouček* at the National Theatre. I have spoken about it with Director Schmoranz and he likewise agreed with my proposal.

Also nothing stands in the way of a production; it will be necessary somehow to find a definitive solution for just two things if you visit Prague this month, so that we could soon make a move towards preparations.

---

1 During March he sent her another seven reminders, see JA vi, 76–85.

First we must come to an agreement about production changes, especially solving the impossibility of Pegasus's flying[1] and reach a definitive agreement on the type of stage sets and costumes on the moon.

The second thing which it seems to me might cause problems will be casting the role of Brouček, which demands absolute competence from the point of view of both singing and acting, if the whole thing is not to suffer through the performance of this tricky role. [...]

F. S. Procházka to Janáček   *Prague, 15 June 1918*   BR206

[...] By chance I spoke with Josef Peška, Schmoranz's theatrical adviser – Peška is a long-standing good friend of mine – he told me that he read the libretto with great interest, that it is 'something quite different' and new, and that he warmly recommended the thing, and he pronounced that the National Theatre must stage your opera. I'm thus writing to you immediately: the libretto, then, seems to be suitable. Everything suggests to me that your work will be staged soon. Schmoranz apparently also mentioned what difficulties will be involved with the costumes of the moon-beings in their gauze robes, but Peška remarked that such a minor consideration cannot be an obstacle. For the second part [i.e. the fifteenth century] they have a perfect set from Jirásek[2] and elsewhere. Perhaps it would not be in vain if you went again to Prague. [...]

Unless he was being diplomatic, Peška's views on the libretto had changed markedly since he last saw it (BR56). Matters lapsed over the summer, much clouded by Janáček's bad-tempered negotiations with Universal Edition (BR178–83). When agreement with the publisher had finally been reached, however, Janáček wrote at once to Kovařovic, two letters on the same day: the first requested him to deal only with Universal Edition (rather than Hudební matice) over the opera and promised that a vocal score would be printed 'within six weeks' (BR207, 19 October 1918); a second letter urged its immediate production now that the patriotic inspiration of the second Excursion (see BR95) had become even more relevant. (The breakup of the Habsburg Empire was imminent and with it the emancipation of the Czechs.)

---

1 Many of the arrivals and departures (including Mr Brouček's escape from the moon) are made on the flying horse Pegasus.

2 Alois Jirásek wrote three Hussite plays, though in June 1918 only *Jan Hus* (1911) was currently in the National Theatre repertory.

BR208   Janáček to Karel Kovařovic   *Brno, 19 October 1918*

I write to you with a request not to put off preparations for the production of *The Excursions of Mr Brouček*. I know, also, that the work is topical: the prophecy which the Apparition of Svatopluk Čech pronounces is coming true.[1]

[. . .]

As far as casting is concerned: perhaps Mr Mařák could nevertheless be talked into taking on the comic role of Brouček?

That tenor from the Plzeň theatre is [also] being praised.

If the role of Etherea was not suitable for Mrs Horvátová, then I would go for Miss Miřiovská.[2]

In your hands, from your mind and from your conception I know that the work will come over healthily and effectively.

So don't put it off!. [. . .]

Otakar Mařák (1872–1940), a favourite Cavaradossi of the period, was an unrealistic and unsuitable suggestion for the character tenor part of Brouček. As it was, Mařák left the National Theatre in 1919 for America. The 'tenor from the Plzeň theatre', was Karel Hruška (1891–1966), who joined the National Theatre that year, but took the part of Duhoslav rather than that of Brouček. Ema Miřiovská did indeed create the part of Etherea, a much more suitable choice than Gabriela Horvátová might have been. That Janáček could contemplate Horvátová's not singing Etherea is eloquent of the rift that took place in their passionate friendship at the time (his last letter to her from this period is dated 23 June 1918). She had succeeded Kovařovic as the dedicatee of the work and the title page of the Hudební matice brush proofs of *The Excursion of Mr Brouček to the Moon* carries her name as such.[3] Presumably, as Kovařovic before her (JP115), she accepted the honour, but, like him, was supplanted, now by the third and final dedicatee, in the words of the first edition of the vocal score, 'the liberator of the Czech nation, President Dr T. G. Masaryk'. The President accepted the dedication in a letter from his daughter Alice's office on 5 May 1919 (**BR209**), and Janáček made energetic efforts to have a score ready to present to him on his visit to Brno on 23 August (**BR210**: Janáček to Universal Edition, 4 August 1919), only to find that the provisional vocal score that Universal Edition obligingly provided had printing errors in the Czech title and that the visit was cancelled (**BR211**: Janáček to Universal Edition, 29 August 1919).

1 In his appearance near the beginning of the Hussite Excursion, Svatopluk Čech celebrates the past glories of Hussite victory in 1420 and wonders whether a happier poet than himself will welcome times when tired hands will rise 'in freedom' (VS178–82).
2 Ema Miřiovská (1891–1974), employed 1913–39 at the Prague National Theatre for light soprano and soubrette roles.
3 'Věnováno / Paní Gabriele Horvátové / Noltschové / 'Kostelničce' [Dedicated to Mrs Gabriela Horvátová-Noltschová, 'Kostelnička'], BmJA, A42.826.

The production was held up at this stage by the delay in publishing the vocal score, though, as Kovařovic reported to Janáček on 20 January 1919 (**BR212**), providing Universal Edition could get him the vocal scores 'within a few weeks' (the writing out of chorus and orchestra parts had begun 'long ago'), he could have the opera produced that summer season. The central role was also a problem: 'an absolutely terrifying worry for me is casting the part of Brouček. Lebeda [see p. 79, fn.1], whom I had to count on, continues to be ill.'

By the summer Universal Edition reported to Janáček (**BR213**, 25 August 1919) that Schmoranz, whom they had asked about it, said that *Brouček* could be performed 'when difficulties over the casting had been overcome – the way the parts are written no-one is able to or wants to sing them'. This had two consequences: the thought of staging the opera in Brno, and the revision of the voice parts. Presumably Janáček himself made local soundings and reported (as usual) more optimistically on the case than was warranted: '*Brouček* will I hope be performed this season in Brno' (**BR211**). In this Janáček was encouraged by Procházka, who concluded that intrigues were getting in the way: 'Perhaps they don't have tulle for the ballets, perhaps they don't have something else, but most of all they don't have a good and honourable will' (**BR214**, 12 September 1919). The Brno plan came to nothing, and it was not until several years after the opera's production in Prague that Brno took it up, and then only the first excursion (see BR247+).

The revision of the voice parts bore more fruit. This was suggested to Janáček by Kovařovic (**BR215**, 25 September 1919) and readily accepted by Janáček the next day:

Janáček to Karel Kovařovic   *Brno, 26 September 1919*   **BR216**

[...] It goes without saying that with your help I will gladly revise passages motifs [too] high for the voice, and even two [whole] parts (one bass, and one baritone).

The practical side and emotional heat during composition – these often don't go together with me. [...]

On 18 October 1919 Janáček reported to Universal Edition that he had seen Kovařovic about this 'a week ago' (**BR217**, 18 October 1919), and that same day wrote to Kovařovic with the results of his own deliberations.

Janáček to Karel Kovařovic   *Brno, 18 October 1919*   **BR218**

I have gone through *Brouček* carefully and in detail.

The fifteenth-century part is now in a *single* act: as a whole the piece thus has three acts: Vikárka, moon, fifteenth century.

There are now of course fewer scene changes in the fifteenth century: just two. In this way the work has gained two great climaxes.

I think that it has gained in effectiveness.
I have adjusted the voice parts.[1]

1. Sacristan – Domšík – Lunobor, is a bass with the range

2. Würfl – Čaroskvoucí – Alderman is a baritone with the range

3. Mazal – Blankytný – Petřík is a large tenor part (Mr Schütz)
4. Málinka – Etherea – Kunka large soprano part (Mrs Bogucká)[2]
5. Young Waiter – Child Prodigy – Student mezzo-soprano with the range

6. Artist – Harfoboj – Miroslav – Virtuoso is a tenor part with the

range  – important (Mr Lebeda?)

7. Oblačný – Vacek is a baritone part with the range  a recitation part, an important acting role!

8. Duhoslav – Vojta is a small tenor part with the range

9. Kedruta – an alto part with the range

10. Brouček I have revised, so as not to have very high passages

---

1 See pp. 246–7.
2 Marja Bogucká (1885–1957), soprano of Polish origin, employed at the Prague National
Theatre 1908–24 mostly in the non-Czech repertory (Gilda, Tatyana, Mélisande, Mimi).

11. The Apparition of the Poet is now a high baritone part

 (Mr Vávra)[1]

So it has quite a number of solo parts.

I have left the choruses as they were; offstage they will be able to sing at the [original] high pitch – and some extra help with the singing can always be found.[2]

Some of the lower modulations (p.146) succeed easily; also on pp. 148, 149, 157, 162.[3]

So I put my work into your hands with the conviction that I have at least written something new in our musico-dramatic literature.

At the same time I am sending a corrected vocal score.

A printed vocal score with Janáček's corrections, pitch adjustments, and many new stage directions written in red ink survives in the Janáček archive[4] but it is unclear how much notice was ultimately taken of it. For instance Janáček's odd division of the work, with the earth act (Act 1 Scene 1) comprising a whole act comparable to the whole Hussite Excursion (Acts 3 and 4), was not observed. In order to achieve a single fifteenth-century act Janáček deleted the direction for a curtain on VS260 (originally marking a division before the old 'Act 3') and, more surprisingly, the curtain between the previous two acts (VS203). In the process he cut the whole Act 2 prelude (VS204 to 206 bar 3) and the scene description of a room in Domšík's house. Similarly, not all of Janáček's casting suggestions were taken up (see BR220+).

Janáček to Karel Kovařovic   *Brno, 18 November 1919*   **BR219**

What's happening with *The Excursions of Mr Brouček*?

Mr František Procházka tells me that 'the National Theatre has no stomach to give it'.

1 Jan Hilbert Vávra (1888–1950), baritone, employed at the Prague National Theatre between 1912 and 1930 in parts such as Don Giovanni and Eugene Onegin. After the First World War he attempted briefly to retrain as a tenor, but returned in 1920 as a baritone. In the end the Apparition of the Poet was taken by Bohumíl Soběský.

2 Janáček is referring to the male-voice chorale 'Slyšte, rytieři boží' (VS193–203), with its extraordinarily high-lying tenor parts. It is heard first offstage, then *fortissimo* onstage bringing the act to an end. The 'extra help' that it ended up with was audible backing from a harmonium, about which Janáček duly complained (BR237).

3 These references refer to the semitonic shifts which occur in Harfoboj's song and its repetition by the artists celebrating Würfl on earth.

4 BmJA, A 23.495.

I'm afraid the story of *Jenůfa* could be repeated!
Please tell me how the matter stands to put my mind at rest.

BR220   Karel Kovařovic to Janáček   *Prague, 20 November 1919*

Mr Procházka's assertion belongs to the realm of Prague theatrical gossip. The musical material of *Brouček* is prepared and we will begin rehearsing it next month.

Further, I mention that I am forced to entrust the rehearsal of your opera to the newly named operatic dramaturg, Mr Otakar Ostrčil, because my poor health precludes me in the foreseeable future from engaging intensively in theatrical work.

I hope that you will be fully satisfied with this information.

PS After consultation with the dramaturg Mr Ostrčil I can give you a proposal for casting the roles in your *Brouček*:

[...]

I ask for your view in regard to this plan.

Kovařovic's list followed Janáček's suggestions for both Harfoboj (Lebeda, the Prague Števa) and the Apparition of the Poet (Vávra), though the part of Mazal (etc.) was given not to the Prague Laca (Schütz), but to Miloslav Jeník[1] and the part of Málinka was shared between Ema Miřiovská and Markéta Letnianská.[2] Kovařovic had originally suggested Letnianská for the Young Waiter, though in a letter to Ostrčil of 2 January 1920 (**BR221**), Janáček mentioned that he had heard Miss Ludmila Prokopová[3] and suggested her for the part (Letnianská, he thought, was too tall in comparison with the suggested Etherea, Miřiovská). Although Ostrčil accepted this at the time (BR227) the part was ultimately taken by Marie Crhová.[4] The role of Brouček was given to Mirko Štork, the resident buffo tenor, whom Peška had suggested for the part five years earlier (see BR55). For all Kovařovic's agonizing over the casting of this role, it was surprisingly trouble-free. Much

---

1 Miloslav Jeník (1884–1944), engaged by Prague National Theatre in 1919 as a lyric tenor, though he also sang many *Helden* roles such as Florestan, Otello and even Siegfried.
2 Markéta Letnianská (1891–1957), employed at the Prague National Theatre for coloratura and light soprano roles.
3 Ludmila Prokopová (1888–1959) appeared in guest performances in Brno 1920 and Prague from 1918 and was with the Prague National Theatre company 1920–3 singing roles such as Cherubino, Oscar and Pamina.
4 Marie Crhová (1885–1973), soloist at the Prague National Theatre 1920–5, mostly in soubrette roles (she sang Esmeralda in *The Bartered Bride* 562 times).

more difficulty came from his choice of Václav Novák[1] for the role of Würfl-Čaroskvoucí-Alderman. After the second rehearsal Novák refused to sing the part, though Ostrčil persuaded him to carry on. On 30 January Novák wrote a fierce letter to Schmoranz (**BR222**), again refusing the role on the grounds that Janáček was a madman who knew nothing about voices and did not care whether something was singable or not, and that the part of Würfl was damaging his voice. Ostrčil's diplomacy won out in the end and Novák sang in nine of the ten performances in Prague.[2]

Janáček to Karel Kovařovic   *Brno, 22 November 1919*   BR223

If I could give you half of my own health – you wouldn't have much – but I'd be happy to do it.

I completely agree with the casting. So you have a dramaturg? I will write to Mr Otakar Ostrčil.

This was to be Janáček's last communication with Kovařovic, who died of cancer in December 1920. Janáček's dealings with Ostrčil at that time were thoroughly cordial and uncomplicated (see JP109, 109+) and under new management things at last began to move. By 19 December 1919 Janáček could announce to Universal Edition (**BR224**) that the work was being diligently rehearsed and that the soloists would be ready in mid-January, though a month later he had revised his estimate of the première to 'the beginning of March' (**BR225**: Janáček to Universal Edition, 25 January 1920).

Janáček to Otakar Ostrčil   *Brno, 29 January 1920*   BR226

You are with my *Brouček* on the moon and in the fifteenth century; aren't you sending me to the fires of hell?

I would so like to hear the orchestral rehearsals – to fill in things if I felt the need!

Should you consider some colouristic retouching good – don't hesitate to carry it out.

Otakar Ostrčil to Janáček   *Smíchov, 31 January 1920*   BR227

Be assured that I'm not sending you into the fires of hell but, on the contrary, I am overjoyed that I was allowed to rehearse your masterly

1 Václav Novák (1881–1928), engaged from 1917 at the Prague National Theatre for heroic baritone roles (Holländer, Wolfram). Although he was an outstanding singer and original actor, his explosive temperament led to his dismissal from the company in 1923, but he returned in 1925. For all his grumbles about the part of Würfl, he went on to create a much-acclaimed Wozzeck in 1926 and Jaroslav Prus in the Prague première of *The Makropulos Affair* in 1928.
2 Pala 1962, 211–12.

work. It is a real treat for me, though the work – I admit – isn't easy. In the orchestra – so far I have had sectional rehearsals – no need has been felt so far for any retouching. Besides, I think that the orchestral part will sound colourful without any retouching just as in that respect your *The Fiddler's Child*[1] sounded very rich, although not a single note was revised. On the other hand, we were forced to [make] further transpositions in the voice parts, since the high tessitura created great difficulties for the singers. I have made every endeavour not to harm the spirit of the work anywhere. Today we had the first blocking rehearsal at the piano. Miss Prokopová has taken over the part of the Young Waiter according to your wishes.

Ostrčil invited Janáček to the rehearsals beginning on Monday, 9 February (**BR228**, 4 February 1920), though Janáček had flu and could not attend (**BR229**: Janáček to Ostrčil, 10 February 1920) and later rehearsals had to be postponed owing to the illness of the producer, Schmoranz (**BR230**: Ostrčil to Janáček, 20 February 1920).

BR231   Otakar Ostrčil to Janáček   *Smíchov, 18 March 1920*

We are now rehearsing diligently. Today was the first blocking rehearsal on stage with the chorus for Acts 1 and 2. With the orchestra we are at the beginning of Act 2. I observe with delight how your work is captivating more and more listeners, except for a few stupid ones who would like to sing only knights in shining armour in Italian operas. We will continue next week. On Monday [22 March] there will probably be a rehearsal on stage with the piano, the orchestra will have the day off, so that the orchestral rehearsal will be only on Tuesday. *On Wednesday and Saturday* stage rehearsals are out of the question and orchestral rehearsals unlikely because there are usually two opera performances. Also next week there is a holiday,[2] when one cannot rehearse on stage. If you still want to come and risk it, it would be very pleasant for me.

BR232   Otakar Ostrčil to Janáček   *Smíchov, 25 March 1920*

The arrangements for Monday and Tuesday [29 and 30 March] are as follows: on Monday at 9 the whole orchestra, at 11 blocking

---

1 Ostrčil, conducting the Czech Philharmonic, gave the première of Janáček's orchestral 'ballad' on 14 November 1917.
2 There were various free days in the ten days before Good Friday, which in 1920 fell on 2 April.

rehearsals at the piano at Žofín.[1] On Tuesday at 9 the whole orchestra, at 11 *Sitzprobe* – soloists, chorus, orchestra for Acts 1 and 2.

It will greatly please me if you can come.

Janáček was in Prague for at least the Monday rehearsal. Later, in a flurry of letters over 8–9 April to his wife from Prague he announced 23 April as the firm date for the première with the first repeat performance on Sunday 25 April (**BR233**, 8 April 1920) and that he had had enough of rehearsals: 'The days before 23 April and the rehearsals in them will be sufficient for me' (**BR234**, 9 April 1920). One can sense some disappointment in this short note: 'Not every theatre will master *Brouček*. Two singers could be better. Well, what is one to do?'

The première was not a great success. Osvald Chlubna, who accompanied Janáček that day, found him silent and depressed when before the performance they went to buy a congratulatory wreath for Ostrčil. After the performance little notice was taken of the composer; there was no first-night celebration (**BR235**: Osvald Chlubna: 'Reminiscences of Leoš Janáček', 1931–2, 126). In comparison with the easy relationship with the Prague singers in *Jenůfa*, Janáček felt so uneasy with the Brouček cast that he did not even thank them properly, as a later letter to the singer of Würfl indicates.

Janáček to Václav Novák   *Brno, 2 February 1921*   **BR236**

I looked you up at Královské Vinohrady, but I did not catch you at home. And the first letter after arriving back from Prague I am writing to you.

The reason for it is the frank words of Mr Jeník; I am grateful to him for them.

It made me write these lines.

He spoke for all the soloists singing in my *The Excursions of Mr Brouček* and reproached me in the name of them all for not even thanking them for their work.

I regret that such a talk took place only after a year – and in front of Director Schmoranz.

I am not one of those composers who don't know how to value and esteem performers' achievements. Surely these words are apt for them: the word became flesh. They embody the composer's word, they give life to his work. How could I be indifferent to such people!

But do bear this in mind: that people made it their business that I should know how my work was belittled on the part of these very soloists.

1 See p. 79, fn.3.

Believe me, I have not experienced more bitter moments than during the dress rehearsal of *Brouček*.

How could I dare to draw closer, more intimately to Mr Štork, to you, to Mr Jeník? It seemed to me that from your side I was hated outright for my work.

And that is certainly painful.

When thanks to Mr Jeník an open discussion has taken place from my side as well, there is nothing left for me to do than assure you, Mr Štork and Mr Jeník of my sincere gratitude for your outstanding and unique performances, demanding and exhausting for you. I ask you please to be my spokesman and disperse the misunderstandings, and take up with at least a little love my work that some have condemned as heretical.

Janáček did not stay in Prague for the second performance but instead returned to Brno, hardly pleased by the reviews, which in general found the work experimental and lacking in lyricism.[1]

BR237   **Janáček to Otakar Ostrčil**   *Brno, 25 April 1920*

It is 9 o'clock in the evening; I am thinking of you at the ending of the *Excursion to the Moon* section![2] Today I read the reviews in the Prague newspapers. Why do they pontificate in such a learned fashion? If I have written such music and so much of it for those who have eyes to see and ears to hear for them to laugh sincerely, then I have already done my bit. To laugh at these Broučeks; that's enough. And he [Nejedlý? see fn.3] advises me to write my scores *in pencil*!? Why doesn't he advise me not to write at all? In these words there was lots of poison, but he will choke on it himself.[3]

For the 'Apparition of the Poet' to be effective a tenor voice will be necessary, so that the tune does not have to suffer transposition. I'm concerned with the motif

[cf vs178; Janáček was quoting from memory] and it disappeared.

1 Reviews are quoted extensively in Pala 1962, 208–11.
2 Janáček wrote his letter at the time of Ostrčil's second performance of the opera.
3 Seemingly a reference to the writer and scholar Zdeněk Nejedlý (1878–1962), one of Janáček's fiercest critics (whose surname translates as 'inedible'); his review did not appear until June (*Smetana*, x (1920), 60–3).

I want then to have a look at the passage 'V sud!' ['Into the barrel'!] and tighten it up a bit, so that the somersault into the courtyard of the Vikárka will be more sudden.

And if only one didn't hear that harmonium during the first Hussite chorale! What is needed here is the facility [to sing] *a cappella*; at that distance horns in the orchestra[1] wouldn't help, even not to mention the absurdity of a Hussite chorale to such accompaniment!

What do you think of the recommended 'retouching'? [. . .]

FINAL CHANGES

Janáček to Otakar Ostrčil   *Brno, 27 April 1920*   BR238

That place 'V sud! V sud!' – was too slow, it was diluted. I felt it and even a layman pointed it out to me, the writer Mr Procházka.

I have thought about how to improve it without special difficulties and unpleasant corrections.

So we'll do it like this:

Janáček's revision of the passage affected vs287–9 and consisted of the omission of a total of ten bars (some of the repetitions of 'V sud!'), with the remaining exclamations of 'V sud!' rewritten for full chorus instead of either male or female voices. There were also some adjustments in Kedruta's part and in particular the insertion of a chorus part underneath her 'K satanu jeď a i k jeho bábě!' ['Go to Satan and to his grandmother!', vs289, Maestoso].[2]

Thus we will achieve a greater gradation and reach the Maestoso at fig.69 [vs287] without let-up.

But that Maestoso! Still much slower than it was played! Four times slower than the Allegro at fig. 67 [vs283, Con moto] and the whole chorus will burst in with the words: 'K satanu jeď i k jeho bábě!' [. . .]

And now in the following bars a gentle decrescendo and only at

---

1 Janáček is discussing the unaccompanied high-lying male-voice chorus 'Slyšte rytieři boží', vs193–203. Such demanding writing was not beyond the specialist male-voice choral societies that Janáček had written for a decade earlier (e.g. *The Seventy Thousand*), but evidently the tuning gave problems to the Prague theatre chorus. It sounds as though one suggestion was for Janáček to add an accompaniment for horns in the orchestra to replace the obtrusive support of a harmonium in the wings.
2 Janáček's handwritten amendments are printed in JA ii, 35–8.

the 9th bar before fig.70 [i.e. the 3rd last bar on VS290] is it *soft* and a faster, humorous tempo.

This scene will certainly appear more lively.

Could you please correct it like this? Will I hear it like this when I come to see you again?

Ostrčil replied (**BR239**, 28 April 1920) that he would not be able to incorporate the changes without rehearsals, so it would have to wait, and furthermore Janáček, when he next came to hear the work, would probably hear it 'more objectively': it was already growing in audience esteem. There was a more positive response to Janáček's next request.

BR240   Janáček to Otakar Ostrčil   *Brno, 16 May 1920*

The appearance of the ballet is delightful in *Brouček* – but short!

I am writing to Director Schmoranz and Mr Berger[1] to *extend* the ballet up to Čaroskvoucí's words 'Přátelé, teďk malému občerstvení' ['Friends, now for some small refreshment!', VS96–7]. *Surely my dance music ends only here!* I don't know how it could have been overlooked! The ballet could develop to a climax. Would it could be done!

And you know what else would be necessary to give it a lift! That of course I will leave until the holidays.

1. 'Křížaci přebrodili Vltavu!' ['The Crusaders have forded the Vltava!', VS247] – it will be necessary to strengthen something in the orchestra here.

2. The transition of the comedy of the fifteenth century to the courtyard of the Vikárka – this transition will *have to be more sudden, sharper*.

The motif

– leave this *fortissimo* in all its variants (including p. 294 of the vocal score)[2] and always the chorus bursts into it with 'V sud!'

---

1 Augustin Berger (1861–1945), solo dancer at the Prague National Theatre (1883–1900), ballet master at Dresden Court Opera (1900–10), Warsaw (1910–12), Prague (1912–23) and the New York Metropolitan Opera (1923–32).

2 The motif does not occur on VS294. It is last heard on VS290–1, starting soft and getting continually softer.

The motif

remains as its gentle opposite.

Thus no *piano* and *diminuendo*! Mr František Procházka was right to alert me to the weakness of this transition. The bustle on the stage – the wild rushing around – should stay.

And when I heard the last performance and its orchestral clarity – I thank you once again for your great work.

Otakar Ostrčil to Janáček   *Smíchov, 18 May 1920*   BR241

I have now spoken with the director and with the ballet master about the extension of the ballet and I hope that it will be modified by the next performances in accordance with your wishes. As far as the passage 'Křižáci přebrodili Vltavu' is concerned, I think that it is necessary for Petřík here to sing at full *fortissimo on stage*. It's true that the director objected during blocking that it was right to be sung faintly at first since Petřík sings this somewhere outside, but this realism is too shortsighted. In the theatre it must be heard above all by the audience and in this case *very prominently*. As for the transition from the fifteenth century to the Vikárka, you must excuse me, Maestro, that I am also here of a different opinion. Just as it is now, is simply a stroke of genius, that sudden disappearance of the dream as it often is in real life, that at the most critical moment the dream dissolves into nothing. And this is caught in the music in a masterly fashion with that sudden *pianissimo*. I don't know however whether the staging goes hand in hand with it. A *sudden* darkening would be necessary here, shutting off [the stage] with a black cloth, in short as sudden a disappearance of the scene on stage as the disappearance of the *fortissimo* in the orchestra. If the *fortissimo* is not sudden, [if there is] running around on stage etc., there will be an actual real-life transition from the fifteenth century to the Vikárka of the nineteenth century, but in no way an awakening from a dream. This is of course only my opinion and it goes without saying that the decisive view is *yours*, and I will act according to it. But then of course it would be necessary to reorchestrate that interlude.

Another change seems to have come from Schmoranz, who objected to the fact that when the army commander Jan Žižka enters with his captains (vs269–71) there is joyous music in the orchestra, but no choral reaction:

BR242   **Gustav Schmoranz to Janáček**   *Slatiňany, 15 August 1920*

Whether you let Žižka enter at the same time as Petřík[1] will not change anything essential. The fault lies in the fact that the *people* are mute. The enthusiasm of a crowd is never, and was never, expressed silently. Respect yes, but enthusiasm never, NE–VER.

I'm amazed that you won't accept this. No production will be able to remedy this fault.

BR243   **Janáček to Otakar Ostrčil**   *Hukvaldy, 23 August 1920*

[...] The criticism that Žižka is not welcomed verbally pains me. Mr Schmoranz has now answered me angrily. And yet I welcomed Žižka! I had no words, but look at p. 270 of the vocal score where at fig.55[2] the motif 'Vítajte po vítězení' ['Welcome after victory'] is heard. I thought then about having Žižka welcomed as well. But I had no words in the libretto.

I enclose then that verbal welcoming. Take it up then and perform it. [...]

BR244   **Otakar Ostrčil to Janáček**   *Smíchov, 25 August 1920*

[...] With your letter I also received your suggestion for filling out the chorus during the heroes' welcome in *Brouček* and I gave it immediately to the copyist of the choral parts to write into all the parts.[3] At the next opportunity I will also rehearse it in the chorus.

Further changes were suggested by Brod, who on 7 June 1920 (**BR245**) had suggested suppressing the Hussite excursion in the German version, for three reasons: its local patriotic colour, which would be unintelligible to Germans and unsympathetic; its undramatic nature (debates and theological discussions without action); and its glorification of war, which offended Brod's pacifist principles. Janáček did not respond at first, so that Brod needed to appeal two weeks later (**BR246**, 23 June 1920), mentioning that he had still

1 Petřík enters a little earlier, on vs265, to cries of 'Vítajte!' ['Welcome!'] from the people.
2 Rehearsal figures in the first edition disappeared in later reprints. Fig. 55 is on vs270, bar 9.
3 Extra choral parts have been written in pencil into the full score Ostrčil used (BmJA, A11.488). They begin on the equivalent of vs270, bar 8 (last beat) and continue (combining with Petřík's cries of 'Dítky!') until the 12/16 bar (vs271).

more thoughts on how to make the piece more dramatic. These were set out in a later letter (**BR247**, 17 July 1920) and included suggestions for strengthening the parallels between the earth and moon characters and making their motivations more consistent. He modified his proposal that the Hussite Excursion should be suppressed by suggesting that the moon scene could end with the burning of Brouček. He would quite understand if Janáček declined the proposal, but Janáček would similarly have to understand that to undertake the translation of the piece in its present form would go against his principles. Janáček continued to ignore all such suggestions and it was not until 1959 that Universal Edition issued *The Excursions of Mr Brouček* with a German translation (by Karlheinz Gutheim), and in a slightly abridged and adapted version. A more authentic (but nevertheless adapted) German version was issued in 1964. It is ironic that the only other production of the work in Janáček's lifetime (and in his home town) unwittingly carried out Brod's proposal: on 15 May 1926 František Neumann presented merely *The Excursion Of Mr Brouček to the Moon*.

Janáček: 'The Excursions of Mr Brouček'   BR248

Have I managed to get to the core of irony and sarcasm and to pluck out a smile of agreement on the face of the listener?

Have I managed at the right moment to uncover the depths of the profound, bitter moral truth, to force the listener to be mindful of it in the quite ordinary tale of Mr Brouček and in his dreamt-up adventure?

Have I found in the colours of the orchestra both the gossamer web of the dream and the reflection of outer space, the mystery of the lunar landscapes and the gloominess of long-past ages?

Hudební revue, xiii (1919–20)

These were some of the questions that Janáček asked himself in an article solicited by the *Hudební revue* to coincide with the Prague première. They speak of some uncertainty in the piece's reception, an uncertainty thoroughly justified by later events. *Brouček* was in many senses Janáček's *Schmerzenkind* (as Hertzka had characterized it, **BR249**, 21 December 1920). It took up ten years of his creative life, the making of its libretto involved a comically large number of people, most of whom he managed to alienate; its publication led to a temporary rift with Universal Edition; Brod refused to translate the work. The production in Prague was much delayed and fraught with difficulties, especially over the singers, and the piece lasted only a year in the Prague repertory and was not produced there again until 1948.

But *Brouček* was an important turning point. For all its dramatic problems, it was a much richer and even more innovative score than *Jenůfa* and, with *Fate*, contained the seeds for the four last operas. And after Janáček's problems with its librettists there grew the realization that they were probably more trouble than they were worth (and much too expensive); thereafter Janáček wrote all his own texts with virtually no help. The last, wonderfully productive, phase of his operatic life had begun.

*   *   *

CHARACTERS IN *THE EXCURSIONS OF MR BROUČEK*

The following list was printed in the vocal score:

BROUČEK, a landlord	tenor
MAZAL, a painter – *Blankytný* – Petřík	tenor
SACRISTAN at St Vít [Cathedral] – *Lunobor* – Domšík od Zvonu	bass-baritone
MÁLINKA, his daughter – *Etherea* – Kunka	soprano
WÜRFL, publican at the Vikárka – *Čaroskvoucí* – Alderman	bass
YOUNG WAITER – *Child Prodigy* – Student	soprano
MR BROUČEK'S HOUSEKEEPER – Kedruta	contralto
ARTISTS – *Oblačný* – Vacek Bradatý	baritone
Duhoslav – Vojta od pávů	tenor
Harfoboj – Miroslav the goldsmith	tenor
Větroboj – Voice of the professor	tenor

Dancers, Etherea's companions
The Apparition of the Poet
First and Second Taborite. People

The Three Worlds
Characters in CAPITALS appear in the Earth scenes.
Characters in *italics* appear in the Moon scenes.
Characters in normal type appear in the fifteenth-century scenes.
Brouček appears in all scenes.
His housekeeper appears in only the last act of *The Excursion of Mr Brouček to the Moon*, which was suppressed in final version.

Moon names
In the Čech novel usually a first name and a surname are provided for the individual artists (but not for Lunobor, his daughter Etherea or for the Maecenas Čaroskvoucí):
    Hvězdomír Blankytný (a poet)
    Slunovít Oblačný (a poet)
    Větroboj Hvězdný (a rival poet)
    Duhoslav Žárný (a painter)
    Harfoboj Hromný (a musician)

The 'surnames' are all Czech adjectives, mostly inclining toward poetical vocabulary: *blankytný* (sky-blue), *hvězdný* (starry), *oblačný* (cloudy), *žárný* (glowing), *hromný* (thundery), *čaroskvoucí* (magically shining). Čech coined the first names by combining Slavonic name endings such as (*-mír, -vít, -slav, -boj, -bor*) with the following words: *luna* (poetical word for moon), *hvězda* (star), *slunce* (sun), *vítr* (wind; inflected form *větr-*), *duha* (rainbow), *harfa* (harp). The full names are sometimes used in early drafts and letters (not always accurately, see BR33), but only the surnames are given in the vocal score.

Other names
Brouček — a beetle
Mazal — a dauber
Málinka — see BR32+
Domšík — see p. 207, fn.1
Kunka — see p. 207, fn.2

Voice types
Janáček changed his mind about some of these; see his letter to Kovařovic, BR218.

6 Káťa Kabanová

KK1   **Janáček to Kamila Stösslová**   *Brno, 12 January 1919*

[...] There will be no more cold spells this year. Primroses are flowering now for the third time this winter. The days are getting longer again and with them the joys of life. I've put my first opera in order, written thirty-one years ago. Now I have nothing to do – until something occurs to me again. [...]

After the acceptance of *Jenůfa* by Kovařovic in 1916, Janáček had been systematically looking through and revising his other operas. *Brouček*, still then a single 'Excursion', was first in line. By the end of 1917 he had finished and revised it and had added a completely new 'Excursion'. Between January 1917 and September 1918 he had contemplated revising *Fate*, but was so discouraged by the reactions of people such as Brod (see OS108–11) that he finally abandoned the attempt. But when the score of *Šárka* turned up in the peasant chest in January 1918 he set about getting the third act orchestrated and then revised the whole opera (SAR13–21). When *Šárka* was done, he turned his hand to his operatic song cycle *The Diary of One who Disappeared*, begun in 1917 and then left aside; it was completed by 6 June 1919. The only large new work he wrote at the time, an occasional piece to celebrate the creation of a new, independent Czechoslovak state in 1918, was the symphonic poem *The Ballad of Blaník*. This was given its première on 21 March 1920 and was probably written in the latter part of 1919. Despite the claims of Václav Jiřikovský, then director of the Brno National Theatre, that he had interested Janáček in Ostrovsky soon after the Vienna première of *Jenůfa* (16 February 1918), there is no other evidence that Janáček had considered *The Thunderstorm*, the basis for his opera *Káťa Kabanová*, before 1919.

KK2   **Václav Jiřikovský: 'Reminiscences of Leoš Janáček'**

Jenůfa was triumphing in Vienna with Jeritza [see JP141] and the desire grew in Janáček to write a new stage work. He was looking for a subject. He also came to me and confided in me about his plan. I drew his attention to a number of interesting subjects from poems and plays which in my opinion might suit him, among them also Hviezdoslav's poem *The Forester's Wife*,[1] Ogrizović's *Hasanaginica*[2] and Ostrovsky's *The Thunderstorm*.[3] Janáček got hold of the books at once.[4] After a while he returned. He was taken by the Ostrovsky. He saw in *The Thunderstorm* a raw earthiness which agreed with him. And then also that desire for truth he saw in Ostrovsky suited his nature. Janáček personified the elemental force of Ostrovsky's dramatic language; his passionate partiality for real-life dialogue and for melodic realism are indeed the most interesting facets of Janáček's artistic character. And he had been so strongly taken by the Ostrovsky that he talked about it with complete assurance, although he still had his doubts about a few character traits, and about some situations. He debated these in a very committed manner, and I felt that these doubts were for him already [part of] the creative process. He talked about the characters of Ostrovsky's play in such a real way, and with such interest in their fates, that the seeming weaknesses of these characters, which as he came to see them, were only childish slips in the eyes of their creator, slips which only then gave rise to the dramatic conflict of Janáček's *Káťa Kabanová*.

I was highly delighted that I had attracted Janáček's interest to *The Thunderstorm* to such an extent and had correctly understood his creative urge. In order to encourage him still further in his decision I had *The Thunderstorm* put on in the theatre on 29 March 1919 [actually 18 March 1919], produced by Auerswald.[5] The performance itself, which went very well at the time, completed Janáček's creative preparation, and he began to sketch *Káťa Kabanová*.

Divadelní list, vii (1931–2)

One of the books that Janáček acquired was the Czech translation of the play by Vincenc Červinka,[6] which was published in the spring of 1918,[7] and it was this translation which prompted the Brno and Prague productions of the

---

1 Hviezdoslav, pseudonym of Pavol Országh (1849–1921), Slovak poet; his epic poem *The Forester's Wife* was published in instalments 1884–6.

2 Milan Ogrizović (1877–1923), Croatian writer; his play *Hasanaginica* (= the wife of the Aga Hasan) was given in 1909.

3 Alexander Nikolayevich Ostrovsky (1823–86); his play *The Thunderstorm* was written and first performed in 1859, and published in 1860.

4 If he did so, he seems not to have acquired personal copies of them all. Only Ostrovsky's *The Thunderstorm* survives in his library (L 8).

5 Jaroslav Auerswald (1870–1931), actor, theatre producer and stage designer. He was a member of the Brno National Theatre from 1899 to 1931.

6 Vincenc Červinka (1877–1942), translator from Russian, editor and critic.

7 Burjanek 1955, 374, fn.65.

play the next year (18 March and 19 March 1919 respectively) and from which Janáček was to fashion his libretto. Červinka later reported (KK7) that Janáček missed the Prague production and that his knowledge of the play came through reading Červinka's translation – which suggests that Janáček had not seen the play in Brno either. Whatever combination of circumstances pointed Janáček in the direction of Ostrovsky's play it was a sympathetic subject for someone with a deep love of Russia. He had given Russian names to both his children; his trip to Russia in 1896 had left a deep impression; the following year he helped found a Russian Circle in Brno, serving as chairman in 1909–15 and 1919–21; and he was well acquainted with a wide range of Russian literature. Many years before he composed *Káťa Kabanová* he had begun sketching operas on Tolstoy's *Anna Karenina* (1907) and *The Living Corpse* (1916), the former directly in Russian; his last opera was to be based on a Dostoyevsky text. A masterpiece by Russia's best-known dramatist before Chekhov, *The Thunderstorm* was a most suitable subject for an opera, if a shade conventional for Janáček.[1]

KK3   **Adolf Červinka[2] to Janáček**   *Prague, 27 October 1919*

In answer to your inquiry of 21 October concerning the translation of Ostrovsky's *The Thunderstorm*, allow me to inform you that you have probably confused me with Mr *Vincenc* Červinka, the writer and sub-editor of *Národní listy*, who, according to the newspapers, is at this moment returning across the Pacific Ocean to Bohemia. His address here is Jakubská 12, Smíchov [Prague]. [...]

Should you not wish to wait until Mr Červinka's return to Bohemia, I will ask, when I have the opportunity at the meetings of the Committee of the Syndicate, to whom Mr Červinka has entrusted such affairs during his absence, and I will write to you about this.

KK4   **Janáček to F. S. Procházka**   *Brno, 5 November 1919*

I'd like to have the rights to the Czech translation of Ostrovsky's *The Thunderstorm*.

Who represents Mr Vincenc Červinka, the writer and sub-editor at the *Národní listy*? He's said to be in America.

---

1 The subject appealed to Tchaikovsky (his overture, op.76) and at least six other opera composers. The first of these settings, by Vladimir Nikitich Kashperov, was based on a libretto by Ostrovsky himself (1867); see Štědroň 1973.
2 Adolf Červinka (1875–1936), writer and translator. Trained as a lawyer, he was an expert on authors' rights and from 1919 served as secretary of the Syndicate of Czech Writers and Composers.

Could you find out in the Syndicate to whom he has entrusted his affairs? He's the translator.

Dr Adolf Červinka told me this. [. . .]

F. S. Procházka to Janáček   *Prague, 9 November 1919*   KK5

Editor Vincenc Červinka is on his way home now; I've just had a postcard from him. So be patient for a little while. He didn't entrust his affairs to anyone. Červinka wrote to me that he'll certainly be home by Christmas.

The contents of Procházka's letter was confirmed in a further letter from Adolf Červinka (**KK6**, 22 November 1919), who also offered the opinion that although the Syndicate thought that Vincenc Červinka would make no objections to Janáček's use of his text, Janáček would need to deal with him personally to determine the fee.

Vincenc Červinka: 'How *Káťa Kabanová* came into being'   KK7

I returned home that year (1919) only just before Christmas, whereupon the then secretary of the Syndicate of Czech and Slovak Writers [sic, see p. 250, fn.2] Dr Adolf Červinka, now dead (who as a great expert in authors' rights was also our legal adviser) told me that Maestro Leoš Janáček had long been trying to get hold of me, that he wanted to set Ostrovsky's *The Thunderstorm* and would I write to him. Before I got round to writing, a letter from Janáček arrived on 29 December 1919: he wanted to compose music to my text, and would I let him know my conditions. He had sought me in vain from the summer onwards, he was in a hurry, and I should to reply to Brno, Kounicova 30.[1]

As a layman in music I shook my head over how it was possible to compose music to a prose text, but I answered him by return. That of course I gladly gave my permission, but he might perhaps want some revision from me, at least the form of the dialogue, also surely some cuts and so on. In the very first days of January 1920 Leoš Janáček visited me and assured me that he would adapt the text himself, that he had it almost ready in his head. And he complimented me that while the original Ostrovsky, which of course he did not know,[2] may

---

1 Janáček's home address in the grounds of the Brno Organ School, by then the Brno Conservatory.

2 Janáček had attempted to acquire the complete works of Ostrovsky in Russian in 1902 (Burjanek 1955, 368, fn.53); presumably unsuccessfully, since no Russian edition of any of Ostrovsky's works is to be found among Janáček's books.

have been rhythmic, certainly my translation was so much so that it clothed itself effortlessly with his music and so on.[1] He had not seen the production of *The Thunderstorm* at the National Theatre; he'd unfortunately missed it, he said, but he'd read the translation in 'Světovka'[2] and had been greatly taken by the action and its dramatic development.

[KK13]
Národní politika (18 October 1938)

KK8 Vincenc Červinka to Janáček   *Smíchov [Prague], 31 December 1919*

I am very pleased that you are devoting attention to Ostrovsky, in my opinion the greatest Russian dramatist.

I give my permission most willingly for the use of my translation of *The Thunderstorm*, and in the case of a stage production I would ask for a 2% royalty.[3] If, with my modest knowledge of Russian conditions and background, I can be of any assistance to you it goes without saying that I am always at your disposal.

KK9 Janáček to Vincenc Červinka[4]   *[Brno,] 10 January 1920*

Should I need any explanations, naturally I will turn to you. I saw the Volga and its life in Nizhni Novgorod.[5] Even General Inspector Machar[6] rates Ostrovsky's work highly. It contains much that is touching, soft (in the Slav manner); what depth of feeling! If only I can find the right expression, just as deep!

With Červinka's permission secured, Janáček began work and composed straight from his Czech translation. Though he had eventually found a helpful librettist in Procházka, there had also been that unpleasant haggling over his

1 These reported words are almost identical to those which Preissová used to describe Janáček's reaction to the previous play he had set, *Her Stepdaughter* (see JP3).

2 Světovka = informal name for Světová knihovna [The World Library], a series published in Prague by J. Otto.

3 Janáček noted on this letter 'I answered 10 January 1920 that I accepted his conditions.' The question of Červinka's royalties was not so easily solved. Some twenty-five letters were exchanged on the subject and it was only in May 1928, a few months before Janáček's death, that Universal Edition determined that Červinka should receive 15% of Janáček's royalty, i.e. not 2% of the gross takings.

4 Janáček's letters to Červinka have disappeared; the texts have been translated from Červinka's quotation of them in his 1938 newspaper article (KK7).

5 Called Gorky 1932–90; Janáček went there during his visit to Russia in 1896.

6 Josef Svatopluk Machar (1864–1942), poet whose disillusioned view of contemporary society influenced the Czech poetry of the 1890s. A friend of President Masaryk, he took part in the organization of the Czechoslovak army in the function of General Inspector 1919–24. Janáček mentioned a meeting with him in February 1918 in Vienna, before the première of *Jenůfa* (JA vi, 71).

royalty (BR191–3), and in his last four operas, even those not based on stage plays, Janáček became his own librettist. He was much more bold than in his previous adaptation of a stage play, *Jenůfa*. Here the six scenes that he fashioned out of the five-act play imaginatively overrode the original act divisions and created new climaxes. He amalgamated or eliminated several characters. His copy of the play[1] is thick with annotations, mostly crossing out or transposing lines or whole passages.[2] The first, and only, date that Janáček wrote in his copy of the play, 1 March 1920, comes at the end of Act 1. But by then he was well into the composition of the music.

Janáček to Kamila Stösslová   *Brno, 9 January 1920*   **KK10**

[. . .] I have begun writing a new opera.[3] The chief character in it is a woman, gentle by nature. She shrinks at the mere thought [of hurting, of evil]; a breeze would carry her away – let alone the storm that gathers over her.

Janáček to Kamila Stösslová   *Brno, 23 February 1920*   **KK11**

[. . .] I'm working happily and industriously on my new opera.

I tell myself all the time that the main character, a young woman, is of such a soft nature that I'm frightened that if the sun shone fully on her, she would melt, yes even dissolve.

You know, such a soft, good nature. [. . .]

Another source of inspiration in Janáček's conception of the part of Kát'a seems to have been Puccini's *Madama Butterfly*; he attended a performance shortly before he made a start on the opera. Its relevance to *Kát'a Kabanová* is clear from the musical links that exist between Kát'a and Puccini's heroine (for instance in their entrance music) and from the identification that Janáček made between both characters and Mrs Stösslová (see also KK45). Janáček had met Kamila Stösslová (1892–1935) at Luhačovice in the summer of 1917 and initiated a friendship, increasingly intense, that was to last to the end of his life.

Janáček to Kamila Stösslová   *Brno, 5 December 1919*   **KK12**

[. . .] I have just come from the theatre. They gave *Batrflay*,[4] one of the most beautiful and saddest of operas. I had you constantly before

1 BmJA, L 8.
2 For an example see Tyrrell 1982, 50–1.
3 According to Marie Stejskalová's diary, composition began on 5 January 1920 (Smetana 1948, 113).
4 Janáček's Czech transliteration of 'Butterfly'.

my eyes. *Batrflay* is also small, with black hair. You must never be as unhappy as her.

[. . .]

I am so unsettled by the opera. When it was new, I went to see it in Prague.¹ Many places still move me deeply. [. . .]

KK13   Vincenc Červinka: 'How *Káťa Kabanová* came into being'

In the summer I met up with Janáček in Luhačovice² and at that time he told me enthusiastically with what relish he was working, and how it flowed from his hand. He was looking forward to the thought that this time he would make a breakthrough in Prague more quickly than for instance with *Jenůfa*, which Kovařovic had held up there for such a long time.

[KK7]
Národní politika (18 October 1938)

Červinka's report is borne out by Janáček's dates in the score.³ By the time he saw him, Janáček had finished a first version of Act 1 (1 July 1920) and after the summer holidays quickly added the remaining acts: Act 2 between 14 September and 15 October 1920, and Act 3 by 24 December 1920. In a letter to Ostrčil on 6 December he mentioned that his 'big work' was at the 'final chords' (**KK14**). But as usual Janáček then made a thorough revision, which went on far beyond his announcement of completion of the work to Kamila Stösslová and Červinka. This took place between January 1921 and 27 March 1921, with a second revision dated 17 April 1921.

KK15   Janáček to Kamila Stösslová   Brno, 6 March 1921

[. . .] After unusually hard work I have finished⁴ my latest opera. I don't know whether they will call it *The Thunderstorm* or *Katěrina*. Against *The Thunderstorm* is the argument that another opera of that name already exists;⁵ against *Katěrina* that I write nothing but

---

1 Janáček saw it at the Prague German Theatre on 16 February 1908 (Racek 1955, 24), where it had opened on 29 September 1907. What he saw in December 1919 was a new production by the same company; the opera was not given at the Prague National Theatre until 1921.

2 Janáček stayed in Luhačovice from 12 July to 2 August 1920 (Štědroň 1939, 23).

3 BmJA, A 7441, a-b.

4 Often a relative term with Janáček: see dates on autograph score in commentary above.

5 A prominent Czech example was Fibich's *The Tempest* (1895).

'female' operas. *Jenůfa – Katěrina*. The best thing, instead of a title, would be to have three asterisks.

*   *
*

[. . .]

Another possibility that Janáček considered was the Russian *Jekatěrina*, by which title Otakar Nebuška referred to it when proposing a contract for its publication, by Hudební matice (**KK16,** 22 March 1921). A week later Janáček wrote to Vincenc Červinka about it, and it was Červinka who came up with the final solution.

Janáček to Vincenc Červinka   *Brno, 31 March 1921*   **KK17**

I have finished the opera. The trouble is what to call it. There are already several *The Thunderstorms* in music and opera. So that name is not a good idea. Furthermore this natural phenomenon is not the mainspring of the action.

It is *Katěrina* who holds the psychological interest of the story. Director Schmoranz mentioned to me that the title Katěrina might be taken as Catherine II ['the Great']. He suggested the name *Káťa*. Boris and also Tichon call her that. I'd therefore be in favour of this title. What do you think about it?

For musical reasons it was of course necessary to shorten much of the 'talking'. Also to concentrate the action on fewer characters. Mr Machar had already drawn my attention to this. Many of the characters were just 'stuck on' to the action. They are of course purely Russian background figures.

'Kuligin–Kudrjáš' is a single character in my version. I have compressed the mad old lady into the 'evil woman' with a few shouts.

I worked on it with relish and quickly. The full score is now being copied; Professor Veselý will make a vocal score by the end of the holidays.[1] Mr Ostrčil, head of the [Prague] opera, and Director Schmoranz know about the work. So nothing remains except for people to like it.

This is an important letter in that it makes clear that the storm of the title was relatively unimportant to Janáček and that it was the character of Káťa herself who was 'the mainspring of the action'. For all Janáček's Russophilism, he was clear-headed about eliminating the 'Russian background figures' so as to concentrate the action emphatically on the title role. Janáček's amalgamation of Dikoj's clerk Kudrjáš with the older Kuligin (village

---

1 He did not; see KK29.

intellectual and sympathetic commentator) was also a sensible way of reducing the cast, though one whose execution was confused by renaming one of the other subsidiary characters Kuligin. The 'mad old lady' who prophesies Káťa's doom in Act 1 Scene 2 of the play virtually disappeared from the opera; the 'few shouts' are those of an otherwise unidentified woman from the crowd in the storm scene.[1] When suggesting the opera's final title Červinka was remarkably agreeable to all these changes.

KK18   **Vincenc Červinka to Janáček**   *Prague, 3 April 1921*

I completely agree with you that the name of your new opera composed after Ostrovsky's *The Thunderstorm*, to which I am already warmly looking forward, will have to be differentiated from all earlier *The Thunderstorms*. This occurred to me myself some time ago, and your calling it *Káťa* would perhaps be the happiest solution. *Káťa Kabanová* might possibly be a little broader. Anyone who had at least a passing acquaintance with Russian plays would then realize at once that it was on a subject taken from Ostrovsky – for it is a famous name in Russian theatre. Years ago I read in a Russian literary journal that (at an approximate guess) Ostrovsky's *The Thunderstorm* had been played at least 3000 times in the towns of European Russia alone! Likewise in literary handbooks, anthologies, biographical dictionaries of leading Russian actors, the role is usually given as 'Káťa Kabanová' and that of Tichon's mother (also very important) as 'Kabanov's mother, or Kabanicha'.

But otherwise certainly do what you think best. The brevity of the title is also important. Underneath the title of the opera, and also on theatre posters and programmes it will surely be mentioned that the opera is composed after Ostrovsky's tragedy, so the matter will be clear.

The shortening of the action and amalgamation of two characters into one, in my opinion, though it is not for me to decide, will help to concentrate the action and the impact of the tragic climax. I am anyway such a Russophile and so much in love with great Russian literature, chiefly the earlier works, that I cannot but greatly welcome that you have gone for Russian material and a plot so universally human, in which the gloomy fate of feudal Russia is truly incorporated.

---

1 For more details of Janáček's changes to the play see Tyrrell 1982, 54–60.

PUBLICATION

That Janáček accepted Červinka's suggestion for the title is clear from his letter to Otakar Nebuška of 14 April 1921 (**KK19**) in which he called it *Káťa Kabanová* for the first time. Janáček was responding to Nebuška's suggestion (KK16, 22 March 1921), that Hudební matice bring out the vocal score together with a number of other works. The very next day (**KK20**, 15 April 1921), however, Janáček informed Universal Edition of Hudební matice's interest in the work, a ploy which found so immediate a response from Universal (**KK21**, 21 April 1921) that Janáček omitted *Káťa Kabanová* from the Hudební matice contract.

Otakar Nebuška to Janáček   *Prague, 25 April 1921*   **KK22**

In your proposal of 23 April 1921 for a publisher's contract we are missing any mention of the opera *Káťa Kabanová*. Since we negotiated that Hudební matice would publish it immediately together with the male-voice choruses and female-voice choruses, and with *The Diary of One who Disappeared*, and that Roman Veselý would complete the vocal score before the holidays, we assume that this is a simple oversight. Thus we suggest that as a model for the agreement between you and Hudební matice we should use your *Jenůfa* contract with Universal Edition. We have a copy at hand and can then draw up a contract. The author's fee will not of course be two Austrian crowns per copy of the vocal score, but 10% of the retail price of all copies sold.

Despite Nebuška's enthusiasm, Janáček gave him only the choruses. He had the *Diary* published by the Brno firm of Pazdírek, and continued his negotiations over *Káťa* with Universal Edition. By 31 August (**KK23**, Nebuška to Janáček) Hudební matice had had to settle for the rights to sell the Universal Edition score in the Czechoslovak Republic, as was the case in *The Excursions of Mr Brouček* (BR169). Janáček was evidently tempted by the advantages of a publisher which would be able to promote his opera in the German-speaking world and to comply with his demand (**KK24**: to Universal Edition, 17 September 1921) of an advance of K2000. After some bargaining,[1] Janáček returned an agreed contract on 11 November 1921 (**KK25**). The published vocal score appeared on 20 February 1922 and ten copies were immediately despatched to Janáček (**KK26**: Universal Edition to Janáček, 20 February 1922). The K2000 were sent off a few days later (**KK27**: Universal Edition to Janáček, 23 February 1922).

The actual publication was delayed in the latter stages by Janáček's last-minute additions (see KK83 ff) but initially by the preparation of the vocal score. After the full score had been professionally copied it went to Roman

1 See Janáček 1988, 169–71.

Veselý (see KK17 and KK22), who had made the vocal score of *Mr Brouček's Excursions* (see BR155–7, 197–9). In a letter to Veselý of 30 May 1921 (**KK28**) Janáček inquired how he liked the first act, asked if it would be ready before the holidays, and promised the remaining two acts by 1 July. Since Gustav Homola[1] finished his fair copy of the full score by 5 May, these dates indicate that Janáček was still tinkering with the score: as late as 18 August Janáček was continuing to 'clean it up' (KK40). Veselý, however, reneged on his promise to prepare the vocal score, suggesting that one of Janáček's pupils might take it on instead (**KK29**: Veselý to Janáček, 23 June 1921). Janáček turned to Břetislav Bakala, who began with Act 2 and had much of it done by the time he went off on holiday (**KK30**: Bakala to Janáček, 9 July 1921). He sent the complete vocal score to the printer on 2 September 1921, as he informed Janáček by card that day (**KK31**).

PRODUCTION

Janáček had so far made strenuous efforts to have his first productions in Prague, though, except in the case of *The Excursions of Mr Brouček* he had never succeeded. But *Brouček* had had its problems in Prague, which culminated in Janáček's gloomiest première and the antagonism of the singers (see BR235–6). The postwar conditions for Czech opera in Brno had greatly improved, with regular access to the splendid German opera house, and the company headed by an extremely able and experienced conductor, Janáček's own recommendee František Neumann (1874–1929). Janáček was thus more tempted to heed Neumann's local-patriotic invitation, though this did not prevent his offering the opera to Prague at the same time. From *Káťa Kabanová* onwards, all Janáček's operatic premières took place in Brno. This had the advantage of giving the composer the opportunity to attend rehearsals easily and to make last-minute adjustments. A pattern thus grew up of Brno staging the work soon after its completion – in the case of *Káťa Kabanová* in a mere six months – with the Prague première, under Otakar Ostrčil, following about a year later.

KK32	**František Neumann to Janáček** **for the Brno National Theatre**	*Brno, 26 April 1921*

May I ask that you entrust your opera *Katja Kabanova*[2] to us for its first performance?

---

1 Gustav Homola (1899–1953), composer, Janáček's pupil at the Organ School 1916–19 and in composition master classes 1920–2, during which time he was evidently prevailed upon to make the first fair copy of Janáček's autograph score.
2 Neumann had reacted promptly to the news, buried at the end of a review by Max Brod in the *Prager Abendblatt* (21 April 1921), that Janáček had completed an opera, '*Katja Kabanowa*'. The topic was taken up at greater length by *Lidové noviny* (26 April 1921) on the basis of firsthand information from Janáček.

It is very important to me that the new work of our foremost Moravian composer be also performed for the first time in Moravia.

Janáček to Otakar Ostrčil
Brno, 2 May 1921   KK33

News had reached the papers that I have finished *Káťa Kabanová*.

Immediately, a letter arrived from Neumann, head of the local National Theatre, asking me to give them this new work for next season.

Today he came to see me personally.

I told him that I also wanted to give *Káťa Kabanová* to the Prague National Theatre.

But after the experiences with *Brouček* it isn't all that tempting! To announce a performance four times, and four times not to give it, is evidence of strange goings-on.[1]

I also mentioned my work to Director Schmoranz; but his only reaction was a reminiscence of an excellent stage performance (of Ostrovsky's *The Thunderstorm*).[2] [. . .]

Otakar Ostrčil to Janáček
Smíchov [Prague], 5 May 1921   KK34

Please don't be angry with me about *Brouček*. The last postponement really was because of illness. [. . .] As for *Káťa Kabanová* I am happy that you will entrust it to the Prague National Theatre as well. You mustn't be surprised that Schmoranz was not able to react to your reference to the work other than as a man of the theatre.

As for me, during my stay in Brno I hadn't taken the opera to be ready yet, and so I didn't ask much about it. I know it's unpleasant for a composer to talk about a work still not entirely finished.

Now of course I understand that your opera is completely finished, and so ask you to send us the full score as soon as possible, and possibly the vocal score – I believe that Roman Veselý is working on it. You know my attitude to your work and perhaps I need not assure you that it will be an honour and a pleasure for me to study your new work. [. . .]

---

1 There was a long gap between the last two performances of *The Excursions of Mr Brouček* at the Prague National Theatre (19 September 1920 and 22 June 1921) caused by the continued illness of Václav Novák.

2 Schmoranz had been the producer of the Prague National Theatre's staging of the play in 1919.

KK35   **Janáček to Otakar Ostrčil**   *Brno, 7 May 1921*

You were upset by my letter? Don't take it so badly. I know that there was illness among the soloists – I only go by the outcome – work put off for so many months. I don't look for reasons.
[...]
You can't buy a pig in a poke – and I don't even want to sell it like that. [...]

KK36   **Janáček to Kamila Stösslová**   *Brno, 23 May 1921*

[...] *Káťa Kabanová*, that latest opera of mine, is going to be given in Brno and perhaps even in Prague. But I don't have much stomach for the Prague theatre. [...]
What can I say about myself? You know I dream up a world for myself, I let my own dear people live in my compositions just as I would wish. All of it purely invented happiness.
Real joy, real happiness smiles on you at least sometimes. But on me? When I finish a work – even this dear *Káťa Kabanová* – I'm sad about it. As if I were parting with someone dear to me. [...]

On 25 June Janáček received a more formal offer of production from the directorate of the National Theatre in Brno (**KK37**) proposing the theatre's maximum fee of 10%. By 3 August, however, Janáček had not yet sent back the contract, and had to be reminded about it by Neumann (**KK38**). This would appear to be forgetfulness on Janáček's part rather than evidence that he was still hoping for an earlier Prague production: his correspondence that month both with Universal Edition and with Kamila Stösslová, shows that he was clearly taking a Brno première for granted.

KK39   **Janáček to Universal Edition**   *Brno, 11 August 1921*

The vocal score of my
                    Káťa Kabanová
will be finished shortly. [...]
I asked Dr Max Brod today if he would take on the translation. The libretto is based on *The Thunderstorm* by Ostrovsky (a Russian writer).
The printing would have to be done as soon as possible. The Brno National Theatre have already begun rehearsing. [...]

Janáček to Kamila Stösslová   *Brno, 18 August 1921*   KK40

[...] I've now had plenty of work. I've been completely cleaning up
the music of *Káťa Kabanová*.

Yesterday the conductors from the theatre were at my house; the
work was played, and was liked. I'll see.

Perhaps you will be at the première, more likely in Brno. It will be
here probably at the beginning of November. [...]

Janáček's information about the première evidently came from his pupil
Břetislav Bakala, who since 1920 had worked at the Brno Theatre as a
repetiteur, and who had prepared the vocal score of *Káťa Kabanová*
(KK30, 31).

Břetislav Bakala to Janáček   *Brno, 24 August 1921*   KK41

Today I received Act 3 from Nešuta.[1] He made a fair number of
mistakes there! So I still have to correct them tomorrow and will take
it immediately to the theatre. We will send my score to the printers
because Svozil[2] talked about it with the chief [Neumann], who
apparently expressed the view that we must have that clean vocal
score since we will begin to rehearse *Káťa* straight after *Faust*[3] and
will not wait for printed scores. But it would probably be as well if
you, Maestro, were to write yourself to Universal Edition, to get them
to hurry up with the printing and send us at least a brush proof.[4] You
see I'm counting on the première [taking place] *at the latest* by the
beginning of November; I think, however, that it will be possibly in
the second half of October. After *Le nozze di Figaro*, which is set for
20 September,[5] we will get going with rehearsals at full steam. [...]

Janáček's contacts with the Prague National Theatre over the work went
back to May 1921 (KK33–35), but it was some months before Janáček could
redeem his promise not to sell Ostrčil a 'pig in a poke'. In a letter to him
dated 22 August 1921 (**KK42**) Janáček promised the full score 'as soon as the
Brno people have copied out the vocal score', in the event a fortnight later
(**KK43**: Janáček to Otakar Ostrčil, 9 September 1921).

1 František Nešuta (1868–1924), trumpeter, member of the Brno opera orchestra 1915–
24.
2 Hynek Svozil, see p. 315, fn.1.
3 The première of this production was 27 September 1921.
4 See p. 227, fn.1.
5 It opened two weeks later, on 5 October 1921.

KK44   Otakar Ostrčil to Janáček   *Prague, 20 September 1921*

I have looked through both the text and full score of your new opera *Káťa Kabanová*. Unfortunately I did not get the vocal score from Dr Brod; it is apparently in Vienna with Universal Edition and he will send it to me as soon as it is returned. Thus I cannot so far give my definitive verdict since I was not able to study the full score thoroughly in such a short time. It is essential that I play through the vocal score myself in detail, so I ask for your indulgence. Besides I hope that we will soon hear the opera in Brno. Can the full score stay here, or would you like it returned to you for the time being?

KK45   **Janáček to Kamila Stösslová**   *Brno, 29 October 1921*

[. . .] Come to the Brno première: everything promises that it will be beautiful.

And you know, when I became acquainted with you in Luhačovice during the war and saw for the first time how a woman can love her husband – I remember your tears – that was the reason why I turned to *Káťa Kabanová* and composed it.

I invite you, then, now that the work is finished. [. . .]

KK46   **Directorate of the Brno National Theatre to Janáček**   *Brno, 12 November 1921*

At your request we have discussed the set for the second scene of your new opera with the producer Vladimír Marek[1] and the chief designer Vladimír Hrska[2] and we were told that there are only twenty seconds for the scene-change for scene 2, in which time it is impossible to arrange the room other than with a so-called *backdrop*. The same thing happens in Act 2. Nevertheless we have given new instructions and have had additions to the sets painted which in all our opinions should wholly satisfy you.

As far as the symmetry of the furniture is concerned, which you objected to, Mr Marek will do everything possible given the time available. We are convinced that you will be pleased with these new arrangements.

1 Vladimír Marek (real surname Heidrich; 1882–1939), drama and opera producer at the Brno theatre 1919–23.
2 Alexander Vladimír Hrska (1890–1954), stage-designer, head of design at the Brno National Theatre in the 1921–2 season. He designed the cover for the vocal score of *Káťa Kabanová* (1922).

The première was originally set for 10 November 1921 (**KK47**: Janáček to Universal Edition, 26 October 1921). Because of the illness of Marie Veselá,[1] who was singing the title role (KK25: Janáček to Universal Edition, 11 November 1921), the Brno première was postponed until 23 November and was well received by the Brno critics[2] and by Brod:

Max Brod on the première   KK48

Success in the theatre. To assess it correctly you would have to ask the Brno theatre experts who could compare it with other Brno successes. The general opinion is that the success of *Káťa Kabanová* was unprecedented. – After only Act 1 the audience was not content merely to recall the performers more than ten times to the stage. 'Author! Author!' thundered again and again as the curtains parted. Until Janáček himself appeared with that touchingly courteous smile of his on his great kind face. When he bowed it seemed that he murmured some unheard words, for his lips moved. It was uncommonly moving to see this youthfully vigorous old man on the stage which still reverberated with the magical sounds of his passion. —— This scene was repeated and more intensely so after every act. I have heard that the temperature of theatrical enthusiasm in Brno is a few degrees lower than in Prague. Well then, on this occasion it was really a Prague temperature in Brno.

Sternenhimmel (1923)

Janáček to František Neumann   *Brno, 27 November 1921*   KK49

We meet up once again at an artistic event – unarranged – just like the encounter of water and lightning.
    The performance of *Káťa Kabanová* is one of these meetings.
    It seems that the times of Smetana[3] are being reborn in Brno.
    Should I thank you, the orchestra, the singers?
    We are certainly glad that we have all grown into our parts, on our own ground.
    We can all honour one another, and like one another!

1 Marie Veselá (1892–1969), member of the German theatre in Brno 1914–18, then of the Czech theatre in Brno 1919–22. She joined the National Theatre, Prague in 1922, once again taking the title role in *Káťa Kabanová*. She excelled in dramatic soprano roles, particularly in Verdi (Aida) and even Isolde. She is sometimes confused with Marie Calma-Veselá (1881–1966; see JP54 ff.).
2 Extracts from some of the Brno reviews are printed in Tyrrell 1982, 98–100.
3 Smetana's eight completed operas and his tenure of the conductorship of the Provisional Theatre in Prague 1866–74 are intimately bound up with the flowering of Czech national opera.

To you and all those involved in the performance of *Káťa Kabanová*.

KK50   Otakar Ostrčil to Janáček   *Prague, 28 November 1921*

I heartily congratulate you on the great success of *Káťa Kabanová* and much regret that I wasn't able to attend the première since that day I was conducting [Fibich's] *The Bride of Messina* at our theatre. Also the next performances coincide with rehearsals for the concert of the Orchestral Association,[1] but as soon as I have a free evening *I will definitely come.*

KK51   Janáček to Kamila Stösslová   *Brno, 14 December 1921*

[...] I have had a decided success with *Káťa Kabanová*. Olomouc, Ljubljana and Prague have already taken it.   Reichenberger [see JP139+] of the Vienna Staatsoper is coming to have a look at it.

 And the *Diary* [*of One who Disappeared*] with that gypsy girl is also popular! [...]

Ostrčil was as good as his word. He came to see *Káťa Kabanová* on 8 December and there and then agreed to stage it in Prague, as Janáček excitedly reported back to Universal Edition (**KK52**, 9 December 1921). Performances in the other towns Janáček mentioned were all preceded by performances elsewhere. Ljubljana waited until 1934, Olomouc until 1948 and Vienna until 1974, by which time the opera had become well established on the German stage.[2]

KK53   Otakar Ostrčil to Janáček   *Smíchov, 24 December 1921*

[...] I have already reported to the administration about *Káťa Kabanová* and announced that we will put it on as soon as Universal Edition delivers the material to us. I also said that they must draw up a contract directly with you. I advise you, Maestro, not to forget to stipulate a *deadline for its performance* on the contract. In the present circumstances this is very important. Of course don't tell anyone that this initiative comes from me.

On 1 March 1922 (**KK54**) Ostrčil, now in possession of the recently published vocal score, wrote to Janáček suggesting casting. Singers associated

---

1 Orchestrální sdružení v Praze; Ostrčil conducted this, the chief amateur orchestra in Prague, in 1908–22.
2 See Přibáňová 1984b for a full list of productions.

with *The Excursions of Mr Brouček* included Miloslav Jeník[1] (Boris), Karel Hruška[2] (Kudrjáš), Markéta Letnianská[3] (Glaša) and Marie Crhová[4] (Fekluša). The only casting that Janáček commented on was that suggested for Kabanicha, Marie Rejholcová,[5] who had sung the Mayor's Wife in the Prague *Jenůfa*:

Janáček to Otakar Ostrčil   *Brno, 3 March 1922*   KK55

Thank you for your letter.

I have just one fear about the casting of Kabanicha – as regards her acting.

Good, true-to-life, natural acting has an effect all round, on the others taking part.

Weak acting, all the worse.

From the acting point of view Mrs Horvátová would be more suitable.

But you know both of them better. Decide for yourself. [. . .]

By 1921 Janáček's intense friendship with Gabriela Horvátová, the creator of the Kostelnička in the Prague production of *Jenůfa*, had been over for three years, and he made only the smallest attempt to secure her for what would have been a powerful casting of the role. Rejholcová sang the part, and all Ostrčil's other proposals were followed except for the title role (for which Ostrčil had suggested Božena Petanová)[6] and the small parts of Kuligin and Fekluša. In the event, Káťa was sung by the Prague Jenůfa, Kamila Ungrová (see JP87+), alternating with Marie Veselá, the creator of the part in Brno, who had recently joined the Prague National Theatre company.

The printed full score of *Káťa Kabanová* came out in August, and September 1922 (**KK56**: Universal Edition to Janáček, 12 September 1922, announcing the publication of Acts 2–3), in time for the Prague rehearsals, though the orchestral parts were available only at the end of November (**KK57**: Universal Edition to Janáček, 25 November 1922) and had to be borrowed from Brno. Janáček expressed particular interest in the Prague stage-sets.

Janáček to Otakar Ostrčil   *Brno, 21 September 1922*   KK58

Universal Edition tells me that they have sent you the printed full score of *Káťa Kabanová.*

1 Mazal, see p. 236, fn.1.
2 Duhoslav, see BR208+.
3 Málinka, see p. 236, fn.2.
4 Young Waiter, see p. 236, fn.4.
5 See p. 81, fn.3.
6 Božena Petanová (1888–1958), a dramatic soprano at the National Theatre 1919–30.

Director Neumann also said that they have sent you the orchestral material.

Can I draw your attention to the fact that the printed score departs in many places from the written score from the Brno theatre. It's the printed score that's correct!

I am curious how you will design the work. It's not easy.

In Brno it turned out coarsely and tastelessly; it was not even set in the period 1840–60. [...]

KK59   Otakar Ostrčil to Janáček   *Prague, 23 September 1922*

[...] It goes without saying that we will lay great store on the *Káťa* designs in order to satisfy you. If you have any special wishes kindly let me know.

KK60   Janáček to Otakar Ostrčil   *Brno, 26 September 1922*

[...] I think that the [printed] parts will soon be ready.

I had the proofs six or seven weeks ago! [Janáček returned the corrected string parts to Universal Edition on 28 July 1922, KK61].

Nevertheless it would be as well to compare the written Brno parts with the printed score and insert whatever is necessary into the parts. There is something in the trombones and in the second violins (Acts 2 and 3).

Director Neumann wanted to have it done.

When the soloists know their parts I'd like to hear them at the piano – on account of the tempos. The metronome is like a milestone; it shows distances; we can pass them any way we like. [...]

KK62   Otakar Ostrčil to Janáček   *Prague, 17 October 1922*

[...] *Káťa Kabanová* is at the stage of ensemble piano rehearsals and orchestral rehearsals.[1] I'm delighted to tell you that not only I but the soloists involved are very taken with the work.

[...]

[PS] NB In addition to Mrs Veselá I have cast Mrs Ungrová as Káťa; the part will suit her excellently both as a singer and an actress.

---

1 Soloists' rehearsals with repetiteurs began on 16 July 1922, orchestral rehearsals on 29 September, and blocking rehearsals began on 19 October, two days after Ostrčil's note. Altogether there were 198 individual and ensemble rehearsals for the Prague première (Pulkert 1978, 220).

Janáček to Otakar Ostrčil   *Brno, 24 October 1922*   **KK63**

I'm going to be in Prague on Sunday evening, Monday and Tuesday (29, 30, 31 October).

I have a [folk]song [commission] meeting.

On Tuesday I would like to come to see you at the theatre.

Will you be having a rehearsal of *K.K.*? [. . .]

Janáček to Otakar Ostrčil   *Brno, 2 November 1922*   **KK64**

I was pleased with your apt understanding of *Káťa Kabanová*.

You yourself sensed the faster tempos [needed for] Kudrjáš's songs [in Act 2 Scene 2].

The rest good down to the smallest detail.

From what I heard of the orchestral rehearsals it's necessary to take that passage with the sleigh bells at fig.3 [vs6] a shade faster. It's a bit difficult for the flute, but it's playable.

Would you be kind enough to have both clarinets additionally write in this passage from the violas

in the bar before fig.6 (Act 1) [vs8]:

thus for B flat clarinet:

It got lost – and so it's necessary to double the violas.

I think you will be rehearsing again on Monday and Tuesday [6–7 November]; so I'll come and listen.

But I now know for sure that in your hands the work is safe.

I'm looking forward to it and have no fears!

Janáček to Kamila Stösslová   *Brno, 2 November 1922*   **KK65**

Neither sight nor sound of you!

The Prague première of *Káťa Kabanová* will be around 19 November. Thus in a fortnight!

So get ready to come with your husband.

I go to Prague again on Sunday [5 November]; I will be there until Tuesday evening.

KK66   Janáček to Otakar Ostrčil   *Brno, 17 November 1922*

Please tell me in good time when the *final* rehearsals will be.

I badly need to hear the effect of those harmonics on the second violins (Act 3, full score from p. 78) [vs107 ff].

[on back of envelope:] NB It is in Act 2, not Act 3.

KK67   Otakar Ostrčil to Janáček   *Prague, 18 November 1922*

Allow me to inform you that the last rehearsals for *Káťa Kabanová* are set for Tuesday, Thursday and Friday – 21, 23 and 24 – the première then on Sunday 26 November, providing we don't have to change these arrangements because the sets from Vienna are still not here. In that case I will let you know of any change.

KK68   Otakar Ostrčil to Janáček   *Prague, 20 November 1922*

Allow me to inform you that the première of *Káťa Kabanová* must be postponed because the sets have not yet arrived. Therefore the Thursday [23 November] rehearsal this week falls away and will instead be on Friday.

KK69   Janáček to Zdenka Janáčková   *Prague, 28 November 1922*

[...] Newspapers are already criticizing the theatre because of the sets; that's the only form of publicity they know. But Scenes 1 and 2 and Scenes 2 and 3 [3 and 4] are broken up! Bakala [was] unlucky with the corrections!

Otherwise fine.

KK70   Janáček to Kamila Stösslová   *Prague, 29 November 1922*

[...] I have my première tomorrow; it will be magnificently staged. – So it's a pity that you aren't here. [...]

As was common practice at the time, the sets for *Káťa Kabanová* were not made locally (in this case they were ordered from Kautsky, the well-known Viennese scenic studio). When they eventually arrived they turned out to be too elaborate to be changed without stopping the music in the middle of Acts 1 and 2. The reviews of the delayed première on 30 November 1922 were mixed.[1] Antonín Šilhan (*Národní listy*, 2 December 1922) criticized the libretto and found the music mosaic-like. Jaromír Borecký (*Národní politika*, 2 December 1922), although he liked the performance and designs and praised Janáček's characterization and dramatic qualities, found the music 'considerably impoverished, especially in melodic invention', the orchestra just 'mood painting'. A key to his reaction is his alignment with a current attitude towards Smetana that brooked no rivals. '[*Káťa Kabanová*] cannot stand as a model. It would be a mistake were it to become a school. Czech opera has only one way forward: Smetana.' One of the most sympathetic was Boleslav Vomáčka (*Lidové noviny*, 2 December 1922), who knew and admired the work from its Brno performance, and energetically attacked the sets and the primitive acting, a view that evidently reflected Janáček's own feelings.

Janáček to Otakar Ostrčil   *Brno, 2 December 1922*   KK71

On the way back I came across the reviews in *Národní listy* and *Národní politika*, and at home *Lidové noviny*.

A fellow could lose his reason at the contradictions he reads! What malice!

Having got to the end of all the critical comments I must say against it that the opera soloists were inadequate as *actors*, apart from Mr Huml.[2] But that is a result of their training as singers, in the old school.

This could not be changed at one go during *Káťa Kabanová*.

In this connection could you help along Act 2 Scene 1 with a generally slightly faster tempo – especially at the passage 'Tak mi srdce přestalo bít' ['So my heart stopped beating', VS78] – quicker, and before that fig.7 [VS77], the Più mosso always more lively in contrast to that Adagio.

And from fig.10 [VS79] a passionate tempo.

Otherwise be true to yourself in everything.

I would be pleased if *Káťa* were to be given everywhere as magnificently as you did it.

The first foreign production of the opera was in Cologne in December 1922. In advance of the première, Janáček received a request for information about the

---

1 The abridged texts of Borecký's and Vomáčka's reviews are printed in Tyrrell 1982, 106–9.

2 Jiří Huml (1875–1948), originally an actor, trained as a singer and had considerable experience, notably in Munich and Dresden, before his permanent engagement at the Prague National Theatre 1910–39. One of the leading members of the company, he excelled both in Wagnerian bass parts and in Smetana's comic bass parts. He played Dikoj in *Káťa Kabanová*. Ironically he was reluctant to take on the part and did not begin rehearsing until 22 September (Pulkert 1978, 220).

opera from a Cologne journalist, the pianist and writer Julius Wolfsohn (1880–1944).

KK72   **Janáček to Julius Wolfsohn**   *Hukvaldy, 2 September 1922*

I am pleased that *Káťa Kabanová* will be performed in Cologne. But how exactly can I help you?

The work flowed from my pen just like the beautiful river Volga.

Should I now catch the waves? Impossible. The motifs transform themselves in my work as if 'of their own accord.'

It seems to me that even when a motif rises up threateningly it has its germ in the still, dreaming waters. For instance the motif

threads its way through the whole work. The whole weight of the drama lies in it.

But also the cause: the departure of Tichon.

And the motif flies now into the flutes, the sleighbells and the oboes

And when a motif becomes so fundamentally different, I feel that it must be so, I don't think anything more about it.

Nor do I think any more about *Káťa Kabanová*. I am already taken up with another, different work.

I have asked Dr Max Brod to stand by to help you.

[...]

Brod, despite Janáček's appeal to him (**KK73**, 22 August 1922), seems not to have helped, and Wolfsohn wrote to Janáček again (**KK74**, 1 November 1922), this time sending him a series of themes from the opera for Janáček's comments and explanations. In view of Janáček's original refusal to 'catch the waves' it seems all the more odd that with his second letter Wolfsohn was able to coax Janáček into describing the 'meaning' of the motifs he had wrtitten out from the opera, the only instance in any opera where Janáček provided such a direct interpretation. In his second letter (**KK75**, 2 November 1922), Janáček simply took Wolfsohn's piece of manuscript paper and labelled the motifs, providing lengthier explanations overleaf.[1] None of Janáček's comments is particularly startling. In his view the two themes in the overture

represent respectively 'lightning' and 'Kát'a's bearing the reproaches of Kabanicha'; the music at Kát'a's first entrance in the opera (vs27) represents 'Kát'a's unstained purity'; and the music at the beginning of Act 2 (vs71) represents 'suffocating atmosphere', 'air filled with evil'.

Sadly, Wolfsohn's efforts to publicize the work in Cologne went for little. Despite its distinguished conductor, Otto Klemperer, the opera was received with puzzlement and disdain by the critics, and was taken off after one performance, on 8 December 1922. Its second showing in Germany, four years later at the Berlin Städtische Oper (31 May 1926) under Fritz Zweig (1893–1984), was a much more distinguished affair, attended by Janáček, Schreker and Schoenberg among others. Janáček was especially delighted with the orchestra: 'And how the storm raged in Act 3 in an orchestra of ninety-five players! Performances like these are dazzling. They open wide the work's gate into the world' (**KK76**: Janáček: 'The sea – the land', 13 June 1926).

TRANSLATION AND CHANGES

Janáček had turned to the German translator of *Jenůfa*, Max Brod, to translate the work (KK39, 11 August 1921). Brod readily agreed the very next day (**KK77**, 12 August 1921) and indeed continued to make German translations of all Janáček's later operas. As a creative spirit himself, a novelist, critic and composer, he was full of suggestions for additions and improvements, some of which in *Kát'a Kabanová* eventually led to revisions of the music. He received the vocal score on 4 October[2] and, as he states in his letter to Janáček of 5 October (**KK78**), was at work the next day. On 20

---

1 See Tyrrell 1985, 85 for a complete translation.
2 He had also seen it in September, during his negotiations with Universal Edition over payment (Janáček 1988, 163–6).

October (**KK79**) he wrote to Janáček to say that he had 'practically finished' Act 1 and a few days later was vigorously proposing amendments:

KK80   **Max Brod to Janáček**   *[undated, postmarked Prague, 25 October 1921]*

Here are my proposed changes:

Act 2 Scene 1
Evil as she is, Kabanicha shouldn't be hypocritical as well. She is *not* so in *Ostrovsky*, and thus remains a bit likeable after all, as a symbol of the old discipline and order *that she has voluntarily subjugated herself to!*

(a) The passage 'Půjdu se modlit! Nevyrušujte mne' ['I'm going off to pray. Don't disturb me!'(vs73)] is *repulsive*. I can't recommend strongly enough replacing these words with something else. (They are *not* in Ostrovsky either.) I suggest adding to the words 'bylo by to slušnější' ['it would be more proper'] something like 'but nowadays there's nothing in the world but mischief and confusion'. Compare *The Thunderstorm* on this point, p. 50 [of Červinka's published Czech translation] 'to je ta pomatenost, lid je zmatený' ['it's madness; the people are confused']. – p. 44 with Kabanicha's beautiful monologue 'A toholeto taky by chtělo žít po svojí vůli' ['And they (young people) would also like to live in just the way they please']. It's clear from this passage that *my* view of Kabanicha is correct. – Her morality is *honest in intent*; she is consistent!

(b) Vocal score, p. 15 [vs78]:[1] 'Vítá Dikoje' ['She welcomes Dikoj'] – The word 'ostražitě' ['vigilantly'] should be cut.

p.16 [vs78]. – I consider it very misguided to have Kabanicha lead Dikoj away and then reappear. The audience will think they've been up to goodness knows what with one another . . . Besides, this coming and going of the two is completely *unmotivated*. – I suggest *either* leaving both on stage talking quietly to one another while Káťa sings *or* postponing Dikoj's entrance to p. 20 [vs80]. Then the words on p. 15 [vs78] 'Přišel jsi s něčím usw' ['You came for something etc'] would be dropped, and Káťa's words 'Někdo přichází' ['Someone's coming'] would be a mere figment of her imagination resulting from her state of excitement, which indeed I find much better than the

---

1 Page numbers quoted by Brod refer to the manuscript vocal score from which he was working (each act was paginated separately). The vs numbers in square brackets that follow refer to the equivalent page numbers in the Universal Edition printed vocal score.

present clumsy motivation. – It's up to you which of these two possibilities I should choose.

(c) At the end of this scene Kabanicha adds the words: 'Nemuč se' ['Don't torture yourself'] – sit down here, I want (to have a sensible talk with you), to comfort you – but don't forget your manners!'. The curtain falls *slowly*.

Brod was wrong about Kabanicha's going off to pray, and thus about the hypocritical aspects of her character to which he took such exception. The line does indeed occur in the original Ostrovsky.[1] Janáček nevertheless accepted Brod's suggested addition under (a) and omitted 'se modlit' (to pray). He also accepted the additions under (c), writing words over the existing orchestral music: all of Kabanicha's part on vs85 was added in this way. Apart from a few minor changes, however, Janáček accepted neither of the two 'possibilities' under (b) and has kept the world guessing ever since about what Kabanicha and Dikoj might have been up to.

Scene 2
(d) You were going to send me an addition to the song 'Donský Kozák' ['The Don Cossack'].

(e) Bottom of p. 37, top of p. 38 [vs91]: 'Kdo by to mohl být? Zamiloval jste se do někoho' ['Who could it be? You've fallen in love with someone']. – This line will simply *not do* now that *Boris* has already confessed *everything* to *Kudrjáš* in Act 1. – I suggest having Kudrjáš say here: 'But I warned you! Are you two really so hopelessly in love?' Then the dialogue can continue. – Next, p. 41 [vs93]: 'To je tedy Kabanová?' 'Ano.' 'Vida, vida' ['It's the Kabanová woman then?' 'Yes.' 'Well, well!'] – This is again superfluous since they have both known for a long time who's involved. Here Kudrjáš should say: 'You're forgetting the sort of people you're living among'. Boris: 'Ano' ['Yes']. [Kudrjáš:] 'Do be careful!'

(f) p. 63 [vs107]: 'Co na tom – ze dvora vedou vrátka, která se zevnitř zavírají. Bude klepat, odejde. Ráno ji řeknu, že jsme tvrdě spaly.' ['What of it? – the gate from the courtyard locks on the inside. She'll knock, then go away. The next morning I'll tell her we slept heavily.'] – Instead of these dull lines I suggest: 'Incidentally, her visitor is still there. Dikoj. Strange, those two old brutes, they quarrel with everyone and get along only with each other.'

---

1 A detailed analysis of Brod's suggested changes and their partial realization is given in Tyrrell 1982, 201–2, fn.10–29.

Brod's inquiry about the 'Donský Kozák' song is evidence of the late stage at which Janáček substituted for Ostrovsky's original another Russian folksong whose translator had to fit his new text to Janáček's already written music.[1] Again Janáček was selective about what he took from Brod. The inconsistency that Brod pointed out under (e) had arisen from Janáček's economical reluctance to invent lines and instead adapting something from elsewhere in the play, in this case from a later scene. Here he took up Brod's suggestion though not his idea for omitting the 'superfluous' identification of Káťa. He also retained the 'dull lines'. Brod's advice here, however, led to one of the most magical moments in this double love-scene. Against the slow soaring offstage unison of Káťa and Boris – heard on its own in Janáček's original version – Varvara continues her more matter-of-fact conversation with Kudrjáš by adding a shortened version of Brod's lines for her at the end of (f).

Act 3

(g) p. 43 [VS140–1]. 'Utéci' ['Escape'] is repeated *four times*. Suggestion: 'Utéci?' Varvara: 'But where?' Kudrjáš: 'To Petersburg.' Varvara: 'Yes, to a new merrier life!'

[(h)] p. 63 [VS154]. 'Strýc mě vyhání' ['My uncle is sending me away']. – From here it should read: 'to a business contact in Jachta, far away near the Chinese border, in Siberia' (Ostrovsky's original p. 88!).

Now, please send me the altered passages as soon as possible with corresponding *music* (*legible*, please) so that I can get on with the translation.

Janáček accepted Brod's variations in place of 'utéci', though plumped for Moscow rather than Petersburg and worked in 'Jachta' (in a Czech transliteration – Kjachta) in the final scene, but without its fussy geographical location.[2] Janáček's response to this letter is known only through his alterations to the score, though it is clear from Brod's next letter (KK81) that he received two letters from the composer, one of them giving him the text of the folksong. Janáček's answer to Brod's letter is also lost. Some of Brod's letter is concerned with errors in the music notation,[3] but part of it explains the changes he made in his German translation to make the work accessible to German audiences:

1 Tyrrell 1982, 58–60.
2 Tyrrell 1982, 202, fn.20 and 21.
3 The full text is printed in JA ix, 92–4 (original German) and Tyrrell 1982, 66–7 (English translation).

Max Brod to Janáček *Prague, 4 November 1921* **KK81**

[...] In many passages, as you will note, I have not translated word for word, but have made *slight* alterations to the text with German theatres in mind.

I have high hopes that this work will conquer the German stage. And to this end I have tried to emphasize the Russian setting more clearly, as it is more remote and unclear to Germans than to Czechs. – Take p. 39 [VS92], for instance: 'Here in your little town women are locked indoors', which I added from Ostrovsky's original since these words clarify the setting! – On p. 63 [VS107] I added a trait to Kabanicha's character that is more interesting than the garden-gate story from the preceding scene.[1] I consider this way of characterizing old Kabanicha a good one, as it meets the German public's need to understand her psychology more fully.

On pp. 5, 7 and 8 [VS115–17] of the last act I've added a few things to make the Russian setting more precise. I've also taken pains in the German to have the Russian words pronounced with their original syllabic stress (Russian accentuation), while the Czechs use a Czech accentuation. For example p. 16 [VS121], German: 'The poet Der-*schá*win' (Czech: *Děřžavín*). – You will note similar changes in many other passages. I hope in this way to have helped your piece along the road to success in Germany.

On 22 October I sent Act 1 to Hertzka [Universal Edition]. Still no acknowledgement of receipt.

Now I'll send off Acts 2 and 3 with a request to acknowledge receipt. [...]

PS When is K.K.'s first performance in Brno? As I want to make my arrangements in time please send a precise, *definitive* date soon!

Max Brod to Janáček *Prague, 9 December 1921* **KK82**

A few remarks on Act 1 of *Kát'a*:

(1) I'm *disturbed* about the note in the list of characters 'mezi III. jednání a jeho proměnou uplynou dva dny' ['Two days elapse during the scene-change in Act 3']. I think it would be more *dramatic* if this scene-change were to follow *immediately* after the first part of Act 3, with the time-lapse being no more than a couple of hours.

---

1 Brod replaced the garden-gate story with Varvara's observation that it would never occur to Kabanicha that she was being hoodwinked.

Should I translate it or leave it out? – Naturally I will do just as you
see fit.

(2) I also enclose two pages from the vocal score as I think you
ought really to have Boris sing another short lyrical passage. An
opportunity to do so is provided on p. 24, bar 6 (oboe entry).[1] *Boris,
at the same time as Fekluša*, could perhaps sing the following lines:
'Hubím svoje mládí! – I'm destroying my youth! (repeated) I'm
destroying my youth! Year after year I saw nothing around me but
misery – happiness was always far, far away, like a glimmer on the
horizon after sunset.'

Fekluša doesn't actually have to sing anything here and would best
begin at the top of p. 25: 'Jací lidé bohabojní, štědří, ti Kabanových'
['What pious people they are, and generous, these Kabanovs!'] At
which Boris starts up from his dream: 'Kabanových!'

This, too, is merely a suggestion for you to consider; please feel free
to reject it if it doesn't suit you. – I know from my *own* experience
that an outsider always fancies changes much more readily than the
author himself!

[...]

(4) I would also suggest shortening the Boris-Dikoj scene. – 'Najdeš
si práci, jenom chtít' ['You would find work if you wanted to'], delete
to fig.16: 'Kam se zvrtnu, všude tě potkám' ['Wherever I turn I bump
into you'], etc. – I found this scene weak during the performance;
perhaps, though, that was only the fault of the acting.

[...]

After seeing to these matters I will send off the proofs to Hertzka.

KK83   **Janáček to Max Brod**   *[undated, after 10 December 1921]*

[1.]   In Act 3 Káťa replies to Boris's question: 'And what about your
husband?'

Káťa: 'Bije, mne bije!' ['He beats me!'] 'Chvíli je laskav!' ['For a
while he's kind!', a slightly misremembered version of vs155–6]. Is
he still like that even after he *knew* of Káťa's misdemeanour?

If so it would need *at least those two* days to elapse between the
two scenes of Act 3.

Had Tichon been like that immediately he returned – not even
knowing Káťa's misdemeanour – then the two days wouldn't be
necessary and it could stand as I wrote it, i.e. Káťa does not return

---

1 Brod is now quoting from the printed vocal score.

home after the storm; she runs out into the storm; the others look for her.

So put *'after some hours'* instead of two days.

2. And now that addition to Boris's part! You know, when a ripe apple has fallen from the tree – how could one want it to go on growing?

But it can *sweeten*!

A good idea occurred to me after you drew this to my attention!

Both Boris and Fekluša will sing! From p. 24, bar 6: [Janáček here writes out Boris's and Fekluša's voice parts from vs24, bar 6 to the end of the page in what was to be virtually their final version, making a 'duet' out of what was originally a solo for Fekluša]. The rest stays at it is! It will be good like that. So now please translate it!

[. . .]

4. It's a shame that there isn't *another* exchange between Dikoj and Boris! God forbid that I should shorten it!

[PS] NB the Prague National Theatre has accepted *Káťa Kabanová*. Director Ostrčil was very taken with it.

Even here people are getting to like it.

Wish me luck with *Liška Bystrouška* as well!

[. . .]

NB 3. Please write that change, for Boris, into the libretto!

A clue to the dating of this letter is of course the receipt of Brod's, but more especially the date of Janáček's letter to Universal Edition of 10 December 1921 (**KK84**) where he rejected Hertzka's suggestion of extending the part of Boris. This was not advisable, he wrote, with no deeper motivation, and anyway there were no more words for him in Ostrovsky. But Brod's letter seems to have changed his mind: the chief outcome of this exchange was the surprising 'duet' for Boris and Fekluša made at a very late stage – on the proofs – by Janáček's inserting extra lines for Boris (from his repetition of '[Ó] hubím svoje mládí' on vs24. The tricky question of the time-lapse in Act 3 was ducked altogether by omitting any reference to it, though the beginning of the act is described as being 'towards evening' and after the scene-change 'the thick twilight turns to night'.

In later years Janáček's greatest concern was with the failure of opera houses to observe his requirement that each act should be played continuously. He had noted this shortcoming in a letter to his wife during the Prague rehearsals (KK69, 28 November 1922) and his misgivings grew as he saw more productions of the work.

KK85   **Janáček to Universal Edition**   *Brno, 19 February 1923*

The conductor Břetislav Bakala has once again made a thorough check of the full score of *Káťa Kabanová*; he noticed that there are still many printing errors.

He will let you know about them; it would be good if these corrections, copied out or in some other way, could be enclosed with each full score. It must also be stated that the two scenes of each Act, 1, 2 and 3, should follow *immediately* after one another.

In Prague this was ignored and so the performance fell apart.

In Cologne on the other hand they omitted the first scene of Act 2 (Dikoj-Kabanicha)![1]

[...]

KK86   **Janáček to Otakar Ostrčil**   *Brno, 4 March 1924*

[...] I have read that *Káťa Kabanová* is to be given during the international festival celebrations[2] at the end of May.

I earnestly beg you not to let the work be broken up by the scene-changes.

In Act 1 the living-room need not be so richly furnished.

Similarly in Act 2 the room could be so simple that in a few seconds it could be cleared away and the sunken path, prepared in advance, would just appear.

Similarly the ruins in Act 3 could be simpler so that they could be cleared away quickly and the previously prepared view of the Volga would then just appear.

In other words the two scenes of Acts 1, 2 and 3 could be stage-set at the same time.

[...]

I don't want more magnificent sets.

Do please comply with my wishes.

When the music is performed so very splendidly by you in Prague don't let it be broken up by the scene-changes.

[JP160]

Presumably after further badgering from Janáček, J.M. Gottlieb,[3] the Prague

---

1 The short dialogue for Dikoj and Kabanicha (VS81–5) is the last part of Act 1 Scene 2.
2 A festival staged in Prague 25 May to 8 June 1924, partly coinciding with the ISCM orchestral festival, which opened in Prague on 31 May; *Káťa Kabanová* received its ninth performance at the Prague National Theatre on 29 May 1924.
3 Josef Matěj Gottlieb (1882–1967), stage-designer, head of design at the Prague National Theatre 1919–42. He designed the sets for the Prague première of *Káťa Kabanová*.

scene-designer, announced to him that he was 'redoing the two rooms for *Káťa Kabanová* so that the quick scene-changes can be effected according to [his] wishes' (**KK87**, 15 May 1924). This, however, seems not to have avoided the breaks in mid-act, and, three years later, Janáček decided to expand the musical links connecting the two scenes of Act 1 and the two scenes of Act 2 into short interludes. In Act 1 he simply developed existing material, but in Act 2 he wrote a brisk little march, reminiscent of the march in Act 2 of the opera he was then working on, *From the House of the Dead.*

Janáček to Universal Edition   *Brno, 9 November 1927*   **KK88**

[...] The music for the scene-changes in Acts 1 and 2 of *Káťa Kabanová* was too short. I have extended the interludes to give more time for setting the stage.

The word *attacca* is also missing before these scene-changes.

Because of this the work got broken up into *six* parts rather than into *three* acts.

I will send on everything to you at the beginning of next week so that the Prague performance can make use of it.

The 'Prague performance' Janáček referred to was not at the Prague National Theatre, but at the German Theatre. Its repertory naturally tended to be German-biased, but it had given *Jenůfa* in 1926. Its première of *Káťa Kabanová* took place on 21 January 1928 under Hans Wilhelm Steinberg (1899–1978) and was the first production of the opera to include Janáček's newly written interludes. Steinberg not only performed each act continuously, but played Acts 1 and 2 without a break, a notion which greatly took Janáček's fancy, and he added this to his requirements for the opera:

Janáček to Universal Edition   *Hukvaldy, 25 January 1928*   **KK89**

Káťa in Prague under

Steinberg

was outstanding!

His delightful idea:

to play the first two acts in one span, without a break, please *promote* this most urgently in my name wherever *Káťa* is given. My insertions work marvellously. [...]

Janáček to Zdenka Janáčková   *Hukvaldy, 26 January 1928*   **KK90**

[...] That review of *Káťa* is marvellous! You can't imagine how splendidly they performed it. They compressed everything into *two* acts! Brno and the Prague National Theatre were not a patch on it. [. . .]

[PS] *Kát'a* will now go round the world!

DEDICATION

Janáček dedicated *Jenůfa* to the memory of his daughter Olga, and *The Excursions of Mr Brouček* (eventually) to President Masaryk. *Kát'a Kabanová* carries no dedication on its title page, but it was most certainly Kamila Stösslová's opera. Janáček acknowledged the source of inspiration in his letter to her of 29 October 1921 (KK45), when he invited her to the Brno première. She did not go, but, in one of her few letters to Janáček that has survived, she asked for a score.

KK91   **Kamila Stösslová to Janáček**   *Písek, 13 January 1922*

If you want to be nice, send me a score of *Kát'a Kabanová*. And I would ask you to write something in it for me, so that I or my children would have something from you as a keepsake. [. . .]

The inscribed score has indeed survived as a keepsake for future generations.[1] Janáček wrote a conventional dedication in it ('To Mrs Kamila Stösslová in remembrance, Leoš Janáček'), but his letters of the time continued to emphasize the source of its inspiration.

KK92   **Janáček to Kamila Stösslová**   *Brno, 10 February 1922*

[. . .] In the next few days they should have finished printing the vocal score of *Kát'a Kabanová*. I'll send you a copy; after all I had you much in mind during *Kát'a Kabanová* [. . .]

KK93   **Janáček to Kamila Stösslová**   *Brno, 25 February 1922*

[. . .] So you have *Kát'a Kabanová*. During the writing of the opera I needed to know a great measureless love. In those beautiful days in Luhačovice tears ran down your cheeks when you remembered your husband. It touched me. And it was your image I always placed on Kát'a Kabanová when I was writing the opera. Her love went a different way, but nevertheless it was a great, beautiful love!

1 In the Okresní muzeum [District Museum], Písek.

Janáček to Kamila Stösslová *Prague, 14 March 1922* **KK94**

Can't you even say thank you for *Kátá*?

Kamila did say thank you a couple of days later, but in a letter (**KK95**, 16 March 1922) full of domestic distractions and signally unaware of the honour that was being bestowed on her. She would also have been quite unaware of the irony of Janáček's words 'So you have *Kátá Kabanová*', echoing those with which Kabanicha is given the lifeless corpse of Kátá in the final moments of the opera. In the last few months of his life, however, Janáček gave her one of the most beautiful dedications ever written by a composer:

Janáček to Kamila Stösslová *Písek, 12 February 1928* **KK96**

Mrs Kamila!

And it was in the summer sun. The slope was warm, the flowers almost fainting bowed towards the earth.

At that time the first thoughts about that unhappy Kátá Kabanová – her great love – went through my head.

She calls to the flowers, she calls to the birds – the flowers to bow to her, the birds to sing to her the last song of love.

'My friend', I said to Professor Knop.[1] 'I know a marvellous lady, miraculously she is in my mind all the time. My Kátá grows in her, in her, Mrs Kamila Neumannová! The work will be one of my most tender!'

And it happened. I have known no greater love than in her. I dedicate the work to her. Flowers, bow down to her; birds, never cease your song of eternal love!

Dr Leoš Janáček

---

1 Bohumír Štědroň (1946, 214) suggested that Janáček meant 'Khodl', an acquaintance in Písek.

7 The Cunning Little Vixen

GENESIS

LB1 Marie Stejskalová's reminiscences (1959)

The morning edition of *Lidové noviny* was brought to us by delivery boys, I'd go to a news stall for the afternoon one. When *Bystrouška*[1] was coming out I'd open the paper first thing on the way home to see if there was another instalment; and if there was I'd rush home and read it quickly before giving it to the master, who anyway was working and got round to newspapers only in the evening. I was reading it like this once – it was when there was a picture of Bystrouška [the Vixen] going hand in hand with Zlatohřbítek [the Fox] and carrying a flower. It seemed to me terribly funny how they strutted about like that. I thought no-one could hear me laughing aloud: the mistress wasn't at home, and the master was in his study. But suddenly he appeared at the kitchen door.

'Woman, what's so funny?'

'Just *Bystrouška*, sir.'

'What *Bystrouška*?'

'But don't you read it? It's written by Editor Těsnohlídek from the *Lidové noviny*.'

I handed him the newspaper, he looked at the picture, read to himself, and began to smile, and I said to him:

'Sir, you know so well what animals say, you're always writing down those bird calls – wouldn't it make a marvellous opera!'

He didn't say anything. But he began collecting every instalment of *Bystrouška*. And what didn't happen next! He went to see Mr Těsnohlídek, then Mr Těsnohlídek came to us, they reached an agreement, and the master began to study animals for *Bystrouška*. At six in the morning he would get up, drink his Karlsbad water – every year in May he'd take a Karlsbad cure at home – and go off to the Lužánky park to listen to the birds singing, the trees rustling, and the

---

1 Těsnohlídek's novel about the Vixen *Bystrouška* with Lolek's illustrations; see LB2+.

bumblebees buzzing. He would return full of life and joy and say: 'What you people have been sleeping through!'

The serial publication of *Liška Bystrouška* in fifty-one parts went from 7 April to 23 June 1920, thus at the rate of four or five instalments a week. If the Janáčeks' servant, Marie Stejskalová, remembered the right picture (which came in the forty-sixth instalment), this incident took place in the week beginning Monday 14 June, i.e. a good fortnight after Janáček finished taking his Karlsbad water. A more serious objection arises from studying the complete run of newspaper cuttings in the Janáček archive. If Janáček 'began collecting every instalment of *Bystrouška*' from the time of the incident as described by Stejskalová, he would have ended up with only six out of the fifty-one instalments; if she had been collecting them herself she would surely have said so. However, the initial impulse could have come equally well from any other of the many readers of Brno's popular and liberal daily paper, the *Lidové noviny*, or from Janáček's acquaintance on the editorial board: he himself was a regular contributor. Even after Stejskalová allegedly drew Janáček's attention to the subject he did nothing further about it for some time. Until April 1921 he was still hard at work on *Káťa Kabanová*. It was 1922 before he actually approached Těsnohlídek about the matter.

Rudolf Těsnohlídek: 'The youthful old man' LB2

[. . .] Liška Bystrouška has played her tricks in the newspapers. I don't know why people liked her so much. Perhaps because she moved close to the ground.[1]

I did not suspect that she had a diligent reader and admirer in a man with silver hair and sparkling eyes. I know him only at a distance since he is a musician and I don't understand much about music. Suddenly I heard that *Liška Bystrouška* had bewitched him and that he wanted to describe her frequently trivial words and even more trivial actions in the language of notes, which of all human things, is the least earthbound.

I didn't believe it and took it for a joke. Later I was pursued by a new direct question: what would I say about it? I said nothing. I was surprised and had the feeling that in the end someone was making a fool of me. Then one spring day two years ago, I received a written invitation from Maestro Janáček.

My heart was heavier than that of Bystrouška when they caught

---

1 i.e. appealed to an unsophisticated readership, which is why Těsnohlídek could not really believe that Janáček was thinking of making a libretto from it.

her in the larder during the *zabíjačka*.[1] I summoned up my courage
and went. It was a day in May, and birdsong pealed over the Brno
streets, above the roofs and beneath the heavens as if it were somewhere in the meadows down by the Svitava river.

Leoš Janáček was waiting in the little garden of the Conservatory.[2]
He sat among the bushes, with thousands of tiny little blossoms
above his head; that head of his was just as white, and seemed to be
the largest of the flowers. He smiled; and I knew at once that this was
the smile which life awards us like a gold medal for bravery in the face
of the enemy. For bravery in sorrow, humiliation and anger. At that
moment I believed that Liška Bystrouška was sitting, tamed and quite
overcome by the kindliness of the man in the tiny garden, and that
unseen she would draw near to sit at our feet and listen to our
conspiracy. Janáček made a few remarks about the story and then
began talking about his forests there in Valašsko,[3] which I don't
know, about his studies of bird noises and I became aware that he had
succeeded in knowing the happiness of a smile [. . .].

Lidové noviny (3 July 1924)

Rudolf Těsnohlídek (1882–1928) had been employed by the *Lidové noviny*
since 1908 as a law reporter and feuilletonist. Dr Bohumil Markalous, one of
the paper's editors, had come across some 200 sketches by the painter
Stanislav Lolek (1873–1936). Drawing on his experience as apprentice
forester, Lolek depicted in them the adventures of a clever vixen, constantly
outwitting the local forester. Těsnohlídek was instructed to produce a text to
accompany the pictures ('he charged me to write little lines to it', LB3). The
result was not so much a cartoon strip – as it has sometimes been called – but
a short novel with a large number of illustrations. The author's initial
reluctance to take on the assignment is ironic: among his novels, children's
books and volumes of poetry, it was his only work to achieve real popularity
or critical success (it won a state prize in 1923) and is still regularly published
in Czechoslovakia.

There were problems with the title from the start. In the collective article in
Lidové noviny to mark the première of Janáček's opera (LB3: 'Liška Bystrouška in the theatre', 1 November 1924), Těsnohlídek described how the
printers mistook the original name of 'Liška Bystronožka' (Vixen Fleetfoot)

---

1 Pig-slaughtering, a time of celebration when all sorts of delicacies are made from the pig.
This incident is not directly included in the opera, though the Vixen refers to it when she
describes her life to the Fox.
2 Janáček's Organ School had been turned into a Conservatory in 1919 after Czechoslovak
independence the year before. After its nationalization in 1920 he was replaced as director,
but continued to live in the house in the grounds.
3 Těsnohlídek confused Valašsko with its neighbouring region, Janáček's native Lašsko
(see map).

for 'Liška Bystrouška', and Bystrouška she then remained. This word is usually translated as 'sharp (little) ears' (as deriving from *bystro-ouška*), but, as Charles Susskind has pointed out,[1] it could also be taken as the affectionate diminutive noun of the adjective *bystrý* (sharp, quick, acute; thus 'sharp little one'), an interpretation upheld by Janáček's setting of the word in three syllables (*by-strou-ška*) rather than in the four of *by-stro-uš-ka*. The novel was called simply *Liška Bystrouška*, the opera expanded to *Příhody Lišky Bystroušky* ('The Adventures of the Vixen Bystrouška', see LB56), though Janáček usually referred to it as *Liška Bystrouška*, or one of these two words on their own.

As in *Káťa Kabanová*, Janáček put together his own libretto. A letter from Těsnohlídek (**LB4**, 16 May 1922), written evidently soon after their May meeting in Janáček's garden, supplied a song entitled 'Verunko!' (Verunka, a variant of Veronika). 'I'm sending you both stanzas of that slightly juvenile song to choose from. I made it fit the elegiac tearfulness of the schoolteacher and the mirthful tearfulness of his companions. If it doesn't suit you, I'll gladly have another go'. Janáček used the song (at the beginning of the tavern scene in Act 2), but treated it in the same cavalier way that he handled Těsnohlídek's book as a whole, selecting seven lines somewhat at random from the total of fourteen. Apart from having written the book in the first place, this seems to have been Těsnohlídek's only contribution to the libretto. The other songs that Janáček introduced were folksongs. Harašta's song at the beginning of Act 3 ('Déž sem vandroval' – 'When I went a-wandering') is quoted briefly in Těsnohlídek's novel; Harašta's second song, heard offstage against the duet of the Vixen and the Fox ('Když jsem já šel okolo hája zeleného' – 'As I went past the greenwood') is a well-known folk text, existing in many variants. The text of the Fox Cubs' song, 'Běží liška k Táboru' ('A vixen runs to Tábor'), comes from the best-known of all collections of Czech folksongs, Erben's *Czech Folksongs and Nursery Rhymes*.[2] Janáček's attention to it, however, was probably drawn by its appearance in the *Lidové noviny* under the heading 'Liška Kořenářka' ('The herbalist vixen'), accompanied by a drawing of a vixen with a large bag, walking on hind legs to Tábor (according to the helpful road sign).

Těsnohlídek disappeared at this early stage, having signed a contract with Janáček for 10% of Janáček's Czech-language performance royalties of the opera (**LB5**), and Janáček proceeded alone. By the time he did so, the novel had come out in book form (1921). Janáček possessed a set of the cuttings from the newspaper, but it is clear from his copious annotations in the book that he worked chiefly (and more conveniently) from the latter:[3] he crossed out unwanted chapters or small sections and occasionally jotted down extra

1 Susskind 1985, 76–7; Susskind goes on to point out that the translation of 'bystrouška' as 'sharp little one' provides a justification for Brod's much-disparaged translation *Das schlaue Füchslein*, and its English version, *The Cunning Little Vixen*. In the light of these different interpretations I have left 'Bystrouška' untranslated.
2 See Cígler 1975, 210–23 for a detailed study of these sources.
3 The cuttings are held in the BmJA at shelfmark L19, the annotated novel at L20.

comments. His most frequent marks were underlinings, added names of characters to identify speakers, and page numbers to direct himself to the next passage.

Těsnohlídek's *Liška Bystrouška* in no way reflected the author's basic pessimism (he took his own life a few years later) but is instead a genial account, from an 'animal' viewpoint, of the adventures of a vixen cub, found by a forester, who takes her home and brings her up with his dachshund and his farmyard hens. The vixen makes friends with the dog, but gradually picks off the hens until, when threatened by the irate forester's wife, she bites through her leash and escapes back to the forest. Here she finds a den for herself by evicting a badger from his sett, but as winter approaches and food is scarce she returns to the farmyard for a number of successful raids. On the last of these she is cornered, but still manages to escape. The forester, despite many attempts, never recaptures her, a source of amusement for his drinking companions, the local schoolmaster and the priest. Meanwhile the vixen meets a fox, who courts her and marries her.

Janáček's order of events in Act 1 and the first half of Act 2 follows Těsnohlídek's closely, but thereafter the two diverge. While Těsnohlídek devoted the next section to a description of Bystrouška's raids (taking up a quarter of the book), Janáček omitted this entirely and made the courtship and marriage scenes (which bring the novel to a close) the culmination of Act 2. The events of Act 3 are thus Janáček's redaction, partly drawn from earlier incidents in the novel, and partly his own invention. Těsnohlídek had introduced the vixen's altercation with Harašta the poultry-dealer as yet another example of her quickwittedness. In the opera, however, Harašta shoots her and this single stroke gives an entirely different slant to the piece. Instead of a light-hearted tale the opera becomes a serious work which, for all its comic touches, is able to include and comprehend death. 'A merry thing with a sad end', was how Janáček characterized it to Kamila Stösslová as he began work on it (LB10).

CHRONOLOGY

LB6   Janáček's autobiography (1924)

One thing is certain, that each of my operas has grown for a good year or two in my thoughts without my hindering its growth by a single note.

For a long time I had a real headache with every work.

I played with *Liška Bystrouška* as if she was tame. It's strange how the rusty red of her fur continually blazed in my eyes.

Although Janáček may well have begun thinking about *Liška Bystrouška* as a potential opera while it appeared in *Lidové noviny* in 1920, the first public indication of the fact came a year later, after his final revision of *Káťa Kabanová* in the spring of 1921. In an interview for *Lidové noviny* Janáček confirmed the story that had got around that he was going to compose *Liška Bystrouška*:

adv [Adolf Veselý]: 'Leoš Janáček's new work' **LB7**

[...] How I'm looking forward to the work! In the summer in Luhačovice I thought over the matter, I carry it about with me, I'm working on it. Well, it will certainly take two years...

'Will it be an opera in the ordinary sense?', I ask.

– People will act in it as well as speak, but like animals. Foxes, old and young, frogs, mosquitoes – but you know it from the book. It will be an opera as well as a pantomime.[1]

'What', I say, like Rostand's *Chanteclaire* [sic]?'[2]

–The human-animals in *Chanteclaire* just philosophize. In my *Vixen* there will be dramatic action, stage action. And then the animals! For years I have listened to them, memorizing their speech; I'm at home with them.

Lidové noviny (15 May 1921)

To prove the point Janáček published a feuilleton a fortnight later about a goldfinch, the first of several in which he notated birdsong. The piece ended as follows: 'Why all these words about the rugged notes of the goldfinch [...]? In the first place I liked him (or her). And second, I'm collecting suitable companions for Liška Bystrouška' (**LB8**: 'The little goldfinch', *Lidové noviny*, 1 June 1921). *Káťa Kabanová* still occupied Janáček, however, with final corrections to the score up to the Brno première on 23 November 1921. And Max Brod's German translation, which went ahead that autumn, threw up more possibilities for tinkering with the score. It was only in his final, undated letter to Brod on the subject, written after 10 December 1921 (**LB9**; KK83) that he mentioned his new opera again in a sudden postscript: 'Wish me luck with *Liška Bystrouška* as well!' The actual writing began in the new year:

---

1 i.e. mime; it is interesting that even at this stage the important ballet/mime element of the opera was firmly in place, as is confirmed by Janáček's annotations of 'ballet' in his copy of the the novel.

2 Edmond Rostand's four-act verse drama *Chantecler* (1910), an allegory in which farm and forest animals are depicted as experiencing human feelings.

LB10   Janáček to Kamila Stösslová   *Brno, 10 February 1922*

[. . .] I have begun writing *Liška Bystrouška*. A merry thing with a sad end: and I am taking up a place at that sad end myself.

And so I fit in there! [. . .]

LB11   Janáček to Kamila Stösslová   *Brno, 18 March 1922*

[. . .] I'm now out of that bad-tempered, in fact tiring, mood. I have been working on the girl's novel *Liška Bystrouška*. So I don't have a moment now to think about *myself*.

What is remarkable in the genesis of this opera is how seldom Janáček referred to it during composition. It was not until the autumn that either Brod or Stösslová heard about it again, though his contacts with Těsnohlídek in May 1922 (LB2, LB4) would suggest that Janáček was now confident of his subject and going ahead with it. In fact by the summer he seems to have completed the first two acts in a first draft, and was even looking ahead to the next opera. His head was so full of *The Vixen* that when asked by Julius Wolfsohn (see KK72–5) to write something for the Cologne première of *Kátá Kabanová*, he tried to pass most of the task on to Max Brod:

LB12   Janáček to Max Brod   *Hukvaldy, 22 August 1922*

[. . .] Though I will also write to him myself, I don't want to stir up that mental brew [again].[1] In fact I can't: I'm already in a different atmosphere.

Have you also had a break?

I am now at Hukvaldy near Příbor. Quiet solitude, slumbering forests. I am writing out the libretto of *Bystrouška* up to where I've got.

Roughly up to the last act.

Do you know Čapek? *R.U.R.*, *The Insect Play*. His sister said something about a libretto.[2]

Unlike in *The Excursions of Mr Brouček*, where he endeavoured to prepare a libretto before composing, Janáček had gone ahead simply with the annotated book in front of him, though he felt the need to see how the story was shaping up before he pressed ahead with the next act, in which he was no longer able to follow Těsnohlídek so closely. There seems to have been something of a gap in composition, both from the evidence of this letter and

1 One of Janáček's more striking metaphors: literally brain-porridge (*mozkovou kaši*). Janáček is unwilling to re-enter the heady emotional world of *Kátá Kabanová*.
2 See VM2+.

from another reference to the opera in his autobiography (**LB13**: 'I was occupied in my mind with *Liška Bystrouška* in Luhačovice in August 1922; I set it down in notes in the autumn of 1922 until 1923 – January, February 1924.') What this account does not say, however, is that by August 1922 two acts were already written in a first draft. By September 1922 Janáček was at work again, as can be gathered from a brief reference in his letter to Kamila Stösslová of 30 September 1922: 'Write cheerfully. I am now writing a merry opera' (**LB14**). An approach from the local theatre suggests that the first version of the opera was complete in November 1922 and that Janáček had passed the word round.

Václav Štech to Janáček for the National Theatre in Brno

Brno, 20 November 1922   **LB15**

I learn that you have just finished your new opera *Liška Bystrouška*.

If this is so, I ask you to be so kind and entrust the first performance of your work to the National Theatre.

Janáček's autograph score[1] provides some clues about the writing of the opera. He added a starting date of '22 January 1922', i.e. nearly three weeks before his letter to Stösslová on the subject (LB10), and over a month before Stejskalová got to hear of it.[2] He completed Act 1 on 26 March 1922. The present Act 2 was originally divided into two acts. Janáček completed the first of these on 5 June 1922 and began the second (the Fox-Vixen scene) two days later, 7 June 1922. The autograph date for the end of this act (2 October 1922) seems too late in view of his letter to Brod (LB12). Janáček dated the end of the whole opera to 25 October 1922, a few weeks before the Brno theatre picked up the news (LB15). This of course was merely a first version and, as usual, the opera was substantially revised.

Janáček completed his revision of Act 1 on 22 February 1923; the fair copy by Jaroslav Kulhánek[3] was dated 29 March 1923. An autograph date of 29 June 1923 is probably that of Janáček's revision of Act 2 (Kulhánek's copy is 20 July 1923). Břetislav Bakala was once again making the vocal score, and on 22 August 1923 (**LB16**) reported to Janáček that he had nearly finished Act 2. Janáček had revised Act 3 by 10 October 1923, and Kulhánek's copy was completed rather later, by 12 January 1924. Janáček had always made extensive corrections to the copyist's fair copy, but in *The Vixen* he began using his copyists additionally as amanuenses, giving verbal instructions for additions. 'I didn't go anywhere for the holidays; I'm up to my neck in work with the copying of *Bystrouška*', he wrote to Kamila Stösslová on 3 April 1923 (**LB17**; i.e. during the copying of Act 2, whose autograph is remarkably

---

1 BmJA, A 7455a-c; additional sections at A 7455d and A 33.819.
2 Her diary records 24 February 1922 as the starting date and 12 March 1923 as the finishing date of *The Vixen* (Smetana 1948, 113).
3 Originally held (and used until 1982) by the Brno Theatre; now in BmJA A 52.663.

patchy in places). This formulation suggests substantial involvement on the composer's part in the 'copying'. Furthermore the late completion date of Act 3 seems to have been caused by difficulties in finding an available helper. On 5 July 1923 (**LB18**), while on holiday in Štrbské Pleso, Janáček wrote to his pupil František Míťa Hradil (1898–1980): 'I will arrive about 20 July at Hukvaldy. We could finish writing that third act by 1 August. I will inform you further in good time.' In his memoirs Hradil (**LB19**) recounts that he had begun helping Janáček with *The Vixen* in Brno (and was surprised by the K90 he received on 3 July 'For copying', as the postal order described it). However, he wrote to Janáček on 7 July 1923 (**LB20**), that he had to be in Prague for the second half of July and could help out only from 1 August. By that time Janáček would be returning to Brno and since Hradil was based in Ostrava, Janáček then thought of another of his copyists, Václav Sedláček.

| LB21 | **Janáček to Zdenka Janáčková** | *Hukvaldy, 25 July 1923* |

[. . .] What will come of all this, I don't know. A copyist here would be expensive for me. If Sedláček will be in Brno at the beginning of August, we will write a bit before Luhačovice.

The Brno copy of the full score, however, is in Kulhánek's hand; it seems that in the end Janáček waited until he was available.[1]

During his work on the opera Janáček seems to have made some attempt to 'research' some of the more detailed aspects of behaviour of foxes and turned for help to one of his Hukvaldy friends, Ludvík Jung, a landowner and lessee of the Hukvaldy brewery.

| LB22 | **Ludvík Jung to Janáček** | *[?Hukvaldy,] 26 January 1923* |

I thank you for your note and answer your question:

The vixen/fox (technically: bitch and dog) matures in the second year and comes on heat in the months of January and February (the older vixen earlier; the younger later). The vixen is usually pregnant (technically: with cub) for sixty days and has a litter of five to six cubs (the young animals fewer, the older ones more). Once a year!

---

1 A copy of the score by Sedláček turned up in Prague in 1972 (it subsequently disappeared), and was hailed in the press as the 'original score' (Přibáňová 1980, 167). The dates of Kulhánek's copy of the first two acts suggest that he was following very closely in Janáček's footsteps. In Act 3 however, Kulhánek may have been copying out a score that Janáček had worked on with Sedláček, a conclusion supported by the fact that Janáček, when offering the work to Universal Edition (LB24), reported that the vocal score would be ready 'in the next few days' – i.e. towards the end of October, and thus months before Kulhánek's full score was ready.

Janáček also made use of his acquaintance with the Sládek family, with whom he stayed in Hukvaldy before buying his own house. Vincenc Sládek (1865–1944) was the local forester. The incident below is described by Sládek's nephew and godson, quoting the words of Ruda Červenka, an old friend of the family:

Jan Václav Sládek's reminiscences (1979)   LB23

Your father, godfather, Janáček and I set off for Široká mez. We didn't wait long. Janáček came in a white suit. We burst out laughing.

'You're more likely, Dr Janáček, to catch sight of a magpie on a willow[1] than a vixen, who sees everything.' Mr Janáček had to return and change into less striking clothes.

We reached Babí hora [Old Woman Mountain] by way of the Ondřejnice valley and Rybí stream. And indeed, as if to order, the vixen's family emerged from the den and began to show off and frisk about. Janáček started fidgeting [with excitement] until in the end he frightened the foxes away.

'Why couldn't you keep still Dr Janáček? You could have gone on looking!'

Janáček, completely exhilarated and happy, just brushed this aside with the words 'I saw her!, I saw her!', and there was no holding him any more. We hurried home.

Janáček had offered *The Vixen* to Universal Edition on 22 October 1923 (**LB24**). The firm cautiously suggested waiting until the première (**LB25**: Universal Edition to Janáček, 14 November 1923). Janáček thereupon threatened (**LB26**, 10 November 1923) to turn to Hudební matice, who on 9 January 1924 told Janáček that they would be glad to publish the opera, if financially possible (**LB27**). After Universal Edition saw the score early in 1924 (it was temporarily lost in the Christmas post), the firm pronounced that they would be able to have it out only the next year (**LB28**, 16 February 1924). Janáček responded by pleading for it to be ready by his seventieth birthday (**LB29**, 19 February 1924); Universal Edition in turn responded that a printed vocal score was not possible by 4 July[2] (**LB30**, 22 February 1924) and four days later, on 26 February 1924, returned the manuscript (**LB31**).

Janáček was now in an embarrassing position, as he wrote to Universal Edition: he had already turned down the Hudební matice offer on the understanding that Universal Edition was committed to the opera. The première in Brno had been postponed until the autumn, which allowed more

---

1 'vidět straku na vrbě'; possibly a reference to 'malovat [i.e. paint] straku na vrbě', i.e. to hoodwink, bamboozle someone.
2 The date that Janáček mentioned in LB29 as 'a bit significant'; it was in fact the seventieth anniversary of his christening, rather than of his birth the day before.

time for the score to be out in advance. Did Universal Edition not care about it at all? (**LB32**: Janáček to Universal Edition, 28 February 1924). This appeal had its due effect, and in his next letter Hertzka offered to have the opera published in vocal score by the end of June (**LB33**, 4 March 1924). Work then proceeded extremely quickly; proofs began arriving the following month (**LB34**: Universal Edition to Janáček, 25 April 1924). By 30 July 1924, not quite by Janáček's seventieth birthday, but well before the Brno première, Universal Edition was able to send him a copy of the printed vocal score (**LB35**).

PERFORMANCES AND REACTIONS

The Vixen received its first performances both in Brno and in Prague under the now traditional conductors – František Neumann in Brno, and Otakar Ostrčil in Prague. In Brno rehearsals were well under way by the beginning of September, as Janáček reported to Universal Edition (**LB36**, 1 September 1924). By 10 October, when Janáček was planning to send the score to Prague for Ostrčil to have a look at, this proved impossible because orchestral rehearsals were in progress. Furthermore, as Janáček wrote, he 'might perhaps add a note here and there. I'd write it in so that the score would then be completely in order' (**LB37**, 10 October 1924). By the end of the month, he felt confident enough of his new opera to send out invitations.

LB38   **Janáček to Otakar Ostrčil**   *Brno, 31 October 1924*

Today I heard *Liška Bystrouška* all through – and I think I can invite you to it.

So come on 6 November [for the première].

By chance there are here in the theatre people born for the parts, i.e. very small and small.

The score is now in order.

But I'll wait with it until you come here.

Wouldn't your wife like to come too?

Ostrčil had to excuse himself since he had a new première coming up shortly in Prague (**LB39**, 1 November 1924). It seemed too, that Brod would be unable to come to the première: he was busy and wrote that he would hear *The Vixen* in Prague (**LB40**, 30 October 1924). Janáček countered by emphasizing the near-perfect casting: 'In Prague you won't hear *The Vixen* so soon and not like here. There are performers on stage as if made for every part' (**LB41**, 31 October 1924). Later, however, Janáček had second thoughts on this subject, which he passed on to Ostrčil:

Janáček to Otakar Ostrčil *Brno, 8 January 1925* **LB42**

[...] When you come to casting *The Vixen*, please put right some-thing that stuck out here in Brno:

The Cock and the Hens,

and also *Lapák* [the dog] are too big!

Cast the *chickens* with children, the Cock and the Hen and Lapák with girls about fifteen years old.

Their voices will then be well differentiated from those of the humans.

As a whole, however, Janáček was pleased with the Brno production:

Marie Stejskalová's reminiscences (1959) **LB43**

The master took great pleasure from the Brno première of *The Vixen*. He would come back from rehearsals laughing at how the singers were learning to crawl on all fours. The opera chief Neumann, the producer Zítek, and the painter Milén,[1] who designed the sets, made such a beautiful work out of the *The Vixen*, that it surprised even the master.

Janáček's enthusiasm for the Brno production led him to propose to Ostrčil that Prague take over the Brno sets and production (**LB44**, 14 February 1925), an idea Ostrčil firmly rejected:

Otakar Ostrčil to Janáček *Prague, 16 February 1925* **LB45**

It is natural that we want to solve *The Vixen* in our own way, of course fully respecting your intentions. Because of the difficulty of the problem I made arrangements some time ago and have already assigned both the production (to Pujman)[2] and the stage sets (to J. Čapek).[3] For this reason then I could not satisfy the wishes of Messrs Milén and Zítek.

A month later Čapek announced that his set and costume designs for *The Vixen* would be with Pujman for Janáček to see when he next came to Prague (**LB46**, 24 March 1925). 'I had a good time in Prague', Janáček reported to

---

1 Eduard Milén (1891–1976), painter, illustrator and stage-designer.
2 Ferdinand Pujman (1889–1961), freelance producer at the Prague National Theatre from 1921, house producer 1921–59 (with interruptions).
3 Josef Čapek (1887–1945), painter and stage-designer, brother of the writer Karel Čapek (see VM1+).

Kamila Stösslová (**LB47**, 29 March 1925). 'They already know *The Vixen* well. The designs of the painter Mr Josef Čapek will be most effective.' Ostrčil was less successful in satisfying Janáček's wishes over the casting. Janáček later commented to Brod: 'The Fox Cubs and the Hens must be a children's chorus. It was again Mr Ostrčil's arbitrary decision to let monsters on to the stage' (**LB48**, 16 June 1925).

Janáček attended the Prague rehearsals, but not as zealously as those for *Jenůfa*. Two weeks before the première he slipped down to Prague to see how things were going (**LB49**: Janáček to Zdenka Janáčková, Prague, 4 May 1925). The next day he announced to Zdenka his return on 6 May (**LB50**), and the day after that he wrote to Mrs Stösslová with his impressions:

LB51   Janáček to Kamila Stösslová   *Brno, 7 May 1925*

[. . .] The Vixen grows remarkably at the Prague National Theatre. In a week her fur-coat will already be like red gold. It will be something to laugh at. They perform it excellently. But I had to get away from Prague: those rehearsals within the gloomy walls of the theatre from morning to late afternoon, day after day, killed me with exhaustion. And outside the sun shone and the warmth spread around.

The Vixen was given in Prague on 18 May as part of the ISCM festival, which took place in Prague that year, a circumstance which led to the first radio broadcast of a Janáček opera. All concerts from the festival were being broadcast and Radiojournal, the Czech radio organization, duly applied to Janáček for his permission (**LB52**, 25 April 1925). Janáček was delighted that his première would be 'going out into the world' – 'eine gute Propaganda', he announced to Universal Edition when inquiring into conditions (**LB53**, 28 April 1925). Foreign critics were there for the festival, including Rosa Newmarch representing the *The Times* (**LB54**). A now well-established admirer and correspondent, she described the première as 'the most discussed event' of the festival. She commented enthusiastically on the orchestration, detecting – one wonders how – a 'specially constructed "occarina" [sic], [which] adds to the strange unearthly quality of the woodland voices', and hinted at what for the time being turned out to be the most frequent criticism of the work: 'The libretto evoked some impatient criticism from those who did not understand it.'[1] Fears on this count explained Brod's original lack of interest in the work when Janáček first described it to him:

LB55   Janáček to Max Brod   *Brno, 11 March 1923*

I remember one incident in my native village.

The mayor's son in a fit of passion – his sweetheart had left him –

---

1 The whole of Mrs Newmarch's review is reprinted in Janáček 1986, 83–5.

would have massacred all the wedding guests. He shot at them through the windows of the room where the wedding of his former sweetheart was being celebrated.

He was tried and sentenced.

Well, what of it? When he returned to the parish after serving his term do you think people avoided him?

No. Just as if nothing had happened.

They spoke with him and associated with him as before.

For me it was confirmation that ordinary people don't take evil as a lasting stigma. It happened – and is no more.

My Vixen Bystrouška is like that too: she stole, she throttled [chickens] but besides that she is also capable of noble thoughts.

In Act 2 she wanders about; she turned out the badger from his sett; she settled down comfortably in his warm lair. She makes merry in taverns, steals – and roguishly plays games with the Schoolmaster and the Priest, who return tipsy from the tavern.

The Vixen falls in love, genuinely in love.

The Schoolmaster proclaims his love to the sunflower in full bloom at the fence, the Priest recalls his beloved from his student days.

The Vixen Bystrouška runs everywhere through the wood.

The Forester, the last to return from the tavern, frightens her off with a wild cry – and with a shot from his rifle.

The Schoolmaster and Priest pick themselves off the ground and seek to get offstage as fast as their legs will carry them.

In Act 3 the Vixen Bystrouška now has many of her cubs around her. Family happiness.

In the forest the poultry-dealer-cum-poacher puts down his basket with the poultry he has bought. The Vixen Bystrouška plays a trick on him. She positions herself right before his eyes. Harašta goes after her with his gun. There's a chase. Meanwhile the young cubs make quick work of the poultry basket.

'Strike me, kill me just because I'm a vixen?' she shouts at the poacher. His hair stands on end when he sees nothing but the red of the Fox cubs all over his ducks in the basket. He shoots without aiming – and it's all over with the Vixen Bystrouška.

The Forester and the Schoolmaster grow old; the Priest has moved away.

It is spring in the forest – but also old age.

In a dream the forest with all its animal kingdom appears to the Forester; he looks for his Vixen Bystrouška. It's not her. But here is a tiny fox cub, just like her, toddling up to him! 'The spitting image of her mother.'

And thus good and evil turn around in life afresh.

The end. [. . .]

LB56   **Janáček to Max Brod**   *Brno, 20 March 1923*

On the way to Brno probably the most apt title occurred to me:

The Adventures of Liška Bystrouška[1]
opera-idyll

And in place of Act 1, Act 2, Act 3 I would give titles: Bystrouška caught. In the farmyard of 'Lakeside', the Forester's lodge. Bystrouška dispossesses. Bystrouška's courtship. Bystrouška brings up a family. The end of Bystrouška. [. . .]

The final version was in fact a compromise: act numbers were retained, but expanded versions of the above titles were given to designate individual scenes.

LB57   **Max Brod to Janáček**   *[Prague,] 23 March 1923*

I have read your text. To be frank it seems very strange to me. I am not yet able to relate to it, perhaps because I know so little about animals. – In any case what you have created is something most odd. Whether it is suitable for the stage – on this matter allow me to reserve judgement for the time being until I have seen the vocal score. At any rate I find the subtitle 'opera-idyll' very suitable. It will avert false expectations. – Instead of 'jednání' ['acts'] you could perhaps simply say 'scenes'.

The thoughts about good and evil with which Janáček introduced and concluded his synopsis, and the reference to spring and old age, were evidently uppermost in Janáček's mind. (Eleven days later he wrote to Stösslová, 'I caught Bystrouška for the forest and the sadness of the late years', LB17.) They help explain why into such a light-hearted subject he was prepared to introduce the Vixen's death. Other clues to Janáček's intentions for the work include the animal–human parallels that he added. Apart from Těsnohlídek's suggestive juxtaposition of the news of Terynka's engagement with the description of Bystrouška's marriage to the Fox, there is no hint of

---

1 *Lišky Bystroušky příhody* (literally: 'Of Liška Bystrouška the adventures'). Later 'příhody' was put first and the genre became simply 'opera'. In the first version of the autograph, the opera is described as a 'bajka' [fable].

this in the novel. But when Janáček read and annotated his copy of the novel he began jotting down ideas for other animal–human parallels. Many were tried and many abandoned. For instance Janáček noted 'sparrow – schoolmaster' in one place; 'schoolmaster – fox' in another. In the end he omitted the sparrows from the opera (their dialogue discussing their growing family was given over to a conversation between the Vixen and the Fox in Act 3), coupled the Schoolmaster with the Mosquito, and left the Fox without a human counterpart. Not all the parallels that survive into the opera do much more than help to reduce the size of the cast. Though there is something to be said for linking the sanctimonious Badger with the Priest, the almost random linking of the Schoolmaster with the Mosquito, or the Owl with the Forester's Wife are harder to explain. Generally, however, they could be seen as a part of Janáček's vision of the wholeness and continuity of nature.

Two years later Brod became much more receptive to the subject matter, though, as he got down to work on the German translation, he felt that the text could be improved:

Max Brod to Universal Edition   *[Prague], 2 June 1925*   **LB58**

I have already begun the translation – and hope to be able to deliver Act 1 in about a fortnight. The remainder will then follow a fortnight later. – The work is difficult. I am reading the original novella and am trying in this way (through changes, with Janáček's permission) to produce a German libretto that is clearer than the Czech.

This suggestion had an enthusiastic response from Emil Hertzka (**LB59**, 10 June 1925), which Brod then enclosed in his next letter to Janáček (**LB60**, 13 June 1925; LB62) as further pressure to allow him 'a completely free hand'. The Czech text, he wrote, 'is very poor and unclear' and needed major changes to equip it for the German stage. Brod then outlined the changes he had in mind. These were repeated more succinctly in a letter to Janáček once the translation was complete:

Max Brod to Janáček   *[Prague], 11 July 1925*   **LB61**

The translation finished today. Here I'm sending you a copy of Acts 2 and 3. – Unfortunately I have no carbon of [Act] 1. But it doesn't matter since there are only a few places changed.

On the other hand you will find in almost every line of the enclosure my efforts to make the thing (a) clearer, (b) more concentrated.

All three love-stories (of the Priest, the Schoolmaster and the Forester) are all concentrated around a single figure – that of the gypsy girl Terynka,[1] who stands as a parallel to the figure of the Vixen.

This has necessitated a number of changes which (as I believe) contribute considerably to the dramatic intensification of the text.

In the music only very few notes are slightly changed, as usual. No more than in *Jenůfa*.

I must say, frankly, that this time I am rather proud of my work – for I really believe that I have forged the text, which is confused in many ways, into a unity.

The animal scenes are less altered – but the human scenes thoroughly so. Of the animal scenes only that with the Badger is changed so as to clarify the parallels with the Priest.

In Act 1 the main change is that here as well (just as at his appearance 'byl jsem tak zmatrovaný' [vs10]) the Forester thinks not about his wife, but of Terynka. His wife comes across only as a jealous old woman. [. . .]

[LB66]

Janáček generally gave his approval, though reacted strongly against Brod's suggestion about the ending.

LB62   Max Brod to Janáček   *[Prague], 13 June 1925*

[. . .] What's to be done now with the *end*? In Prague it looked on the stage as if the Forester was going to die. Kitsch! There is absolutely no motivation for this!!! I can imagine the end as a vision of eternal love, which comforts the *Forester* – as I have intimated in the book about you (which has just come out in German).[2] Thus as a *dream* of the *eternalness* of *nature* and the *love of life*!'

[LB60]

LB63   Janáček to Max Brod   *Luhačovice, 16 June 1925*

The source of possible misunderstandings was and is the pairing
the Vixen Bystrouška – Terynka.

---

1 Těsnohlídek's Terynka in the original novel is rather more prosaic than the mysterious unseen heroine in Janáček's opera (let alone Brod's 'gypsy girl'). As in the opera she is referred to rather than seen, but far from having any great symbolic significance, is the prosperous middle-aged owner of a sweetstall.
2 Max Brod's *Leoš Janáček: život a dílo* [Life and works] (Prague, 1924) appeared in its original German in 1925. In the final sentences of the book (completed in February 1924), Brod worked in a brief reference to the Vixen's death and to the Forester's welcoming the arrival of a new brood of fox cubs.

In my conception, to which on the evidence of your letter you also incline, there is a parallel between the *symbol* (the Vixen Bystrouška) and *reality* (Terynka).

The symbol is also exhausted with the death of Liška Bystrouška; the reality does not get so far as that (Harašta marries Terynka); but certainly that end will come even to Terynka! How could it be otherwise when she marries such a layabout (Harašta)!

That *prophecy* ought to be expressed by the Forester! Perhaps in that place where he talks about the 'counterpoint' to the Schoolmaster [vs167: Brod ignored this suggestion].

Your interpretation attached to these lines of mine will explain everything; speculation will be unnecessary. So kindly elaborate this and in the new edition the Czech text will also be changed accordingly.

In the vocal score it is written that in the final scene the Forester's gun simply slips from his hand. Nothing more; let everyone work out for himself what he will.

What Mr Pujman wanted to make of it – the Forester convulsed in death throes etc., etc. – was horrible. [...]

Brod replied on 22 June 1925 (**LB64**), by which time he had sent Act 1 to Vienna. The work was giving him much pleasure, he wrote, and he outlined two suggestions for Act 2, strengthening the connections between the Badger and the Priest. One was to redesign the end of the scene between the Vixen and the Badger at the beginning of Act 2. In Těsnohlídek and Janáček the Vixen takes over the Badger's sett by fouling it; Brod thought this scenically impossible and made the Vixen ironically kiss the Badger (after having told the chorus of forest animals that the Badger/Priest had made improper suggestions to her during confirmation classes). Another was to parallel the anti-Badger animal chorus (which then helps the Vixen evict him) by an offstage chorus of angry parishioners heard briefly in the Act 2 inn scene with the repeated word 'Milostpán' ('sir'). Brod was also unhappy about the end of the opera: 'Then I would like to ask you to compose [music for] some words of the Forester *for the last page of the vocal score*, with which he could sink into rumination. To end with the Frog is impossible'.

Janáček to Max Brod   *Brno, 26 June 1925*   **LB65**

1. It's impossible for Liška Bystrouška to kiss the Badger! The reason for the scene: expropriative–communistic is the only one possible!
2. And the end of the opera! Surely it's charming when the little Frog ends it! The music is absolutely made for it. And it is original – and

the merry-go-round of life is thereby truthfully and faithfully depicted!

Also it's impossible now to insert any voice part at the very *Coda* (the music on the final page 182).[1] Just bring the curtain down here!

The enrapt Forester lets the gun slip – a milestone of life – and the little Frog proclaims a new horizon for him.

I think that the suggested words:

So kehret alles zurück,
alles in ewiger Jugendpracht!

['So everything returns, everything in the eternal splendour of youth!']

are already intelligible through the stage action.

3. On the other hand I completely agree with your proposal that on p. 69 *the second bar be repeated* and for the 'people' to be identified as the rabble ([from the] Badger [scene]) in the inserted motif [see ex. on p. 301].

Otherwise I am pleased that your 'poeticizing' is going well. But please comply with my wishes in these two places.

And Brod did, even coming round to liking the Frog, as he reported at the end of his letter of 11 July 1925 (**LB66**; LB61): 'I am very eager about your verdict. – The ending I have left unchanged. It really is, as it stands, quite charming – especially when the Forester in the previous words expresses himself a little more clearly than is the case in the Czech text. There I have also had to intervene quite energetically.'

Brod's suggestions about the offstage parishioners meant a slight adjustment to the vocal score, which had come out in the summer of 1924. The edition had been merely a Czech one: Brod's German translation was now laid under the Czech text. The original plates were retained with a few exceptions such as p. 69, which needed resetting. The offstage parishioners were inserted on this page above the existing orchestral part (the last bar before the 2/4 – this bar was then repeated). Janáček did not accept the chorus in Brod's version:

Mi - lost - pán!__   Mi - lost - pán!__

---

1 The *maestoso* section now on vs183.

and instead wrote his own:

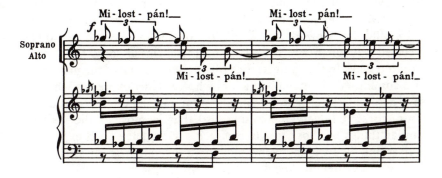

Other changes seem to be have been prompted by the Brno performances. The most important was the addition of the horn fanfares just before the Forester's final scene, presumably to help with the scene-change from the inn to the forest. Here Janáček wrote 27 new bars,[1] which resulted in the renumbering of the remaining ten pages of the vocal score. Janáček advised Universal Edition about the new passage in a letter of 6 July 1925 (**LB67**), in which he suggested that someone in Vienna could do the piano reduction from the full score. However on 25 July Universal Edition announced to Janáček that the fanfares could not be found (**LB68**) and Janáček, then in Hukvaldy in the midst of work on the Sinfonietta and *The Makropulos Affair*, wrote urgently to his wife:

Janáček to Zdenka Janáčková   *Hukvaldy, 27 July 1925*   **LB69**

[...] I am writing to Bakala to do what is still missing in the piano [score] of *The Vixen immediately*. Those fanfares! His corrections (they are lying on the piano) and the additions he should send *immediately* to Universal Edition.

I am writing to him, but best to give him the message.

Universal Edition issued a new version of the vocal score with the fanfares, and with Brod's German translation, but despite flickers of foreign interest (even in Leningrad), the only theatre to take on *The Vixen* during Janáček's lifetime was the Mainz Städtisches Theater, which gave the German première on 13 February 1927 under its music director Paul Breisach. It was not a great success, and Hertzka later reported to Janáček about its problems as he saw them:

1 One bar before the *vivo* section on VS171 up to the pause chord on VS172.

LB70   Universal Edition to Janáček   *Vienna, 9 March 1927*

We have asked the conductor of the Mainz performance of *The Vixen*, Mr Generalmusikdirektor Breisach, about the effect of the work and his view of its likelihood of success, and have today received a letter of which we pass on the enclosed copy. We would like to remark in this context that Mr Breisach is one of the most able and committed German conductors who certainly expresses what he says here only after mature consideration and the intensive study of your work. It is very regrettable also that in most of the reviews similar things to those in Mr Breisach's letter have been expressed concerning the text, and we would like to say quite frankly after these reviews and after the remarks which Mr Breisach has made to us, both in this letter as well in a personal discussion, that we do not believe that *The Vixen* will establish itself on the stage in Germany. The idea has now come up to make use of the orchestral interludes, which Mr Breisach also writes of with quite exceptional enthusiasm, for concert performances. Naturally we don't want to give any verdict on this idea for the time being, but first want to have your view. Certainly it has often been the case that orchestral interludes of this sort have had great success in the concert hall, and we would like to ask whether you consider this idea practicable and what form you would imagine such a realization would take. [. . .]

LB71   Janáček to Universal Edition   *Brno, 12 March 1927*

It's a pity I didn't see the Mainz performance of *The Vixen*.

I ran away from the Prague première.

It's a pity that Mr Breisach sees only little particles and sequences[1] in the music.

It's a pity that his singers couldn't enunciate the text well.

The orchestra in Brno and Prague played outstandingly; it wasn't necessary to reorchestrate anything at all.

The Vixen is a forest idyll; only a hint should surface of the sameness of our cycle and that of animal life.

That is enough – it is true that for most this symbolism is too little.

The much-praised interludes belong to the work, they would not work on their own; they are too short.

Nevertheless I am very thankful to Mr Breisach for his frank letter.

---

1 Hans Redlich, writing in the *Musikblättern des Anbruch*, ix/3 (1927), 136, mentions the 'division of motifs into motif-particles' and 'the principle of building up whole scenes on the basis of short sequences'.

I will endeavour to step aside from the little particles and sequences. But *The Vixen* can only eat rabbits, not romances and arias.

Janáček declined to produce an orchestral suite from *The Vixen*. A note to his pupil Břetislav Bakala inviting him to visit him in connection with *The Vixen* (LB72, 17 May 1928), however, suggests that he may have had second thoughts on the subject a year later, and was thinking of delegating the task to him. In fact it was not for another decade that a suite became available, arranged by the conductor Václav Talich in connection with the Prague revival in 1937. And it was not until the celebrated Felsenstein production at the Berlin Komische Oper in 1956 that Janáček's opera showed itself capable of appealing to foreign audiences, and began to establish itself in the international operatic repertory.

8 The Makropulos Affair

VM1   Janáček to Kamila Stösslová   *Hukvaldy, 28 December 1922*

[...] They have now been giving *Makropulos* in Prague. A woman 337 years old, but at the same time still young and beautiful. Would you like to be like that too?

And you know that she was unhappy? We are happy because we know that our life isn't long. So it's necessary to make use of every moment, to use it properly. It's all hurry in our life – and longing.

The latter is my lot. That woman – the 337-year-old beauty [–] didn't have a heart any more.

That's bad. [...]

Janáček saw Karel Čapek's play *The Makropulos Affair* in Prague on 10 December 1922, three weeks after it opened at the Vinohrady Theatre, directed by Čapek himself. Janáček kept his programme, though unusually left no annotations in it other than underlining in blue the date and the genre description 'Comedy in three acts with one scene-change. Written by Karel Čapek'.[1] He did, however, note the date in his diary, taking down a speech melody on the embankment of the National Theatre, and seems to have overheard Čapek too, since another speech melody, labelled 'in the theatre at *Makropulos*', records Čapek's virtually monotone delivery of the unlikely phrase 'jelito krevní' ['blood sausage'].[2]

Karel Čapek (1890–1938) was then thirty-two, already very successful locally as a writer and soon to make his European reputation (he was the only Czech writer, apart from Jaroslav Hašek, the creator of *The Good Soldier Schweik*, to win international recognition between the wars). Čapek's English reputation was established the next year, 1923, when his two best-known plays, *R.U.R.* (1920; = Rossum's Universal Robots) and *The Life of the Insects* (1921, written with his brother Josef), both received London productions. By the time Čapek went to England in 1924 he was a well-known figure, cordially received by authors such as Shaw, Wells, Chesterton and Galsworthy. Though *The Makropulos Affair* appeared in English only in 1927 (staged in 1930), news of the play had already reached England; Edith

1 BmJA, Programy Národního divadla v Praze.
2 BmJA, Z56, pp.137 and 145.

Evans, whom Čapek saw in her celebrated portrayal of Millamant in Congreve's *Way of the World*, told him of her interest in the title role.

Many of Čapek's plays and novels deal with science-fiction themes: atomic fission, the world taken over by giant newts, or by robots (a word he introduced from Czech into the international vocabulary). In *The Makropulos Affair* Čapek deals with longevity. Elina Makropulos, a young Cretan girl born in 1575, has been given, experimentally, an 'elixir of life' devised by her father, court physician to Rudolf II, the last Habsburg ruler to keep his court in Prague. The potion worked, and Elina has lived out her long life as a singer, working in different countries, changing her name from time to time. She is now back in Prague, the sensation of the moment, billed as 'Emilia Marty'. She has remained young and beautiful all these years and is fascinating and attractive to everyone who meets her. But her heart has died, and her life has become a burden. She is also aware that her 300-year span is drawing to its close, and, fearing death even more than life, she needs to take the potion again, the formula of which she had given to a former lover. The action of the play, which collides with the final stages of a centuries-old court case, concerns her attempt to recover it. The 'věc' of the Czech title means simply 'thing' and refers ambiguously perhaps to the document with the formula or more likely to the whole 'affair' connected with it.

At the time, the play was considered an answer to Shaw's *Back to Methuselah*, which had also appeared in 1922 and which postulated that an increased life-span would result in increased wisdom and happiness. Čapek, who came to the opposite conclusion in his play, dismissed any connections with Shaw: he had had the idea for some years, he wrote in the preface, and originally had intended it as a novel. Within a few months of seeing the play Janáček was in touch with Karel Čapek about the rights. Janáček's letters to Čapek are lost (he gave them to a collector),[1] but Janáček kept Čapek's answers.

Karel Čapek to Janáček

[undated, postmarked Prague, VM2
27 February 1923]

As I have already told you, I have too high an opinion of music – and especially of yours – to be able to imagine it united with a *conversational*, fairly unpoetical and over-garrulous play, as is my *Makropulos Affair*. I fear that you have in mind something different and something better than what my piece can really provide – apart from that 300–year-old character. But there is no need to pay regard to these sincere doubts of mine; what is worse – as I have found out from my agent, František Khol[2] – is that I am constrained in this

1 JA ix, 177, fn.329.
2 František Khol (1877–1930), writer, dramaturg at the Prague National Theatre 1915–25, and owner of the theatrical agency Centrum, which represented Čapek's interests.

regard, namely by a contract with the American (and world-wide) agent Hans Bartsch,[1] to whom I had to guarantee, as is common practice, that for ten years the work would not be filmed or set to music. I think that this clause of the contract cannot be changed.

But on the other hand, dear Maestro, there is nothing to prevent you, without regard to my piece, devising an action where a 300-year-old life and its sufferings would be the pivot and centre within a more suitable framework than my piece affords. After all it's not my patent; as a basis you could use Ahasuerus [the wandering Jew], the witch from Langer's tale (in the collection *Murderers and Dreamers*),[2] and even Miss Makropulos, and adapt the action quite independently yourself and also – insofar as you have told me about your inspiration – just as you see the material. After all you have no need of a long tale about a law case, about a lost formula, and its use etc. In all this, my text would have to be changed so extensively that it is already perhaps more profitable not to stick to it and to create your own conditions. I repeat that I do not consider the fiction of an eternal or 300-year-old person as my literary property and that therefore nothing stands in the way of your using this fiction in your own manner.

To his sister, Helena (1886–1962), Čapek was rather more frank. Janáček knew her from Brno, where she worked in the editorial offices of the *Lidové noviny*, and it may have been her suggestion that put Čapek into Janáček's mind in the first place, as a chance remark Janáček made in a letter to Max Brod indicates: 'Do you know Čapek? *R.U.R., The Life of the Insects*. His sister said something about a libretto.' (VM3, 22 August 1922; LB12). Janáček seems to have approached her to act as go-between over *The Makropulos Affair*.

VM4   Helena Čapková: *My Dear Brothers* (1962)

When, through me, Leoš Janáček asked him [Karel Čapek] for permission to make a libretto for a new opera from the play himself in

---

1 1884–1952.

2 František Langer (1888–1965); his collection of short stories *Dreamers and Murderers* (Čapek muddled the title) came out in 1921 and included one called 'Eternal youth', which describes a woman who has lived for about two centuries (from the Council of Trent to 1608), but who has remained in the prime of youth. Every generation she changes her name and moves somewhere else. Her secret, which she learnt from an old hag, is to bathe in the blood of an innocent girl-child. This ten-page tale has the effect of a thriller (the last murder is described in great detail) and there is none of the philosophical speculation found in Čapek.

his own way, Karel simply brushed it aside and grumbled: 'That old crank! Soon he'll even be setting the local column in the newspaper. It's good that he is not asking me to help him with it; I don't feel like working up a libretto from it, I probably wouldn't bring it off, I don't have the time, and even if I had, I wouldn't even want to do it.'

Perhaps because of Čapek's rather discouraging news about the rights Janáček did not immediately settle on *The Makropulos Affair* as the subject of his next opera. He was still working hard on *The Cunning Little Vixen* [LB15+ff] and there was another competitor, the play *The Child* (1923), by the Czech writer František Xaver Šalda (1867–1937). This recent play had come with a warm recommendation from Max Brod, who saw parallels in it with *Jenůfa*.[1] Janáček dutifully took a copy of it on holiday with him to the Slovak mountain resort of Štrbské Pleso and made his usual annotations in the book, beginning with the date '10 July 1923' on the title page.[2] But he also took *The Makropulos Affair*[3] and began reading it that same day, duly noting his surroundings from time to time, for instance (at the end of Act 1) the 'gigantic flies' whose low buzzing he captured with a few tremolo notes in his copy of the play. The sun set as he got to p. 42 and Janáček took up the play the next morning, 11 July (a date on p. 46), reaching the end with the annotation '11 July 1923, Štrbské Pleso'. Apart from noting the wild life, Janáček made a few encouraging comments along the way: he liked the idea that Emilia Marty got drunk (p. 70), and decided that Gregor would be a tenor virtually at his first speech. By the end of his holiday he had rejected *The Child* for its stilted diction (he scribbled 'it's not alive, it's artificial' in his copy) and decided in favour of *Makropulos*. He described this decision later in an interview:[4]

[VM61]

Adolf Veselý: 'Chats with Leoš Janáček' VM5

It captivated me immediately, when I saw the repeat of Čapek's play in Brno. It's true that, as with everything else, I went off to the Tatra mountains or to Luhačovice. At Štrbské Pleso it occupied my thoughts. I was also taken by Šalda's *The Child* – I hesitated and decided: the modern historical opera, as it is called, won the contest.

Národní listy (20 October 1925)

---

1 See JA ix, 124–6; Straková 1955, 443–4.
2 Straková 1955, 443.
3 Janáček's annotated copy of the play is in BmJA, L 26.
4 This is a longer version of what Janáček had already told Veselý while dictating his autobiography (1924), 99. A much later version, published in *Literární svět* (8 March 1928, just after the Prague première), goes on to comment on how fast it all went ('like a machine'), and that he laid particular store on Act 3 and its climactic effect.

The Makropulos Affair won the contest from a position of weakness since Janáček still needed permission to set it.[1] Some time after his July trip to Štrbské Pleso he wrote to Čapek again for permission, possibly stressing the fact that he would be setting the piece in Czech, which would hardly affect Bartsch's rights in America.

VM6   **Janáček to Rosa Newmarch**   *Brno, 3 August 1923*

[. . .] I am searching in vain for a libretto for a new opera. I cannot reach an understanding with Karel Čapek; he has a nice thing [called] *The Makropulos Affair*.

And when I do not have ideas for a new work, I am like an empty shell.

VM7   **Karel Čapek to Janáček**   *Prague, 10 September 1923*

Forgive me that I have not replied for so long to your letter concerning *The Makropulos Affair*. I have been waiting for my agent [see p. 305 fn.2], who was on his travels and without whom I did not want to do anything.

I must say I think that the American agent (the owner of the world rights) cannot make objections to a musical setting in Czech. You are consequently free to make use of my piece for a musical setting; and because I myself would simply not get round to any sort of reworking or revision, I therefore give you the right to arrange my text as you need.

I would have liked to have given you something better to set than this particular piece; but if you are drawn to it, you will surely make something great from it, and from my whole heart I most fervently wish you much happiness.

PS   Kindly agree conditions with my agent Engineer František Khol, Prague VII, Nad Rudolfovou štolou 6.

Khol's conditions, which he announced in a letter to Janáček of 24 September 1923 (**VM8**), were steep: 33% of performance receipts and 50% of anything printed where Čapek's text appears. Janáček's draft reply (**VM9**, 28 September) asked for clarification: was the 33% to be taken from the composer's standard 10% performance royalty? He also asked for it to be lowered to 30% in view of the lack of permission for foreign-language rights, a condition to which Khol acceded when he sent the contract on 10 October 1923 (**VM10**).

1 It also turned out that Šalda would not have granted him permission to set *The Child* (JA ix, 125, fn.196).

Three days after receiving the contract Janáček announced to Kamila Stösslová that: 'I will compose [a piece] about a beautiful woman and one who is already 300 years old – and who does not want anyone' (**VM11**, 13 October 1923). The work began a little later, on 11 November 1923, judging by the first date on Janáček's autograph score.[1]

Janáček to Kamila Stösslová   *Brno, 12 November 1923*   **VM12**

[...] I have begun a new work and so no longer have time on my hands.

A 300-year-old beauty – and eternally young – but only burnt-out feeling! Brrr! Cold as ice! About such a woman I shall write an opera. [...]

Janáček to Max Brod   *[undated, Brno, winter 1923–4]*   **VM13**

[...] I already have around 200 pages of *The Makropulos Affair*; you know this time it just flies along unrestrained. Heaps of motifs; how to draw them together I will see only at the end of Act 1. But for the holidays I will nevertheless go off to the Tatra mountains. That white, silent, snowy covering, as far as the eye can see, forces a fellow to be silent and to think. [...]

Janáček's reference to the 'holidays' suggests Christmas and New Year, thus dating this letter to late December 1923. But unless he got the number of pages wrong, or the 'flying along' got considerably slower, he was more likely to have got to p. 200 (out of 269) in January 1924, since he completed his first version of Act 1 only on 19 February 1924. He began Act 2 on 19 March 1924.

Janáček to Kamila Stösslová   *Brno, 4 December 1923*   **VM14**

[...] I am now doing that brrr! But I will warm her up, so that people sympathize with her. I might still fall in love with her. [...]

After a summer break, Act 3 was completed by 18 February 1925 (or perhaps a day or two later, in the light of VM18).

---

1 BmJA, A7422. This score is the source of all subsequent dates of composition given below. The dates that Janáček himself supplied (15 August 1924–15 November 1926) in a letter to Universal Edition (19 November 1926; see Janáček 1988, 285–6) are less reliable. The completion date may be that of final adjustments during rehearsals, but by 15 August 1924 he had already completed the first version of Acts 1–2.

VM15   **Janáček to Kamila Stösslová**   *Brno, 5 February 1925*

[...] I am now a merry fellow again and hard at my work. I am now near the end of that 300-year-old beauty.

She is already freezing with horror – and doesn't want to live any longer when she sees how happy we are, we who have such a short life. We look forward to everything, we want to make use of everything – our life is so short.

That part of my opera is touching. I think that I will be finished with it by Easter. [...]

VM16   **Janáček to Max Brod**   *Brno, 13 February 1925*

[...] I am now finishing the final scene of *The Makropulos Affair* – nevertheless 'children's rhymes'[1] with their melodic and harmonic somersaults get into my fingers [holding] the pen. [...]

VM17   **Janáček to Kamila Stösslová**   *Brno, 15 February 1925*

[...] With my cold 300-year-old one there can only be serious talk. But I won't stay at home with her. She is, it's true, near to my heart – but when I have finished with her that will be a load off my mind.

VM18   **Janáček to Kamila Stösslová**   *Brno, 19 February 1925*

[...] When in the next few days I finish my 300-year-old beauty, I fear that I shall – be sad.

VM19   **Janáček to Kamila Stösslová**   *Brno, 23 February 1925*

[...] I am now as in a trance. I've finished the 300-year-old; but now comes the worst work: copying it out. I would like to teach you to paste over the crossed-out stuff, to square it up, tear off, replace – then it would go quickly for me. [...]

To 'finish his 300-year-old' meant of course merely finishing the first version. Janáček was right in his letter to Brod (VM13) to draw attention to the many motifs. His well-established routine was to make a continuous draft – basically a written-down improvisation – in which a large number of themes would be generated. In the second version he would abandon many of these and instead work more systematically with a select number, drawing them together. The graphic description in his letter to Kamila Stösslová (VM19) of

---

1 A reference to Janáček's *Nursery Rhymes* for nine voices and chamber ensemble, which he is thought to have begun composing in summer 1925.

his 'scissors-and-paste' approach sounds more fastidious than his usual methods suggest. There was much crossing-out, writing over and replacing; rather less squaring up and tearing off.

Janáček to Kamila Stösslová   *Brno, 3 March 1925*   **VM20**

[. . .] What to do with that 300-year-old! They take her for a liar, a fraud, a hysterical woman – and at the end she was so unhappy! After that, I want everyone to like her. Without love it won't work for me.

After a short break, the tidying up began on 15 March 1925. The autograph does not make clear when Act 1 was completed in this way. However the end of Act 2 is dated 27 July 1925. Janáček's comment to Kamila Stösslová on 9 July (VM21) that 'at Hukvaldy I want to "tidy up" Act 2 of that cold one' suggests that the revision of this act had not started any earlier.

Janáček to Kamila Stösslová   *Hukvaldy, 12 July 1925*   **VM22**

[. . .] I will stay here about a month. I work here easily; as I have already written to you, I want to have Act 2 of 'that cold one' cleaned up, so as to have peace then in Brno. [. . .]

Janáček to Zdenka Janáčková   *Hukvaldy, 24 July 1925*   **VM23**

[. . .] I work diligently in the mornings; I'm still lacking two scenes, naturally the longest ones. [. . .]

Janáček to Kamila Stösslová   *Hukvaldy, 27 July 1925*   **VM24**

[. . .] I have finished tidying up Act 2 of that 'icy one'.
  Eternally beautiful – everyone falls in love with her -
  anyone would die for her –
  oh, what a muddle it is! But I sorted it out. [. . .]

There was another break before he revised Act 3. This was done by 12 November, and a final revision is indicated by more dates at the end of the opera, 27 November 1925 and 3 December 1925, the last corroborated by a letter two days later:

Janáček to Kamila Stösslová   *Brno, 5 December 1925*   **VM25**

[. . .] I'm finished with *The Makropulos Affair*. Poor 300-year-old beauty! People thought she was a thief, a liar, an unfeeling animal. 'Beast', 'canaille' they called her, they wanted to strangle her – and her fault? That she had to live long.

I was sorry for her. Three years of work at an end. What now?

PUBLICATION

'What now?' probably referred to further creative plans. As far as *The Makropulos Affair* was concerned, there was now the question of publication and an immediate consideration of whether to enter it in an opera competition in Philadelphia:

VM26   Janáček to Universal Edition   *Brno, 14 January 1926*

In 1926 there is a World Exhibition in Philadelphia. They have also announced competition prizes for an opera, symphony etc. Should I take part in it with the opera
                    The Makropulos Affair?
Is there not someone already chosen? Mascagni?
The deadline – four months – is incomprehensible.
In four months one surely cannot produce an opera in full score – [and] vocal score!
It would be tempting to win. But my method is:
to let finished work lie for a little while,
them look it through again,
then during the rehearsals make any necessary corrections.
All that would be impossible by 1 February.
And to fail, even though in America, that I also wouldn't like.
Can you find out any further details?
I am sending you the *Šárka* contract at the same time.
We will talk about *The Makropulos Affair* when the fair copy of the score is before me.
    [...]

PS   I must still speak with 'Centrum' (the agent of Karel Čapek, the librettist) concerning *The Makropulos Affair*.

                                                                    [SR36]

The music competition was organized by the organist of St Clement's Church, and was offering a prize of $3,000 for the best opera, to be delivered by 1 March 1926.[1] Janáček did not take part. Universal Edition believed that

---

1 Janáček 1988, 250.

it was technically unfeasible and did not recommend entrusting the work to an 'anonymous company' (**VM27**, 16 January 1926).

Janáček to Universal Edition   *Brno, 22 January 1926*   **VM28**

In 1923 I entered into negotiations with the writer Dr Čapek.

His agent made the enclosed contract with me.

They are tough conditions.

Would you be so kind as to read them through and lower it to an acceptable percentage.

Not 70–30%.

Not 50–50%.

Dr Čapek is understanding, and is prepared to make a new agreement.

Translations are ready in all languages.

But the German translation is not much use. Dr Brod would have to rework it according to the music.

I will request the proceeds of the libretto be given to Dr Čapek, those of the vocal scores to me.

The full score would not be published?

I await a prompt answer and the return of the contract Dr Čapek–Janáček. [. . .]

Hertzka of Universal Edition considered the contract unfavourable for Janáček and offered to act on his behalf (**VM29**, 25 January 1926). This resulted in Khol's sending an amended contract to Janáček on 2 April 1926 (**VM30**). Janáček's own contract with Universal Edition was signed a few months later (**VM31**, undated, 16 July 1926) with only a few changes, including the demand for 5% for his contribution to the libretto.

Preparations for printing the vocal score proceeded equally smoothly. Universal Edition received the manuscript vocal score (made by Janáček's pupil Ludvík Kundera) on 19 June 1926 (**VM32**) and on 9 September announced to Janáček that engraving had begun (**VM33**). Proofs, originally promised in time for the Brno rehearsals (**VM34**: Universal Edition to Janáček, 25 October 1926), were however sent only at the beginning of December (**VM35**: Universal Edition to Janáček, 3 December 1926). On 15 December 1926 (**VM36**), just a few days before the Brno première, Universal Edition despatched to Janáček ten copies of the vocal score and five copies of the Czech libretto.

The vocal score contained Max Brod's German translation. Janáček had originally suggested that all it needed was for someone to adapt the standard German translation of the play (**VM37**: Janáček to Universal Edition, 7 June 1926). This was an unrealistic suggestion and, anyway, Universal Edition was keen to employ Brod once again to hasten the work's arrival on the

German stage (**VM38**: Universal Edition to Janáček, 10 June 1926). Brod was a fast worker. As he reported to Janáček on 19 October 1926 (**VM39**), he aimed to finish Act 1 by the end of the week, having received the score a few days earlier. Within the allotted time he had sent Act 1 to Universal Edition, promising the complete translation in 'two to three weeks' (**VM40**: Brod to Janáček, 22 October 1926). As usual he insisted on 'clarifying' passages which had become unclear in Janáček's hasty adaptation (**VM41**: Brod to Janáček, 25 October 1926). Janáček, who had made a number of changes to *Káťa Kabanová* on Brod's urging (KK80 to KK84), and had even permitted Brod to make a far-reaching adaptation of his Czech text in *The Cunning Little Vixen* (LB60 to LB66+), this time attempted to stand his ground.[1] In particular he resisted Brod's attempt to sort out the confusion that might arise between the two 'envelopes' (one containing the contested will and another containing the recipe for the miraculous elixir of life) on the sensible grounds that the changes Brod proposed would need to be reflected in the music and he had no intention of writing any more (**VM42**: Janáček to Brod, 9 November 1926). After the première he announced in a lengthy letter to Brod (**VM43**, 2 January 1927), that he had been made aware 'from several quarters' of considerable freedom in his translation of Act 3 and proceeded to list fifty-two discrepancies. Brod was somewhat taken aback by this (**VM44**, 4 January 1927), and over the next month conceded eleven of Janáček's demands (**VM45**: Universal Edition to Janáček, 7 February 1927). Janáček was hardly satisfied. Although the changes could be incorporated in the German libretto (which came out in January 1928), there was nothing to be done about the printed vocal score. As Janáček complained to Universal Edition (**VM46**, 18 February 1927), Brod's adaptation harmed not only Janáček, but also Čapek, whose words had directly inspired his music. Brod's changes did not fit the music at all: why could he not simply translate? Janáček's relations with Brod remained cool ever after.

PRODUCTION

At the end of a letter which told Kamila Stösslová of his plans to travel to England, of the forthcoming première of the Sinfonietta and the unveiling of a memorial plaque at his birthplace, Janáček also announced: 'And yesterday I submitted my 300-year-old to the theatre' (**VM47**, 24 April 1926). Janáček's pre-eminent position in Brno musical life and his good working relationship with the conductor and producer at the Brno Theatre over several premières of his operas did not mean that things now ran entirely smoothly. The new opera made more musical demands than his earlier works, and no doubt this led, once rehearsals got under way in the autumn,

---

1 These exchanges are described in more detail in Susskind 1985, 100–5 and in JA ix, 204–20.

to the odd caustic comment and possible threat of changes or cancellation, duly reported back to Janáček by one of his copyists, Hynek Svozil.[1]

František Neumann to Janáček   *Brno, 7 October 1926*   **VM48**

Mr Svozil is not an executive organ of the director and neither of his communications is based on the truth.

No-one has stopped rehearsing *The Makropulos Affair* and Mr Zítek is not making any changes. If any such changes will be necessary I will make them myself after agreeing them with you.

Ota Zítek to Janáček   *Brno, 16 November 1926*   **VM49**

From several quarters I have been asked for an essay, analysis and lecture about your *Makropulos Affair* (Philharmonic Club, Hudební matice, [*Die*] *Musik*).[2] I am, of course, quite well informed about the work, but I feel it my duty to find out from you if you have any special remarks that perhaps I have still missed. Permit me nevertheless to inquire, despite the fact that I feel in recent times an inexplicable grudge from your side towards me; kindly let me know, perhaps by phone at the theatre, when in the afternoon in the next few days I might visit you, or whether you could come sometime towards noon to the theatre, since we would have the full score and piano scores to hand.

Janáček to Ota Zítek   *Brno, 16 November 1926*   **VM50**

What sort of rumour is this? What grudge? I am grateful to you for your work on *Šárka*, *The Vixen*, on *The Excursion*. I have said this publicly.

And I think that in *The Makropulos Affair* you will approach the work in the same happy way.

Copyists whispered to me that you have been retouching, correcting the score of *Makropulos*. To that I said simply: surely not!

In the next few days the corrected print of the vocal score will arrive. Let's wait for it. A discussion will be easier.

Yesterday I sent back the final proofs of Act 3.

Having been originally announced for 11 December 1926 (**VM51**: Janáček to Universal Edition, 22 October 1926), the première was then projected for 17

---

1 Hynek Svozil (?-1933), second violinist at the Brno National Theatre 1910–19, then archivist there 1919–33 (Krtička, 100).
2 Zítek published articles about *The Cunning Little Vixen*, but seems not in the end to have published anything on *The Makropulos Affair*.

December (**VM52**: Janáček to Kamila Stösslová, 23 November 1926). In the event it took place on 18 December 1926, with rehearsals in full swing in November. As usual, Janáček made last-minute adjustments to the orchestration.

VM53   Janáček to Jaroslav Ušák[1]   *[undated, Brno, ? December 1926]*

You know about that solo for the third trombone? We added half a bar at its beginning in the strings, then another half bar.[2]

Please write it into the parts; I wrote it then in pencil into the full score. And yesterday I didn't hear it.

VM54   Janáček to Kamila Stösslová   *Brno, 14 December 1926*

[...] These have been bad days for me. It's the last rehearsals for that 'icy one'; I thought that the theatre was not up to it. Even the 'icy one' didn't want to warm herself up for this role. It was agony to listen to the scraping for a whole week. Now it's going well and the 'icy one' has warmed up.

[...]

The theatre is sold out, and I don't know myself where I will be. Apart from this opera I have finished another three works;[3] it struck me how the greatest work should finish now with me. [...]

VM55   Janáček to Universal Edition   *Brno, 17 December 1926*

So the rehearsals have ended and I believe that the performance will be successful.

Enclosed are insertions for the *full score* – the *vocal score remains unchanged*.

When one hears one's things, here and there [extra] filling in the orchestra occurs to one.

I will send you some more smaller insertions in the orchestra.

And now about the dynamic marks:

A larger theatre, a larger orchestra needs different markings. The main thing is: *not to drown the singers!*

For the theatre here Conductor Neumann took trouble and put in

---

1 Jaroslav Ušák (1891–66), trombonist and writer. He was a member of the Brno National Theatre orchestra 1921–40.
2 Possibly the repeated figure in the bass at Act 2, figure 28 (vs87).
3 The Sinfonietta (completed 1 April 1926), the Glagolitic Mass (completed 15 October 1926) and the Capriccio for piano left hand and chamber orchestra (completed 30 October 1926).

dynamic phrasings into his full score.

Should one take them over into the Vienna full score?

Will someone from Universal Edition be present at the performance on Saturday [18 December]?[1]

Then one could discuss the matter and decide.

The clean copy of the vocal score has not yet arrived here.

Ludvík Kundera: 'Janáček's *The Makropulos Affair*' VM56

I remember the joyful première of *The Makropulos Affair*. We all felt at the time that a great artistic work had been born here, which we would continue to admire more and more, which would excite us for a long time yet, and the longer the more so. And amongst us a highly delighted Janáček! He praised Neumann and his orchestra, he praised the main characters, especially the unforgettable Alexandra Čvanová[2] for her poetic and *mondaine* qualities, the excellent tenor Olšovský[3] and others. But again and again he returned to the performance of Mrs Ježićová,[4] who took the quite tiny part of the Cleaning Lady, and in particular to the manner with which she 'spoke' her few words. What he appreciated in it was that her *parlando* preserved the exact musical notation, but at the same time was completely natural.

Opery Leoše Janáčka na brněnské scéně, ed. Václav Nosek (1958)

Janáček to Kamila Stösslová Brno, 21 December 1926 VM57

That 'icy one' had unsuspected success! To the extent that everybody had cold shivers down their spines. They say it is my greatest work.

But it's still possible to go higher!

Have a nice Christmas!

---

1 Hans Heinsheimer from Universal Edition was present at the première (Janáček 1988, 291).

2 Alexandra Čvanová (1897–1939) joined the Brno company in 1926, having made a great impression at a guest appearance as Tatyana in *Eugene Onegin*. The title role in *The Makropulos Affair* was one of the many demanding parts she took on in Brno. Later she was to be an outstanding Káťa.

3 Emil Olšovský (1890–1945), was a member of the Brno company 1911–17, 1923–44, singing most of the *Heldentenor* repertory (Prague borrowed him for Siegfried). An experienced Janáček singer (he sang Laca in *Jenůfa* for the 1913 revival in Brno), he was the first Tichon in *Káťa Kabanová*, Gregor in *The Makropulos Affair* and Luka in *From the House of the Dead*.

4 Jelena Ježićová (1894–1934), contralto of Croatian birth. She settled in Moravia at the end of the First World War and from 1923 to 1930 was one of the mainstays of the Brno company.

VM58   Janáček to the Brno Orchestra   *Brno, 24 December 1926*

Gentlemen, during the first rehearsals I went down the steps of the theatre like Jeremiah amongst the ruins of Jerusalem.

I flushed hot at the thought that you would not bring it off, and that I had not brought it off. We walked past one another without speaking.

And nevertheless you brought it off superbly under Neumann's baton – and well, I brought it off too.

I thank you for your performance.

VM59   Janáček to Ota Zítek   *Brno, 24 December 1926*

A single new chord, if it is a bleeding knot of emotions, will save a composition: your idea of a cast shadow in Act 2 lifted the mystery of Emilia Marty to unsuspected heights.

Thank you for all your work with *The Makropulos Affair* but especially for that idea of yours.

You helped the work.

VM60   Ota Zítek: unpublished memoirs of Janáček

He regarded *The Makropulos Affair* as his most dramatic work. Emilia Marty should be a beauty with burnt-out feeling, ice. He required little movement but nevertheless she had to be passionate in such a way that people felt sympathy with her. For 300 years she has held on only as an immobile mummy; her fault was that she had to live a long time. It is necessary to depict on stage the fear of a woman who will never have an end. 'Would it not be possible in the long run to make her a weeping stone, an immobile statue from whose eyes tears trickle down?'

In contrast to the heady lyricism of *Káťa Kabanová*, the melody of *The Cunning Little Vixen* redolent of the forest, there was a great new problem. Tunes were not to be developed, he wanted those short, aphoristic little motifs to coincide with the aphoristic movement of people. He also demanded something similar during the rehearsals for *The Excursion of Mr Brouček to the Moon*.[1] Everyone had to be excited by the presence of Emilia, thus these short, terse little motifs. [...] Only Kristina is someone of a different type from the others [...] because she is a woman in love. Dr Kolenatý was to be a

[1] The Brno première of this single *Excursion*, with Zítek as producer, took place on 15 June 1926, seven months before the première of *The Makropulos Affair*.

cynic, Gregor choleric.[1] The opera *The Makropulos Affair* was above all to be theatre, music theatre, and not stage music.

Helena Čapková: *My Dear Brothers* (1962)   VM61

[Karel Čapek] came to the Brno première of the opera. And how charmed and pleased he was! The piece, which he had not thought about for ages, turned out nobly, even magnificently, in Janáček's nice arrangement and splendid music, and the performance was outstanding. Karel simply glowed, drinking mutual toasts with the Maestro at our [offices].

'He did it a hundred times better than I could ever have even imagined!', he proclaimed. But that tireless one [i.e. Janáček] was now looking elsewhere, far ahead.

[VM4]

Janáček to Kamila Stösslová   *Brno, 28 January 1927*   VM62

[...] Well now, she [the 'icy one'] is liked in spite of it all, and universally. Those outfits of hers! In Act 1 a sort of greenish fur as a lining. Those pearls and long gold earrings [!] In Act 2 a white fur, a long train, in Act 3 a dress made out of gold, as if out of gold scales. What a sight! And everyone falls in love with her. Yes, it will be in Prague, in Berlin. Plzeň also wants it; I still don't know if they will be up to it.
[...]
So come and see that 'icy one' in Prague; perhaps you will see your photograph.[2] [...]

After the successful performance of *Káťa Kabanová* at the Berlin Städtische Oper (31 May 1926), both Berlin opera houses, the Staatsoper and the Städtische Oper, competed for Janáček's latest opera (**VM63**: Janáček to Universal Edition, 3 June 1926). The favourites were Erich Kleiber and the Staatsoper, who had given the Berlin première of *Jenůfa* in 1923; on 27 January 1927 Universal Edition received their acceptance of the conditions (**VM64**: Universal Edition to Janáček), promising a production 'in the next season'. By the end of the year Universal Edition announced to Janáček that

1 Albert Gregor, awaiting the outcome of a court case over his family's claims to a vast estate, falls passionately in love with Emilia Marty. The cynical Dr Kolenatý is his lawyer; Kristina, at the beginning of her career as a singer, is the daughter of Dr Kolenatý's clerk.
2 Janáček suggested an alternative model in the feuilleton 'It's dusk' (1928): a 'lady from Kounicová avenue' (where the Brno Conservatory was), with 'an icy, beautiful face', and wearing 'a fur coat as black as if it had been shed by the moles themselves'.

it was in rehearsal at Berlin (**VM65**, 13 December 1927); the première was scheduled for May (**VM66**: Janáček to Kamila Stösslová, 30 April 1928). At the last moment the production was cancelled, allegedly because Barbara Kemp[1] refused to sing the principal part;[2] the German première was eventually conducted by Josef Krips (1902–74) at Frankfurt on 14 February 1929, six months after Janáček's death.

Prague, however, produced the work during Janáček's lifetime. Almost a year before the Brno première of *The Makropulos Affair* and during the tense correspondence with Janáček over *Šárka*, Ostrčil had 'look[ed] forward to' Janáček's new opera and declared that it would be 'an honour if [Janáček] were to entrust it to the National Theatre in Prague for its first performance' (sr41, 31 January 1926). Ostrčil was not allowed the première, and at one stage Janáček did not want him to have the piece at all if he were not prepared to take on *Šárka* as well (see sr42–5). After the Brno première Ostrčil asked again for the opera (**VM67**, 13 January 1927). Janáček acceded, but urged him to see the Brno production in order to 'understand the reason for some of [his] wishes' (**VM68**, 19 January 1927), an idea he elaborated during a further exchange of letters.

VM69   Janáček to Otakar Ostrčil   *Brno, 27 January 1927*

[. . .] There are many things which I will have to fill in, to draw attention to; it would be good if you had your own vocal score with you.

I think that every further production of *The Makropulos Affair* ought to get more perfect.

And it is advisable to point out and sort out those passages in which it has to be [perfected].

This meeting presumably took place, since Janáček reported on 9 February to Universal Edition (**VM70**) that Ostrčil had been to Brno hear *The Makropulos Affair*.

VM71   Janáček to Otakar Ostrčil   *Hukvaldy, 20 February 1927*

Universal Edition informs me that you are thinking of giving *The Makropulos Affair* next season and are asking to know conditions.

I have told Universal Edition that it is necessary [for you] to make an agreement separately with them and with me.

At the same time I indicated what I would want.

It was the production in particular which failed in *Káťa Kabanová* [and] in *The Cunning Little Vixen* in Prague.

---

1 German soprano (1881–1959), leading soprano at Berlin 1913–32.
2 Vogel 1963, 315; Vogel 1981, 332.

Therefore in this respect I would like to reserve a decisive influence for myself in *The Makropulos Affair*.

Otakar Ostrčil to Janáček   *Prague, 8 June 1927*   VM72

I would like to make a start on studying *The Makropulos Affair* before the holidays. Since you had some wishes regarding the production please let me know which of our producers you would like. At your disposal are the following gentlemen: Munclinger, Pollert and Pujman.

Janáček had disliked Ferdinand Pujman's production of *The Cunning Little Vixen* in Prague (see LB63), so the choice was between Emil Pollert (1877–1935), a bass at the National Theatre who had also begun producing operas in 1921, and Josef František Munclinger (1888–1954). Munclinger was another converted bass, but Janáček already knew his work as a producer from the production of *Káťa Kabanová* in Bratislava in 1923, which he had seen and liked.[1] Munclinger was permanently engaged at the National Theatre from 1925, and had also produced the 1926 revival of *Jenůfa* and was accordingly chosen for the première of *The Makropulos Affair* (no answer to Ostrčil's letter survives.)

First reports from Prague were that the première would be at the beginning of January (VM73: Janáček to Kamila Stösslová, 24 November 1927). This was much too optimistic, and it was only on a visit to Prague on 13 December 1927 that Janáček found out about the casting: 'the very best', as he reported to Kamila that day (VM74). After the contretemps over *Šárka*, there seems to have been much less official communication with Janáček over rehearsals. It was only through a chance meeting with a member of the orchestra during another trip to Prague that he discovered that 'the whole orchestra is already playing Act 2' (VM75: Janáček to Zdenka Janáčková, undated, ?11 February 1928). Soon afterwards, Ostrčil made contact again:

Otakar Ostrčil to Janáček   *Prague, 15 February 1928*   VM76

In the material for *The Makropulos Affair* which we got from Vienna, there are children's drums rewritten for xylophone. Please let me know what you would like here. The première is set for 1 March, orchestral rehearsals for 23, 24, 27 and 28 February. We should be pleased if you would honour us with your presence.

---

1 JA ii, 72.

VM77 **Janáček to Otakar Ostrčil** *Hukvaldy, 17 February 1928*

They are ordinary children's drums, toys.

They can be got hold of easily, cheaply; *just so that they make a sound at least approximating the notation.*[1]

Forget the xylophone!

It was Janáček's original plan to go to some of the rehearsals, but not however to attend the première. He intended to send his wife there instead as his 'representative' (**VM78**): Janáček to Kamila Stösslová, 17 February 1928), an idea that he had proposed to Zdenka a few days earlier (in VM75), but the course of the rehearsals changed his mind.

VM79 **Janáček to Zdenka Janáčková** *Prague, 23 February 1928*

Today they rehearsed from 11 to 6!

The theatre [piece] and the Capriccio.[2]

In the theatre the orchestra is excellent here; Miss Kejřová[3] has a magnificent voice. Mr Kubla[4] – still doesn't know it.

They rehearsed Act 1 and half of Act 2.

[...]

Tomorrow there are again rehearsals for both works.

On Sunday [26 February] I will go to Písek for the day.[5]

On Monday there will already be stage rehearsals.

They say it will be nice [...]

1 Janáček uses the 'tamburo piccolo' most memorably at the height of Marty's interrogation, when she is asked for the last time who she is; the accompaniment consists of empty two-note chords on the brass and a crescendo on the toy drum (VS178–9).

2 Janáček's Capriccio for piano left hand and orchestral ensemble was given its première in Prague on 2 March 1928, the day after the première of *The Makropulos Affair*. Janáček went from one set of rehearsals to the other.

3 Naďa [Anna] Kejřová (1899–1983), a full member of the National Theatre ensemble 1925–39, took parts such as Pamina, Mimi, Butterfly and many Smetana roles. She sang the Fox at the Prague première of *The Cunning Little Vixen*.

4 Richard Kubla (1890–1964) had experience in Vienna and in the Prague German Opera House before regular engagement at the National Theatre in 1923. One of the stars of the period, he sang both the *Helden* and lyrical tenor repertory and was best known in foreign opera, in parts such as Cavaradossi, Radamès and Des Grieux. He had trouble learning the part of Siegfried in Czech; Gregor in *The Makropulos Affair* seems to have caused similar problems.

5 To see Mrs Stösslová during the weekend break from rehearsals. Písek was three hours from Prague by express train; Prague to Brno took five hours.

Janáček to Zdenka Janáčková   *Prague, 24 February 1928*   **VM80**

Now I will also have to go to the première!

It has been rehearsed marvellously; Elina Makropulos is outstanding both in voice and acting. The Brno orchestra is of course rather poor in comparison with the one here.

Everybody was pleased that I praised it. Ostrčil valued that praise at half a million. The Šašecís[1] were here, I met Markalous. Tomorrow and on Sunday [25–6 February] there is nothing here. I look forward to basking in the sun in Písek.

I already need that rest. But to hear that third act – [!] then it must be said that only —— knows how to do it; you can fill in the blank yourself.

[. . .]

I shall ask for a box for us and the Brods [. . .]

Janáček to Zdenka Janáčková   *Prague, 27 February 1928*   **VM81**

The weather is beautiful. In Písek I would most gladly have sold the fur coat; the sun was as warm there as if on St Joseph's day [19 March]. The ear has stopped aching. Today the rehearsal lasted from 11 to 3. Well, Ostrčil is sweating it out!

The casting of Prus,[2] the lawyer[3] is excellent and that old fellow,[4] yes and Elina Makropulos.

What is merry in the opera is done merrily; and in Brno it was just sad.

Tomorrow, 28 February, is the dress rehearsal.

Čapek's[5] sets [see Plate 8] weren't a success. [. . .]

You will be arriving at 10.38 at the Wilson Station.

I shall come to meet you.

Today I put on my raglan and now will remain with it.

---

1 Bohumír Šašecí (1854–1930), the chief district attorney, and his wife Marie.
2 Václav Novák, who had so disliked singing the part of Würfl in *The Excursions of Mr Brouček* (see BR221+ and BR222).
3 The lawyer Dr Kolenatý was played by Emil Pollert, the Priest in the Prague première of *The Cunning Little Vixen*, and offered to Janáček as a potential producer for *The Makropulos Affair* (see VM72).
4 i.e. Hauk, played by Karel Hruška, who had already played Duhoslav in *The Excursions of Mr Brouček*, Kudrjáš in *Káťa Kabanová*, and the Schoolmaster in *The Cunning Little Vixen*. Hauk was in line with the character tenor parts (such as Triquet in *Eugene Onegin*) in which Hruška specialized.
5 Josef Čapek, brother of Karel (see LB45).

VM82   Janáček to Kamila Stösslová   *Prague, 28 February 1928*

So the main, final rehearsal is over. I think that it will turn out well.
Mrs Kejřová, who is taking that 300-year-old, has movements like
you. You know that time when you told me about your childhood
adventures, those 'four fingers' – that lady seems just like you in her
gait and her whole appearance. [. . .]

VM83   Janáček: letter to the editor

Dear Mr Jaromír John[1]
    I'm in Prague, in fact with two little pieces.[2]
    Sometimes it makes one angry, but this time it's a pleasure.
    I most like listening to that din in the orchestra before the rehearsal
when all over the place the most difficult motifs are still being learnt.
Oh yes sir, with that trumpet: how many times has it already gone
wrong [?!]

    I will strain my ears at the première to see if that D flat cracks!
And those twiddly bits on the horns!

    Even I learn things in those moments, not just you gentlemen.
    It is unnecessary to praise the way the whole stage is directed from
the conductor's stand – ; but, I wrote sobbing for Hauk – and it made
one sad, and you, Mr Hruška, sob excellently – and it was funny!
    So it should be.
    In the Capriccio, which Mr Hollmann will play, already defiantly[3]
the famous trombonists of the famous Philharmonic learn their parts
at home! At home!

---

1 i.e. Dr Bohumil Markalous. Perhaps it was at their meeting on 24 February (VM80) that
Janáček got the idea, or encouragement, to write this short newspaper article.
2 See p. 322 fn.2.
3 *ve vzdoru*; a pun on the original title of the piece *Vzdor* [Defiance], written for the pianist
Otakar Hollmann (1894–1967) who had lost his right arm in the First World War.

It is necessary to record that to their eternal memory.

Pestrý týden (1 March 1928)

Karel Čapek to Janáček   *Prague, 1 March 1928*   **VM84**

I wish most warmly that this evening you will again reap a great and full success. I will come to one of the repeat performances to applaud your great work which I had the honour in a small way to inspire.

Janáček to Kamila Stösslová   *Brno, 3 March 1928*   **VM85**

[. . .] And there was the première. I had two boxes, no guests in them! So I invited the Krečmers;[1] they came and brought a nice little picture as a present. The première began; success mounted to an unprecedented storm. [. . .]

Janáček to Universal Edition   *Brno, 7 March 1928*   **VM86**

[. . .] I will send you a few minor corrections with the request to send them to Mr Kleiber [for the German première, see VM63 + ff]. They occurred to me at the performance in Prague, which was outstanding, particularly Elina, Baron Prus, Baron-Idiot [i.e. Hauk].

The set not nice. The orchestra splendid. [. . .]

Janáček to Zdenka Janáčková   *Prague, 23 March 1928*   **VM87**

[. . .] They keep on inviting me to attend the Monday performance [26 March] of *The Makropulos Affair*. Rather no than yes. [. . .]

Twenty-five reviews of *The Makropulos Affair* they gave me to read. In some I stand terribly high, in one I'm not worth talking about. It didn't hurt me. [. . .]

At last, just a few months before his death, Janáček could afford to be magnanimous about the reviews. He could always count on a warm reception in Brno, but his relationship with Prague was scarred with decades of disparagement, if not hostility. Apart from *Jenůfa* in 1916 *The Makropulos Affair* was to be his only unequivocal success amongst his Prague operatic premières.

---

1 Otto Kretschmer (1875–1945) and his wife Marie Louisa (1891–1957). Kretschmer had a large private art collection which Janáček described in one of his *Lidové noviny* feuilletons a year before (see Janáček 1958a, 189).

9 *From the House of the Dead*

SUBJECT AND SCENARIO

ZD1   Janáček to Max Brod   *Brno, 3 December 1926*

[...] You know, *Šárka – Jenůfa – Káťa – Brouček – The Vixen – Makropulos*.

Well, I had to do *Makropulos*.

I stuck my nose into everything.

All I want now is to come across a free libretto; so as not to be limited, bound; from a rather different world – in short, I don't know yet myself: whether it will be gouged in the earth – or in some sort of spiritual sphere. [...]

Janáček was writing to give Brod notice of the Brno première of *The Makropulos Affair*, and found himself surveying his operatic life's work. It is interesting that *Šárka* opens the canon, that *Fate* is omitted and that *Brouček* and *Káťa Kabanová* are in reverse order. But most surprising of all is that he clearly had no notion at this stage what he was going to do next. Nor had the position changed by the end of the month: 'For the first time I have an empty head, i.e. I'm not preparing anything' (ZD2: to Kamila Stösslová, 27 December 1926).

Although Janáček claimed in May 1928 (ZD29) that it was the third year of his work on the opera, there is no evidence that he considered it at all in 1926. Nor would there have been much time. Large non-operatic works such as the Sinfonietta, the Capriccio and the Glagolitic Mass occupied him throughout the year, and probably the Violin Concerto too.[1] It is in the Violin Concerto, written in two drafts probably by February 1927,[2] that the musical seeds of the new opera can be found: much of its material was taken over when it was revised as the overture to *From the House of the Dead*. Whether its various subtitles 'The pilgrimage of a soul', 'Soul', 'Little soul', relate to the opera, or to another contemplated opera (based on William Ritter's[3] play *L'âme et la chair*), or indeed to Kamila Stösslová (whom

---

1 Chlubna (1929–30) reported at the time of the première of *From the House of the Dead* that on Janáček's return from London in May 1926 'with sudden haste he began to write a violin concerto', which he equally suddenly abandoned.

2 BmJA, A 33.746.

3 William Ritter (1876–1955), French-Swiss critic and novelist, and enthusiast for Czech and Slovak music.

Janáček had taken to addressing as 'soul' or 'little soul')[1] can only be a matter of speculation. But if the work originally had no relation to *From the House of the Dead*, it is curious that 'chains' (i.e. prison chains emblematic of the opera's prison setting) are specified among the percussion. At about the time that he completed the second draft of the Violin Concerto he made his first recorded reference to the subject of what would be his final opera.

Janáček: open letter to Brod, published as 'What I profess'	ZD3
	Brno, 12 February 1927

[...] were I thinking as a composer, I would go right to the *truth*, right to the harsh speech of the elements, and I would know how to advance a bit with the help of art.

On this path I do not stop by at Beethoven, or Debussy, or Dvořák or Smetana; because I will not meet any of them there. I do not borrow anything from them, for it is now impossible to pay them back.

Here I am close to Feodor M. Dostoevsky. He found in the *Dead House* a good man's soul even in Baklušin, in Petrov and in Isaj Fomič.[2]

Good fellow, Isaj Fomič!

[...]

Lidové noviny (13 February 1927)

It is surprising that Janáček was prepared to publish this letter with its virtual announcement of his new opera when his work on it was at such a preliminary stage. The references to Dostoevsky's novel in the final paragraph (the last phrase 'Good fellow, Isaj Fomič' is actually written in Russian, and in Cyrillic characters) are themselves evidence that Janáček had not by then progressed very far in his conception of the opera. None of these characters were to figure in the opera he ultimately wrote. Petrov and Isaj Fomič got no further than being included in a draft scenario (see ZD6); Baklušin had a small part in Janáček's earliest musical draft of Act 1, though in the revision this part was reallocated to the more important figure of Skuratov. The characters who dominate the opera with their long narrations – Luka, Skuratov, Šiškov – are not mentioned.

After *Káťa Kabanová* and Janáček's two unfinished attempts at operas on Tolstoy subjects (see KK2+), the Russian provenance of the subject was no surprise, though the actual material certainly was. Dostoevsky's *Memoirs from the House of the Dead*, published in serial form from 1860 to 1862, was a novel only in name. It presents as the purported memoirs of an

---

1 See Štědroň and Faltus 1988, 88–91; Procházková 1989.
2 For convenience all characters referred to in this chapter are given in the Czech transliterations used in the opera (or in Janáček's earlier scenarios and drafts).

aristocrat, Alexandr Petrovič Gorjančikov, Dostoevsky's own experiences in the prison camp of Omsk, where he served four years (1850–4) for his membership of a revolutionary circle. The result is a remarkably modern-sounding attempt at reportage, with the physical conditions of day-to-day life in a nineteenth-century Siberian prison camp described in clear, straight-forward detail. After several chapters dealing with first impressions, Dostoevsky devoted chapters to particular prisoners and their crimes. Then there are chapters concerned with festivities (Christmas, theatricals), several chapters describing life in a prison hospital, and others on 'summer time', 'prison animals' etc. Apart from the arrival and departure of the narrator there is no continuous story.

In much the same way that Janáček had compiled a libretto from *The Cunning Little Vixen* by simply working through the novel and extracting narrative, Janáček now went through Dostoevsky's novel marking passages that interested him. In *The Vixen* Janáček copied such lines into a draft libretto before he began composing: in *From the House of the Dead* he eliminated even this stage, relying on rough scenarios, lists of incidents with page references to his copy of the novel, and some small-scale rearrangements of dialogue jotted down on the pages of the novel.

ZD4 Scenario in Janáček's diary (between 23 and 28 February 1927)[1]

[Act] I
night; the last little light goes out.

Dawn

Act II
P[etrovič] summer
work in the brickyard
they dismantle a boat
on the river
during which B[aklušin] tells about his love[2]
There at Petěrburg [i.e. St Petersburg]
in the interval.
'Story' [in Russian][3]

---

1 BmJA, Z 64, 18, 21–3. Janáček's roman numerals denote acts, with 'jed[nání]' added only to Act 2. The diary entries begin at Act 2; Act 1 has been added at the end (p.23) though is given above at the beginning. Some words are in Russian, as shown.
2 Later Janáček suppressed the character of Baklušin and gave his story about his love for the German girl Luise ['Lujza'] to Skuratov.
3 *razkaz*, perhaps Janáček's incorrect creation of a 'Russian' word, the equivalent of the Czech *rozkaz* ('order'). There are orders in the opera, but not here; so perhaps he meant *rasskaz* ('story', in Russian).

[Act] III
Holiday [in Russian]
'You lie, you lie' singer
Theatre → climaxes in Don Quixote[1]
Hell
tea hatred

[Act] IV
night in the prison
death and[2]
dawn
announcement Commandant
Eagle!!
to be released only!

Not everything is readily comprehensible, but many of the outlines of the opera, especially Act 2 (here spread over 'II' and 'III') are already in place. Remarkable absences are the narrations in the outer acts, and virtually all the action of Act 1. The single idea here – night in the prison with the last light turned out, and then the dawn – was incorporated in the first musical draft, but then jettisoned with the act opening instead at dawn.

This preliminary scenario is complemented by another (**ZD5**, two sheets) for Act 3 set in the hospital ('after ten years') with a floor plan including an oven and eight beds arranged in two rows of four, flanking a candle. There are numbered references to the characters: the old man prays; Skuratov (confused); Petrovič listens to the story (this function was ultimately taken over by Čerevin); another dies. Then follow events of the previous scenario (zD4) slightly expanded (with 'Spring again', *'Freedom'*). A continuation designated 'Final scene' provides the most interesting passages:

Final scene[3]
They strike off Petrovič's chains
Petrovič spoken monologue
Aljeja Eagle tsar!
the prisoners off to work Petrovič [illegible: ?hears] the cry of Aljeja

1 The subject of the second of the three plays in Dostoevsky (Janáček omitted the first), is Don Juan (under the Russian folk version of 'Kedril the Glutton'). On the back of a leaflet (dated 7 March 1927) Janáček jotted down a list (transcribed in Firkušný 1936–7) of dramatic treatments of the Don Juan story. Janáček included the operas by Righini and Mozart, Molière's play, Gluck's ballet, Pushkin's *The Stone Guest* and Don Quixote, in whose quest he evidently saw parallels with that of Don Juan.
2 This line has been arrowed into a new position, after 'Commandant.'
3 Petrovič is designated by a single Russian P; Aljeja's name is written in Russian.

Curtain

Aljeja in a white hospital robe remains as a symbol of *the spark of God in man*.

Reminiscence [?] of the introduction.

Janáček was soon to find a different association for Aljeja (see ZD8) but he nevertheless inscribed his final autograph score with the words 'In every creature a spark of God'. A further stage of preliminary work was Janáček's more detailed list of events (often just characters' names) followed by the respective page numbers (**ZD6**, four sheets). It is here that a more recognizable version of Act 1 can be found, though several of the names he included (e.g. Orlov, Isaj Fomič, Sušilov, Petrov) were not taken even into the first musical draft.

There is reason to believe that Janáček compiled this list of events in stages. The two sheets relating to Act 1[1] are not labelled as such and flow without a break into events that take place in the remaining acts. These sheets are written mostly in Russian. Acts 2 and 3[2] (both specifically labelled as such), are almost entirely in Czech.

The mixture of Russian and Czech stages is symptomatic of the fact that Janáček was working directly from the Russian original. Janáček owned two copies of Dostoevsky's novel, one in Russian and the other a Czech translation.[3] It is the Russian edition which is much more heavily annotated; all the page-numbered references to the novel refer to this edition; the translation of the text in the opera is Janáček's rather than that printed in the Czech edition. For the first draft of the opera Janáček translated the Russian text into Czech as he went along. He worked hastily, even carelessly, sometimes transliterating rather than translating many words or phrases; some were even left in their original Cyrillic. The literary progress of the opera through its many versions (including those after Janáček's death) is one of increasing, but never complete, elimination of the Russian words. Even by the final version Janáček could not resist spelling the name of Petrovič with a Cyrillic rather than a Latin 'P.'

PROGRESS OF THE OPERA

Janáček left no dates in either his Russian or his Czech edition of Dostoevsky's *Memoirs from the House of the Dead*, but did add '18 February 1927' to the title page of his final autograph score. In the light of the probable dating of the first scenario in his diary (ZD4), this seems reasonable

---

1 First published in Firkušný 1936–7, 14 and 16.
2 First published in Procházka 1966, 229 and 232.
3 Held in BmJA, JK 11 and JK 10 respectively.

as a starting date for serious work on the opera, though even then he had some doubts: 'I don't know what work to take up', he wrote to Kamila Stösslová the next day (**ZD7**, 19 February 1927). 'One is within reach, but every person in it is in chains. And I would prefer to have smiling people.'

It was some months before the subject came up again in his now very frequent correspondence with Kamila. 'You are in my new opera under the name Aljeja:[1] such a tender, nice creature' (**ZD8**, 27–8 May 1927). He made another, similar, brief reference the next month (**ZD9**, 8 June 1927), and in the feuilleton 'They caught them' (**ZD10**, *Lidové noviny*, 28 June 1927), whose undeclared subject was Kamila Stösslová, he developed this theme further: 'Dostoevsky would have called you the tortured Akulka;[2] and I would have called you Aljeja, of the childlike pure soul.' A month later *Lidové noviny* attempted to make a news item out of Janáček's new opera, but found the composer reluctant to say much about it:

Anon: 'Leoš Janáček's new opera'   ZD11

Dr Leoš Janáček is working on a new opera, which is already finished in rough outline. It is, as we have already been briefly reported, an opera in three acts called *Memoirs from the House of the Dead* whose libretto the composer wrote himself after the novel of the same name by Dostoevsky. The première of the opera could be some time towards the end of 1928. The composer has not yet been in contact with any theatre about the first performance since he meant, for serious reasons, to keep his new work a secret. His intention, however, has been marred by indiscretion. Answering our question Dr Janáček informed us that the libretto does not depart on the whole from Dostoevsky's novel. It appealed to him because it gave him the possibility of a play within a play and, further, that 'in each of these criminals there is a spark of God'. The new opera has no main hero. Thus its novelty lies in some sort of collectivism.

Lidové noviny (29 July 1927)

The reference to the opera's being complete in 'rough outline' was something of an exaggeration; it is thus hardly surprising that Janáček had not yet negotiated with any theatre. A few days after his death *Lidové noviny* printed as a memorial tribute a fuller version of this interview purportedly in the composer's own words.[3] The substance is identical except that the reason for Janáček's unwillingness to talk about the work is now disclosed: it is linked with a heated commentary on the Prague National Theatre's

1 The Tartar lad whom Petrovič befriends and teaches to read.
2 The long-suffering heroine of Šiškov's story in Act 3.
3 'Janáček's last opera', *Lidové noviny* (15 August 1928), reprinted in Firkušný 1937.

opera competition, for which he apparently wished to enter the work.[1] Another reason for Janáček's silence might also be the foreboding that this would be his last opera. Not even Kamila Stösslová heard any more about the work until he had nearly finished the first version.

ZD12   **Janáček to Kamila Stösslová**   *[Brno,] Sunday, [16] October 1927*

[...] I'm feeling lonely again today. I am finishing a big work – probably my last opera, so it seems to me. And I'm always sorry when I take my leave of those whose lives I've lived for as much as two to three years. [...]

ZD13   **Janáček to Kamila Stösslová**   *Brno, 16–17 October 1927*

[...] So, my dear soul, yesterday [i.e. 16 October] and today I have finished that opera of mine

From the House of the Dead.

A terrible title, isn't it? Also yesterday, at the end [of Act 1], one criminal described how when killing the major, he said to himself, 'I am God and tsar!' And in the night I dreamt that in the eiderdown a dead man was lying on me, so strongly that I felt his head! And I cried, 'but I've done nobody any harm!' The eiderdown fell off me; and I was so relieved. –

    [...]

But now that work with my copyist! I'd rather load gravel! And it will go on certainly right up to Easter, if not longer! [...]

The phrase 'at the end' makes it sound as though Janáček had got only to the end of Act 1: the incident occurs near the end of Luka's story in the last few minutes of this act. In fact a rare date, '2 April 1927', can be found at the end of Janáček's first, rather short, draft of Act 1 and so provides a date for its original completion. This version is, surprisingly, without the Luka story. Later, as is attested by the manuscript, Janáček went back to Act 1 and added Luka's account of how he killed the major. Janáček's description of his nightmare suggests that this substantial addition to the act, giving a quite different slant to its conclusion, may have been made as late as October 1927.

    Janáček's normal method, as he frequently stated and which is corroborated by his work on all operas from *Káťa Kabanová* onwards, was to write a first draft fairly quickly and let it lie a while before beginning full-scale revisions. But here something drove him on. There is a date, a week

---

1 This question is explored in Procházka 1966, 222–5.

later (24 October 1927), on the manuscript, just after the beginning of Act 2 announcing the 'cleaning-up' of Act 1. That he must have gone straight into revising the opera immediately after finishing the first draft is corroborated by his letter to Kamila (ZD14) describing two numbers, the first of which, the brawl between the Big Prisoner and the Small Prisoner, occurs soon after the opening of Act 1:

Janáček to Kamila Stösslová   *Brno, 22 October 1927*   **ZD14**

[. . .] Today I did two numbers – pieces from the opera: a merry one – two rascals are fighting, having stolen sour milk and bread from an old woman [vs15–18]; and a second one, sad, fateful.[1] I think that I succeeded with both. [. . .]

The sense of urgency and strain as he continued work on the opera is evident from Janáček's letters to Kamila Stösslová throughout November:

Janáček to Kamila Stösslová   *[undated, postmarked Brno,*   **ZD15**
                                                       29 November 1927]

[. . .] And that black opera of mine is giving me plenty of work.

It seems to me as if in it I am gradually descending lower and lower, right to the depths of the most wretched people of humanity. And it is hard going.

You are my comfort here and the ray of light which gives me persistence in my work. [. . .]

Janáček to Kamila Stösslová   *Brno, 30 November 1927*   **ZD16**

[. . .] So I am finishing one work after another – as if I had to settle my accounts with life. We have prepared a thousand folksongs for printing.[2] That's work from 1901; thus twenty-six years!

With my new opera I hurry like a baker throwing loaves into the oven! [. . .]

---

1 The best candidates for this would seem to be Petrovič's arrival and offstage flogging (vs18–24) or the sad song that the prisoners sing as they go off to work for the day (vs30–3).
2 *Moravian Love Songs*, ed. with Pavel Váša (Orbis, Prague, 1930–6); there are 150 numbered songs, though most of them in several variants and subvariants.

ZD17   **Janáček to Kamila Stösslová**   *Brno, 1–2 December 1927*

[...] And I am completing perhaps [my] greatest work – the latest opera – excited almost to the pitch where my blood would want to spurt out. – [...]

By mid-December he seems to have finished revising Acts 1 and 2 of the opera:

ZD18   **Janáček to Kamila Stösslová**   *Brno, 18 December 1927*

[...] From my work there now remains for me to tidy up just the last act. Then a heavy weight will fall from me! [...]

The hospital scene of the last act clearly cost Janáček much effort. Against the background of the groans and unquiet dreams of the sick prisoners, Šiškov tells the searing story of the murder of his wife Akulka. Despite all that she has suffered at the hands of her previous lover Filka Morozov, Akulka readily confesses to Šiškov that she loves only Filka. This is too much for Šiškov and he kills her. Šiškov's story is the longest in the opera and gave rise to Janáček's most extended description of the opera in his correspondence:

ZD19   **Janáček to Kamila Stösslová**   *Brno, 30 December 1927*

[...] And now, just think, what hard work I still have with this difficult opera!
    There is a sad story there, about the marvellously beautiful Akulka.
    Oh, a big story! The man who took Akulka's life tells, broken-hearted, his whole life story and the whole story [of Akulka]. How he loved her! I will tell it to you some other time, that story of theirs.
    He tells it during the night, in whispers. All round are lying those who are gravely ill.
    And now to hear such a confession from him –
    to hear – and know that it is night,
    to hear – that he is speaking furtively,
    to hear – that the sick [lying] around sigh deeply,
    to hear – and to feel his terrible suffering during his speech!
    It isn't easy, Kamila! But now I have had a good idea. It will be as if it were painted.
    What about us! We also put out the lights,
    we also do not cry out to make the house shake and bring it down,
    we also talk to one other in intimate voices.

But my Akulka – Kamila – and I are merry. There is much laughter and fooling around and meanwhile the light burns red in the stove and spreads its glow. And I had a similar idea! Except it wasn't the light – but the heavy breathing of the sick prisoners.[1] [...]

Janáček to Kamila Stösslová   *Brno, 3 January 1928*   **ZD20**

[...] I am finished with this difficult story about Akulka in my opera. In the last few days I sat up working from 8 in the morning till noon, and in the afternoon until evening. I myself was excited until my blood raced – and for me there was no pity and understanding.[2]

Janáček to Kamila Stösslová   *Brno, 4 January 1928*   **ZD21**

[...] Opera finished.
The work finished. [...]

All Janáček's mature operas took at least two years to compose, but his last opera, his most original and in many ways his greatest, had been written in less than eleven months, a remarkable achievement for a man of seventy-three. This however was not the end of the matter. He made a final revision, finishing Act 3 (on 24 April 1928) before Act 2 (7 May 1928), and then supervised the copying of the score. On this occasion he brought in simultaneously his two most experienced and loyal copyists, Václav Sedláček, who finished copying Act 1 by 28 March 1928, and Jaroslav Kulhánek, who completed Act 3 by 14 May 1928. They divided Act 2 between them; Kulhánek's initials are at the end of the act (his work in this act began on p. 157), dated 23 May 1928.[3] That they worked beyond these dates is attested by Janáček's references to his work with them in his letters to Kamila and by entries in his diary (**ZD22**) recording payments in June to Sedláček (K252 on 11 June 1928 – he had already paid him K400 for Act 1 on 27 March) – and to Kulhánek (K860 on 20 June 1928 'for the second half of Act 2 and for Act 3'). Janáček's personal involvement in the 'copying' meant that he was able to give personal instructions for further changes as they went along.

1 This resulted in one of Janáček's most magical inspirations – the wordless humming of the male chorus in three parts, which several times interrupts or is heard against Šiškov's narrative (vs147–58, *passim*).
2 An oblique reference to his wife.
3 Dates written into their copy of the score, BmJA, A11.489.

ZD23   **Janáček to Kamila Stösslová**   *[Brno,] Saturday 10 March [1928],*
                                                                         at night

[. . .] And yesterday with those copyists of mine I worked hard for five hours, and my head seemed to be going round. It's because I don't have anything else here apart from work that would otherwise take my fancy. [. . .]

ZD24   **Janáček to Kamila Stösslová**   *Brno, 18 March 1928*

[. . .] All these past fourteen days I have really not gone out of the house, I have not spoken with anyone else except during my work with the copyists, or at home: 'What will we have for lunch?' [. . .]

You know, my little soul, I am glad that I like my new opera, now that I have been cleaning it up for a year. That's a good sign. [. . .]

ZD25   **Janáček to Kamila Stösslová**   *Brno, 2 April 1928*

[. . .] I will not begin any other work now in addition to that copying. I've always been hanging around the writing desk. I haven't done much walking and because of it, I've got quite a lot of rheumatism. [. . .]

Even at this late stage certain details of the opera were unresolved, for instance the way Skuratov's story in Act 2 is interrupted by the cries of a drunken prisoner and is eventually overwhelmed by the singing and dancing of the others (ZD26). Another problem was the 'devils' which occur in the tale of Don Juan, presented by the prisoners as part of the summer festivities (ZD27).

ZD26   **Janáček to Kamila Stösslová**   *Brno, 1 May 1928*

Today's the first of May. Everything is in bloom, everything is green. On this holiday [celebrating] work I have been working very hard. I have – perhaps successfully [–] got round one very complicated passage in the opera. Skuratov is telling about his Lujza, about his love for her, and at the same time high-spirited prisoners are getting drunk, are shouting, dancing. You know, it's like someone wanting to cross the mud without getting dirty. [. . .]

ZD27   **Janáček to Kamila Stösslová**   *Brno, 2 May 1928, at night*

[. . .] I need devils on stage; I just cannot find the thread to pull them out of my brain. I keep on throwing it into the bin. Well, it's spring now and it drags me outside from the writing desk. [. . .]

If only I could get these devils finished! [. . .]

Janáček to Kamila Stösslová   *Brno, 3 May 1928*   ZD28

[. . .] I have to correct another little bit in my opera. I bang my head, I tear up one idea after another. And in irritation I wait until that right one comes. And it's been going on now for several days. [. . .]

Janáček to Kamila Stösslová   *Brno, 5 May 1928, afternoon*   ZD29

[. . .] I've had news from Hukvaldy, that the extension[1] is continuing fast. Just as soon as I've finished here tidying up the opera, I will go off there immediately.

I really feel that it is high time to put down my pen – and walk from the Augustinian [house] to Aloiska,[2] not to think any thoughts, just to listen to you, to look at you. I am now so exhausted. [. . .]

Kamila, the copyist has just left. You can't imagine what a load will fall from my soul when this *House of the Dead* will be finished. This is the third year it has been oppressing me, night and day. Only when I was with you did I forget it. And what it will be I still don't know even myself. Now notes upon notes just pile up into a mountain; a tower of Babel grows. When it collapses on me, I will be buried. In Luhačovice I will dig myself out from these ruins [. . .]

Janáček to Kamila Stösslová *[Brno,] Saturday 5 May [1928], at night* ZD30

[. . .] I am still waiting for an idea from above about the beautiful miller's wife.[3] The miller, before leaving, orders: 'Don't let anyone in!'. Hardly has he gone than a neighbour knocks; she lets him in; flirtation.

At that very moment someone else knocks. A clerk; she lets him in, having first hidden the neighbour. Flirtation. At that very moment someone else knocks. A bearded monk – a devil [–] enters after she has hidden the clerk. Flirtation.

At that very moment her husband knocks furiously. The doors fly open – what happens next you can imagine for yourself!

1 To the holiday house he had bought there in 1921.
2 References to places in Luhačovice: Augustiánský dům was where Janáček generally stayed; Aloiska is the name of one of the springs.
3 The last of the plays that the prisoners enact. In essence it is the folktale elaborated by Gogol in his *Christmas Eve* and set as an opera by several Russian composers (e.g. Tchaikovsky in his *Vakula the Smith*).

I must finish that tomorrow. And then I will throw down my pen and be off! So, sleep well!

[6 May 1928]

So my little soul, today, 6 May, I've done it! From 8 in the morning to 12.30, from 3 to 5 – and the devils have taken off the false miller's wife. A load off my chest, emptiness in my head. Open the gates, let me live like any other man. [. . .] For such a long time, the third year, it was being moulded inside me without ceasing. You were the only shining cloud with which I liked to run about to have a rest from my work. All finished!

While Act 1 had been duly copied out by Sedláček in March, Janáček had gone on working on the central portion of Act 2 which he had found especially troublesome. Even four days after he announced to Kamila that it was finished, he reported that he 'just wanted to sleep, sleep after this hard work!' (ZD31, 10 May 1928). He now, however, needed to continue supervising the copying of Acts 2 and 3. The next day he reported: 'Today I was already more cheerful with my copyist; when he could go no further, I almost overturned the rocking chair.' (ZD32, 11 May 1928). Act 3 was finished first in this way, on 14 May 1928, Act 2 on 23 May 1928. But revision with the copyists continued after these dates. Janáček reported to Kamila continuing work with them on 7–8 June 1928 (ZD33), Kulhánek added 'corrected by Janáček, 8 June 1928' to his previous finishing date in Act 3, though even that was not quite correct.

ZD34   **Janáček to Kamila Stösslová**   *[Brno,] 9 June [1928], at night*

[. . .] Today it was a furnace in Brno. 22 degrees in the shade! But there was also a furnace in my room the whole day. In the morning the copyist finished Act 3 by 10; part of Act 2 remains still to be looked through and the thing will be now 'washed clean' in the first water.
[. . .]
In the afternoon some madman photographed me; then the copyist came again.
[. . .]

The next day one copyist (Sedláček) had finished (ZD35: Janáček to Kamila Stösslová, 10 June 1928), a week later (Janáček having had four days in Hukvaldy) there were 'only about twenty pages still to write up' (ZD36, 18 June 1928), and finally, on 19 June 1928 Janáček announced to Kamila that 'The copyists will be finished here tomorrow, on Wednesday' (ZD37), a date confirmed by Janáček's payment to Kulhánek on 20 June (ZD22).

Thus by 20 June a complete, copied-out full score existed, based on Janáček's autograph, which itself had gone through three (in parts of it more) stages of drafting. Janáček made further changes by replacing some of the original copyists' pages with newly copied sheets. Furthermore, Janáček made additional corrections in his own hand. He mentioned on 9 June (ZD34) that he still had to look through the last part of Act 2; and his final checking is evident from his many minor adjustments written directly into the copyists' full score. By the time he went off on his usual summer break to Luhačovice (1–21 July 1928), he had checked through both Act 1 and Act 2 in this way. Act 3 he took with him to Hukvaldy (see ZD38). Here he caught a chill which developed rapidly into pneumonia. He died on Sunday, 12 August, leaving the copy of the last act of *From the House of the Dead* unchecked.

POSTHUMOUS HISTORY OF THE OPERA

Osvald Chlubna: 'On the revision . . . *From the House of the Dead*' ZD38

[. . .] By the end of July 1928, when Janáček returned from Luhačovice and was making preparations for his departure for Hukvaldy, I visited him as usual in the afternoon at 4 o'clock. I didn't catch him at home, however. He was already off on a walk. Mrs Janáčková, who was glad I had come, placed all at once before me three bound volumes – full scores – and asked me to have a look at them, [saying] that it was Janáček's new opera, which had the title *From the House of the Dead*, and asked me what I thought about it. Thus for the first time I had in my hands the full score of this opera, for the first time I leafed through it and glanced at it. I was surprised how many pages had little writing on them, how thinly it had been orchestrated, and at the strange mixture of Czech words and perhaps Russian which formed the basis of the text. This was my first impression from reading it. [When seeing] my doubtful surprise, Mrs Janáčková added that Janáček wrote this opera for himself and that there were no women's roles in it, just men, those disinherited and outlaws from life, and that Janáček himself had great misgivings about this work because of its unusual subject. And she added further that the first and second act had been looked through by Janáček and were ready, and that Janáček would take the third to Hukvaldy, where he would finish it. Today, when I look through the pages of the first and second act, I can see in fact that Janáček corrected the copyists' entries but that he also composed many additional things, as was his habit.

Janáček left for Hukvaldy on 30 July 1928 and also took with him
the third act to look through. However he did not touch *From the
House of the Dead* any further at Hukvaldy. Mrs Janáčková brought it
back on 20 August when Dr Krampus asked for it for Universal
Edition. She was lucky that she was still able to find the manuscript and
she put it together with the earlier two acts. And so *From the House of
the Dead*, incomplete, fell into forgetfulness for a while; writers of
essays and even musicologists steered well clear of it. And even
František Neumann hesitated to perform it in the National Theatre in
Brno. He would have preferred to have given a concert performance of
it.[1] Furthermore, the material was not accessible for a while since it was
involved in the settling of his estate and was needed to estimate estate
duty.

But Břetislav Bakala and Ota Zítek had not forgotten about the
opera. Though the score was not in good order, it was nevertheless in a
state where it was possible to consider its stage performance if someone
was willing to look through it to make playable the impossible things in
it, and partly add what was necessary to the orchestration. Bakala took
care of preparing the score for performance and Director Zítek,[2] as
producer and dramaturg of the National Theatre in Brno, accepted the
opera for performance. Bakala invited me to help – it was in the
autumn of 1929 – and so began the process of realizing our wishes, to
see and hear Janáček's opera *From the House of the Dead* on stage. I
met up with Bakala every afternoon in his flat in Bayerova street and
we went through the score bar by bar and played through it again. And
I must just mention that at that time there was still no vocal score at our
disposal and that all our work was based on the full score. We were not
concerned about the orchestral, technical and instrumental disposi-
tions. That would, on the whole, have been simple work for both of us.
More was at stake in this opera and its completion. We were concerned
above all that Janáček's work, although apparently completed and two
acts of which were checked, should be placed before the public by us
just as Janáček himself planned and executed it though because of his
sudden death it had not reached a final version. We had mastered
Janáček's style as well as his orchestration so thoroughly that we could
allow ourselves to take on this revision. Therefore we first studied
Dostoevsky's *Memoirs from the House of the Dead*. I borrowed it
from Mrs Janáčková in a Czech version from the library of Leoš

1 Even this was denied him; Neumann died on 25 February 1929 at the age of 55.
2 Zítek became director of the Brno National Theatre after Neumann's death in 1929.

Janáček. In it I found quite a few of Janáček's notes on the text which Janáček had taken over unchanged into the full score in such a way that he had not drawn up any previous text, any libretto, at all. And because he was, additionally, using the Russian original at the same time,[1] a mixture of Czech and Russian words, even whole Russian sayings and sentences, consequently accumulated. His only aid was just four octavos of paper,[2] which contained the dramatic structure of the opera.

When through this route we had picked up the action we then began to realize the work in such a way that Janáček's version, insofar as it was legible, and the groupings of instruments that he had chosen to realize the sound of his musical palette, was used to the very last note. Only in the most pressing cases did we make changes and add instruments simply so that the continuity as well as the contrasts of the instrumentation would not disturb Janáček's instrumental style through the choice of instruments and would preserve the characteristics of his score. Of course it was necessary to fill in gaps in the sound which Janáček had overlooked, to strengthen the melodic and also the rhythmic phrases, and to prepare the dramatic climaxes. How we did this, I will say later with reference to the relevant pages of Janáček's score.[3] All this we did with the most devoted love to Janáček's last work, and need not perhaps assure anyone that we respected the work as Janáček's final heritage to us, his pupils. [. . .]

Opery Leoše Janáčka na brněnské scéně, ed. Václav Nosek (1958)

Chlubna was writing almost thirty years after these events, in justification of his and Bakala's version, which had come under increasing criticism. It is understandable, despite the presence of a partly corrected copyists' score, that Janáček's pupils believed the work to be incomplete. For the first time in an opera, Janáček had gone over to the method he had employed increasingly in all other genres of doing without printed music paper, and instead drawing his own stave lines (freehand!) as he needed them. The score thus looks quite different from, say, that of *The Makropulos Affair* and consists of small oblong sheets of paper often with very little on them. However, this was not simply a continuity sketch since Janáček continued with this method through all stages of drafting. Furthermore, in his daily work with his copyists, Janáček had ample opportunity to fill out the orchestration, had he chosen to. The spare, often chamber-like, orchestration was clearly deliberate and in keeping with the subject matter.

1 The Russian text was in fact Janáček's primary source (see ZD6+).
2 Chlubna overlooked the first scenario in Janáček's diary (ZD4); the 'four' octavos (ZD5, ZD6) turned to six with the discovery of two more (see p. 330, fn.2).
3 A page-by-page verbal description of the changes is appended to Chlubna's article.

Nevertheless Chlubna and Bakala filled out the score in a somewhat lusher late-Romantic style. They were also puzzled by the grim ending, so much at variance with the 'positive' endings of many of Janáček's earlier works: their most portentous intervention was the addition of a concluding 'freedom chorus' for male chorus worked contrapuntally against a major-mode version of Janáček's motto theme from Act 1. It was in this version, with verbal additions by Zítek to fill out some of the sparser moments of dialogue, that the work received its première in Brno on 12 April 1930 under Bakala, produced by Zítek. It was this version, too, which was published in vocal and full score (both 1930) by Universal Edition. The usual Prague première followed in 1931 (Prague National Theatre 21 February 1931), no longer with Ostrčil, but with Maixner conducting and produced by Pujman, with a German première in Mannheim two months earlier (14 December 1930).

In 1964 Universal Edition published an edition of the vocal score with Janáček's original ending added as an appendix. This appeared a few years after they had issued a new version of the full score by Rafael Kubelík, based on Janáček's autograph, which excised many, but not all of the additions. Kubelík conducted this version in a concert performance in Munich (17 November 1961), and it was heard subsequently in the first English stage production at Sadler's Wells conducted by Charles Mackerras (28 October 1965). A final phase in the rehabilitation of the opera was the preparation by Charles Mackerras and myself of a score based on Sedláček's and Kulhánek's supervised fair copy and including all of Janáček's final additions to Act 1 and 2. This version was used in the Decca recording of 1980 and in subsequent stage productions.

ZD39   Janáček: 'On the way to the House of the Dead'

Why do I go into the dark, frozen cells of criminals with the poet of *Crime and Punishment*? Into the minds of criminals and there I find a spark of God. You will not wipe away the crimes from their brow, but equally you will not extinguish the spark of God. Into what depths it leads – how much truth there is in his work!

See how the old man slides down from the oven, shuffles to the corpse, makes the sign of the cross over it, and with a rusty voice sobs the words: 'A mother gave birth even to him!'

Those are the bright places in the house of the dead.

(found in the clothes returned from the sanatorium after Janáček's death)

Epilogue

It's said that at the dress rehearsal, when they'd got to the end of Act 3, with the Forester dreaming of the young Bystrouška and, instead of her, catching the little Frog, who sings to him: 'It's not me! That was granddad. They told me all about you,' the master wept and said to the producer Zítek standing next to him: 'You must play this when I die.'

Stejskalová's reminiscences (1959)

A painful, unforgettable moment occurred. It was half-past ten, and from the orchestra, placed on the other side of the foyer, behind the coffin, was heard the music from the end of the opera *The Cunning Little Vixen*, played by the orchestra of the Brno National Theatre under the direction of the head of opera, František Neumann. Adolf Flögl sang the words of the Forester. It was the scene into which the deceased Maestro placed his philosophical ideas of life and death. [. . .] And when, at the word *'láska'* (love), rang out that broadly arching melody, so simple and so warm and expressive, everyone felt instinctively that truly during those sounds 'people will walk with heads bowed and will realize that a more-than-earthly joy has passed amongst them'.

Adolf Vašek: In the Steps of Dr Leoš Janáček (1930)

Chronologies of Janáček's Operas

ABBREVIATIONS

BT = Brno (National) Theatre
GT = German Theatre (Prague)
NT = National Theatre (Prague)
UE = Universal Edition
VS = vocal score
VT = Vinohrady Theatre (Prague)

ŠÁRKA

1880?	Zeyer writes libretto for Dvořák.	SR1—
1 Jan–1 Feb 1887	Zeyer publishes libretto in periodical.	SR5+
?Feb–?July 1887	Janáček composes Šárka, 1st version.	SR5+
6 Aug 1887	Dvořák receives Janáček's opera for his verdict.	SR7
10 Nov 1887	Zeyer refuses Janáček permission to use his text.	SR9
18 June 1888	Štross completes fair copy of VS, 2nd version.	SR12+
1888?	Janáček orchestrates two acts of 2nd version.	SR12+
25 Jan 1917	Šourek asks for information about Šárka.	SR14
14 Jan 1918	Janáček finds full score of Šárka Acts 1–2.	SR13
25 May 1918	Janáček asks Chlubna to orchestrate Act 3.	SR15
2–25 Aug 1918	Chlubna orchestrates Act 3.	SR15
20 Oct 1918	Janáček applies to Zeyer's trustees for use of text.	SR16
28 Dec 1918	Janáček obtains permission to use text.	SR17
early 1919?	Janáček revises VS (= 3rd version).	SR19
10 Jan 1919	Janáček invites Chlubna to revise orchestration in light of the revisions to VS.	SR19
16 April 1919	Janáček asks Procházka for extra lines.	SR20
6 May 1919	Procházka sends additional lines.	SR21
12 May 1919	Janáček tells UE of the opera.	SR23
15 Nov 1924	Helfert writes approvingly of Šárka.	SR27
2 June 1925	Janáček asks for Zítek to supply new words.	SR29
4–7 June 1925	Janáček makes final revisions to score.	SR30
31 Oct 1925	Janáček finalizes title.	SR32

11 Nov 1925	Première of *Šárka* at BT.	SR32+
14 Jan 1926	Janáček returns signed contract to UE for publication of VS.	SR36
Jan 1926	Prague unwilling to stage *Šárka*.	SR37ff
4 June 1926	UE reports many errors in VS.	SR46
14 Aug 1926	Janáček tries to make production in Prague of *The Makropulos Affair* conditional on taking *Šárka*.	SR42
23 Feb 1927	UE states engraving of *Šárka* under way.	SR45
28 Dec 1927	Publication delayed by German translation.	SR47
4 Feb 1928	Janáček thinks he has persuaded Brod to translate opera	SR53
13 Feb 1928	Brod returns *Šárka* to UE.	SR55

THE BEGINNING OF A ROMANCE

July–Aug 1885	Věšín's painting *The Beginning of a Romance* exhibited in Brno.	PR1−
1886	Preissová publishes short story *The Beginning of a Romance*.	PR1
2 April 1891	Preissová suggests Červinková for libretto.	PR4
5 April 1891	Preissová agrees to Tichý's writing libretto.	PR5
13 May 1891	Preissová sends libretto to Šťastný.	PR6
15 May 1891	Janáček begins first version (VS).	PR5+
2 July 1891	Janáček completes first version.	PR7+
Dec 1891	Janáček proposes sending score to NT.	PR13
12 Jan 1892	Score submitted to BT.	PR14
Feb 1892	Janáček sends revised score to NT for approval.	PR19
13 March 1892	Brno singer turns down part of Poluška.	PR17
April 1892	Negative comments by Prague conductors on opera.	PR25–6
5 Sept 1892	Delays in BT production.	PR28
10 Feb 1894	Première at BT.	PR31–3
1 June 1916	Preissová proposes revising opera (Janáček declined).	PR37
1924	Janáček rejects opera.	PR42

JENŮFA

15 Jan 1887	Janáček's review of Kovařovic's *The Bridegrooms*.	JP12
9 Nov 1890	Première of Preissová's play *Her Stepdaughter*.	JP1+
Nov 1893	Contacts between Preissová and Janáček.	JP4–5

18 March 1894 to 11 Feb 1895	Reading of play and preliminary sketching of *Jenůfa*.	JP9+
31 Dec 1894	Completion of 'Jealousy' Overture.	JP9+
16 Feb 1895	Composition in full score begun.	JP9+
1897	Act 1 complete in full score?	JP9+
1897–1901	No work on *Jenůfa*.	JP9+
late 1901	Act 2 begun.	JP10
summer 1902	Act 2 complete (Štross's fair copy of VS completed 8 July 1902).	JP9
Feb 1903	Janáček plays *Jenůfa* to his daughter Olga.	JP7
26 Feb 1903	Death of Olga.	
18 March 1903 (or earlier)	Act 3 complete.	JP11+
? March 1903	Janáček offers *Jenůfa* to NT.	JP13
28 April 1903	NT turns down *Jenůfa*.	JP15
?summer 1903	Janáček persuaded to submit *Jenůfa* to BT.	JP17
3 Oct 1903	Janáček makes last-minute changes to score.	JP18
8 Oct 1903	BT's terms for production of *Jenůfa*.	JP19
9 Oct 1903	Score entrusted to BT.	JP20
Christmas 1903	Soloists and chorus (but not orchestra) rehearse.	JP22
?19 Jan 1904	First full rehearsal of Act 1.	JP26
21 Jan 1904	Première at BT.	JP28 ff.
9 Feb 1904	Janáček offers *Jenůfa* to NT again.	JP35
4 March 1904	Kovařovic undertakes to attend a performance of *Jenůfa*.	JP37
April–May	Kovařovic has still not seen *Jenůfa*.	JP39
5 Dec 1904	Janáček invites Mahler to hear *Jenůfa*.	JP42
9 Dec 1904	Mahler cannot come, but asks for VS.	JP44
11 July 1906	Hrazdira suggests cuts.	JP48
1906–1907	Janáček revises score.	JP48+
late Dec 1907– mid-Feb 1908	Janáček works on proofs of VS.	JP50–1
by 18 March 1908	VS published by Friends of Art Club.	JP52
28 Aug 1908	Janáček meets Marie Calma-Veselá.	JP54
Feb 1911	Appeal by Friends of Art Club to NT to produce *Jenůfa*.	JP56
25 March 1913	Final performance of BT production of *Jenůfa*.	JP57+
? Sept 1915	Schmoranz hears *Jenůfa* and is enthusiastic.	JP60
29 Sept 1915	Kovařovic turns down *Jenůfa* again.	JP62
3 Oct 1915	Peška attacks Schmoranz.	JP63
after 20 Oct 1915	Peška attacks Kovařovic.	JP66
by 10 Nov 1915	Kovařovic's resistance weakens.	JP67
12 Nov 1915	Janáček 'tidies up' score.	JP70

8 Dec 1915	Calma sings extracts to Kovařovic and convinces him.	JP76
26 Dec 1915	Janáček in Prague for consultation with Kovařovic.	JP82
5 Feb 1916	Janáček recommends Schütz for Laca.	JP87
by 25 Feb 1916	Casting complete; Calma not cast as Jenůfa.	JP88
21 March 1916	Kovařovic studies *Jenůfa*.	JP91
17 April 1916	Daily rehearsals at piano.	JP93
25 April 1916	First orchestral rehearsal.	JP94
[4] May 1916	Janáček attends rehearsals (Act 1, orchestra; soloists blocking; Act 2).	JP96
5 May 1916	Kovařovic working on full score (Act 1 nearly ready).	JP97
11 May 1916	Janáček at Act 2 orchestral rehearsals; work on Act 3 chorus and soloists' movement.	JP98
12 May 1916	Janáček at Act 1 stage rehearsals.	JP99
13 May 1916	Janáček at orchestral rehearsals (Act 2).	JP100
14 May 1916	Censorship forbids Jenůfa's prayer.	JP101
15 May 1916	Orchestra's final work on Act 3; Orchestra and soloists work on Acts 1–2.	JP101
17 May 1916	First full rehearsal.	JP99
18 May 1916	Full rehearsal of Acts 1–2 with stage action.	JP102
19 May 1916	Orchestra polishes Acts 1–2; full rehearsal Acts 1–2.	JP103
19 May 1916	Censorship allows Jenůfa's prayer, but requires change of words in Recruits' chorus.	JP103
21 May 1916	Janáček and Kovařovic adjust words for Recruits.	JP105
22 May 1916	Orchestral rehearsals for Acts 2–3; Chorus and soloist rehearsals for Act 3.	JP107
22 May 1916	Final permission from police censorship.	JP107
26 May 1916	NT première of *Jenůfa*.	JP108
4 June 1916	Janáček dedicates *Brouček* to Kovařovic in gratitude.	JP114
3 Dec 1916	Janáček persuades Brod to take on German translation.	JP135–7
20 March 1917	Brod's translation complete.	JP139
5 May 1917	VS (2nd edn) published by Hudební matice.	JP119
4 Dec 1917	UE publishes German VS.	JP133
16 Feb 1918	Vienna première of *Jenůfa*.	JP141
9 Sept 1918	UE publishes German full score.	JP134
28 May 1923	Kovařovic's widow threatens action over royalty.	JP146
21 Sept 1923	Janáček attempts to suppress Kovařovic's changes.	JP150

1 Jan 1924	Janáček plans to go to arbitration over changes.	JP157
19 Feb 1924	The Kovařovic case collapses; his version stands.	JP162
1982	Recording (by Mackerras) of original version.	JP166+

FATE

Aug 1903	Janáček meets Kamila Urválková.	OS2
9 Oct 1903	Janáček thinks about libretto.	OS6
? Oct 1903	Janáček draws up first scenario.	OS7
early Nov 1903	Bartošová agrees to collaborate on a libretto.	OS8
12 Nov 1903	Janáček sends Bartošová scenario of part of Act 1.	OS9
17 Nov 1903	Janáček sends scenario of more of Act 1.	OS11
25 Nov 1903	Bartošová returns final part of libretto of Act 1.	OS8+
26 Nov 1903	Janáček begins sketching scenario of Act 2.	OS14
29 Nov 1903	Janáček sends scenario of Act 2.	OS15
8 Dec 1903	Janáček sends Act 3 scenario.	OS18
by 8 Dec 1903	Composition of Act 1 begun.	OS18
22? Dec 1903	Bartošová takes final part of libretto to Brno.	OS20
Christmas 1903	Janáček shows libretto to friends.	OS22
10? April 1904	Janáček suggests revisions to Acts 1 and 2 libretto.	OS23
12? April 1904	Janáček suggests revisions to Act 2 libretto.	OS24
22 April 1904	Composition of Act 1 finished.	OS25
28 April 1904	Janáček receives new material from Bartošová.	OS26
11 May 1904	Bartošová meets Janáček in Luhačovice for revisions.	OS28
3 July 1904	Janáček's last recorded contact with Bartošová.	OS29
12 June 1905	Štross's fair copy of opera (1st version) completed.	OS29+
22 June 1906	Janáček agrees to submit *Fate* to BT.	OS33
30 July 1906	Janáček receives fair copy of revised (2nd) version and begins to check it.	OS36
9 Oct 1906	Janáček asks BT to collect score and states conditions.	OS39
11 Dec 1906	BT accepts conditions.	OS40
3 Jan 1907	BT designer asks questions about sets and costumes.	OS41

26 March 1907	BT producer asks questions.	OS43
12–14 May 1907	Rektorys suggests submitting *Fate* to VT.	OS44
29 May 1907	Janáček submits *Fate* to VT.	OS47
18 June 1907	Skácelík agrees to revise libretto.	OS53
27 Sept 1907	Skácelík reports (negatively) on libretto.	OS58
10 Oct 1907	Janáček suggests changes to Act 1 of libretto.	OS59
3 Nov 1907	Janáček's corrections to Act 1 complete.	OS63
14 Nov 1907	Janáček suggests changes to Acts 2–3 of libretto.	OS65
19 Nov 1907	Janáček sends corrected score (3rd version) to VT.	OS66
1 Dec 1907	Parts being copied by VT.	OS68
29 July 1908	BT begs to perform *Fate*.	OS73
31 July 1908	Janáček temporizes over BT's request.	OS74
4 Nov 1908	VT states that *Fate* will not be given before 1909.	OS77
4 Oct 1911	VT states there is no contract to perform *Fate*.	OS80
20 Dec 1911	Janáček sent contract for VT to perform *Fate* 1912–13.	OS84
4 Feb 1913	VT preparations going badly.	OS86
5 April 1913	VT states that *Fate* is unperformable.	OS91
by 6 April 1913	VT hears from Janáček's solicitor.	OS92
4 June 1913	First hearing of Janáček's court case against VT.	OS95–6
10 July 1913	Court case adjourned until 27 Aug 1913.	OS97
17 July 1913	Čelanský tries to settle out of court.	OS98
1 Sept 1913	VT proposals for out-of-court settlement.	OS101
20 Sept 1913	Case against VT adjourned.	OS103
by 18 Oct 1913	Janáček formally withdraws case against VT.	OS105
27 Feb 1914	Janáček withdraws *Fate* from VT.	OS106
3 July 1914	BT producer states *Fate* will be performed next season.	OS107
9 Jan 1917	Janáček asks Procházka for help with revision of libretto.	OS108
8 Sept 1918	Max Brod 'at a loss' over libretto.	OS111
13 March 1934	Broadcast performance of *Fate*.	OS112
25 Oct 1958	First stage performance (in Brno) of *Fate*.	OS112

THE EXCURSIONS OF MR BROUČEK

Notes

1. BRI–94 refer exclusively to *The Excursion of Mr Brouček to the Moon*.
2. In BRI–76 the act numbering refers to the original four-act version of *The Excursion of Mr Brouček to the Moon*; thereafter act numbers are as today, while 'Act 3' refers to the discarded epilogue act.
3. *The Excursion of Mr Brouček to the Fifteenth Century* Act 2 was originally divided into Acts 2 and 3; references throughout 1917 are to this form.
4. ME = *The Excursion of Mr Brouček to the Moon*
   FCE = *The Excursion of Mr Brouček to the Fifteenth Century*

1 Feb 1888	Janáček reprints part of Čech's novel in *Hudební listy*.	BRI
12 March 1908	Janáček asks to meet Čech's publisher.	BR2
21 March 1908	Janáček gains permission to use Čech's text.	BR6
22 March 1908	Janáček's outline of libretto.	BR9
29–30 March 1908	First contacts with Mašek.	BRIO–II
17 May 1908	Mašek sends beginning of libretto.	BRI5
28 Oct 1908	Mašek's final refusal to work on libretto.	BR23
8 Nov 1908	Holý refuses to write libretto.	BR28
15 Nov 1908	Janke agrees to write libretto.	BR29
16 Dec 1908	Janke sends first scene of libretto.	BR30
22 Jan 1909	Janke's libretto upset by Janáček's new plan.	BR31
8 March 1909	Janáček's cast-list with earth-moon parallels.	BR33
26 Sept 1909	Janáček claims to have composed Act 1 four times.	BR36
18 Feb 1910	Janáček begins Act 2.	BR37
April 1911	Act 2 finished; Janáček begins Act 3.	BR42
29 April 1912	S.K. Neumann refuses to work on libretto of opera.	BR46
June 1912	Janáček's first contacts with Gellner (Act 3).	BR47
23 Oct 1912	Janáček's contacts with Gellner over Act 4.	BR50
12 Feb 1913	Act 3 complete.	BR49+
17 June 1913	Gellner's final contributions to Act 4.	BR52
12 Oct 1915	Peška agrees to look at *Brouček* libretto.	BR55
19 Dec 1915	Peška recommends Procházka as librettist	BR57
31 Dec 1915	Janáček sends *Brouček* libretto to Procházka.	BR58

3 April 1916	Procházka sends Mazal–Málinka scene.	BR61
29 May 1916	Procházka sends Act 4 libretto.	BR63
June 1916	Janáček's first contacts with Mahen.	BR64
4 June 1916	Janáček dedicates opera to Kovařovic.	JP114
mid-June 1916	Janáček's first contacts with Dyk.	BR71
19 July 1916	Mahen sends Act 3 of his libretto.	BR65
21 July 1916	Janáček receives Dyk's revisions to Act 1.	BR74
8 Sept 1916	Mahen reacts to report about Dyk's involvement.	BR69
14 Sept 1916	Dyk sends revision of Mazal–Málinka scene.	BR76
	[FROM NOW FINAL ACT-NUMBERING]	
18 Sept 1916	Dyk sends corrections to end of Act 2.	BR77
23 Sept 1916	Dyk sends Lunobor's 'three chapters'.	BR78
30 Sept 1916	Janáček sends Act 2 for additions.	BR79
1 Oct 1916	Dyk's first instalment of Act 2 additions.	BR80
5 Oct 1916	Veselý's VS of Act 1 Scene 1 complete.	BR155
7 Oct 1916	Janáček's settlement with Mahen.	BR83
9 Oct 1916	Dyk's second instalment of Act 2 additions.	BR81
16 Oct 1916	Dyk provides new drinking song.	BR84
25 Oct 1916	Janáček begins Act 3 (epilogue).	BR86+
26 Oct 1916	Veselý's VS of Act 1 Scene 2 complete.	BR155+
26 Oct 1916	Composition just before 'climax' of Act 2.	BR162
5 Nov 1916	Janáček ends revisions of Act 2.	BR162
11 Nov 1916	Dyk sends his Act 3 libretto continuation.	BR85
20 Nov 1916	Dyk arrested for high treason.	BR86
22 Nov 1916	Act 1 with publisher Hudební matice for engraving.	BR158
5 Dec 1916	Janáček completes Act 3.	BR86+
19 Dec 1916	Sedláček's copy of Act 3 complete.	BR92+
24 Dec 1916	Veselý's Act 2 complete.	BR157
25 Dec 1916	Proofs of Act 1 in progress.	BR160
17 Jan 1917	Brod makes suggestions for ends of Acts 2 and 3.	BR87
22 Jan 1917	Act 2 engraved.	BR160+
22 Jan 1917	Discussions over staging ME.	BR166
31 Jan 1917	Janáček asks Procházka for help with additions.	BR89
1 March 1917	Procházka sends additions for Act 3.	BR90
15 March 1917	Sedláček's copy of Act 3 (revised).	BR92+
16 March 1917	Janáček asks Procházka for more additions to Act 3.	BR93
18 March 1917	Procházka sends additions.	BR94
24 March 1917	Janáček proposes FCE to Procházka.	BR95
29 March 1917	Sedláček's copy of final revisions to Act 3.	BR92+

?11 April 1917	Janáček and Procházka meet to discuss FCE.	BR98
30 April 1917	Procházka begins FCE libretto.	BR103
1 May 1917	Procházka finishes Act 1.	BR104
?5 May 1917	Janáček begins composition of FCE.	BR109
31 May 1917	Procházka finishes Act 2.	BR114
23 June 1917	Procházka sends Act 2.	BR121
1 July 1917	Janáček completes Act 1.	BR123
31 Aug 1917	Act 1 ready in fair copy.	BR129
27 Dec 1917	Interest in ME by Drei-Masken Verlag.	BR168
18 Sept 1917	Janáček finishes Act 2.	BR134
22 Oct 1917	Procházka working on Act 3.	BR135
28 Oct 1917	Procházka finishes Act 3.	BR137
5 Nov 1917	Procházka sends off Act 3.	BR138
23 Nov 1917	Janáček working on Act 3.	BR140
3 Dec 1917	Procházka sends Act 3 changes.	BR143
3 Dec 1917	Janáček finishes Act 3.	BR145
12 Dec 1917	Janáček makes small addition to Act 3.	BR150
23 Dec 1917	Janáček describes *Brouček* in *Lidové noviny*.	BR167
by 29 Dec 1917	Maixner agrees to make VS of FCE.	BR195
18 Jan 1918	Janáček abandons ME epilogue.	BR154
8 Feb 1918	Hudební matice agrees to waive rights to ME.	BR169
28 Feb 1918	Janáček asks Veselý to make VS of FCE.	BR197
13 March 1918	UE sees brush proofs of ME.	BR174
27 April 1918	Janáček takes libretto to Kovařovic.	BR201
17 May 1918	Kovařovic asks to see full score.	BR203
5 June 1918	Janáček's proposals to UE over edition.	BR176
11 June 1918	Kovařovic agrees to stage *Brouček*.	BR205
21 June 1918	Drei-Masken Verlag turns down ME.	BR173
8 July 1918	UE sends contract for edition.	BR178
before 16 July 1918	Negotations with Procházka over royalty.	BR191
5 Aug 1918	Procházka agrees royalty with Janáček.	BR193
22 Aug 1918	Veselý's VS of FCE ready.	BR199
15 Sept 1918	Janáček returns signed contract for edition.	BR180+
24 Oct 1918	Amended contract for edition signed.	BR183
11 April 1919	Vocal score ready for printing.	BR184
5 May 1919	President Masaryk accepts dedication.	BR209
20 May 1919	Novák completes cover design for VS.	BR188
24 Sept 1919	Vocal score printed and distributed.	BR190
25 Sept 1919	Kovařovic suggests revising voice parts.	BR215
18 Oct 1919	Janáček sends back revised VS.	BR218
20 Nov 1919	Kovařovic suggests casting.	BR220
19 Dec 1919	Opera in rehearsal in Prague.	BR224

March 1920	Rehearsals resume after Schmoranz's illness.	BR231
23 April 1920	Première at NT.	BR233+
25 April 1920	Janáček suggests changes to Ostrčil.	BR237
27 April 1920	Janáček sends Ostrčil changes in FCE.	BR238
16 May 1920	Janáček sends Ostrčil more changes.	BR240
23 Aug 1920	Janáček sends choral welcoming to Žižka to Ostrčil.	BR243
15 June 1926	Première (of ME) at BT.	BR247+

KÁŤA KABANOVÁ

Spring 1918	Červinka's translation of *The Thunderstorm*.	KK2+
18 March 1919	Brno production of *The Thunderstorm*.	KK2+
19 March 1919	Prague production of *The Thunderstorm*.	KK2+
21 Oct 1919	Janáček writes to Adolf Červinka for permission.	KK3
27 Oct 1919	Adolf Červinka writes that Vincenc Červinka is away.	KK3
29 Dec 1919	Vincenc Červinka receives letter from Janáček .	KK7
31 Dec 1919	Červinka gives permission for use of translation.	KK8
early Jan 1920	Janáček visits Červinka.	KK7
5 Jan 1920	Janáček begins *Káťa Kabanová*.	KK10
1 July 1920	Janáček completes Act 1.	KK13+
14 Sept 1920	Janáček begins Act 2.	KK13+
15 Oct 1920	Janáček completes Act 2.	KK13+
24 Dec 1920	Janáček completes Act 3.	KK13+
Jan 1921	Janáček begins first revision.	KK14+
22 March 1921	Nebuška proposes publication by Hudební matice.	KK16
27 March 1921	Janáček completes first revision.	KK14+
3 April 1921	Červinka suggests title of *Káťa Kabanová*.	KK18
17 April 1921	Janáček completes second revision.	KK14+
21 April 1921	Universal Edition offer publication.	KK21
26 April 1921	Neumann asks for *Káťa Kabanová* on behalf of BT.	KK32
2 May 1921	Janáček tells Ostrčil he has completed *Káťa*.	KK33
5 May 1921	Homola completes fair copy of full score.	KK28+
23 June 1921	Veselý refuses to make VS.	KK29
25 June 1921	Formal request from BT for *Káťa Kabanová*.	KK37
July 1921	Bakala works on VS.	KK30

12 Aug 1921	Brod agrees to translate *Káťa Kabanová*.	KK77
18 Aug 1921	Janáček continues to check score.	KK40
31 Aug 1921	Hudební matice agree to sell UE's edition.	KK23
2 Sept 1921	Bakala sends VS to printer.	KK31
5 Oct 1921	Brod begins to translate libretto.	KK78
22 Oct 1921	Brod sends Act 1 to UE.	KK81
25 Oct 1921	Brod proposes changes.	KK80
4 Nov 1921	Brod about to send Acts 2 and 3 to UE.	KK81
10 Nov 1921	Original date of BT première.	KK47
11 Nov 1921	Janáček signs contract with UE.	KK25
23 Nov 1921	BT première of *Káťa Kabanová*.	KK47+
8 Dec 1921	Ostrčil sees and accepts *Káťa Kabanová* for NT.	KK52
after 10 Dec 1921	Janáček makes changes on Brod's suggestion.	KK83
20 Feb 1922	UE VS published.	KK26
1 March 1922	Ostrčil suggests casting for NT production.	KK54
16 July 1922	NT solo rehearsals begin.	KK62
Aug-Sept 1922	UE publishes full score.	KK56
29 Sept 1922	NT orchestral rehearsals begin.	KK62
19 Oct 1922	NT blocking rehearsals begin.	KK62
31 Oct 1922	Janáček hears orchestral rehearsal at NT.	KK63–4
21–4 Nov 1922	NT final rehearsals.	KK67
22 Nov 1922	UE publishes parts.	KK57
26 Nov 1922	Original date for NT première.	KK67
28 Nov 1922	Janáček has misgivings about continuity of acts.	KK69
30 Nov 1922	NT première of *Káťa Kabanová*.	KK70+
8 Dec 1922	German première of *Káťa Kabanová* (Cologne).	KK75+
4 March 1924	Janáček asks for quick scene changes at NT.	KK86
31 May 1926	Berlin première of *Káťa Kabanová*.	KK75+
9 Nov 1927	Janáček extends interludes in Acts 1 and 2.	KK88–9
21 Jan 1928	First performance (Prague GT) with new interludes.	KK88+
12 Feb 1928	Janáček's dedication of score of Kamila Stösslová.	KK96

THE CUNNING LITTLE VIXEN

| 7 April to 23 June 1920 | Publication of Těsnohlídek's *Liška Bystrouška* in *Lidové noviny*. | LB1+ |
| 15 May 1921 | Janáček admits to plans to compose *The Vixen*. | LB7 |

22 Jan 1922	Janáček begins composition (1st version).	LB15+
26 March 1922	Janáček completes Act 1.	LB15+
early May 1922	Janáček meets Těsnohlídek for permission to use *Liška Bystrouška* for an opera.	LB2
16 May 1922	Těsnohlídek provides one song.	LB4
5 June 1922	Janáček complete Act 2 (1st half).	LB15+
7 June 1922	Janáček begins Act 2 (2nd half).	LB15+
22 Aug 1922	Janáček 'roughly up to the last act'.	LB12
25 Oct 1922	Janáček completes first version?	LB15+
20 Nov 1922	Approach from BT for *The Vixen*.	LB15
22 Feb 1923	Revision of Act 1 completed.	LB15+
29 March 1923	Kulhánek's copy of Act 1.	LB15+
29 June 1923	Revision of Act 2 completed?	LB15+
20 July 1923	Kulhánek's copy of Act 2.	LB15+
July 1923	Difficulties with copyists/amanuenses.	LB18–21
22 Aug 1923	Bakala VS of Acts 1–2 nearly complete .	LB16
10 Oct 1923	Revision of Act 3 completed.	LB16+
22 Oct 1923	Janáček offers *The Vixen* to UE.	LB24
9 Jan 1924	Hudební matice offers to publish VS.	LB27
12 Jan 1924	Kulhánek's copy of Act 3.	LB16+
4 March 1924	UE undertakes to publish VS by end of June.	LB33
30 July 1924	UE publishes VS.	LB35
1 Sept 1924	Rehearsals under way in BT.	LB36
6 Nov 1924	BT première of *The Vixen*.	LB38
16 Feb 1925	NT producer and designer in place for *The Vixen*.	LB45
29 March 1925	Janáček reports that NT already know *The Vixen* well.	LB47
4–6 May 1925	Janáček attends rehearsals at NT.	LB49–51
18 May 1925	NT première of *The Vixen*.	LB51+
by 2 June 1925	Brod begins German translation.	LB58
26 June 1925	Janáček rejects most of Brod's arrangement.	LB65
11 July 1925	Brod completes German translation.	LB61
27 July 1925	Janáček asks for fanfares to be sent to UE.	LB69
13 Feb 1927	German première of *The Vixen* (in Mainz).	LB69+

THE MAKROPULOS AFFAIR

10 Dec 1922	Janáček sees Čapek's play *The Makropulos Affair*.	VM1+
27 Feb 1923	Čapek unable to give Janáček permission to set *Makropulos*.	VM2
10–11 July 1923	Janáček reads *Makropulos* on holiday.	VM4+

3 Aug 1923	Janáček unable to reach agreement with Čapek.	VM6
10 Sept 1923	Čapek gives his permission for Janáček to set *Makropulos*.	VM7
24 Sept 1923	Khol sends Janáček conditions for use of text.	VM8
10 Oct 1923	Khol sends revised conditions.	VM10
11 Nov 1923	Janáček begins work on *Makropulos*.	VM11+
19 Feb 1924	Janáček completes Act 1 (1st version).	VM13+
19 March 1924	Janáček begins Act 2 (1st version).	VM13+
18? Feb 1925	Janáček completes Act 3 (1st version).	VM14+
15 March 1925	Janáček begins revising *Makropulos*.	VM20+
27 July 1925	Revision of Act 2 complete.	VM20+
12 Nov 1925	Revision of Act 3 complete.	VM24+
3 Dec 1925	Final revision of *Makropulos* complete.	VM24+
14 Jan 1926	Janáček considers submitting *Makropulos* for opera competition in Philadelphia.	VM26
22 Jan 1926	Janáček suggests to UE that it renegotiate his contract with Čapek.	VM28
31 Jan 1926	Ostrčil asks to give première.	SR41
2 April 1926	Khol sends amended contract.	VM30
24 April 1926	Janáček submits *Makropulos* to BT.	VM47
3 June 1926	Both Berlin theatres competing for German première of *Makropulos*.	VM63
?16 June 1926	Janáček signs contract with UE.	VM31
19 June 1926	UE receives manuscript VS from Janáček.	VM32
9 Sept 1926	Engraving of VS begun.	VM33
before 7 Oct 1926	*Makropulos* in rehearsal at BT.	VM48
19 Oct 1926	Brod received VS 'a few days previously'.	VM39
22 Oct 1926	Brod sends off translation of Act 1.	VM40
9 Nov 1926	Janáček resists Brod's proposed changes.	VM42
3 Dec 1926	VS proofs sent for BT rehearsals.	VM35
11 Dec 1926	Proposed date of BT première.	VM51
15 Dec 1926	VS and libretto published and sent to Janáček.	VM36
18 Dec 1926	BT première of *Makropulos*.	VM52+
2 Jan 1927	Janáček complains of Brod's changes in Act 3.	VM43
13 Jan 1927	Ostrčil asks to perform *Makropulos*.	VM67
7 Feb 1927	Brod concedes some of Janáček's demands over German translation.	VM45
9 Feb 1927	Ostrčil attends BT performance of *Makropulos*.	VM70
8 June 1927	Ostrčil suggests producers for NT production.	VM72

13 Dec 1927	*Makropulos* allegedly in rehearsal at Berlin.	VM65
13 Dec 1927	Janáček hears of NT cast for *Makropulos*.	VM74
?11 Feb 1928	Orchestral rehearsals under way at NT.	VM75
23–8 Feb 1928	Janáček attends rehearsals at NT.	VM79–81
1 March 1928	NT première of *Makropulos*.	VM84–5
May 1928	German première scheduled at Berlin.	VM66
14 Feb 1929	German première at Frankfurt.	VM66+

FROM THE HOUSE OF THE DEAD

after May 1926	Janáček begins Violin Concerto.	ZD2+
12 Feb 1927	Letter to Brod with reference to Dostoyevsky's novel.	ZD3
18 Feb 1927	Janáček begins sketching opera.	ZD6+
?23–8 Feb 1927	Scenario in Janáček's diary.	ZD4
2 April 1927	Janáček completes Act 1 (1st version).	ZD13+
27–8 May 1927	Janáček refers to opera in correspondence.	ZD8
28 June 1927	Janáček refers to opera in *Lidové noviny*.	ZD10
29 July 1927	News item in *Lidové noviny* about opera.	ZD11
16–17 Oct 1927	Janáček finishes opera (1st version).	ZD13
22 Oct 1927	Janáček at work on 2nd version (Prisoners' brawl near beginning of Act 1).	ZD14
by 18 Dec 1927	Act 1 and 2 (2nd version) complete.	ZD18
30 Dec 1927	Janáček working on Šiškov's story (Act 3).	ZD19
3 Jan 1928	Janáček finished with Šiškov's story.	ZD20
4 Jan 1928	2nd version of opera complete.	ZD21
10 March 1928	Janáček working with copyists.	ZD23
28 March 1928	Sedláček's copy of Act 1 complete.	ZD21+
24 April 1928	3rd version (Act 3) complete.	ZD21+
1 May 1928	Janáček working on Skuratov's story (Act 2).	ZD26
2 May 1928	Janáček working on Don Juan and Kedril play scene (Act 2).	ZD27
5–6 May 1928	Janáček completes Beautiful Miller's Wife play scene (Act 2).	ZD30
7 May 1928	3rd version (Act 2) complete, i.e. whole opera.	ZD21+
11 May 1928	Janáček continues supervising copying.	ZD32
14 May 1928	Kulhánek's copy of Act 3 complete.	ZD21+
23 May 1928	Sedláček and Kulhánek's copy of Act 2 complete.	ZD21+
7–8 June 1928	Janáček continues supervising revision of fair copy.	ZD33
9 June 1928	Revisions to fair copy of Act 3 complete.	ZD34
10 June 1928	Sedláček finishes revisions to fair copy.	ZD35

11 June 1928	Janáček pays off Sedláček.	ZD22
18 June 1928	Twenty pages 'still to write'.	ZD36
20 June 1928	Kulhánek finishes revisions to fair copy.	ZD37
20 June 1928	Janáček pays off Kulhánek.	ZD22
1–21 July 1928	Janáček on holiday in Luhačovice.	ZD37+
end July 1928	Chlubna reports seeing bound scores of opera.	ZD38
end July 1928	Janáček has checked final copy of Acts 1 and 2; Act 3 still needs to be checked.	ZD38
30 July 1928	Janáček goes to Hukvaldy.	ZD38
12 Aug 1928	Janáček dies of pneumonia, Act 3 still unchecked.	ZD38+
autumn 1929	Chlubna and Bakala revise opera.	ZD38
1930	VS and full score published by UE.	ZD38+
12 April 1930	BT première (in Chlubna–Bakala arrangement).	ZD38+
14 Dec 1930	German première in Mannheim.	ZD38+
21 Feb 1931	NT première.	ZD38+
17 Nov 1961	Kubelík performs version without Chlubna–Bakala additions.	ZD38+
1964	UE issue VS with Janáček's original ending.	ZD38+
1980	Recording by Mackerras based on Sedláček–Kulhánek copy with Janáček's additions.	ZD38+

Glossary of Names and Terms

This glossary contains names (and a few terms) that occur in more than one chapter of the book. Information on those occurring only in one chapter is given in the footnotes or within the text of the chapter. All persons in the glossary are Czech, unless otherwise stated.

Bakala, Břetislav (1897–1958), conductor. Janáček's pupil at the Brno Organ School (1912–15), he was repetiteur and conductor at the Brno Opera 1920–5, where he helped Neumann in the preparation of several Janáček premières. He made the piano arrangements for the vocal scores of *Káťa Kabanová*, *The Cunning Little Vixen* and *From the House of the Dead*.

Bartoš, František (1837–1906), folklorist and dialectologist. From 1888 director of the Czech Gymnasium in Old Brno, where Janáček also taught. Janáček collaborated with him on several collections of Moravian folksongs.

Bartošová, Fedora (1884–1941), schoolteacher, poet and friend of Janáček's daughter Olga. She published poems in *Lidové noviny*, *Moravská orlice* and other journals, at first under the pseudonym of Kamila Talská. She wrote the first libretto for *Fate* (see os7+ ff, especially p. 114, fn.1).

Bendl, Karel (1838–97), composer. His operas included *The Child of Tábor* (1892).

Beseda, a friendly conversation, neighbourly gathering for a chat. From this primary meaning several subsidiary meanings developed in the nineteenth century, notably that of a social organization, e.g. the Umělecká beseda [Artists' Society]. The building erected in Brno for the Czechs' cultural gatherings and and other entertainment in 1874 was called the Besední dům [Meeting House].

The Starobrněnská beseda [Old Brno Beseda] was founded in 1888 in Old Brno (the Czech quarter) as a cultural club for Czechs in German Brno. It had its own library, and organized lectures, various entertainments and patriotic evenings; the Brno Orchestral Society was founded under its aegis. The society met in hired rooms, from 1891 in the house of Janáček's neighbour Mrs Kusá. This house was acquired for it in 1900 and remained its home until 1917, by which time its heyday was over.

Branberger, Dr Jan (1877–1952), writer on music. He was professor and secretary of the Prague Conservatory (1906–18) and music critic of the journal *Čas* (1903–10).

Brod, Max (1884–1968), German-speaking writer, born in Prague, the friend and biographer of Kafka and of Janáček, many of whose librettos he translated into German (see JP134+). Janáček sought his advice on many occasions (see for instance OS110+, 111), and Brod contributed several details to the final shape of *Brouček* (BR87ff), *Káťa Kabanová* (KK80–4) and *The Cunning Little Vixen* (LB57–66).

Chlubna, Osvald (1893–1971), composer. In 1914–15, he studied at the Brno Organ School with Janáček, who later entrusted him with the orchestration of the final act of *Šárka* (SR14+ to SR19). After Janáček's death he reorchestrated and revised *From the House of the Dead* (see ZD38).

Doubravský, Alois [Staněk, Alois] (1867–1924), tenor. He took his professional name Alois Doubravský from his birthplace, Doubravčice. A stalwart member of the Brno Czech theatre, he sang in 1039 performances there between 1897 and 1913. He was the first Laca in *Jenůfa* in 1904 and as director of the Brno National Theatre (1903–4) was responsible for the opera's introduction into the repertory.

Družstvo (pl. *Družstva*), consortium. *Družstva* were formed by wealthy Czech patriots to administer the companies in the new Czech theatres in Prague, Brno and elsewhere, tendering for fixed-term contracts. The *Družstvo Národního divadla* ran the Prague National Theatre from 1881 to 1900, with František Adolf Šubert as director (from 1883). When ousted by the newly formed *Společnost Národního divadla*, Šubert and his *Družstvo* went on to found a new Czech theatre in the Vinohrady district of Prague (see OS45+).

Dvořák, Antonín (1841–1904), the leading Czech composer of his generation, befriended Janáček and advised him on some of his early compositions, including *Šárka* (SR7–8). Julius Zeyer originally wrote the libretto of this opera for him (SR1–3).

Elgart, Dr Jaroslav (1872–1955), executive officer of the *Družstvo* of the Brno Czech theatre, brother of Karel Elgart Sokol. A medical doctor, he was later chief surgeon in the Kroměříž general hospital. He treated Janáček and in gratitude Janáček dedicated his *Fairy Tale* for cello and piano to him.

Elgart Sokol, Karel (1874–1929), writer, brother of Jaroslav Elgart. A pupil of Janáček at the Teachers' Training Institute, he was an enthusiastic contributor to Brno cultural life, as a teacher at Vesna, a functionary of the *Družstvo* of the Brno Czech theatre and as a member of the literary committee of the Club of the Friends of Art (1905–10).

Fibich, Zdeněk (1850–1900), the most prominent Czech opera composer after Dvořák in the last decade of the nineteenth century. His best-known opera, *Šárka* (1897) was written a decade after Janáček's first opera, and to a different libretto.

Foerster, Josef Bohuslav (1859–1945), composer. A younger contemporary of Janáček, he achieved early success with his opera *Eva* (1899), based, like *Jenůfa*, on a play by Gabriela Preissová (see JP3 to JP5+).

Frýda, Josef Antoš [Friedl, Antonín Josef] (1857–1922), actor and theatre director. He was director of the Brno National Theatre 1905–9 and thus particularly involved with its proposed production of *Fate* in 1906–7 (see OS35 and OS39–42).

Hanusová-Svobodová, Leopolda (1875–1941), soprano (see JP29). She was the first Kostelnička in *Jenůfa*, and the proposed Míla for the abortive Brno production of *Fate* (OS94).

Helfert, Vladimir (1886–1945), musicologist. He taught at the newly instituted Masaryk University in Brno from 1922, from 1931 as full professor. He was responsible for establishing the university's Janáček collection, later taken over by the Moravian Museum in Brno, whose music archive he had founded in 1919. In 1939 he published the first (and only) volume of what was planned to be a multi-volume biography of the composer.

Hertzka, Dr Emil (1869–1932), publisher, managing director from 1907 to 1932 of the Viennese firm of Universal Edition (q.v.).

Horvátová [married name: Noltschová], **Gabriela** (1877–1967), mezzo-soprano/dramatic soprano (see JP86+). She sang the Kostelnička at the first Prague performance of *Jenůfa*. Horvátová conducted a passionate correspondence with Janáček from early 1916 to 1918 and provided enthusiastic moral support during the final stages of the composition of *The Excursions of Mr Brouček*.

Hudební matice, music publishing organization, founded in Prague in 1871 under the aegis of the Czech cultural society, the Umělecká beseda [Artist's society]. After 1907 publications came out under the imprint of Hudební matice Umělecké besedy, conveniently abbreviated to its original form, Hudební matice. The Hudební matice published the second edition of *Jenůfa* (see JP116+ and ff.) and initiated the publication of *The Excursion of Mr Brouček to the Moon* (see BR158 ff), though this was ultimately taken over by Universal Edition.

Janáčková, Olga (1882–1903), the composer's daughter. Janáček dedicated *Jenůfa* to her memory.

Janáčková [née Schulzová], **Zdenka** (1865–1938), the composer's wife. Janáček married his piano pupil Zdenka Schulzová in 1881. They had two children: Olga (1882–1903) and Vladimír (1888–90). The marriage was not a happy one. Soon after Olga's birth the couple separated for two years, and after her early death there was little other than habit and convenience to keep Janáček and his wife together. Holidays tended to be taken separately, and it was during his solitary stays in Luhačovice that Janáček met Kamila Urválková and Kamila Stösslová.

Jirásek, Alois (1851–1930), playwright and novelist, with a particular penchant for historical themes.

Jiřikovský, Václav (1891–1942), administrative director of the Brno Theatre 1915–19.

John, Jaromír. *See* **Markalous, Dr Bohumil.**

Kleiber, Erich (1890–1956), Austrian conductor, general music director at the Berlin Staatsoper, where in 1924 he introduced audiences to an influential production of *Jenůfa*.

Klemperer, Otto (1885–1973), German conductor. He conducted at the German Prague theatre (1907–10) and was music director at Cologne (1917–24), where in 1918 he introduced *Jenůfa* (the first German-language version after Vienna) and the German première of *Káťa Kabanová* in 1922. A Janáček enthusiast who conducted many early performances of the Sinfonietta, he was also a contender for the German première of *The Makropulos Affair* at the Berlin Kroll Opera, to which he moved in 1927.

Kovařovic, Karel (1862–1920), composer and conductor, head of opera at the Prague National Theatre 1900–20. As a composer, he achieved his greatest popular success with *The Dogheads* (1898). Janáček's contemptuous review of Kovařovic's first opera, *The Bridegrooms* (1884, see JP12), soured relations between the two men and resulted in the long delay before Kovařovic accepted *Jenůfa* in Prague.

Krásnohorská, Eliška [pseudonym of Alžběta Pechová] (1847–1926), writer, and librettist of operas by Smetana, Bendl and Fibich.

Kulhánek, Jaroslav (1881–1938), first trombone at the Brno National Theatre 1919–38. Janáček used him as a copyist in his three last operas.

Kunc, Jan (1883–1976), composer, critic and administrator. He graduated from Janáček's Organ School in Brno in 1903 and studied further at the Prague Conservatory (1905–6). A prominent critic, he wrote a study of Janáček's dramatic style (1906) and his first biography (1911). He became administrator (1920–3) and director (1923–45) of the Brno Conservatory (the former Organ School).

Kusá [née Fantová], **Julie** (1858–1908), friend of Gabriela Preissová. Married to the politician Wolfgang Kusý, she settled in Brno and was active in Moravian cultural circles there.

Kvapil, Jaroslav (1868–1950), librettist of Dvořák's *Rusalka*, Foerster's *Debora* and proposed librettist for Foerster's *The Farm Mistress*.

Löwenbach, Jan (1880–1972), lawyer, writer on music and librettist. As an expert on copyright law with Hudební matice from 1908, he often gave Janáček personal legal advice, for instance over his dealings with foreign publishers (see JP120ff) or in his disputes with the National Theatre over *Jenůfa* (see JP164ff).

Mackerras, Sir **Charles** (1925–), English conductor. A pupil of Talich, he conducted *Káťa Kabanová* in London in 1951, the first Janáček opera to be staged in Great Britain. His series of recordings of Janáček operas for Decca include the first authentic versions of *Jenůfa* (without Kovařovic's changes).

Maixner, Vincenc (1888–1946), conductor and composer. He joined the National Theatre as Kovařovic's assistant and repetiteur in 1915; as a conductor there (1918–38) he was responsible for the Prague première of *From the House of the Dead* in 1931.

Markalous, Dr **Bohumil** (1882–1952), writer (under the pseudonym of Jaromír John), and arts editor of the *Lidové noviny*.

Maturová, Růžena (1869–1938), the leading dramatic soprano at the Prague National Theatre 1893–1910, the first exponent of Dvořák's Rusalka and Fibich's Šárka and many other major roles. From 1906 to 1911 she was married to the conductor František Jílek.

Moor, Karel (1873–1945), composer and conductor. He held various conducting posts including that of second conductor at the Brno National Theatre (1908); it was during his tenure as director of an independent theatrical company (1909–10) that his operetta *The Excursion of Mr Brouček to the Moon* was performed in 1910.

Nebuška, Otakar (1875–1952), administrator and writer on music. Trained and employed as a lawyer, he helped establish Hudební matice in 1907 as an independent publishing body and up to 1925 himself prepared for publication much of its extensive output. This included the second edition of *Jenůfa* in 1917 (see JP116+ to JP119) and several smaller non-operatic works by Janáček. The publication of both *The Excursions of Mr Brouček* and *Káťa Kabanová* was initiated by Nebuška in Hudební matice, though ultimately taken over by Universal Edition in Vienna.

Neumann, František (1874–1929), conductor and composer. He gained conducting experience abroad, notably in Frankfurt am Main from 1904. Having attracted Janáček's attention in Prague in 1906 by conducting the Introduction to *Jenůfa* (*Jealousy*), he was invited to take over the newly reconstituted Czech opera in Brno after the First World War at Janáček's suggestion. In the decade that he presided there as chief conductor (and from 1925 as director) Neumann built up a fine company which under his direction gave the premières of *Káťa Kabanová*, *The Cunning Little Vixen* and *The Makropulos Affair* and the belated première of *Šárka*.

Newmarch [née Jeaffreson], **Rosa** (1857–1940), English writer on music. Her earlier writings were on Russian music. When wartime conditions put an end to her visits to Russia, she transferred her interests to Czech music, and in particular to that of Janáček. She became his most important English-speaking correspondent, organizing English premières of many of his works and Janáček's visit to England in 1926. In recognition of her services Janáček dedicated the Sinfonietta (1926) to her.

Novák, Vítězslav (1870–1949), composer. One of the most prominent Czech composers early twentieth century, especially of instrumental music. The Prague production of Janáček's *Jenůfa* fell in between, and overshadowed, the first two works of Novák's operatic career (*The Imp of Zvíkov*, 1915; *Karlštejn*, 1916).

Ostrčil, Otakar (1879–1935), conductor and composer. Successor to Kovařovic at the Prague National Theatre from 1920 until his death, Ostrčil was responsible for the première of *The Excursions of Mr Brouček* and the Prague premières of *Káťa Kabanová*, *The Cunning Little Vixen* and *The Makropulos Affair*.

Peška, Josef (1857–1923), writer [literary pseudonym: Karel Šípek] and librettist. He was a headmaster and a theatre enthusiast, friendly with the chief executives of the Prague National Theatre, Gustav Schmoranz and Karel Kovařovic (for whom he wrote four librettos including that of *The Dogheads*). With Dr František Veselý and Marie Calma-Veselá he was the chief instigator for getting Prague to accept *Jenůfa* (see JP59 ff).

Preissová [née Sekerová], **Gabriela** (1862–1946), writer and dramatist. Her short stories and plays make use of her firsthand knowledge of the ethnographic aspects of the Slovácko region in Moravia. Her short story *The Beginning of a Romance* and her play *Her Stepdaughter* became the basis for Janáček's second and third operas (see PR1 ff and JP1 ff).

Procházka, F(rantišek) S(erafinský) (1861–1939), poet, editor of the magazine *Zvon*. Janáček set three of his *Songs from Hradčany* for female voices in 1916 and employed him in the final revision of *The Excursion of Mr Brouček to the Moon* (BR57–63, BR89–95) and *Šárka* (SR20–2). Procházka wrote the libretto for *The Excursion of Mr Brouček to the Fifteenth Century* (BR95 ff).

Rektorys, Artuš (1877–1971), editor and writer. He was an important Prague contact for Janáček from 1906 and advised him over the staging of *Fate* (see OS44 ff) and over the libretto for *Brouček* (see BR2 ff). He later edited several volumes of Janáček's correspondence, including that between Janáček and himself.

Schmoranz, Gustav (1858–1930), administrative director of the Prague National Theatre 1900–22. Josef Peška tried to get him to persuade Kovařovic to accept *Jenůfa* (he failed, see JP59–63). By training an architect, Schmoranz occasionally produced works at the National Theatre; rather surprisingly he took on the première of *The Excursions of Mr Brouček*.

Sedláček, Václav (1879–1944), flautist and Janáček's copyist. He played the flute from 1910 to 1935 in the Brno Theatre orchestra and in 1916 helped adapt the Brno orchestral parts of *Jenůfa* to the 'Kovařovic version'. Janáček used him later that year to copy his final version of *The Excursions of Mr Brouček* and thereafter employed him systematically as one of his chief copyists. He dedicated the *March of the Blue Birds* (1924, for piccolo and piano) to him.

Šilhan, Dr Antonín (1875–1952), critic (notably in *Národní listy*, 1910–41). A trained lawyer, he was a functionary of the Umělecká beseda.

Šípek, Karel. *See* Peška, Josef.

Smetana, Bedřich (1824–84), composer, the leading Czech nationalist of his generation, and the composer of *The Bartered Bride, Dalibor, Libuše* and *The Kiss*.

Sokol, Karel Elgart. *See* Elgart Sokol, Karel.

Šourek, Otakar (1883–1956), musicologist and critic, the author of the standard four-volume Dvořák biography (1916–33) and many other writings on Dvořák.

Staněk, Alois. *See* Doubravský, Alois.

Stejskalová, Marie [Mářa] (1873–1968), the Janáčeks' servant from 1894 until Zdenka Janáčková's death in 1938. Her reminiscences (1959) are an important source of information about Janáček's daily life, her close relationship with the composer's wife often helping to provide an insight into the latter's views.

Stösslová [née Neumannová], **Kamila** (1892–1935). Janáček met her at Luhačovice in 1917 and thereafter conducted a voluminous correspondence with her that reflects their growing friendship until his death. *Káťa Kabanová* was inspired by her (see KK45) and dedicated to her (see KK91–6). Janáček's letters to Kamila are a valuable source of information about the dating and inspiration of his final works (see for instance LB10, VM1, VM12, VM25, VM62, ZD8, ZD19, ZD21).

Štross [Stross], **Josef** (1826–1912), oboist and the copyist of Janáček's early compositions up to the first version of *Fate*.

Šubert, F(rantišek) A(dolf) (1849–1915), theatre director, producer and playwright. He was administrative director at the Prague National Theatre from 1883 until the management changes of 1900. Appointed and director of the Vinohrady Theatre on its opening in 1907, he resigned in 1908.

Suk, Josef (1874–1935), composer, mostly of orchestral and instrumental music.

Umělecká beseda. *See* Beseda and Hudební matice.

Universal Edition, Viennese music publishing firm, founded in 1901. Its modern bias led to early contacts with such composers as Bartók, Schoenberg, Berg, Webern, Schreker among many others. From 1917 it published most of Janáček's larger-scale works, including six of his operas.

Urválková [née Choutková], Kamila (1875–1956). She provided the inspiration for Čelanský's one-act opera *Kamila* and Janáček's *Fate*. Janáček met her in Luhačovice in August 1903 (os1 to os2) and she encouraged him to write a new opera. The early history of *Fate* is documented by their correspondence (see os3 to os7).

Veselý, Dr František (1862–1923) medical doctor, the creator of the public spa at Luhačovice. Janáček got to know him from his annual visits there (see e.g. os28). He was chairman of the Club of the Friends of Art and from this position began the process, together with his wife Marie Calma-Veselá and the writer Karel Šípek (Josef Peška), of persuading Kovařovic to accept *Jenůfa* in Prague (see jp55 to jp86 passim).

Veselý, Roman (1879–1933), pianist. He made the piano reduction for the vocal score of *The Excursions of Mr Brouček*.

Vomáčka, Boleslav (1887–1965), composer and critic, most notably for the Brno *Lidové noviny* (1921–38).

Vrchlický, Jaroslav (1853–1912), poet and dramatist, the librettist of operas by Dvořák, Fibich, Foerster and Novák.

Zítek, Ota(kar) (1892–1955), opera producer, composer and writer. He was employed at the theatre in Brno as opera producer (1921–6), dramaturg (1926–9) and director (1929–31). During this time he formed a close partnership with the conductor František Neummann and was responsible for the premières of Janáček's last three operas and of the early *Šárka* (sr28, sr31, sr33). Later he became director of the town theatre in Plzeň (1931–9).

List of Sources

Original-language sources are given here for all documents quoted or cited in the book.

    1st column = document code number
    2nd column = location of manuscript (—— = location unknown)
    3rd column = printed location (—— = unpublished)

Notes

1. Library locations are shown with the following abbreviations:

Bma	Brno, Městský archiv
pa	private archive
Pnmla	Prague, Národní muzeum: literarní archiv
Pnmčh	Prague, Národní muzeum: muzeum české hudby
Pnmdo	Prague, Národní muzeum: divadelní oddělení
PSom	Písek, Okresní muzeum
Wue	Vienna, Universal Edition archive
Wuest	Vienna, Universal Edition collection deposited at the Vienna Stadt- und Landesbibliothek
Whhst	Vienna, Haus-, Hof- und Staatsarchiv, Wien, Akten der Direktion des Hofoperntheaters, 1196/1904

2. All other documents are in the BmJA, Janáček Archive of the Music Division of the Moravian Provincial Museum, Brno [Hudební oddělení Moravského zemského muzea]. Individual shelfmarks have been supplied for these documents. No distinction has been made between original documents and copies.

3. If an item has been published more than once, the location of the fullest or most authoritative version, not necessarily the first, is shown here.

4. Most printed locations are shown in an author–date form which can be filled out by reference to the main bibliography (see also under abbreviations there). Smaller anonymous items such as contemporary news reports have not been given in the main bibliography. They are marked [¶] in the source list and their full version can be found at the end of the this list under their respective alphanumerical codes.

5. Documents published in an abridged form are marked with an asterisk at the beginning of the third column.

SOURCES

MS	original language publication

CHAPTER I

SR1	——	*Hudební a divadelní věstník*, i (1877–8), 238
SR2	——	*Dalibor*, ii (1880), 183 [¶]
SR3	——	Sládek 1957, 32
SR4	Pnmčh	Krásnohorská 1940, 177
SR5	——	Šourek 1916–33, ii, 26
SR6	——	Janáček 1924, 69
SR7	Pnmch	Dvořák 1988, 261
SR8	Pnmch	Dvořák 1988, 269
SR9	A 3329	Brod 1924, 69
SR10	——	Brod 1924, 69
SR11	A 3376	Brod 1924, 69
SR12	——	Sládek 1957, 176
SR13	B 2543	JA vi, 58
SR14	A 750	——
SR15	——	Chlubna 1958b
SR16	B 1781	Helfert 1939, 353
SR17	C 177	——
SR18	——	Helfert 1939, 353
SR19	——	Chlubna 1958b
SR20	B 2643	JA iii, 88–9
SR21	B 262	JA iii, 89
SR22	B 2644	JA iii, 90
SR23	B 1923	Janáček 1988, 126
SR24	D 920	——
SR25	B 1081	——
SR26	——	Janáček 1924, 93
SR27	——	Helfert 1924–5, 50
SR28	D 674	——
SR29	Pnmčh	——
SR30	A 5000	——
SR31	A 5901	——
SR32	B 674	——
SR33	B 1725	——
SR34	B 2018	Janáček 1988, 246
SR35	D 1040	——
SR36	B 2023	Janáček 1988, 249
SR37	A 6059	JA ii, 90
SR38	——	JA ii, 90 (in Czech)
SR39	——	*LN* (20 Jan 1926) [¶]
SR40	B 2143	JA ii, 91–3
SR41	B 648	JA ii, 93–4
SR42	B 2035	Janáček 1988, 273
SR43	D 260	——

SR44	B 2059	Janáček 1988, 303–4
SR45	D 1105	——
SR46	D 1073	——
SR47	D 1068	——
SR48	Wuest	Janáček 1988, 336–7
SR49	Wue	Janáček 1988, 337
SR50	B 2082	Janáček 1988, 337–8
SR51	——	JA ix, 229
SR52	B 672	JA ix, 230–1
SR53	A 6027	Janáček 1988, 342
SR54	A 4780	——
SR55	Wuest	Janáček 1988, 343

CHAPTER 2

PR1	——	Preissová 1941–2, 131
PR2	A 17	Straková 1958, 149
PR3	B 939	Straková 1958, 150–1
PR4	A 26	Straková 1958, 150
PR5	A 27	Straková 1958, 151
PR6	A 6107	*Fiala 1964, 204, 207–8
PR7	A 28	Straková 1958, 151–2
PR8	A 30	Straková 1958, 152
PR9	A 31	Straková 1958, 152
PR10	A 32	Straková 1958, 152
PR11	pa	Straková 1958, 153
PR12	A 35	Straková 1958, 153
PR13	Pnmdo	Pala 1955, 89
PR14	——	Straková 1958, 154
PR15	Z 13	Straková 1958, 154
PR16	——	Janáček 1970, 229–30
PR17	A 4697	Straková 1958, 154
PR18	A 37	Straková 1958, 154–5
PR19	Pnmdo	Pala 1955, 91
PR20	Pnmdo	Pala 1955, 91
PR21	Pnmdo	Pala 1955, 91–2
PR22	Pnmdo	Pala 1955, 90
PR23	Pnmdo	Pala 1955, 90
PR24	Pnmdo	Pala 1955, 90
PR25	Pnmdo	Pala 1955, 90
PR26	Pnmdo	Pala 1955, 90
PR27	Pnmdo	Pala 1955, 91
PR28	D 11	Straková 1958, 156–7
PR29	A 4609	Straková 1958, 154
PR30	A 48	Straková 1958, 160
PR31	Pnmdo	Pala 1955, 92
PR32	Pnmdo	Pala 1955, 92
PR33	——	Štědroň 1946, 102–3
PR34	Pnmdo	Pala 1955, 92
PR35	B 34	Pala 1955, 92
PR36	——	Hornové 1903, 144

PR37	D 724	*Vyslouzil 1954, 743		JP44	B 870	Němcová and
PR38	A 3530	——				Přibáňová 1963, 279
PR39	——	Brod 1924, 74		JP45	D 721	——
PR40	——	*HRo*, i (1924–5), 71–2		JP46	A 5449	——
PR41	——	JA ix, 173–5		JP47	A 263	——
PR42	——	Janáček 1924, 93–4		JP48	B 83	
				JP49	A 3958	——

CHAPTER 3

				JP50	A 1904	——
JP1	Pnmla	Závodský 1962, 128		JP51	B 1476	JA iv, 70–1
JP2	B 1857	Janáček 1988, 66–7		JP52	B 1478	JA iv, 74–5
JP3	——	Preissová 1941–2, 51		JP53	A 3432	——
JP4	A 3382	Straková 1958, 158		JP54	A 4950	——
JP5	A 3384	Straková 1958, 158		JP55	——	Calma 1938, 99
JP6	——	Trkanová 1959, 90–2		JP56	——	Kundera 1948, 77–8
JP7	——	Trkanová 1959, 57–8		JP57	B 1670	JA viii, 27–8
JP8	——	Janáček 1924, 98		JP58	B 1635	JA viii, 35–6
JP9	D 1569	Vogel 1963, 130		JP59	——	Mareš 1924–5, 35
JP10	A 3470	Helfert 1933–4, 45–6		JP60	——	Calma 1924–5,
JP11	A 3501	Helfert 1933–4, 45				139–40
JP12	——	Janáček 1886–7		JP61	A 5550	JA viii, 44
JP13	——	Trkanová 1959, 92		JP62	B 1672	JA viii, 44–5
JP14	——	JA vii, 16		JP63	D 1671	JA viii, 45–7
JP15	D 1205	JA vii, 17		JP64	——	JA viii, 47–8
JP16	——	Trkanová 1959, 92		JP65	——	JA viii, 48–9
JP17	——	Trkanová 1959, 92–3		JP66	——	Calma 1924–5, 142–3
JP18	A 6159	Štědroň 1959b, 165–6		JP67	A 473	JA viii, 53–4
JP19	C 10	Němcová 1974, 135–6		JP68	A 472	——
JP20	A 6161	Štědroň 1959b, 167–8		JP69	B 1660	JA viii, 50–2
JP21	A 6164	Němcová 1974, 137		JP70	B 1662	JA viii, 54–5
JP22	A 6169	Štědroň 1959b, 179–80		JP71	A 474	JA viii, 55–6
JP23	A 6172	*Němcová 1974, 137		JP72	B 2219	Štědroň 1962, 42
JP24	B 2217	Němcová 1974, 138		JP73	A 476	——
JP25	D 1235	Němcová 1974, 139		JP74	——	JA viii, 57
JP26	A 6174	Štědroň 1959, 180–1		JP75	——	Calma 1924–5, 144–5
JP27	A 6173	Štědroň 1959b, 181		JP76	A 478	JA viii, 57
JP28	D 138	Němcová 1974, 140		JP77	A 477	JA viii, 59
JP29	——	Kunc 1933–4, 78–81		JP78	B 1664	JA viii, 60
JP30	——	Kaprál 1931–2, 198		JP79	——	JA vii, 27–8
JP31	B 1479	JA iv, 77–8		JP80	A 479	JA viii, 60–1
JP32	A 5130	Němcová 1974, 142		JP81	A 480	——
JP33	A 6175	Štědroň 1959b, 182		JP82	B 1665	JA viii, 62
JP34	——	Němcová 1974, 145		JP83	A 481	JA viii, 62–3
JP35	——	JA vii, 17–18		JP84	——	Calma 1924–5, 146
JP36	D 192	——		JP85	A 5539	JA viii, 64
JP37	D 193	JA vii, 18–19		JP86	B 1666	JA viii, 65
JP38	B 2218	Štědroň 1962, 38–9		JP87	B 1775	——
JP39	B 2495	Pala 1953, 886		JP88	A 575	JA viii, 66
JP40	B 2496	Pala 1953, 886		JP89	——	JA vii, 29–30
JP41	D 36	——		JP90	——	Calma 1924–5, 144
JP42	Whhst	Blaukopf 1979, 287		JP91	A 483	——
JP43	Whhst	Blaukopf 1979, 286		JP92	B 2220	Štědroň 1962, 45–6
				JP93	A 4737	——
				JP94	A 4736	——
				JP95	B 2220	JA vii, 30

JP96	D 1215	——
JP97	D 1211	——
JP98	D 1212	——
JP99	D 1213	——
JP100	D 1214	——
JP101	D 1217	——
JP102	B 1333	——
JP103	B 1334	——
JP104	B 1337	——
JP105	B 1338	——
JP106	A 1781	——
JP107	B 1335	——
JP108	——	Trkanová 1959, 93–4
JP109	A 513	JA ii, 18–19
JP110	A 345	
JP111	——	Štědroň 1946, 177
JP112	D 1349	JA vii, 32–3
JP113	——	JA vii, 33–4
JP114	B 2221	Štědroň 1962, 47–8
JP115	B 250	JA vii, 34–5
JP116	B 2222	Štědroň 1962, 49
JP117	D 143	*JA vii, 104
JP118	A 651	JA vii, 105
JP119	A 654	——
JP120	D 146	Janáček 1958b, 364
JP121	D 228	Janáček 1958b 367–8
JP122	D 222	Janáček 1958b 363
JP123	B 1825	Janáček 1988, 38–9
JP124	D 882	*Janáček 1971, 264–5
JP125	B 1830	Janáček 1988, 43
JP126	B 1818	Janáček 1988, 33
JP127	D 867	JA ix, 240–2
JP128	A 4141	*Janáček 1971, 273
JP129	B 1833	*Janáček 1988, 46
JP130	C 303	Janáček 1988, 48–9
JP131	D 850	*Janáček 1971, 296
JP132	D 884	——
JP133	A 4147	*Janáček 1972, 302
JP134	A 4157	——
JP135	——	Brod 1923, 31–4
JP136	B 1205	JA ix, 16
JP137	C 295	Janáček 1988, 16
JP138	B 1809	Janáček 1988, 23
JP139	D 859	*Janáček 1971, 270
JP140	B 2555	JA vi, 69–70
JP141	——	Mareš 1940
JP142	D 891	Janáček 1971, 259–60
JP143	Pnmdo	JA vii, 81
JP144	D 295	JA vii, 82
JP145	——	Dědeček 1940, 94
JP146	A 3977	JA vii, 86
JP147	B 2132	JA ii, 73–4
JP148	B 1151	——
JP149	B 1019	JA vii, 88

JP150	A 6055	JA ii, 75–6
JP151	B 1985	Janáček 1988, 202
JP152	A 5428	——
JP153	D 766	JA vii, 90 fn
JP154	D 1348	JA vii, 90–1
JP155	——	JA vii, 89
JP156	——	JA vii, 92–3
JP157	D 794	JA ii, 76–7
JP158	D 1322	JA ii, 77–8
JP159	D 1420	JA vii, 94–5
JP160	D 1421	JA ii, 79–80
JP161	B 1990	Janáček 1988, 207–8
JP162	D 471	JA vii, 97 fn
JP163	D 804	JA vii, 99
JP164	Pnmla	Janáček 1958b, 396–7
JP165	D 602	Janáček 1958b, 397
JP166	Pnmla	Janáček 1958b, 398

CHAPTER 4

OS1	——	Trkanová 1959, 96–7
OS2	——	Janáček 1924, 94–5
OS3	A 6164	Štědroň 1959b, 169–74
OS4	——	Janáček 1903, 10–12
OS5	E 1134	*Straková 1956, 211
OS6	A 6161	Štědroň 1959b, 167–8
OS7	A 6164	Štědroň 1959b, 169–74
OS8	B 1727	——
OS9	A 5797	——
OS10	A 176	Straková 1956, 213–14
OS11	A 5798	——
OS12	A 180	Straková 1956, 216
OS13	A 5800	——
OS14	A 5799	——
OS15	A 5804	——
OS16	A 177	Straková 1956, 214–15
OS17	A 5801	——
OS18	A 5803	——
OS19	A 5802	——
OS20	A 178	Straková 1956, 215
OS21	A 178	Straková 1956, 216
OS22	B 1727	——
OS23	A 5806	——
OS24	A 5807	——
OS25	A 5809	——
OS26	A 5811	——
OS27	A 5812	——
OS28	B 1727	——
OS29	A 5813	——
OS30	A 3319	——
OS31	A 3835	——

OS32	D 720	JA iv, 180
OS33	D 722	JA iv, 181–2
OS34	A 5133	Straková 1956, 217
OS35	A 5449	——
OS36	A 6143	——
OS37	A 264	*JA iv, 41fn
OS38	A 6139	——
OS39	Bma	Janáček 1938, 131
OS40	D 719	*JA iv, 182
OS41	A 275	Straková 1956, 220
OS42	D 718	JA iv, 182–3
OS43	A 3422	JA iv, 183–4
OS44	B 316	JA iv, 39
OS45	——	JA iv, 40
OS46	B 317	JA iv, 40–1
OS47	A 5160	JA iv, 41–2
OS48	D 243	JA iv, 42–3
OS49	A 5161	JA iv, 44
OS50	D 242	JA iv, 45–6
OS51	A 5162	JA iv, 46
OS52	D 241	JA iv, 47
OS53	A 3440	JA iv, 176
OS54	——	*Národní listy* (23 Aug 1907)
OS55	A 5164	JA iv, 48–9
OS56	D 240	JA iv, 49
OS57	A 5165	JA iv, 51
OS58	B 816	JA iv, 177–9
OS59	——	Janáček 1947–8, 245–6
OS60	A 4627	Straková 1956, 227
OS61	——	Janáček 1947–8, 246
OS62	——	Janáček 1947–8, 246–7
OS63	A 5167	JA iv, 57
OS64	A 4750	Straková 1956, 228–9
OS65	A 5195	JA iv, 58–61
OS66	A 5170	JA iv, 64–5
OS67	A 5171	JA iv, 65
OS68	D 773	Straková 1956, 230
OS69	B 307	JA iv, 85–6
OS70	——	*Straková 1956, 244–5 [¶]
OS71	A 3425	JA iv, 184
OS72	Bma	Janáček 1938, 132
OS73	B 801	*JA iv, 185
OS74	Bma	Janáček 1938, 132–3
OS75	A 5167	JA iv, 94–5
OS76	B 304	*JA iv, 97–8; *Straková 1956, 235
OS77	D 1251	JA iv, 100
OS78	——	JA iv, 147–8
OS79	B 814	JA iv, 186
OS80	D 770	Straková 1956, 237

OS81	A 3444	Straková 1956, 238
OS82	A 3445	*JA iv, 187
OS83	D 707	JA iv, 188
OS84	D 709	JA iv, 188
OS85	C 172	*Straková 1956, 239
OS86	A 3443	JA iv, 188
OS87	A 3466	*JA iv, 189
OS88	A 444	*Straková 1956, 240–1
OS89	A 450	*Straková 1956, 241–2
OS90	D 796	*Straková 1956, 242
OS91	D 705	JA iv, 189
OS92	B 1014	JA iv, 155
OS93	B 1518	JA iv, 155–6
OS94	A 3931	——
OS95	D 706	*JA iv, 189
OS96	——	*Straková 1956, 243–4 [¶]
OS97	D 704	*JA iv, 190
OS98	D 795	Straková 1956, 246
OS99	A 5536	JA viii, 33
OS100	A 3933	Straková 1956, 246
OS101	C 173	Straková 1956, 248–9
OS102	A 3442	Straková 1956, 249–50
OS103	D 703	*JA iv, 190
OS104	A 3932	Straková 1956, 250
OS105	D 797	Straková 1956, 250–1
OS106	D 713	JA iv, 191
OS107	A 3696	*Straková 1956, 252
OS108	B 2582	JA iii, 23–4
OS109	A 3553	JA iii, 24–5
OS110	A 3462	JA iv, 50
OS111	A 4814	JA ix, 52
OS112	A 5419	Straková 1956, 216, 257

CHAPTER 5

BR1	——	*Hudební listy*, iv (1887–8), 62–4 [¶]
BR2	——	JA iv, 73
BR3	B 308	JA iv, 73–4
BR4	B 1478	JA iv, 74–5
BR5	D 238	JA iv, 81–2
BR6	JK 9	*JA iv, 78
BR7	B 1479	JA iv, 77–8
BR8	Pa	JA iv, 78
BR9	B 1480	JA iv, 79–80
BR10	A 5888	JA v, 13
BR11	A 5889	JA v, 15
BR12	B 1481	JA iv, 82
BR13	A 3554	JA v, 16

BR14	A 3561	JA v, 17
BR15	A 3624	JA v, 18
BR16	B 1486	JA iv, 88–9
BR17	A 3227	JA v, 19
BR18	A 3563	JA v, 19
BR19	A 812	JA iv, 92
BR20	A 5175	JA iv, 93
BR21	A 3548	JA v, 20–2
BR22	A 5176	JA iv, 95
BR23	A 3529	JA v, 22
BR24	——	JA iv, 176
BR25	——	JA iv, 97
BR26	B 304	JA iv, 97–8
BR27	A 5179	JA iv, 99–1
BR28	A 2424	JA v, 24
BR29	B 1263	——
BR30	A 2841	JA v, 11
BR31	B 1264	——
BR32	A 3558	JA v, 12
BR33	pa	
BR34	A 3557	JA v, 12
BR35	B 1494	JA iv, 113–14
BR36	B 1755	JA iv, 121
BR37	——	JA iv, 127
BR38	——	JA iv, 129–30
BR39	B 1503	JA iv, 130–1
BR40	pa	——
BR41	L 32 (e)	——
BR42	pa	——
BR43	B 1583	——
BR44	A 7458	JA v, 25
BR45	A 7450	JA v, 26
BR46	A 372	JA v, 26
BR47	L 30	——
BR48	A 4135	JA v, 49
BR49	D 1195	JA iv, 169
BR50	A 7450	JA v, 49
BR51	A 4136	JA v, 50
BR52	B 1006	JA v, 50
BR53	B 1657	JA viii, 37–8
BR54	B 1662	JA viii, 54–5
BR55	A 820	JA v, 51–2
BR56	A 459	JA v, 52–3
BR57	A 819	JA v, 54–5
BR58	B 2581	JA iii, 11–12
BR59	A 3543	JA iii, 12
BR60	B 2582	JA iii, 13
BR61	A 3541	JA iii, 15–16
BR62	B 2585	JA iii, 16–17
BR63	B 884	JA iii, 17–18
BR64	——	JA v, 39–40
BR65	A 3967	JA v, 28
BR66	——	JA v, 42–3
BR67	B 2497	JA v, 28
BR68	——	JA v, 43
BR69	A 3979	JA v, 28
BR70	B 2498	JA v, 29
BR71	——	JA v, 60–3
BR72	A 3527	JA v, 64–5
BR73	B 2376	——
BR74	A 3518	JA v, 65
BR75	A 5614	——
BR76	pa	
BR77	A 3539	JA v, 67–8
BR78	A 3528	JA v, 68–9
BR79	——	JA v, 70–1
BR80	A 3526	JA v, 71–4
BR81	B 875	JA v, 76–7
BR82	A 3969	JA v, 30–1
BR83	B 2501	JA v, 38
BR84	A 3538	JA v, 76–9
BR85	A 3483	JA v, 79
BR86		JA v, 63
BR87	B 1207	JA ix, 19–21
BR88	B 1674	——
BR89	B 2591	JA iii, 26
BR90	A 3524	JA iii, 28
BR91	B 2592	JA iii, 29
BR92	B 2593	JA iii, 30
BR93	B 2594	JA iii, 30
BR94	B 883	JA iii, 31
BR95	B 2594	JA iii, 32
BR96	A 3549	JA iii, 32
BR97	B 2596	JA iii, 33
BR98	A 3550	JA iii, 33
BR99	B 2597	JA iii, 33
BR100	A 3544	JA iii, 34
BR101	A 3511	JA iii, 34
BR102	B 2598	JA iii, 34
BR103	A 3512	JA iii, 35
BR104	A 3525	JA iii, 35–6
BR105	A 3545	JA iii, 52–3
BR106	B 2599	JA iii, 36–7
BR107	A 5196	JA iv, 168
BR108	D 1318	——
BR109	B 26	JA iii, 37–9
BR110	A 3635	JA iii, 39
BR111	B 2601	JA iii, 40
BR112	B 2602	——
BR113	A 3519	JA iii, 40
BR114	A 3521	JA iii, 40
BR115	B 2603	JA iii, 41
BR116	B 2605	JA iii, 42
BR117	B 2604	JA iii, 41
BR118	A 3641	JA iii, 42–3
BR119	B 2606	JA iii, 43
BR120	A 4837	——
BR121	L 34	——

BRI22	B 2607	JA iii, 44
BRI23	B 2608	JA iii, 45
BRI24	A 3642	JA iii, 45
BRI25	A 3640	JA iii, 45–6
BRI26	B 2610	JA iii, 47
BRI27	A 3636	JA iii, 47
BRI28	L II,3 (25–6)	——
BRI29	B 2611	JA iii, 47–8
BRI30	A 3522	JA iii, 48
BRI31	B 2612	JA iii, 48
BRI32	A 3540	JA iii, 49
BRI33	A 6825	*Janáček 1955, 45
BRI34	B 2613	JA iii, 49–50
BRI35	A 3649	JA iii, 50
BRI36	B 2614	JA iii, 50–1
BRI37	A 3648	JA iii, 51
BRI38	B 2615	——
BRI39	B 2618	JA iii, 53
BRI40	B 2619	JA iii, 54–5
BRI41	A 3513	JA iii, 55–6
BRI42	B 2620	JA iii, 57–8
BRI43	A 3644	JA iii, 58
BRI44	B 2619	JA iii, 54–5
BRI45	E 45	Janáček 1990, 26
BRI46	B 2621	JA iii, 59
BRI47	B 2517	JA vi, 35
BRI48	A 3643	JA iii, 59
BRI49	B 2622	JA iii, 60
BRI50	B 2524	JA vi, 41
BRI51	B 2623	JA iii, 60–1
BRI52	A 3523	JA iii, 61–2
BRI53	B 2624	JA iii, 62
BRI54	B 2546	JA vi, 63
BRI55	B 1638	——
BRI56	B 1636	——
BRI57	B 1634	——
BRI58	D 124	——
BRI59	A 647	——
BRI60	A 463	——
BRI61	B 1620	——
BRI62	B 224	Štědroň 1962, 50
BRI63	B 2225	Štědroň 1962, 51
BRI64	D 134	——
BRI65	D 883	——
BRI66	D 141	——
BRI67	D 215	Janáček 1958b, 369
BRI68	Pnmla	Janáček 1958b, 370
BRI69	D 153	Janáček 1958b, 408
BRI70	Pnmla	Janáček 1958b, 371
BRI71	D 220	Janáček 1958b, 374
BRI72	D 218	Janáček 1958b, 380
BRI73	D 222	Janáček 1958b, 383
BRI74	D 914	——
BRI75	B 1881	Janáček 1988, 90–1
BRI76	B 1883	Janáček 1988, 93–4
BRI77	D 904	——
BRI78	D 898	——
BRI79	B 1891	Janáček 1988, 101
BRI80	B 1892	Janáček 1988, 101
BRI81	D 872	——
BRI82	D 895	*Janáček 1988, 112
BRI83	B 1906	Janáček 1988, 115
BRI84	D 931	——
BRI85	B 155	——
BRI86	B 360	——
BRI87	D 932	Janáček 1988, 124–5
BRI88	D 291	——
BRI89	D 936	——
BRI90	D 939	——
BRI91	B 2631	——
BRI92	A 701	JA iii, 74
BRI93	A 702	JA iii, 81–2
BRI94	Pnmla	Janáček 1958b, 376
BRI95	B 2533	JA vi, 49–50
BRI96	B 2558	JA vi, 73–4
BRI97	B 2161	——
BRI98	A 741	——
BRI99	B 1895	Janáček 1988, 106–7
BR200	B 2625	JA iii, 64
BR201	B 2575	JA vi, 88
BR202	Pnmla	Janáček 1958b, 378
BR203	A 4922	
BR204	——	JA vii, 59
BR205	D 183	JA vii, 59–60
BR206	B 218	JA iii, 72–3
BR207	——	JA vii, 66–7
BR208	——	JA vii, 67–8
BR209	B 361	JA vii, 36n
BR210	B 1925	Janáček 1988, 130–1
BR211	B 1927	Janáček 1988, 132
BR212	——	JA vi, 72–3
BR213	D 937	*Janáček 1988, 132
BR214	B 252	JA iii, 92–3
BR215	D 294	JA vii, 78–9
BR216	B 1930	JA vii, 79–80
BR217	B 1931	Janáček 1988, 137
BR218	B 2230	Štědroň 1962, 56–8
BR219	——	JA vii, 82–3
BR220	D 189	JA vii, 83–4
BR221	B 2111	JA ii, 27
BR222	Pnmdo	Pala 1953, 889
BR223	——	JA vii, 84
BR224	B 1935	Janáček 1988, 140
BR225	B 1936	Janáček 1988, 141
BR226	B 2115	JA ii, 29
BR227	A 903	JA ii, 29

BR228	B 387	JA ii, 30
BR229	A 6037	JA ii, 30
BR230	A 905	JA ii, 31
BR231	A 906	JA ii, 32
BR232	A 907	JA ii, 32–3
BR233	A 908	——
BR234	A 4978	——
BR235	——	Chlubna 1931–2, 126
BR236	——	Pala 1953, 890
BR237	A 6041	JA ii, 33–5
BR238	D 1419	JA ii, 35
BR239	A 911	JA ii, 39–40
BR240	A 6042	JA ii, 40–2
BR241	A 914	JA ii, 42–3
BR242	D 329	JA vii, 110
BR243	A 6048	JA ii, 45–6
BR244	A 921	JA ii, 46
BR245	B 396	JA ix, 65–6
BR246	A 918	JA ix, 67
BR247	B 418	JA ix, 67–8
BR248	——	Janáček 1919–20, 177
BR249	D 955	——

CHAPTER 6

KK1	E 112	Janáček 1990, 56
KK2	——	Jiřikovský 1931–2, 250
KK3	A 886	——
KK4	B 2646	JA iii, 93
KK5	B 2646	JA iii, 93–4
KK6	D 305	——
KK7	——	Červinka 1938
KK8	B 1159	——
KK9	——	Červinka 1938
KK10	E 1142	Janáček 1990, 77
KK11	E 1187	Janáček 1990, 80
KK12	E 156	Janáček 1990, 74
KK13	——	Červinka 1938
KK14	B 2116	JA ii, 47
KK15	E 170	Janáček 1990, 86
KK16	B 408	——
KK17	——	Červinka 1938
KK18	B 426	——
KK19	D 335	——
KK20	B 1949	Janáček 1988, 160
KK21	D 979	——
KK22	D 1121	——
KK23	D 336	——
KK24	B 1952	Janáček 1988, 166–7
KK25	B 1959	Janáček 1988, 172
KK26	A 4175	——
KK27	A 4173	——
KK28	A 5463	——

KK29	A 963	——
KK30	A 1800	——
KK31	A 5611	——
KK32	D 1124	——
KK33	B 2122	JA ii, 53–4
KK34	A 936	JA ii, 54–5
KK35	B 2123	JA ii, 55–6
KK36	E 172	Janáček 1990, 87–8
KK37	D 1125	——
KK38	D 339	——
KK39	B 1951	Janáček 1988, 162
KK40	E 178	Janáček 1990, 90
KK41	A 967	——
KK42	A 6051	JA ii, 57
KK43	Pnmdo	Pulkert 1978, 220
KK44	D 340	JA ii, 58
KK45	E 1144	Janáček 1990, 92
KK46	D 380	——
KK47	B 1955	Janáček 1988, 169–70
KK48	——	Brod 1923, 52
KK49	B 1009	Štědroň 1946, 214
KK50	D 369	JA ii, 61
KK51	E 1145	Janáček 1990, 93
KK52	B 1692	Janáček 1988, 175–6
KK53	A 783	JA ii, 61–2
KK54	D 394	JA ii, 62–3
KK55	B 2124	JA ii, 63
KK56	A 4193	——
KK57	D 998	——
KK58	B 2126	JA ii, 64
KK59	D 407	JA ii, 65
KK60	B 2127	JA ii, 65–6
KK61	A 4192	——
KK62	D 412	JA ii, 66
KK63	B 2128	JA ii, 67
KK64	B 2129	JA ii, 67–8
KK65	E 202	Janáček 1990, 102
KK66	B 2130	JA ii, 68
KK67	D 414	JA ii, 69
KK68	D 416	JA ii, 69
KK69	A 3740	——
KK70	E 205	Janáček 1990, 103
KK71	B 2131	JA ii, 69–71
KK72	——	Plamenac 1981, 125–9
KK73	——	JA ix, 108
KK74	B 463	——
KK75	——	Plamenac 1981, 130
KK76	——	Janáček 1958a, 175
KK77	A 941	JA ix, 82
KK78	B 421	JA ix, 88
KK79	B 1690	——
KK80	B 1691	——
KK81	A 950	JA ix, 92–4
KK82	B 1694	——

KK83	——	JA ix, 89–91
KK84	B 1963	Janáček 1988, 176
KK85	B 1983	Janáček 1988, 200
KK86	D 1421	JA ii, 79–80
KK87	A 1104	——
KK88	B 2077	Janáček 1988, 330–1
KK89	B 2085	Janáček 1988, 340–1
KK90	A 5052	——
KK91	E 885	——
KK92	E 187	Janáček 1990, 96
KK93	E 189	Janáček 1990, 96–7
KK94	E 190	Janáček 1990, 97
KK95	E 888	*Janáček 1990, 97
KK96	PSom	Štědroň 1946, 213–14

CHAPTER 7

LB1	——	Trkanová 1959, 99
LB2	——	Těsnohlídek 1924
LB3	——	Janáček and others 1924
LB4	A 1006	——
LB5	——	Cígler 1957, 751
LB6	——	Janáček 1924, 96
LB7	——	adv 1921
LB8	——	Janáček 1921, 113
LB9	——	JA ix, 89
LB10	E 187	Janáček 1990, 96
LB11	E 191	Janáček 1990, 97–8
LB12	——	JA ix, 108
LB13	——	Janáček 1924, 99
LB14	E 198	Janáček 1990, 100
LB15	B 464	——
LB16	B 481	——
LB17	E 1396	Janáček 1990, 105–6
LB18	A 6116	Hradil 1981, 64
LB19	——	Hradil 1981, 284
LB20	D 438	——
LB21	A 4987	——
LB22	B 4150	——
LB23	——	Sládek 1979, 42
LB24	B 1986	Janáček 1988, 204
LB25	D 1002	*Janáček 1988, 205–6
LB26	B 1988	Janáček 1988, 205
LB27	B 500	——
LB28	D 1104	Janáček 1988, 208–9
LB29	B 1991	Janáček 1988, 209
LB30	D 1034	——
LB31	D 1033	——
LB32	B 1992	Janáček 1988, 210
LB33	D 1007	*Janáček 1988, 211
LB34	A 4236	——
LB35	A 4234	——
LB36	B 2001	Janáček 1988, 221–2

LB37	A 6057	JA ii, 84
LB38	B 2139	JA ii, 85
LB39	B 561	JA ii, 85–6
LB40	A 4820	JA ix, 172
LB41	——	JA ix, 172–3
LB42	B 2140	JA ii, 87
LB43	——	Trkanová 1959, 99–100
LB44	B 2141	JA ii, 87–8
LB45	B 1056	——
LB46	A 3992	——
LB47	E 285	Janáček 1990, 144–5
LB48	——	JA ix, 181–3
LB49	A 3727	——
LB50	A 3729	——
LB51	E 294	Janáček 1990, 147
LB52	D 521	——
LB53	A 5986	Janáček 1988, 235–6
LB54	——	Janáček 1986, 83–5
LB55	——	JA ix, 121–2
LB56	——	JA ix, 123
LB57	B 499	JA ix, 124
LB58	Wuest	Janáček 1988, 237
LB59	——	JA ix, 152
LB60	B 1213	JA ix, 179–81
LB61	B 1215	JA ix, 188–9
LB62	B 1213	JA ix, 179–81
LB63	——	JA ix, 181–3
LB64	B 1214	JA ix, 183–5
LB65	——	JA ix, 185–6
LB66	B 1215	JA ix, 188–9
LB67	B 2014	Janáček 1988, 241–2
LB68	B 1093	——
LB69	A 5007	——
LB70	D 1095	*Janáček 1988, 307–8
LB71	B 2062	Janáček 1988, 307
LB72	A 2418	——

CHAPTER 8

VM1	E 208	Janáček 1990, 104
VM2	B 475	JA ix, 246–7
VM3	——	JA ix, 108
VM4	——	Čapková 1962, 352
VM5	——	Veselý 1925
VM6	——	Janáček 1986, 73–4
VM7	B 965	JA ix, 247–8
VM8	D 790	——
VM9	D 790	——
VM10	B 968	——
VM11	E 214	Janáček 1990, 107
VM12	E 1402	Janáček 1990, 108
VM13	——	JA ix, 130
VM14	E 1403	Janáček 1990, 108

VM15	B 273	Janáček 1990, 140
VM16	——	JA ix, 177–8
VM17	E 275	Janáček 1990, 141
VM18	E 1404	Janáček 1990, 141
VM19	E 277	Janáček 1990, 142
VM20	E 278	Janáček 1990, 142
VM21	E 316	Janáček 1990, 156
VM22	E 317	Janáček 1990, 157
VM23	A 5002	——
VM24	E 320	Janáček 1990, 159
VM25	E 343	Janáček 1990, 169
VM26	B 2023	Janáček 1988, 249
VM27	D 1151	
VM28	B 2021	Janáček 1988, 251
VM29	D 957	——
VM30	B 1119	
VM31	B 2033	Janáček 1988, 265–6
VM32	A 4287	——
VM33	D 1030	——
VM34	D 1029	
VM35	A 4244	——
VM36	A 4245	——
VM37	B 2029	Janáček 1988, 263
VM38	D 1075	
VM39	A 4832	JA ix, 203
VM40	A 4833	JA ix, 204
VM41	A 3817	JA ix, 205–6
VM42	——	JA ix, 206
VM43	——	JA ix, 212–16
VM44	A 4835	JA ix, 217–19
VM45	D 1100	——
VM46	B 2058	Janáček 1988, 301–2
VM47	E 365	Janáček 1990, 177
VM48	D 730	
VM49	D 748	
VM50	B 1753	
VM51	B 2039	Janáček 1988, 277–8
VM52	E 403	Janáček 1990, 192–3
VM53	B 1602	——
VM54	E 405	Janáček 1990, 193
VM55	B 2049	Janáček 1988, 290–1
VM56	——	Kundera 1958
VM57	E 406	Janáček 1990, 194
VM58	D 1436	
VM59	B 1754	Štědroň 1946, 235
VM60	G 160b	
VM61	——	Čapková 1962, 353
VM62	E 410	Janáček 1990, 195
VM63	B 2028	Janáček 1988, 261
VM64	D 1101	——
VM65	D 1067	——
VM66	E 618	Janáček 1990, 355–6
VM67	D 529	JA ii, 96–7
VM68	B 2145	JA ii, 97

VM69	B 2146	JA ii, 98
VM70	A 6015	Janáček 1988, 298
VM71	B 2147	JA ii, 98–9
VM72	D 271	JA ii, 99
VM73	E 512	Janáček 1990, 255
VM74	E 525	Janáček 1990, 264
VM75	A 5049	——
VM76	D 632	JA ii, 100
VM77	B 2148	JA ii, 100
VM78	E 575	Janáček 1990, 303
VM79	A 5054	——
VM80	A 5055	——
VM81	A 5056	——
VM82	E 583	Janáček 1990, 308–9
VM83	B 2216	*Pestrý týden* (March 1928)
VM84	A 1341	Štědroň 1946, 236
VM85	E 588	Janáček 1990, 310–12
VM86	B 2091	Janáček 1988, 347
VM87	A 5057	——

CHAPTER 9

ZD1	——	JA ix, 210–11
ZD2	E 407	Janáček 1990, 194
ZD3	——	JA ix, 222–4
ZD4	Z 64	——
ZD5		Firkušný 1936–7, 18, 20
ZD6	——	Firkušný 1936–7, 14, 16
ZD7	E 413	Janáček 1990, 196
ZD8	E 437	Janáček 1990, 209–10
ZD9	E 444	Janáček 1990, 218
ZD10		Janáček 1927b
ZD11	——	*LN* (29 July 1927) [¶]
ZD12	E 490	Janáček 1990, 234
ZD13	E 491	Janáček 1990, 235
ZD14	E 493	Janáček 1990, 236–7
ZD15	E 6	Janáček 1990, 259
ZD16	E 517	Janáček 1990, 259–60
ZD17	E 518	Janáček 1990, 260–1
ZD18	E 527	Janáček 1990, 266–7
ZD19	E 538	Janáček 1990, 278–9
ZD20	E 543	Janáček 1990, 282–3
ZD21	E 544	Janáček 1990, 283
ZD22	Z 71	——
ZD23	E 592	Janáček 1990, 318–9
ZD24	E 596	Janáček 1990, 327
ZD25	E 605	Janáček 1990, 335–6
ZD26	E 619	Janáček 1990, 356–7
ZD27	E 620	Janáček 1990, 357–8
ZD28	E 621	Janáček 1990, 358–9
ZD29	E 1215	Janáček 1990, 359–60

ZD30	E 622	Janáček 1990, 360–1	ZD35	E 654	Janáček 1990, 392
ZD31	E 624	Janáček 1990, 364–5	ZD36	E 659	Janáček 1990, 395
ZD32	E 625	Janáček 1990, 365–6	ZD37	E 661	Janáček 1990, 396–7
ZD33	E 650	Janáček 1990, 388	ZD38	——	Chlubna 1958a
ZD34	E 652	Janáček 1990, 390–1	ZD39	——	Janáčková 1943

FULL CITATIONS OF ANONYMOUS ARTICLES NOT INCLUDED IN THE BIBLIOGRAPHY

SR2 'Drobné zprávy' [Short reports], *Dalibor*, ii (1880), 183

SR39 'Janáčkova Šárka v pražském Národním divadle' [Janáček's *Šárka* in the Prague National Theatre], *LN* (20 Jan 1926)

OS70 'U dirigenta Vítězslava Čelanského: O Janáčkově opeře Osud [. . .]' ['With the conductor Vítězslav Čelanský: about Janáček's opera "Fate" [. . .]', *Národní obzor* (27 June 1913); abridged reprint in Straková 1956, 244–5

OS96 'Ze soudní síně' [From the courthouse], *Národní politika* (?1913), abridged reprint in Straková 1956, 243–4

BRI 'Význammá slova' [Significant words], *Hudební listy*, iv (1887–8), 62–4

ZDII 'Nová opera Leoše Janáčka' [Leoš Janáček's new opera], *LN* (29 July 1927); reprinted in Firkušný 1936–7, 55

Bibliography

Edited writings and letters, etc. are generally listed under the original writer, not the editor.

Items are arranged alphabetically by author, then chronologically under that author.

Publications that have appeared in more than one edition are cited in the text by an author–date reference to the first publication date; page-number references are to the edition marked with an asterisk (*).

Czech diacritics are ignored in alphabetization.

Abbreviations

ČMM   *Časopis Moravského musea/muzea v Brně: vědy společenské*
DČD   *Dějiny českého divadla* [The history of Czech theatre], ed.
       František Černý (Prague, 1968–)
DL   *Divadelní list Zemského divadla v Brně*; *Divadelní list Národního*
       divadla v Brně; *Divadelní list*
HM   Hudební matice
HMUB   Hudební matice Umělecké besedy
HRo   *Hudební rozhledy*
JA   Janáčkův archiv, first series, general ed. Vladimír Helfert (i) and
       Jan Racek (ii–ix)
       i *Korespondence Leoše Janáčka s Artušem Rektorysem*, ed.
          Artuš Rektorys (HMUB, Prague, 1934) [enlarged 2/1949 = iv]
       ii *Korespondence Leoše Janáčka s Otakarem Ostrčilem*, ed.
          Artuš Rektorys (HMUB, Prague, 1948)
       iii *Korespondence Leoše Janáčka s F.S. Procházkou*, ed. Artuš
          Rektorys (HMUB, Prague, 1949)
       iv *Korespondence Leoše Janáčka s Artušem Rektorysem*, ed.
          Artuš Rektorys   (HMUB, Prague, enlarged 2/1949)
       v *Korespondence Leoše Janáčka s libretisty Výletů Broučkových*
          [Janáček's correspondence with the *Brouček* librettists], ed.
          Artuš Rektorys (HM, Prague, 1950)
       vi *Korespondence Leoše Janáčka s Gabrielou Horvátovou*, ed.
          Artuš Rektorys (HM, Prague, 1950)
       vii *Korespondence Leoše Janáčka s Karlem Kovařovičem a*
          ředitelstvím Národního divadla [Janáček's correspondence
          with Kovařovic and the directorate of the National Theatre],
          ed. Artuš Rektorys (HM, Prague, 1950)
       viii *Korespondence Leoše Janáčka s Marií Calmou a MUDr*

Františkem Veselým, ed. Jan Racek and Artuš Rektorys
(Hudební nakladatelství Orbis, Prague, 1951)
ix *Korespondence Leoše Janáčka s Maxem Brodem,* ed. Jan
Racek and Artuš Rektorys (Státní nakladatelství krásné
literatury, hudby a umění, Prague, 1953)

LN   *Lidové noviny*
OM   *Opus musicum*
2/   Second edition

adv [= Adolf Veselý]: 'Nové dílo Leoše Janáčka' [Leoš Janáček's new work],
LN (15 May 1921)
Blaukopf, Kurt: 'Gustav Mahler und die tschechische Oper, *Österreichische
Musikzeitschrift,* xxxiv (1979), 285–8
Brod, Max: *Sternenhimmel: Musik- und Theatererlebnisse* (Orbis, Prague,
and Kurt Wolf, Munich, 1923); *2/1966 as *Prager Sternenhimmel* ...
(Paul Zsolnay, Vienna and Hamburg)
    Leoš Janáček: život a dílo [Leoš Janáček: life and works] (*HMUB,
Prague, 1924; German original, Wiener Philharmonischer Verlag,
Vienna, 1925, enlarged 2/Universal Edition, Vienna, 1956)
Burjanek, Josef: 'Janáčkova Káťa Kabanová a Ostrovského Bouře' [Janáček's
Káťa Kabanová and Ostrovsky's *The Thunderstorm*], *Musikologie,* iii
(1955), 345–416
Calma[-Veselá], Marie: 'Z boje pro Janáčkovou Pastorkyni' [From the battle
for Janáček's *Jenůfa*], *Listy Hudební matice,* iv (1924–5), 137–47
    'Ze vzpomínek na Leoše Janáčka' [From my recollections of Leoš
Janáček], *Hudební výchova,* xix (1938), 99–100
Čapková, Helena: *Moji milí bratři* [My dear brothers] (Československý
spisovatel, Prague, 1962, *3/1986)
Červinka, Vincenc: 'Jak vznikla Káťa Kabanová' [How *Káťa Kabanová* came
into being], *Národní politika* (18 October 1938)
Československý hudební slovník osob a institucí [The Czechoslovak music
dictionary of people and institutions], ed. Gracian Černušák, Bohumír
Štědroň and Zdenko Nováček (Státní hudební vydavatelství, Prague,
1963–5)
Chlubna, Osvald: 'Dr Leoš Janáček: Z mrtvého domu' [Dr Leoš Janáček:
From the House of the Dead], *DL,* v (1929–30), 177, 189–94
    'Vzpomínky na Leoše Janáčka' [Reminiscences of Leoš Janáček], *DL,* vii,
(1931–2), 101–4, 125–7, 169, 172, 289–90
    'K úpravě opery "Z mrtvého domu"' [On the revision of the opera *From
the House of the Dead*], Nosek 1958 [= Chlubna 1958a]
    'Několik slov k Janáčkově "Šárce"' [A few words on Janáček's *Šárka*],
Nosek 1958 [= Chlubna 1958b]
Cígler, Radovan: 'Janáčkovo libreto a Brodův překlad Lišky Bystroušky'
[Janáček's libretto and Brod's translation of *The Cunning Little Vixen*],
HRo, x (1957), 746–51
    Příhody Lišky Bystroušky: příspěvek k poznání díla a původnosti nové

Janáčkovy operní koncepce [*The Cunning Little Vixen*: a contribution to knowledge of the work and the originality of Janáček's new operatic conception] (doctoral dissertation, University of Brno, 1975)

Dědeček, Pavel: 'Karel Kovařovic a "Její pastorkyňa"' [Karel Kovařovic and Janáček], *Petr* 1940, 91–4

Dlouhý, Ladislav: 'Ctirad a Šárka', *Mélanges dédiés à la mémoire de Prokop M. Haškovec*, ed. Ant. Šesták and Ant. Dokoupil (Globus, Brno, 1936), 75–109

Dufková, Eugenie, and Srba, Bořivoj, eds.: *Postavy brněnského jeviště 1884–1984* [Characters from the Brno stage 1884–1984], i (Státní divadlo v Brně, Brno, 1979–84); *Postavy . . . 1884–1989*, ii (ibid, 1985–9)

Dvořák, Antonín: *Antonín Dvořák: korespondence a dokumenty*, ed. Milan Kuna and others, ii (Supraphon, Prague, 1988)

Dyk, Viktor: 'Vzpomínka na Leoše Janáčka' [A memoir of Leoš Janáček], *Lumír lv/4 (1928), 183–4; reprinted in JA v, 60–4

Fiala, Otakar: 'Libreto k Janáčkově opeře Počátek románu' [The libretto to Janáček's opera *The Beginning of a Romance*] ČMM, xlix (1964), 199–222

Firkušný, Leoš: 'Poslední Janáčkova opera Z mrtvého domu' [Janáček's last opera *From the House of the Dead*] DL, xii (1936–7), 358–68, 386–400; printed separately (*Pazdírek, Brno, 1937); reprinted in Firkušný 1939, 54–70

 Odkaz Leoše Janáčka české opeře [Janáček's legacy to Czech opera] (Dědictví Havlíčkova, Brno, 1939)

Fischmann, Zdenka E.: 'Jewish musicians with roots in Czechoslovakia (part I)', *Review of the Society for the history of Czechoslovak Jews*, iii (New York, 1988), 193–217

Flodrová, Milena, Galasovská, Blažena and Vodička, Jaroslav: *Seznam ulic města Brna s vývojem jejich pojmenování* [Catalogue of streets of the town of Brno with the evolution of their naming] (Muzejní a vlastivědná společnost, Brno, enlarged 2/1984)

Forst, Vladimír, ed.: *Lexikon české literatury: osobnosti, díla, instituce* [Dictionary of Czech literature: personalities, works, institutions] (Academia, Prague, 1985)

Helfert, Vladimír: 'Janáčkovy neznámé opery: 1. Šárka' [Janáček's unknown operas: 1. *Šárka*], HRo, i (1924–5), 48–55; reprinted in *Helfert 1949, 23–38

 'Něco o vzniku "Její pastorkyně"' [Something on the origin of *Jenůfa*], DL, ix (1933–4), 65–72; reprinted in *Helfert 1949, 45–50

 Leoš Janáček, i (Oldřich Pazdírek, Brno, 1939)

 O Janáčkovi [About Janáček], ed. Bohumil Štědroň (HMUB, Prague, 1949)

Hornové, V. and J.: *Česká zpěvohra* [Czech opera] (Grosman a Svoboda, Prague, [1903])

Hradil, František Míťa: *Hudebníci a pěvci v kraji Leoše Janáčka: paměti a dokumentace* [Musicians and singers in Janáček country: memoirs and

Bibliography 381

documentation] (Profil, Ostrava, 1981)

Hýsek, Miloslav: *Paměti* [Memoirs], ed. Dušan Jeřábek (Blok, Brno, 1970)

Janáček, Leoš: review of Kovařovic's *The Bridegrooms*, *Hudební listy*, iii (1886–7), 54; reprinted in Štědroň 1946, 111–12

'České proudy hudební: Šárka' [Czech musical currents: (review of Fibich's) *Šárka*], *Hlídka*, xvi (1899), 36–41; reprinted in *Zdeněk Fibich: sborník dokumentů a studií* [Collection of documents and studies], ed. Artuš Rektorys, ii (Prague, 1952), 311–18 [Janáček 1899a]

'České proudy hudební: Psohlavci' [Czech musical currents: (review of Kovařovic's) *The Dogheads*, *Hlídka*, xvi (1899), 362–6 [Janáček 1899b]

'Moje Luhačovice' [My Luhačovice], *Hlídka*, xx (1903), 836–44; reprinted in *Štědroň 1939, 5–13

'Výlety páně Broučkovy: jeden do měsíce, druhý do XV. století' [*The Excursions of Mr Brouček*: one to the moon, the other to the fifteenth century], *LN* (23 December 1917); reprinted in *Janáček 1958a, 52–5; Eng. trans. in Janáček 1989, 92–6

'Výlety páně Broučkovy' [*The Excursions of Mr Brouček*], *Hudební revue*, xiii (1919–20), 177–9

'Stehlíček' [The little goldfinch], *LN* (1 June 1921); reprinted in *Janáček 1958a, 110–13; Eng. trans. in Janáček 1982, 97–100

Leoš Janáček: pohled do života a díla [Leoš Janáček: a view of the life and works], ed. Adolf Veselý (Fr. Borový, Prague, 1924) [='autobiography']

'Moře – země' [The sea – the land], *LN* (13 June 1926); reprinted in *Janáček 1958a, 172–6; Eng. trans. in Janáček 1982, 133–22 and Janáček 1989, 229–34

'K čemu se přiznávám' [What I profess]; *LN* (13 February 1927); reprinted in *Janáček 1958a, 55–7; Eng. trans in Janáček 1988, 105–7 [Janáček 1927a]

'Schytali je' [They caught them], *LN* (28 June 1927); reprinted in *Janáček 1958a, 179–80; Eng. trans. in Janáček 1982, 108–9 [Janáček 1927b]

'Smráká se' [It's dusk], *Venkov*, xxiii (1928), no. 31 (5 February 1928); reprinted in *OM, vi (1974), 207–8; Eng. trans. in Janáček 1989, 115–19

'Dopisy Leoše Janáčka z archivu Družstva Národního divadla v Brně' [Janáček's letters from the archive of the *Družstvo* of the National Theatre in Brno], ed. Leoš Firkušný, *Musikologie*, i (1938), 130–9

'Leoš Janáček a František Neumann', ed. Bohumír Štědroň, *Smetana*, xxxiv (1942), 58–60, 72–4, 89 [correspondence]

'Janáčkovy dopisy dr. Fr. Skácelíkovi' [Janáček's letters to Dr František Skácelík], ed. František Bartoš, *Tempo*, xx (1947–8), 244–8

O lidové písni a lidové hudbě [On folksong and folk music], ed. Jiří Vysloužil (Státní nakladatelství krásné literatury, hudby a umění, Prague, 1955)

Fejetony z Lidových novin [Feuilletons from the *Lidové noviny*], ed. Jan Racek (Krajské nakladatelství, Brno, 1958) [Janáček 1958a]

'Jan Löwenbach a Leoš Janáček: vzájemná korespondence' [mutual correspondence], ed. Ivo Stolařík, *Slezský sborník*, lvi (1958), 360–411 [Janáček 1958b]

'Leoš Janáček kritikem brněnské opery v letech 1890–1892' [Leoš Janáček as critic of the Brno Opera 1890–2], ed. Bohumír Štědroň, *Otázky divadla a filmu*, i (1970), 207–48

'Janáčkova korespondence s Universal-Edition v letech 1916–1918 týkající se Její pastorkyně' [Janáček's correspondence with Universal Edition 1916–18 over *Jenůfa*], ed. Bohumír Štědroň, *Otázky divadla a filmu*, ii (1971), 249–309

Leaves from his life, ed. and trans. Vilem and Margaret Tausky (Kahn & Averill, London, 1982) [Eng. trans. of selections from Janáček 1958a]

Janáček-Newmarch correspondence, ed. Zdenka E. Fischmann (Kabel Publishers, Rockville, Maryland, 1986)

Briefe an die Universal Edition, ed. Ernst Hilmar (Hans Schneider, Tutzing, 1988)

Janáček's uncollected essays on music, selected, ed. and trans. Mirka Zemanová (Marion Boyars, London, 1989)

Hádanka života: dopisy Leoše Janáčka Kamile Stösslové [The riddle of life: the letters of Leoš Janáček to Kamila Stösslová], ed. Svatava Přibáňová (Opus musicum, Brno, 1990)

Janáček, Leoš, and others: 'Liška Bystrouška na divadle' [Liška Bystrouška in the theatre], *LN* (1 November 1924); reprinted in *Janáček 1958a, 316–25; Eng. trans. in Janáček 1982, 145–54

[for other correspondence by Janáček, see under JA in 'Abbreviations' above]

Janáčková, Věra: 'Den na Hukvaldech' [A day at Hukvaldy], *LN* (5 September 1943); reprinted in Procházka 1966, 219

Jančář, Antonín: *Luhačovice: průvodce* [Luhačovice: a guide] (Olympia, Prague, 2/1988)

Jiřikovský, Václav: 'Vzpomínky na Leoše Janáčka' [Reminiscences of Leoš Janáček], *DL*, vii (1931–2), 248–50

John, Nicholas, ed.: *Janáček: Jenůfa; Katya Kabanova*, N. John (ed.) (John Calder, London, and Riverrun Press, New York, 1985) [ENO and Royal Opera Opera Guide, 33]

Kaprál, Václav: 'Vzpomínky na první provedení "Její pastorkyně"' [Reminiscences of the first performance of *Jenůfa*], *DL*, vii (1931–2), 197–9; abridged reprint in Štědroň 1946, 155–6

Kašlík, Hynek: 'Retuše Karla Kovařovice v Janáčkově opeře Její pastorkyně' [Karel Kovařovic's 'retouchings' in Janáček's opera *Jenůfa*], *Hudební věstník*, xxxi (1938), 112–13, 130–1, 142–3, 159–60; *reprinted separately (Unie čes. hudebníků z povolání, Prague, 1938)

Knaus, Jakob, ed.: *Leoš Janáček-Materialien* (Leoš Janáček-Gesellschaft, Zürich, 1982)

Konečná, Hana, ed.: *Soupis repertoáru Národního divadla v Praze 1881–1983* [List of repertory of the National Theatre 1881–1983] (Národní divadlo, Prague, 1983)

Kožík, František: *Kouzelník z vily pod lipami* [The magician from the villa under the lime trees] (Blok, Brno, 1976)

Krásnohorská, Eliška: *Eliška Krásnohorská – Bedřich Smetana: vzajemná korespondence* [mutual correspondence], ed. Mirko Očadlík (Topič, Prague, 1940)

Krtička, Stanislav: *Brněnská hudební epocha: operní a symfonické děje 1919–1941* [A Brno musical epoch: operatic and symphonic history 1919–41] (MS, 1954) [copy deposited in BmJA]

Kunc, Jan: 'Leoš Janáček', *Hudební revue*, iv (1911), 121–34, 185–9

'Vzpomínky na premiéru Její pastorkyně' [Reminiscences of the première of *Jenůfa*], *DL, ix (1933–4), 74–81; abridged reprint in Štědroň 1946, 153–5

Kundera, Ludvík: *Janáček a Klub přátel umění* [Janáček and the Friends of Art Club] (Velehrad, Olomouc, 1948)

'Janáčkova "Věc Makropulos"' [Janáček's *The Makropulos Affair* Nosek 1958

Mahen, Jiří: 'Jak jsme dělali s Janáčkem libreto' [How I did a libretto with Janáček], *Panorama*, vi (1929); reprinted in *JA v, 39–47

Mareš, Frant.[išek]: 'K sedmdesátinám Leoše Janáčka' [For Leoš Janáček's seventieth birthday], *HRo*, i (1924–5), 33–5

'Vzpomínky na Leoše Janáčka' [Reminiscences of Leoš Janáček], *LN (17 February 1940); abridged reprint in Štědroň 1946, 182–3

Med, Jaroslav: *Viktor Dyk* (Melantrich, Prague, 1988)

Nejedlý, Zdeněk: *Bedřich Smetana* (HMUB, Prague, 1924–33, *2/Orbis, Prague, 1950–4)

Němcová, Alena: *Profil brněnské opery v kontextu s dějinami českého divadla v Brně v letech 1894–1904* [A profile of the Brno opera in the context of the history of the Czech theatre in Brno 1894–1904] (doctoral dissertation, University of Brno, 1971)

'Brněnská premiéra Janáčkovy Její pastorkyně' [The Brno première of *Jenůfa*], ČMM, lix (1974), 133–46; German trans. in Knaus 1982, 7–22

'Na okraj Janáčkovy Její pastorkyně: úvaha před zahájením příprav ke kritickému vydání opery' [On the margin of *Jenůfa*: a reflection before the commencement of preparations towards a critical edition of the opera], ČMM, lxv (1980), 159–64 [includes list of sources in BmJA]

'Otázníky nad Její pastorkyní' [A list of questions about *Jenůfa*], OM, xvi (1984), 24–7

Němcová-Grulichová, Alena: *Opera českého Národního divadla v Brně v letech první světové války* [The Opera of the Czech National Theatre in Brno in the years of the First World War] (MS, Brno, 1963; copy deposited at Český hudební fond, Prague)

Němcová, Alena and Přibáňová, Svatava: 'Příspěvek k dějinám opery Národního divadla v Brně 1884–1919', ČMM, xlviii (1963), 261–82

Němeček, Jan: *Opera Národního divadla v období Karla Kovařovice 1900–1920* [The opera of the (Prague) National Theatre in the time of Karel Kovařovic 1900–20] (Divadelní ústav, Prague, 1968–9)

Newmarch, Rosa: 'New Works in Czechoslovakia' [review of *From the House of the Dead*], *The Chesterian*, xii (1931), 213–19; reprinted in Janáček 1986, 165–9

Nosek, Václav, ed.: *Opery Leoše Janáčka na brněnské scéně* [Janáček's operas on the Brno stage] (Státní divadlo, Brno, 1958) [unpaginated]

Nováková, Eva: *Opera v Prozatímním divadle v Brně v letech 1884–1894* [Opera in the Provisional Theatre in Brno 1884–94] (diploma dissertation, University of Brno, 1956)

Pala, František: 'Janáček a Národní divadlo' [Janáček and the National Theatre], *HRo*, vi (1953), 882–91

'Jevištní dílo Leoše Janáčka' [The stage works of Leoš Janáček], *Musikologie*, iii (1955), 61–210

Opera Národního divadla v období Otakara Ostrčila [Opera at the National Theatre during the time of Otakar Ostrčil], i (Divadelní ústav, Prague, 1962), ii (ibid, 1964), iii (ibid, 1965), iv (ibid, 1970) [see under Pospíšil for vols. v-vi]

Petr, Jan, ed.: *Vzpomínáme Karla Kovařovice* [We commemorate Karel Kovařovic] (I.L. Kober, Prague, 1940)

Plamenac, Dragan: 'Nepoznati komentari Leoša Janáčeka operi "Katja Kabanova"' [Unknown commentaries on Leoš Janáček's opera *Káťa Kabanová*], *Muzikološki zbornik*, xvii/1 (1981), 122–31

Pospíšil, Vilém: *Opera Národního divadla v období Otakara Ostrčila* [Opera at the National Theatre during the time of Otakar Ostrčil], v (Divadelní ústav, Prague, 1983), vi (ibid, 1989) [see under Pala for vols. i-iv]

Preissová, Gabriela: 'Má setkání s Thalií' [My encounters with Thalia (i.e. with the theatre)], *Divadlo a hudba*, i (1941–2), no.8, pp.49–51

Přibáňová, Svatava:: *Opera českého Národního divadla v Brně v letech před první světovou válkou* [The opera of the Czech National Theatre in Brno in the years before the First World War] (doctoral disseration, University of Brno, 1971)

'Operní dílo Janáčkovo vrcholného údobí' [The operas of of Janáček's culminative period], *ČMM*, lxv (1980), 165–71 [includes list of musical sources in BmJA for *The Excursions of Mr Brouček*, *Káťa Kabanová*, *The Cunning Little Vixen*, *The Makropulos Affair* and *From the House of the Dead*]

Leoš Janáček (Horizont, Prague, 1984) [Přibáňová 1984a]

Opery Leoše Janáčka doma a v zahraničí [The operas of Leoš Janáček at home and abroad], *Program* [Státního divadla v Brně] (1984, special no.) [Přibáňová 1984b]

Procházka, Jaroslav: *Lašské kořeny života i díla Leoše Janáčka* [The Lašsko roots in the life and work of Leoš Janáček] (Okresní a místní rada osvětová ve Frýdku-Místku, Frýdek-Místek, 1948)

'Z mrtvého domu: Janáčkův tvůrčí i lidský epilog a manifest' [*From the House of the Dead*: Janáček's creative as well as human epilogue and manifesto], *Hudební věda*, iii (1966), 218–43, 462–83

Procházka, Vladimír, ed.: *Národní divadlo a jeho předchůdci: slovník umělců divadel Vlastenského, Stavovského, Prozatímního a Národního* [The National Theatre and its predecessors: a dictionary of artists of the Patriotic, Estates, Provisional and National Theatres] (Academia, Prague, 1988)

Procházková, Jarmila: 'Duše v očarovaném kruhu' [The soul in the charmed circle], *OM*, xxi (1989), 200–7 [on the Violin Concerto and related pieces]

Pulkert, Oldřich: 'Dramatické dílo Leoše Janáčka na scénach Národního divadlo v Praze' [Janáček's dramatic works on the stages of the Prague National Theatre], *HRo*, lxxxi (1978), 218–24

Racek, Jan: 'Leoš Janáček a Praha' [Janáček and Prague], *Musikologie*, iii (1955), 11–50

Sajner, Josef: 'Patografická studie o Leoši Janáčkovi' [A pathological study of Leoš Janáček], *OM*, xiv (1982), 233–5

Simeone, Nigel: *The first editions of Leoš Janáček: a bibliographical catalogue* (Hans Schneider, Tutzing, 1991)

Sládek, Jan Václav (1): *Sládek-Zeyer: vzájemná korespondence* [mutual correspondence], ed. J. Š. Kvapil (Nakladatelství Československé akademie věd, Prague, 1957)

Sládek, Jan Václav (2): *Hukvaldské miniatury* [Hukvaldy miniatures] (Profil, Ostava, 1979) [Reminiscences]

Smetana, Bedřich, *see* Krásnohorská, Eliška

Smetana, Robert: *Vyprávění o Leoši Janáčkovi* [Stories about Leoš Janáček] (Velehrad, Olomouc, 1948)

Šourek, Otakar: *Život a dílo Antonína Dvořáka* [The life and works of Antonín Dvořák], i-ii (HMUB, Prague, 1916–17; rev. 2/ibid, 1922–8); iii-iv (ibid, 1930–3); i-ii (*rev. 3/Státní nakladatelství krásné literatury, hudby a umění, Prague, 1954–5), iii-iv (*rev. 2/ibid, 1956–7) [author-date references are shown as Šourek 1916–33, i etc.]

    ed.: *Antonín Dvořák přátelům doma* [Dvořák to his friends at home] (Melantrich, Prague, and Oldřich Pazdírek, Brno, 1941)

Štech, Václav: *Vinohradský případ* [The Vinohrady case] (J. Otto, Prague, 1922)

Štědroň, Bohumír: 'Leoš Janáček a Luhačovice', *Vyroční zpráva Městské spořitelny v Luhačovicích za rok 1938* (Luhačovice, 1939)

    ed: *Janáček ve vzpomínkách a dopisech* [Janáček in reminiscences and letters] (Topič, Prague, 1946; partial Eng. trans. in Štědroň 1955)

    ed: *Leoš Janáček: Letters and Reminiscences* (Artia, Prague, 1955) [revised version, in Eng., of Štedroň 1946]

    Dílo Leoše Janáčka: abecední seznam Janáčkových skladeb a úprav [Janáček's works: an alphabetical catalogue of Janáček's compositions and arrangements] (Prague, Hudební rozhledy, 1959: Eng. trans., ibid, 1959) [Štědroň 1959a]

    'K Janáčkově opeře Osud' [Janáček's opera *Fate*], *Živá hudba*, i (1959), 159–83 [Štědroň 1959b]

'Ke korespondenci a vztahu Leoše Janáčka a Karla Kovařovice', *Sborník prací filosofické fakulty brněnské university*, F6 (1962), 31–69

'Ke zrodu opery Leoše Janáčka Její pastorkyňa' [The genesis of Janáček's opera *Jenůfa*], *Sborník prací filosofické fakulty brněnské university*, F9 (1965), 325–45

Zur Genesis von Leoš Janáčeks Opera Jenůfa (University J.E. Purkyně, Brno, 1968, *enlarged 2/1972)

Štědroň, Miloš: 'Neznámý zlomek skici z 1. jednání Janáčkovy Její pastorkyně' [An unknown fragment of a sketch from Act 1 of Janáček's *Jenůfa*], *OM*, ii (1970), 293

'Janáček a opera Groza Vladimíra Nikitiče Kašperova na libreto N.A. Ostrovského (1867)' [Janáček and Vladimir Nikitich Kashperov's opera *The Thunderstorm* to N.A. Ostrovsky's libretto (1867)], *Svazky – vztahy – paralely* (Opus Musicum, Brno, 1973), 128–33

Štědroň, Miloš, and Faltus, Leoš: 'Janáčkův Houslový koncert – torzo nebo vrcholné dílo posledního údobí skladatele?' [Janáček's Violin Concerto – torso or culminative work of the composer's final period?], *OM*, xx (1988), 89–96

Stejskalová, Marie: Reminiscences, *see* Trkanová, Marie

Straková, Theodora: 'Janáčkovy operní náměty a torsa' [Janáček's operatic subjects and fragments'], *Musikologie*, iii (1955), 417–49

'Janáčkova opera Osud' [Janáček's opera *Fate*], *ČMM*, xli (1956), 209–60; xlii (1957), 133–64

'Setkání Leoše Janáčka s Gabrielou Preissovou' [Janáček's encounter with Gabriela Preissová], *ČMM*, xliii (1958), 145–63

'Mezihry v Káti Kabanové' [The interludes in *Káťa Kabanová*], *ČMM*, xlix (1964), 229–36; abridged Eng. trans. in Tyrrell 1982, 134–43

'Janáčkovy opery Šárka, Počátek románu, Osud a hudebnědramatická torza: ke genezi děl, stavu pramenů and jejich kritické intepretaci' [Janáček's operas *Šárka, The Beginning of a Romance, Fate* and the musico-dramatic fragments: on the genesis of the works, state of the sources and their critical interpretation], *ČMM*, lxv (1980), 149–57

Susskind, Charles: *Janáček and Brod* (Yale University Press, New Haven and London, 1985)

Těsnohlídek, Rudolf: 'Mladistvý kmet' [The youthful old man], *LN (3 July 1924); abridged reprint in Štědroň 1946, 218–9

Trkanová, Marie: *U Janáčků: podle vyprávění Marie Stejskalové* [At the Janáčeks: after the account of Marie Stejskalová] (Panton, Prague, 1959, *2/1964)

Tyrrell, John: 'The musical prehistory of Janáček's Počátek románu and its importance in shaping the composer's dramatic style', *ČMM*, lii (1967), 245–70

'Mr Brouček's Excursion to the Moon', *ČMM*, liii–liv (1968–9), 89–122

'How Domšík became a bass', *The Musical Times*, cxiv (1973), 29–30

'Mr Brouček at home: an epilogue to Janáček's opera', *The Musical Times*, cxx (1980), 30–3

Leoš Janáček: Káťa Kabanová (Cambridge University Press, Cambridge, 1982)

'Janáček's forgotten commentary on 'Katya Kabanova', *Janáček: Jenůfa; Katya Kabanova*, N. John, ed. (John Calder, London and Riverrun Press, New York, 1985) [ENO and Royal Opera Guide], 83–6

Czech Opera (Cambridge University Press, Cambridge, 1988); Czech trans. (Opus musicum, Brno, 1992)

Veselý, Adolf: 'Besedy u Leoše Janáčka' [Chats with Leoš Janáček], *Národní listy* (20 October 1925)

Vogel, Jaroslav: *Leoš Janáček: Leben und Werk* (Artia, Prague, 1958; Czech original, Státní hudební vydavatelství, Prague, 1963; Eng. trans., Paul Hamlyn, London, 1962, *rev.2/Orbis, London, 1981 as *Leoš Janáček: a biography*) [Vogel 1963 = reference to Czech edition; Vogel 1981 = reference to revised 2nd Eng. edition]

Vysloužil, Jiří: 'Janáčkova opera "Počátek románu" [Janáček's opera *The Beginning of a Romance*], *HRo*, v (1954), 743–4

Závodský, Artur: *Gabriela Preissová* (Státní pedagogické nakladatelství, Prague, 1962)

Zeyer, Julius *see* Sládek, Jan Václav (1)

General Index

Index of Janáček's works